1/201/ 592-2000

1/223-1360

526-0485

800
908/ 852-8024

908/

Third Edition

INTRODUCTION TO THE FOUNDATIONS OF EDUCATION

ARTHUR K. ELLIS
Seattle Pacific University

JOHN J. COGAN
University of Minnesota

KENNETH R. HOWEY
Ohio State University

PRENTICE HALL, Englewood Cliffs, New Jersey 07632

Library of Congress Cataloging-in-Publication Data

Ellis, Arthur K.
    Introduction to the foundations of education / Arthur K. Ellis,
John J. Cogan, Kenneth R. Howey. -- 3rd ed.
        p.   cm.
    Includes bibliographical references and index.
    ISBN 0-13-488602-X
    1. Education--Philosophy--History. 2. Education--United States.
I. Cogan, John J. II. Howey, Kenneth R. III. Title.
LB17.E42 1991
370'.1--dc20   90-41749
                                                        CIP

Editorial/production supervision and
  interior design: Shelly Kupperman
Cover design: Bruce Kenselaar
Prepress buyer: Debra Kesar
Manufacturing buyer: Mary Ann Gloriande

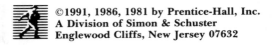 ©1991, 1986, 1981 by Prentice-Hall, Inc.
A Division of Simon & Schuster
Englewood Cliffs, New Jersey 07632

Printed in the United States of America
10 9 8 7 6 5 4 3 2 1

ISBN   0-13-488602-X

PRENTICE-HALL INTERNATIONAL (UK) LIMITED, *London*
PRENTICE-HALL OF AUSTRALIA PTY. LIMITED, *Sydney*
PRENTICE-HALL CANADA INC., *Toronto*
PRENTICE-HALL HISPANOAMERICANA, S.A., *Mexico*
PRENTICE-HALL OF INDIA PRIVATE LIMITED, *New Delhi*
PRENTICE-HALL OF JAPAN, INC., *Tokyo*
SIMON & SCHUSTER ASIA PTE. LTD., *Singapore*
EDITORA PRENTICE-HALL DO BRASIL, LTDA., *Rio de Janeiro*

CONTENTS

6

DEVELOPMENT OF EDUCATIONAL THOUGHT   97
Philosophical Perspectives

7

EDUCATION AND SCHOOLING   117

11   ACCOUNTABILITY   199
How Well Are We Doing?

12   POLITICAL DIMENSIONS OF SCHOOLING   219
Federal, State, and Local

PREFACE

"The more things change, the more they remain the same." The French proverb calls to mind the ebb and flow of ideas across the waters of education. As we stand on the threshold of a new century, the President and the National Council of Governors have issued a set of goals for American education to be achieved by the year 2000, including dramatic advances in the percentage of high school graduates, achievements in math and science. a commitment to global competitiveness, drug- and violence-free schools, and a commitment to the rights and responsibilities of citizenship. These ambitious aims will be analyzed, criticized, argued over, and attempted in a variety of ways.

In this third edition, we have addressed the complexities and development of education in a democratic society, retaining the best from the preceding editions while providing the reader with new insights and information about the continuing story of American education. Among the new features are the latest available figures on the financing and economics of education, new insights into pluralism and multicultural perspectives, recent revisions and recommendations from the reform commissions for the embattled school curriculum, emerging trends in the organization and management of schools, and new perspectives on the nature of teaching as a profession.

Throughout this edition, we have included the reader in perspective setting to involve him or her personally in the saga of American education. We have developed conceptual strands which incorporate the four broad structures of educational foundations: 1. the teacher and the profession, 2. school and society, 3. current and emerging issues in education, and 4. the future of American education.

Our intent is to make the reader aware of the connections between the present-day complex world of schools and the historical, philosophical, political, and social background out of which they have emerged. Today's schools bear little resemblance to their predecessors. The students, the teachers, the social milieu, the technology, and even the goal structure have changed. To be a teacher in today's society represents a far different calling from the school keeping of the past. At its best, teaching asks the professional to enter Robert Reich's "world of real people, engaged in the untidy and difficult struggle with real problems."

We assume full responsibility for any shortcomings which might be found in this book. But with regard to its strengths, the book is better because of the involvement of several talented people including editor Carol Wada and production editor Shelly Kupperman. For their patience, diligence, and creativity, we are deeply grateful.

Arthur K. Ellis
John J. Cogan
Kenneth R. Howey

Chapter 1

THE PERSONAL/ PROFESSIONAL CHOICE
To Teach or Not to Teach

The effort made in this country to spread instruction is truly prodigious. The universal and sincere faith that they profess here in the efficaciousness of education seems to be one of the most remarkable features of America. . . .

Alexis de Tocqueville, a letter to a friend, 1831

The word *education* is generally considered a common component of the vocabulary of most people. After all, people know what *education* is. Or do they?

A person undertaking a study of the many areas of education soon finds that it is quite a complex subject. It is at once concrete and theoretical. It is linked both to public policy and to individuals' hopes and dreams. It can involve people, money, ideas, buildings, methods, knowledge, and a host of other factors—depending on who you talk to or in what particular context you are considering the subject. An unfocused study of the many aspects of education can have the same effect as an attempt to find one's way through a bewildering maze.

In this chapter, we will look at education with a fundamental question: why teach? We will sift through some of the personal motivations affecting the decision whether to teach or not to teach.

A survey of U.S. teachers conducted in the spring of 1984 by Louis Harris for the Metropolitan Life Insurance Company indicated that love of teaching is the most powerful force that keeps teachers in their jobs. Harris found that teachers are "a dedicated group of professionals anxious to improve the educational system."[1]

However, the survey also indicated that teachers face a serious set of challenges: overcrowded classrooms, student apathy, inadequate school funding, and discipline problems. Teachers responded to the following statements thusly:

Strongly/Somewhat Agree

I love to teach.	96%
I would rate my school as excellent or good.	91%
I have to spend too much time on administrative tasks.	72%
I am usually recognized for good performance.	70%
As a teacher, I feel respected in today's society.	47%
The training and preparation teachers receive today does a good job preparing them for the classroom.	46%
I would advise a young person to pursue a career in teaching.	45%
My job allows me the opportunity to earn a decent salary.	37%

[1] *Today's Education*, Annual Edition (Washington, D.C.: National Education Association, 1984–85).

What kinds of inferences can you make about the data from this survey in terms of teaching as a lifetime career?

Of course, not everyone who decides to become a teacher remains one. The Second Gallup/Phi Delta Kappa Poll of Teachers' Attitudes Toward the Public Schools, taken in 1989, revealed a number of reasons why some teachers choose to leave teaching.[2] Here, in order, are the reasons they gave:

1. Low teacher salaries
2. Discipline problems in schools
3. Low status of teaching as a profession
4. Students are unmotivated, uninterested in school
5. Lack of public financial support for education
6. Parents do not support the teachers
7. Outstanding teacher performance goes unrewarded
8. Difficulty of professional advancement
9. Parents are not interested in children's progress

What inferences can you make about a teaching career from these data?

HY TEACH

blic Opinion

The average person can give a number of reasons why teaching is or is not a particularly good career in the 1990s. Do you believe that? Just ask the average person. Find someone outside the teaching profession (a reasonably easy task since teachers make up only 5 percent of the adult American population), and ask him or her to give you several reasons why teaching might or might not be a good career to enter. You might be given encouraging reasons such as the following:

- You would be helping young people to learn.
- You get summers off.
- People respect teachers.
- Teaching is difficult, but rewarding.

Or you might well be given discouraging reasons, such as:

- The pay is low.
- Jobs are scarce.

[2]Stanley M. Elam, "Second Gallup/Phi Delta Kappa Poll of Teachers' Attitudes Toward the Public Schools," *Kappan* (June 1989), pp. 785–798.

- Teaching is just for people who can't do anything else.
- Discipline is too much of a problem.

Now ask this same person to tell you about architecture as a career, or about journalism. Ask this person about another field or two—political science or computer theory—if he or she has not walked away by now.

Possibly you are wondering why we would place an exercise such as this at the beginning of a book which treats such a "solemn" topic as education? The answer is simple. We wish to illustrate an important point: *everyone* has opinions about education, even people who know next to nothing about other professions. Education is public domain. The educator holds a public trust. The person who would become a teacher assumes the deepest set of responsibilities a society can bestow upon a human being. As E. F. Schumacher wrote in his book *Small is Beautiful,* "the task of education would be, first and foremost, the transmission of ideas of value, of what to do with our lives." *What to do with our lives.* How many other professions have had such words written about them?

To give you a sense of both a professional view and the public's perception of the importance of teaching and the contributions of teaching to the general good of society, consider these results, again from the 1989 Second Gallup Poll: Public school teachers ranked teaching as the number one contributor to the welfare of society. The public also registered its support of teachers, ranking teachers number three, just behind clergymen and medical doctors, and *ahead* of judges, lawyers, business executives, bankers, and other professionals.

> But when the American hears the word "schoolteacher" . . . the image will be something like this: . . . She stands in his mind on the borderline of childhood, urging, beckoning, exhorting, patiently teaching, impatiently rebuking a child in whom the impulse is strong to escape the narrow bounds of the schoolroom.
>
> *Margaret Mead*

You, the Teacher

Perhaps, rather than asking the question "Why teach," we should ask the question, "Why should *you* teach?" There are undoubtedly as many reasons for being a teacher as there are people who teach. And, undoubtedly, some of the reasons are not particularly good, or at least do not sound particularly idealistic. Nevertheless, while a reason such as "I love children" may sound good, it may or may not be as important to you as another type of response, such as: "I think it is a career in which I could succeed." It is difficult to make value judgments about an individual person's motivations.

Inventory

To Teach or Not To Teach

Let us take an inventory of some of the factors involved in your decision to teach. Answer as comprehensively as possible.

1. List all the reasons you have for desiring to teach—tangible and intangible.
2. Arrange your reasons in order, beginning with the reason most important to you and proceeding on through reasons less important to you.
3. List the skills and abilities you have that you consider important to teaching. (For example, list such characteristics as "patience," "ability to communicate," "strong voice," "ethical person," etc.)
4. List the skills and abilities you have noted in your favorite teachers.
5. List the skills and abilities you need to be a good teacher.
6. Describe how you envision your life ten years from now.
7. Determine how you feel about your responses.

Let us examine some possible responses from the hypothetical "average person" we interviewed.

- *You would be helping young people to learn.* What do you think of young people? How does one person help another person to learn?
- *People respect teachers.* Do *you* respect teachers? All teachers? What is respect anyway? What about students who refuse to do homework or parents who do not respond to notes from the teacher—do they respect teachers? How important is respect? What about self-respect?
- *Teaching is difficult, but rewarding.* What are some of the difficult aspects of teaching? What is rewarding about it?
- *Teaching is just for people who cannot do anything else.* Is this professional jealousy? Do all people feel this way? Is teaching a profession of incompetents? How do you change the way people think about discipline?

Obviously, some of the statements made by our hypothetical "average person" are true of the teaching profession and some represent misconceptions. Some of the statements are true for some teachers and not true for others. Your own responses to the related questions can help you separate fact from fallacy—and can help you understand your personal motivations in deciding to teach.

Personal motivations for choosing to enter the teaching profession can be based on a number of different types of reasons. For example, you may have altruistic reasons for wanting to become a teacher—you may want to commit yourself to service to the community, you may have a strong rapport with children, or you may have a love of learning that you want to share with others. In addition, you may have some practical reasons for wanting to teach—you may feel that it is a solid career or you may know that you can be hired easily.

Future chapters will illuminate concepts of teaching and education as well as dispel some widely held myths. Your answer to the question "Why teach?" can then be based on acquired knowledge as well as on introspection.

> *When I became a teacher, . . . It was important to sort out the romance of teaching and discover whether, knowing the problems, the hard work and frustration, it still made sense to teach. For me, the answer has been yes, but there are still times I wish I'd chosen some easier vocation.*
>
> *Herbert Kohl*

Society and Teaching

Much of what human beings need to know is not genetically programmed; rather, it must be taught. Each person must acquire anew his or her own culture.

Throughout history, educational arrangements have always been made for the young. These arrangements have varied from highly formal academic experiences to informal life skills experiences. Only in recent times, however, have schools become a worldwide phenomenon. The formalized learning experience for nearly all young people is largely a twentieth-century invention.

How a person acquires the skills, knowledge, and values necessary for survival and prosperity varies considerably from one society to another. Further, the foundations of a person's education cannot, of course, be viewed apart from the goals of his or her society. A case in point is that of the high school dropout in our society. Having completed, let us say, the tenth grade, he or she is reasonably well educated by world standards. But we in the United States brand dropouts as failures because they did not earn a high school diploma. Yet approximately 25 percent of our young people do not complete high school.

Function and Purpose: Two Great Controversies

Over time, some basic purposes of education have evolved. There is—and will continue to be—the debate between those who feel that the basic purpose of education is to serve the individual and those who feel that the basic purpose of education is to serve society. Ours is one of the few societies to place the individual first, with the thought that individuals well served will serve society well.

There is widespread agreement that education ought to serve several functions. Those functions are intellectual development, character development, moral and/or religious training, and citizenship training. The range and depth of the school's responsibility for these four functions has become an object of great controversy, as we will see in subsequent chapters.

WHO TEACHES?

In the past, and in a few cultures of today, parents, elders, priests, and wise men have taken on the teaching role. These people have seen it as their duty to instruct the young in the areas of knowledge, skills, and values. Aristotle wrote that the surest sign of wisdom is a person's ability to teach what he or she knows. Whether the teaching/learning process is informal, as it is in many preliterate cultures, or whether it is highly formalized, as it is in our culture, everyone agrees that the young must be taught by those who know.

Since that time in the dim and distant past when one person first decided to instruct another, the worldwide ranks of teachers have grown, in this closing decade of the twentieth century, to over 20 million. This present-day figure represents only those who make their livings as certified teachers at elementary, secondary, and university levels. The number of uncertified lay teachers, volunteer teachers, and auxiliary teachers would add millions to that figure.

In the United States, teachers are male, female, young, old, white, non-white, experienced, newly trained—a wide variety of people with different personalities, different specializations, different opinions, different goals. Ideally, however, all teachers should have one thing in common: they should all love to teach.

Types of Personalities

Margaret Mead[3] once characterized the subculture of teaching, and of teachers in particular, as having three kinds of value systems or types of personalities. Because the classroom teacher is a primary agent of enculturation, his or her value structure and personal style become an issue of significance in the transmission of culture. Mead's three teacher roles include:

1. The "child-nurse," who helps the learner to be himself and to enjoy his present activities.
2. The "parent," who works for success and wants to prepare the child to succeed in her uncharted future.
3. The "grandparent," whose memories run far back and who enjoys helping children to appreciate their traditions.

The child-nurse teacher derives a sense of satisfaction from the child's enjoyment. The child-nurse readily takes part in activities and tends to be generally uncritical of children's behavior. Happiness and pleasant experiences for children are his or her primary goal.

The parent teacher is committed to teaching skills and new ideas to his or her students. The parent teacher attempts to instill a success orientation and

[3]Margaret Mead, *The School in American Culture* (Cambridge, Mass.: Harvard University Press, 1951), p.16.

creates situations and learning experiences in which students meet new challenges. Ambition and progress are values of paramount importance to the parent teacher.

The grandparent teacher is philosophic in approach and has little concern for utilitarian matters. To the grandparent teacher, the legacy of the past, of the arts, and of tradition are precious and must be passed along to the younger generation. "New" ideas always have their precursors from the past. There is nothing new under the sun.

Types of Teaching

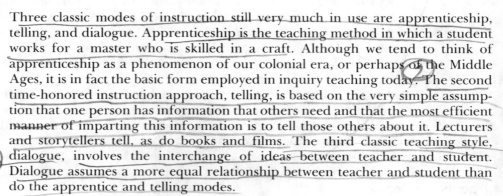

Three classic modes of instruction still very much in use are apprenticeship, telling, and dialogue. Apprenticeship is the teaching method in which a student works for a master who is skilled in a craft. Although we tend to think of apprenticeship as a phenomenon of our colonial era, or perhaps of the Middle Ages, it is in fact the basic form employed in inquiry teaching today. The second time-honored instruction approach, telling, is based on the very simple assumption that one person has information that others need and that the most efficient manner of imparting this information is to tell those others about it. Lecturers and storytellers tell, as do books and films. The third classic teaching style, dialogue, involves the interchange of ideas between teacher and student. Dialogue assumes a more equal relationship between teacher and student than do the apprentice and telling modes.

Teachers and Teaching

Perhaps one of the most important ideas to remember is that *people* teach. And, just as people grow and change with acquired knowledge and experience, so their ideas about teaching grow and change. Trends in education are continuously evolving, recycling, and passing in and out of favor.

The following sections present comments from teachers on teaching. Also included are some interview guides which you can use to obtain your own information and to update some of the ideas about teachers and teaching which we have presented.

Heidi S. graduated from a small liberal arts college in Idaho at the age of twenty-one and began teaching that year in Seattle. She entered graduate school four years later and subsequently reentered the teaching profession as a special education teacher.

> I thought about being a teacher off and on through high school. But I didn't decide to become an education major until my sophomore year of college. I think the strongest influence was my interest in children. I liked to be around them and help them learn. Also, my mother had been a teacher at one time, and that probably had an influence on me. I didn't really have an interest in being anything else. I couldn't see being a technician or a sales representative or anything else but a teacher.

I always thought I wanted to teach third grade until I spent some time observing a third-grade classroom. I don't know if it was because of the control problem the teacher had, or whether her lessons bored the students, or both. I just seemed to get a negative impression of that grade level. I started to reflect on my own school years. I had fond memories of tenth grade and of one teacher in particular. I've often wanted to contact her. She was inspiring to me; she gave me a love of books and an interest in finding out about things—all kinds of things. Curiosity—that's what I'd like to give my students.

After teaching for four years I was ready for a change—so I left the regular classroom and went into special education. I had seen students with real problems, and I wanted to know how to help them. Of course, going into special education also represented a chance to learn something new. But now, more important, I feel needed. And I feel as if I am doing a good job.

Dave R. teaches classes in industrial arts and biology in a small-town senior high school. He attended college after working as a machinist for four years.

I was raised on a farm and always figured I would become a farmer. In high school, I participated in Future Farmers of America (FFA). But when I graduated, I had an opportunity to work as a machinist, so I decided to try it for a while. The time I spent as a machinist convinced me that I like to work with my hands and that I could teach others industrial skills, which I did. I had never thought of teaching before, but I enjoyed training new employees at the shop. I liked sharing my skills.

My years as a machinist gave me a chance to grow up a little. By the time I was in college, I had a much deeper insight into the things that were being said and taught. I found out the key for method courses: apply yourself and then test out the ideas with kids. It's surprising how many method ideas work; it's wonderful when students really respond.

Kathy H. teaches science classes to fourth-, fifth-, and sixth-graders at a private school in St. Paul, Minnesota.

My original idea was to become a nurse. But after working as a nurse's aide, I developed a much clearer picture of what it meant to be a nurse. There were a number of things I liked about it. But there were also some things I had doubts about. When I arrived at college as a freshman, I looked at the schedule of courses I would be taking [in nurse's training] and decided I really wasn't that motivated to take them. The course work, coupled with some doubts I had about nursing, made me quite sure it wouldn't be the right field. So I reevaluated my goals and then changed my major to elementary education because I thought working with children—helping them learn—would be challenging.

I suppose we can all look back on choices we have made and say that we made them either on the spur of the moment or without thinking through all the consequences. But, when you think about it, my own decision to change career plans wasn't that radical. I changed from one service profession to another, so my central goal of service remained the same.

Jack W. teaches first grade at a public school in Chicago. He is the oldest of six children and decided to become a teacher after viewing firsthand the benefits of helping his brothers and sisters with their homework.

When I was a teenager, I used to hate being stuck babysitting the kids. But they were good, and I found out that by reading to them, I could keep them pretty happy. I got cagier after a while—I figured out that if I could interest them in reading themselves, then they'd leave me alone. I was right!

I got a scholarship to college and decided to become a teacher. From the very first, I knew that I wanted to teach elementary school and that I wanted especially to be a reading specialist. For all children, but for minority children in particular, reading is of vital importance. Reading is the whole key to education—and education opens doors.

When I watch the progress that my students make, I get a warm, proud feeling. I say to myself: hey, I'm the one who helped them do that. I don't think I would get the same satisfaction in any other profession.

Laurie F. taught for four years before deciding that teaching just was not for her—at least not in a school. Today she works in a government agency and is a trainer of new personnel.

I probably didn't change my mind often enough as an undergraduate. I didn't keep an open mind—didn't look at all the options. Undergraduate years ought to be that time when a person considers a number of possibilities—and explores a lot of dreams. I didn't. I signed up as an education major my freshman year, and though I didn't particularly enjoy my classes and didn't particularly enjoy student teaching, I thought "Oh well, it's a job."

I finally awakened one morning and admitted to myself that I was not happy teaching a classroom full of students and that they probably weren't happy with me. I looked around for new job possibilities. And—here I am. I'm using my teaching skills, but I'm working with a different age group; it's a different kind of teaching—very goal-oriented and every few weeks I have new people to instruct. It's on-the-job training, and I like it much better. I just wasn't the type to work in a classroom.

The following interview formats can assist you in collecting your own catalogue of impressions, opinions, and facts about the teaching profession. For a fuller picture, compare your interview results with those of another student.

INTERVIEW 1

Name of person interviewed: Occupation:

Ask a nonteacher, parent, or friend who is interested in education the following questions in an interview situation. Record the answers the person gives you in a notebook or on tape.

1. What are some things that you remember about your years in school?
2. Do you remember any teachers in particular?

3. What do you think makes a good teacher?

4. If you were a teacher, what do you think your greatest offering to students would be?

5. How would you compare what you know of schools today with schools when you were a student?

6. What do you think are the problems facing teachers today?

INTERVIEW 2

Name of person interviewed: Position:

Interview a teacher or school administrator. (Because of the wide range of opinions held by people in the field, you may want to repeat this interview with more than one person.)

1. What makes a good teacher?

2. How well do colleges and universities prepare people for teaching?

3. What do you think can be done to improve teacher preparation?

4. What are three major problems facing teachers? Facing the schools?

5. How useful are theories of education to the classroom teacher?

6. What are some of the rewards and difficulties a teacher experiences?

INTERVIEW 3

Name of person interviewed: Position:

Find someone whose job is that of preparing students to become teachers. Ask this person to answer the following questions.

1. What are some differences between an adequate teacher and an outstanding teacher?

2. In what ways are students entering education as a major similar to, and how are they different from students entering education ten years ago?

3. What recent improvements have been made in the way students are prepared by colleges and universities to enter teaching?

4. Why does there often seem to be a gap between theory and practice in education?

5. How are schools of education responding to the apparent oversupply of teachers entering the job market each year?

SUMMARY

In this chapter we examined some of the personal motivations that might explain your answer to the question Why teach? Among these motivators are public opinion (in both its positive and negative views of teaching), the altruistic desire to serve the community, a rapport with children, and the desire to share your love of learning with others.

The next question we posed was, Who teaches? In answering this, we looked at Margaret Mead's characterization of three types of people who teach: the "child-nurse," the "parent," and the "grandparent."

Finally, we turned the stage over to a number of experienced teachers and saw how they answered these questions.

ACTIVITIES

1. Compare your completed interview sheets with those of other students. Are there any similarities in the responses of the various people interviewed? Any differences? Discuss why you think the similarities and the differences exist.

2. Talk to elementary and/or high school students about their teachers. Find out what characteristics they think a good teacher possesses.

3. In a small group of classmates, trade ideas on why group members decided to become teachers. Discuss, as well, the negative feelings you may have about teaching.

4. Interview a teacher who has taught for a number of years. Ask him or her about the changes that have occurred in the schools, in attitudes of students, in professional matters, and in educational trends in general. Ask the teacher how he or she has changed personally.

5. Find out about alternatives for jobs in education and what these alternatives may require. Investigate graduate degrees in education. Discuss whether any of these possibilities appeal to you.

6. List your best and your worst experiences with teachers. Discuss how these situations might have occurred. Who was responsible for these situations? How could you repeat a good experience? What steps could you or the teacher have taken to avoid a bad experience?

SUGGESTED READINGS

BULLOUGH, ROBERT V., JR., *First-Year Teacher: A Case Study.* New York: Teachers' College Press, 1989.

COMBS, ARTHUR, *A Personal Approach to Teaching: Beliefs That Make A Difference.* Boston: Allyn & Bacon, 1982.

ELAM, STANLEY, "Second Gallup/Phi Delta Kappa Poll of Teachers' Attitudes Toward the Public Schools," *Kappan,* June 1989, pp. 785–798.

KIDDER, TRACY, *Among School Children.* New York: Houghton Mifflin, 1989.

KOHL, HERBERT, *Growing Minds: on Becoming a Teacher.* New York; Harper & Row, 1984.

ROWLEY, J., "The Teacher as Leader and Teacher Educator," *Journal of Teacher Education* (May/June 1988), pp. 13–16.

RYAN, KEVIN, et al., *Biting the Apple: Accounts of First Year Teachers.* New York: Longman, 1980.

WARNER, SYLVIA ASHTON, *Spearpoint.* New York: Vintage Books, 1974.

Chapter 2

TEACHING
The Nature
of the Profession

Teachers are caught in a crosscurrent of conflicting points of view regarding the nature of the teaching profession. Idealism conflicts with reality. Educational theory conflicts with teaching practice. Altruism crashes head-on with cynicism.

The person who engages in long and searching thought about the joy of helping students learn and grow is the same person who wonders whether jobs even exist in his or her teaching area. The student teacher who is on the verge of thinking that teachers are the key to an improved tomorrow is the same person who sits in silence listening to burned-out faculty members talk cynically about students who don't care.

Status, power, freedom, jobs, salaries, rights; these are some of the most basic issues in teaching. An exploration of these issues takes one quickly to the heart of the matter. In this chapter we will address these issues and attempt to answer some of the broader questions that must inevitably be posed by anyone who pursues a career in education.

To some extent, the basic issues in the education career are the same issues basic to any professional career. The questions arise regardless of one's chosen field. Can I find work? Can I work where and with whom I want to? How much money will I make? What will be expected of me? Can I advance within the field? What are my professional rights and responsibilities?

Before beginning

ng,
ave
irs.
her
out
ved
our
not
on;

modified, discarded, rediscovered, and repeated again. The teaching profession evolves with these cycles of ideas; salaries and job availability change as priorities of society change. Throughout your education and experience as a teacher, you will note the ebb and flow of many ideals, objectives, and opinions with regard to education and teaching.

Now let us begin our more in-depth analysis of some of the points that the inventory called to our attention.

THE NATURE OF THE PROFESSION

Types of Teaching Experiences

The vast majority of those who choose education as a career will find themselves in the role of public school teachers. There are about 2.3 million public school teachers in America today.[1]

[1]*Estimates of School Statistics as Provided by Department of Education* (Washington, D.C.: National Education Association, 1989).

Inventory

Statements About Teaching

1. The public's concept of the teaching profession is quite low. (True/False)
2. A degree in education has little use if one decides to seek work in fields other than teaching. (True/False)
3. Because the birth rate has declined so dramatically, there will not be many children to teach in the near future. (True/False)
4. Teachers' pay is quite low compared to that of other professions. (True/False)
5. Teaching is one of the most difficult fields in which to find a job. (True/False)

Our Analysis:

1. *The public's concept of the teaching profession is quite low.* We answered FALSE. Recent Gallup polls, in fact, give education a rather high rating and vote of confidence. Education ranks ahead of government, labor, business, and the press.

2. *A degree in education has little use if one decides to seek work in fields other than teaching.* We answered FALSE to this one, too. A statement such as this is very hard to prove one way or the other. However, teaching is a helping profession and one which is based on skills of human relations, communications, and leadership. No wonder schools of education are reporting virtually full employment of their graduates, even though a significant number do not enter teaching.

3. *Because the birth rate has declined so dramatically, there will not be many children to teach in the near future.* We say FALSE. Actually, beginning in 1977, the United States birth rate began to rise. This trend, coupled with the fact that the population of the United States is at an all-time high, has led certain demographers to predict record school enrollments and teacher shortages in the 1990s.

4. *Teachers' pay is quite low compared to that of other professions.* FALSE again. We do not intend to propose that teaching is nothing more than a thinly disguised get-rich-quick scheme. However, of twenty major professions, the average entrance pay for public school teachers is above the median.

5. *Teaching is one of the most difficult fields in which to find a job.* FALSE. It is true that many districts have cut back the size of their school staffs. It is also true that positions continue to be available in certain rural and small-town areas, in work with students who have learning disabilities, and in the outer ring of suburbs surrounding metropolitan areas. In fact, the nationwide placement percentage for students graduating in education has remained at 70 percent for several years. This places education well above such professional fields as architecture, social work, journalism, and numerous others.

However, the private school—though on the decline only a few decades ago—is again alive and well in America. Enrollments in private schools have increased steadily in the past decade. Most private schools are church-related, with Catholic schools representing the single largest group. However, other private schools are founded on other principles: some emphasize preparation for college; some emphasize the trades or the arts; some emphasize discipline and a move back to the basics; others emphasize creative freedom and open education. Salaries at private schools tend to be lower than at public schools. But since private schools are often smaller schools with smaller classes, and since they sometimes have an educational philosophy that may be more compatible with your own, there may be factors overriding salary in making this choice.

Whether in a public school system or a private school, the teacher must also consider what level of teaching most appeals to him or her: elementary school, middle school, junior high school, or senior high school. Further, there are also teaching opportunities in preschool (nursery school) education, adult education, and senior citizen education.

Other decisions the beginning teacher must make include: what subject to teach; whether to consider special education or chapter I reading and mathematics teaching; whether to teach in school—or in another setting; and what some alternatives to teaching are.

Job availability varies from subject area to subject area and from level to level. However, other factors influence job availability as well; these will be discussed in the next section.

Factors Influencing Job Availability

In recent years, the demand for teachers has risen. The number of teachers produced has dropped sharply. This will certainly expand employment opportunities greatly. (See Figure 2-1.)

Many persons who, in the past, would have gone into public school positions automatically, are now considering other professional possibilities. The distinction between schooling and education becomes very important in making these professional considerations. The person who is open to a career that embraces education in a wider sense will find more employment possibilities—and perhaps even more satisfaction—than one who is less willing to explore alternatives.

Many factors affect job availability. The new teacher must have the ability to examine these variants and make career decisions based on an analysis of his or her situation. The factors affecting job availability are: types of schools; specific fields of teaching; level of teaching; geographic location; nonschool possibilities; and alternatives to teaching. Let us examine each factor.

TYPES OF SCHOOLS. The popular press has documented the rise and fall in enrollments in different types of schools. Public school enrollments are rising. Even so, many parents have pulled their children out of public schools because of what they believe to be the deteriorating quality of education in these schools.

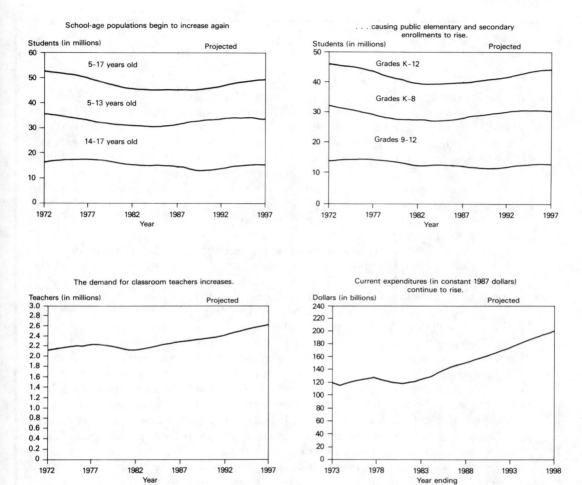

Figure 2-1 Selected Elementary and Secondary Education Statistics
*Source: National Center for Educational Statistics.

Some cities and counties are taking steps to halt this deterioration of educational standards. Further, there is evidence that a more favorable outlook exists in education's future. Nevertheless, when making career decisions, the teacher should analyze the public school/private school picture in his or her community; opportunities may vary in these different types of schools.

Specific Fields of Teaching. Actual teacher shortages exist in some subject areas at the present time. Those areas for which there is a present demand for teachers include special education fields such as education of the deaf and of the mentally retarded, mathematics and science teaching at secondary levels, industrial arts education, and Chapter 1 reading and mathematics teaching.

Teachers*

People who believe that teaching an elementary school class is easy should try doing it. In the past year, I have taught classes in a number of elementary schools and I can attest that it is no simple task. The younger the child, the more difficult the challenge. I have unbounded admiration for the man or woman who spends 180 days a year teaching well in an elementary classroom. Life holds few greater rewards than educating the next generation. Some misguided people make it sound as if it were demeaning to spend the day in a room full of elementary school children. It is surely demanding—to the point of exhaustion, in some cases—but most teachers find it deeply gratifying.

A recent study by the National Center for Education Information provided some keen insights into why people teach. According to NCEI Director Emily Feistritzer, "The vast majority of teachers are in that profession for all the reasons we hope they are. They say it themselves. When asked what is most important to them on a job, teachers say an opportunity to use their own minds and abilities and a chance to work with young people, followed by appreciation for a job well done." This represents no recent burst of altruism, either. A study by Thomas Provenzo and associates showed only 14.2 percent of Dade County teachers listing salary as the primary reward of their profession in 1984—a figure nearly identical to the 14.3 percent who gave that answer in 1964.

With a lot of experienced teachers retiring and with elementary school enrollments rising, close to a million new elementary-level teachers will be needed by 1993. But we are not, in fact, facing a crisis of numbers. As NCEI's Feistritzer points out, those million new teachers represent regular replacement at long-established rates of turnover and attrition. We might wish for greater stability in the ranks of teaching, and there will surely be "spot shortages" in particular specialties and communities. But that suggests the nature of the real challenge: not so much quantitative as qualitative. How do we organize ourselves to harvest a bumper crop of new teachers at a time when we are also demanding drastic improvement in the breadth and depth of their preparation?

*Excerpted from William Bennet, *First Lessons: A Report on Elementary Education in America* (Washington, D.C.: U.S. Department of Education, 1986).

LEVEL OF TEACHING. During the coming years the echo of the post–World War II "Baby Boom" will be felt in the schools; in other words, the products of the baby boom are now adults who are having children of their own. Though the birth rate declined in the 1960s and 1970s, and though the United States birth rate is low compared to other industrialized nations, forecasts show a changing picture: the birth rate is on the up-swing again, and growing school enrollments are projected at the elementary school level through the 1990s. Naturally, job availability will be modified with the changing enrollments.

Another level of teaching to consider is adult education. It is forecast that the demand for trained professionals in the area of adult education will continue to grow in the foreseeable future. When analyzed, an interesting bimodal distribution appears in the adult education picture. On the one hand, there is the pressing need for adult literacy. Exact data on adult literacy are hard to formulate, but estimates on the percentage of illiterate adults in our population run from 10 to 15 percent. The other aspect of adult education is that of providing training to people in business and industry. (See the nonschool education section that follows.)

EARLY CHILDHOOD.   The demand for quality day care and early childhood education represents a real growth industry. Single parents and families with both parents working outside the home will continue to demand care and training for their young children, who range from infants to five-year-olds. The growth will occur both within the private sector, as licensed day-care and nursery schools spring up seemingly on every corner, and within the public school sector. In fact, more and more schools are now providing early morning day care as well as after-school care for children in the elementary grades.

GEOGRAPHIC LOCATION.   Geography is an important factor in job availability. In general, the student-age population has declined in the North and East and has grown in the South and West. States such as Arizona and Florida continue to grow rapidly in student populations, while states such as Pennsylvania and Kansas have shown severe losses of student populations. As industry and business continue to move to the "Sun Belt," the labor force moves with them. The message to the young teacher may well be "Follow the sun," or "Go west."

Geographic location also plays an important part in the type of students the teacher will instruct. Different ethnic groups, different ideals, different types of student problems, different types of school system needs—these are all points to consider when preparing for a career and when searching for a position.

NONSCHOOL TEACHING POSSIBILITIES.   Opportunities for teachers exist in locations other than schools. For example, because of the growing number of families with single parents and the large number of families with both parents working, there is an increasing need for teachers in day care facilities. Further, many parents are interested in providing their children with preschool education experiences and Head Start programs. Therefore, the education of the very young is an area to consider.

Further, the business world and the education world are becoming more closely related. Providing training to employees of business and industry or providing education about the company to persons outside the company are growing concerns of many businesses. At present, it is estimated that there are more than 50,000 persons in the United States who hold education degrees and who are employed in the private sector in various positions.

Other teaching opportunities exist in community centers, in government, and in the health industry.

ALTERNATIVES TO TEACHING. An education degree is a valuable tool in many professions other than teaching. The qualities of teaching are easily adapted to positions in the social services, in counseling, in business, and in the arts. Further, some positions in textbook publishing, in education media development, and in education consulting often require an education degree. In addition, technology and software industries are seeking educators to assist in adapting computers and other equipment to the classroom. For the flexible, imaginative professional, opportunities abound.

Salaries

Salary is probably not the primary motivating factor for a young person to choose teaching as a career. Nevertheless, in an age of rising prices and continuous inflation, salary is becoming an increasingly important consideration of the profession. As school boards struggle to make ends meet, and as the public continues to tighten the education purse strings by such measures as tax reform bills, teachers' salaries cannot avoid being affected.

Nevertheless, teachers' salaries are no longer among the lowest compared to salaries of other professions. In 1927, a beginning teacher would earn about $65 per month; today, the average teacher's salary is about $30,000 per year. This places teachers' salaries below those of lawyers and doctors, but above those of nurses or civil service employees.

Salaries paid to teachers are generally augmented by certain fringe benefits which can include health insurance, sick leave, long-term disability, personal leave, sabbatical leave, extra pay for extracurricular activities, and additional pay for summer work.

Further, teachers with advanced degrees are generally paid higher salaries than teachers with only the baccalaureate degree. With additional pay for experience and advanced degrees, some teachers can make as much as $55,000 per year. Of course, even these salaries may not be high enough to support a family comfortably if the cost of living in a particular area is high. For this reason, many teachers become disillusioned about their inability to make ends meet and the apparent disinterest of the tax-paying public. Salary can become the primary motivating factor leading people to drop out of teaching in order to pursue other, more lucrative careers.

While we have presented average teacher salaries in this section, it is important to point out some of the factors which influence salaries from school board to school board: geographic location, type of school, level of school, experience and education, additional activities. It soon becomes apparent that some of these factors are the same as those affecting job availability. One important point should be made, however: factors which should *not* affect salaries are race, sex, national origin, or age. Federal law prohibits discrimination on this basis—and unequal salaries are a major form of discrimination.

The professional teachers' organizations work for fair salaries and fringe benefits. In many areas, these organizations have won the right of collective bargaining. The U.S. average classroom teacher salary was estimated to be $29,567 for the 1988–89 school year. This represented an increase of 5.6

percent, in current dollars, over the revised figure of $28,008 in 1987–88. Salary gains in "real" or constant-dollar terms for classroom teachers appear more moderate. The average gain in purchasing power for public classroom teacher salaries is estimated at 7.2 percent for the period 1978–79 to 1988–89. While this level of increase was typical for public sector employees during the period, actions taken by state and local governments to enhance the competitiveness of teacher salaries should accommodate effects of these historical losses to inflation.

Figures 2-2, 2-3, and 2-4 highlight the differences between the average classroom teacher salary in current versus constant dollars. The current-dollar increases over the years since 1978–79 appear substantial—from $15,032 in 1978–79 to $29,567 estimated for this year—a 96.7 percent increase in unadjusted terms. When the effects of price inflation are taken into account, the average teacher salary grows by only $1,833 or 12.4 percent over the decade (from $15,032 to $16,895 in 1978–79 dollars).

Public Opinion

Education in the United States represents a public trust. People pay for the schools through taxation. Therefore, many citizens feel a sense of proprietary rights over what occurs in the schools. Perhaps more than the members of any other profession, teachers must come to terms with this fact of public ownership of the schools. Certainly, doctors, lawyers, and businesspeople are affected by public opinion, but compared to the effects of public control over education, control over these and other professions is minimal. In addition to lay opinions

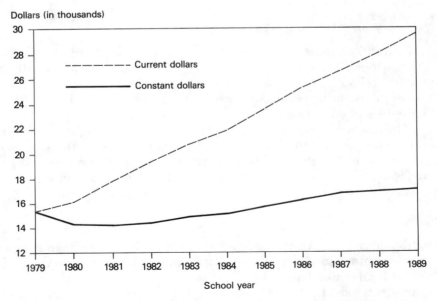

Figure 2-2 Average Classroom Teacher Salary School Years 1978–79 to 1988–89

Source: Estimates of School Statistics (Washington D.C.: NEA Datasearch, 1989).

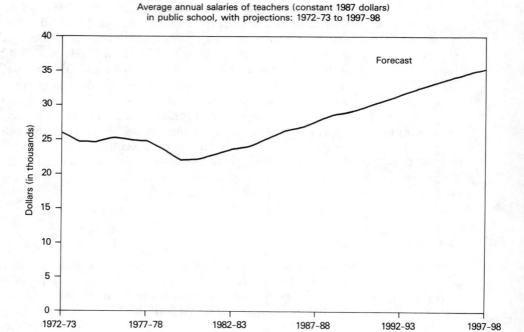

Average annual salaries of teachers (constant 1987 dollars) in public school, with projections: 1972-73 to 1997-98

Figure 2–3 Teachers Salaries Are Expected to Rise Throughout the 1990s.

Source: National Center for Educational Statistics.
(Note: the salary range from 1972–98 does not appear to be very great. This is because the graphic display uses 1987 dollars as its basis.

about education, there are several other groups which have identifiable ideas about this topic. These are the practitioners, those who teach in and administrate the public schools; the teacher educators, the college-level instructors who are involved in preparing people to teach; and the theoreticians, those who develop philosophies of education.

The teacher beginning to develop his or her own thoughts about education would be well advised to develop a greater awareness of the thinking of others. Whether those thoughts are those of an angry parent who thinks the schools have failed his or her child, or those of an educational researcher whose opinions are based on years of systematic inquiry, they are worth hearing.

How to Qualify

Teaching in colonial America was a rather discredited occupation comprised of untrained, unqualified persons who often knew little more than their students. Colorful figures like Ichabod Crane come to mind. Today, of course, specific requirements exist for teachers—although the requirements vary from state to state.

Figure 2.4 Teacher Salary Allocation Schedule 1990-91 School Year (State of Washington)

COLUMNS 1-6 ARE BA PLUS CREDITS OF 15, 30, 45, 90, & 135

Yrs						
0	20,001	20,541	21,101	21,661	23,461	24,621
1	20,656	21,214	21,792	22,389	24,242	25,417
2	21,325	21,900	22,495	23,150	25,034	26,245
3	22,027	22,620	23,232	23,923	25,840	27,104
4	22,742	23,372	24,001	24,729	26,696	27,995
5	23,490	24,136	24,783	25,566	27,565	28,916
6	24,269	24,913	25,596	26,435	28,464	29,849
7	25,061	25,721	26,421	27,314	29,393	30,831
8	25,864	26,561	27,277	28,244	30,352	31,842
9		27,431	28,182	29,184	31,341	32,822
10			29,098	30,172	32,358	33,950
11				31,189	33,423	35,047
12				32,174	34,516	36,189
13					35,636	37,359
14					36,762	38,573
15					37,718	39,597

COLUMNS 1-3 ARE MA PLUS CREDITS OF 45 & 90 OR PHD

Yrs			
0	23,980	25,780	26,940
1	24,708	26,561	27,736
2	25,469	27,353	28,563
3	26,242	28,159	29,423
4	27,048	29,095	30,314
5	27,885	29,884	31,235
6	28,754	30,783	32,168
7	29,633	31,712	33,150
8	30,563	32,671	34,161
9	31,502	33,660	35,201
10	32,491	34,677	36,269
11	33,508	35,742	37,366
12	34,566	36,835	38,508
13	35,659	37,955	39,678
14	36,786	39,154	40,892
15	37,742	40,172	41,955

- $35,200 est. average
- $33,000 state funded
- $ 2,200 locally funded
- Plus state funded benefits, and holidays/ time off (15 weeks)

CERTIFICATION REQUIREMENTS.   All states of the United States and provinces of Canada require that teachers in public and accredited private elementary and secondary schools be certified. In the past, certification was often granted to teachers who had completed a one- or two-year training program. In recent times, however, certification has become contingent upon the successful completion of a professional baccalaureate degree in a particular field of education, such as elementary education or secondary education.

Nothing in my educational background prepared me to be a song-and-dance person. . . . In truth, a master teacher has always been a combination show person and salesman. An instructor's unfeigned love for art, literature, music and nature, if presented with joy and enthusiasm, is contagious. It can raise the curtain on higher mental realms and turn the schoolroom into a state for genuine excitement.

Rosalie S. Lawrence [2]

In addition to certification requirements, credentials in a given subfield of secondary education, e.g., mathematics or physical education, are generally necessary. Specific teaching credentials are used to limit a teacher to a particular subject area.

Thus, just as nurses, doctors, and lawyers are licensed practitioners, so are teachers. Licensure in each case is granted by the state as opposed to the federal or municipal governments.

Because each state has its own certification requirements, a teacher who moves to another state must apply to that state for certification. Basic requirements from one state to another are essentially the same, and it is always possible to receive temporary certification in order to continue to teach while you are making up minor deficiencies.

Certification requirements have not only become more strict over time, but they must also be renewed periodically in order to ensure that students are receiving reasonably up-to-date instruction. Most states require that teachers take college courses and/or inservice courses to keep their credentials current.

COMPETENCY TESTS FOR CERTIFICATION.   A fairly recent development is the requirement that *preservice* teachers pass a competency test for certification. At the present time, twenty-four states require preservice teachers to pass a competency exam prior to the issuance of a teaching certificate. In some states, college students must take a qualifying exam before they begin teacher training. Florida requirements include:

1. An entry examination for students desiring to enroll in a preservice teacher education program in Florida.
2. A comprehensive written examination after completing degree requirements and prior to initial certification.
3. A year-long internship or three years of successful teaching experience prior to regular certification.
4. A single type of teaching certificate regardless of degree level— bachelor's, master's, or doctorate.
5. A five-year validity period for certificates.

[2]From Rosalie S. Lawrence, "Teacher Biz Needs a Little Show Biz," *The New York Times,* January 6, 1980.

Whether the Florida regulation is an indicator of things to come remains to be seen.[3] At any rate, a number of states are moving in the direction of requiring *exit level,* if not entry level, competencies on the part of preservice teachers.

What are these competencies? Robinson and Mosrie[4] summarize illustrative competencies from the Florida state exam:

1. The ability to write in a logical and understandable style with appropriate grammar and sentence structure.
2. The ability to comprehend and interpret a message after listening.
3. The ability to read, comprehend, and interpret, orally and in writing, professional and other written material.
4. The ability to comprehend and work with fundamental mathematical concepts.
5. The ability to comprehend patterns of physical, social, and academic development in students, and to counsel students concerning their needs in these areas.

From all this, one thing is clear. Certification standards are becoming increasingly stringent, and the chances are good that they will continue to do so. If new standards are reasonable and correlated closely with teacher effectiveness, everyone stands to gain from an upgraded profession.

For current information about your state's certification requirements, contact your State Department of Education's Office of Certification.

The NTE or National Teacher's Exam is another example of a test used to screen prospective teachers. There are four parts to the test, examples for two of which (professional knowledge/awareness of classroom techniques; and general knowledge) are given below. School districts using this test set their own standards for passing.

Example 1:
Professional Knowledge
Development of which of the following is likely to be furthered more in a classroom with a competitive atmosphere than in one with a cooperative atmosphere?
a. complex intellectual problem solving
b. social problem solving
c. interest in school and learning
d. affective development
e. drill- and speed-dependent skills

Example 2:

---

[3]For information see *Domains of the Florida Coalition for Development of Performance-based Evaluation System* (Chipley, Fla.: Panhandle Educational Cooperative, 1984).

[4]A. A. Robinson and D. Mosrie, "Florida's New Teacher Certification Law," *Phi Delta Kappan* (December 1979), pp. 263–264.

General Knowledge
Which of these is NOT a correct way to find 75% of 40?
a. 75.0 × 40
b. (75 × 40)/100
c. 75/100 × 40
d. ¾ × 40
e. 0.75 × 40

Example 3:
Professional Knowledge
A teacher with a grievance against the local school board would most likely obtain help and information about teacher rights and the available grievance or arbitration procedures from the
a. U.S. Department of Education
b. state education agency or department
c. local law-enforcement agency
d. local parent-teacher organization
e. local teachers' organization

Example 4:
General Knowledge
"They embrace. But they do not know the secret in the poet's heart." The stage direction above ends a play; the second sentence is not a typical stage direction for which of the following reasons?
a. Poets do not often appear in plays.
b. Plays are not often built around secrets.
c. The direction does not summarize the plot of the play.
d. The direction does not list the names of all the characters.
e. The direction cannot be acted out for the audience to see.

QUESTION	ANSWER	% ANSWERING CORRECTLY
1	e	73
2	a	76
3	e	56
4	e	73

What's Your Opinion?

California is one of many states that requires all would-be teachers to take an elementary reading, writing, and arithmetic test. The California Basic Educational Skills Test, more commonly known as the CBEST, is designed to keep those who are incompetent out of the classroom. The interesting fact is that approximately one out of four test-takers cannot meet the minimum requirements necessary to pass this test. Of added significance is the fact that minorities are failing the test at a much higher rate than Anglos (24 percent). The failure rate for some minority groups is even higher. Some have complained that the tests are culturally biased.

What's in this test? There are several Reading Comprehension passages (the easiest parts of the test); about 78 percent passed this section. About 60 percent of the Math section consists of sixth- and seventh-grade mathematics problems. The rest of the test involves Algebra and Geometry; roughly 70 percent passed this section. The final section is Essay Writing, using questions such as "Why did you choose teaching as a profession?"

The teachers unions have been very active in dealing with this particular issue. One California education lobbyist claims a teacher can fail this test and still be qualified to teach. She goes on to say, "There are a lot of fine test-takers who can not teach their way out of a paper bag."

So what do you think? Will this controversial test insure that you are a competent teacher? Or—for a tougher question—should would-be teachers teach children if they cannot pass a basic skills test?[5]

PROFESSIONAL RESPONSIBILITIES

As a professional, the teacher has wide-ranging responsibilities. He or she is responsible for knowing and supporting the rights of students, for knowing the legal ramifications of his or her own conduct, for knowing his or her responsibilities to provide effective instruction, and for knowing the limits of his or her own academic freedom.

One would undoubtedly prefer to forget about legalities, liabilities, and lawsuits and get on with the business of teaching. Of course, in a more perfect world, this would be possible. But given the way things are, it is necessary to recognize the fact that a teacher must know more than his or her subject matter.

Rights of Students

More and more attention has been paid to the rights of students in recent years. Although schools formerly enforced, without question, policies concerning student behavior, student dress, and student discipline, the situation is now changing. School boards and students often are locked in struggles over who has which rights.

For the most part, the rights of students are the same as the rights of any other American. Simply stated, students shall not be discriminated against on the grounds of race, color, creed, national origin, or sex. But in more specific areas, such as in the area of dress codes or discipline, a clear-cut answer cannot be given. The following situations will illustrate some of the complex issues involved in students' rights.

Take a few minutes to think about the following situations. Give your answers and compare them with the information which we will supply.

[5]"So You Want to Be a Teacher?" *California Magazine* (February 1984), pp. 122–123.

SITUATION 1. The dress code at Wilson School includes a rule on hair length for boys. Several students protest the rule saying that length of hair is an individual choice and that the school has no right to impose such a rule on students. How do you feel about this?

The legal position: The U.S. Supreme Court has refused to consider the issue. Courts of appeal in four circuits have held that the right is protected. Courts of appeal in four other circuits have held that the student has no such right as long as the school rule serves a legitimate goal. In an Eighth Circuit case arising in Minnesota, the court held that a male student could not be prevented from attending a public school because of his hair length, as long as it was clean; and there was no showing that shoulder length hair would materially and substantially interfere with discipline in the school. The court said that the hair restriction invaded private life beyond the school jurisdiction. The school rule was an attempt to impose taste or preference as a standard.

SITUATION 2. Mary was having a difficult time in school both socially and academically. At conference time the teacher told her parents that the records showed that Mary had been a problem student for several years. When Mary's parents asked to see her records, the teacher refused, saying such records were confidential. Do Mary's parents have a right to see her records? Why or why not?

The legal position: Under the Family Educational and Privacy Act of 1974, parents have the right to inspect and review all their child's school records. The school must establish a procedure for complying with a request to see student records and may take no longer than forty-five days to comply with a request. The school must notify parents of their rights under this law.

Parents also have the right to a hearing to challenge any inaccurate, misleading, or inappropriate information in the records. If such information is found, it must be corrected or removed. Parents may insert a written explanation about challenged information in the records.

Before the records are given to anybody, except school officials and the courts, parents have to give the school specific written approval. This approval must include details of the specific records to be given out, the reason for giving the records, and the person to whom the records are to be given. Before records are given to courts, both the student and parents must be notified.

SITUATION 3. A group of students approached their advisor, Mr. Jefferson, to seek permission to meet one night a week at school in order to hold sessions of their political club. Mr. Jefferson said he would look into it and get back to them. Can the students do this? Why or why not?

The legal position: Students should be permitted to hold student meetings on school property during school hours. After school hours, they would be limited, just as any other community group, under the state law. This may mean paying rent or a charge for any damage.

Students also have the right to gather informally as long as they do not substantially disrupt the educational process.

Situation 4.   It's "one of those days," and Angela, a junior high school teacher, has decided she just can't take any more. She paddles a student. What do you think the Supreme Court would say about that?

The legal position: In a 1977 case,[6] an eighth-grade student in Florida was paddled for being slow to answer a teacher's question. The severity of the beating, more than twenty blows with a wooden paddle, caused him to seek medical treatment and miss eleven days of school.

The U.S. Supreme Court, in a 5–4 decision on this case held that (1) the original intent of the Cruel and Unusual Punishment Clause of the Eighth Amendment was to control the punishment of criminals, and does not apply to disciplinary corporal punishment in public schools. The Court accepted the common law rule that teachers may impose reasonable but not excessive force to discipline the child. If the force is excessive and unreasonable, the teacher may be held liable in damages to the child and, if malice is shown, may be subject to criminal penalties; (2) the Due Process Clause does not require notice and a hearing prior to the administration of corporal punishment; and (3) the question of whether to continue corporal punishment in the schools is for legislatures and schools boards to decide.

Teacher Liability

One of the most compelling questions a teacher must consider is "when might I be sued?" Thiemich writes:[7]

Legal action is likely against a teacher when all, or some of the following allegations are made:

1. that a pupil suffered injury, loss, or damage.
2. that the pupil was not at fault for what happened.
3. that the teacher did not exercise sufficient care or supervision.
4. that there is a cause-and-effect relationship between the act (or failure to act) and the incident which caused the injury. This cause-and-effect relationship is referred to as "proximate cause."

Teacher liability, or the question of who is legally responsible, is never automatic. A teacher, or the school district, is liable only if liability is established in a court of law. It is interesting to note that a teacher carries *greater* responsibility for the safety of children than do parents and other adults. Teachers are expected to be even more careful than parents because teachers are considered trained specialists in child supervision, discipline, and pupil control.

---

[6]*Ingraham* v. *Wright,* 430 U.S. 651, 97 Ct. 1402, 51 L.Ed. 2d. 711 (1977).

[7]A. Thiemich, "Tort Liability in Education" (St. Paul, Minn.: Minnesota Education Association, 1980), p. 1.

It is impossible to cover the wide range of potential incidents out of which legal action might be taken against the teacher. Thiemich[8] describes the most likely situations out of which *torts,* or civil lawsuits, could occur.

Torts are likely to relate to certain situations or sets of circumstances. They may rise in relation to all or some of the following conditions when a pupil is injured:

1. an action is taken where a reasonably prudent teacher should realize that there is possible risk to pupils or others.
2. there has been a failure to act when necessary to protect and assist those supervised, or as duty requires.
3. negligence is evident, in the case of someone known to be dangerous, inadequate, or incompetent (i.e., student teachers, lay assistants, aides).

Here is a sample situation. Test your own information about teacher liability against the opinion of the court.

SITUATION. Larry was a first-year teacher. He had made excellent progress and was given a student teacher for the spring semester. Because the student teacher seemed quite capable, Larry would often leave the classroom to use the ditto machine or to correct papers in the faculty room. One day Larry was summoned abruptly because a student had climbed on a desk, fallen off, and broken her hip. Extensive surgery would be needed. Is Larry potentially liable in this case? Why or why not?

The legal position: The use of a student teacher in the classroom should immediately be recognized by a teacher as a possible risk situation. A student teacher or aide can be presumed to be less experienced in the control of pupil behavior and may be less skilled in recognizing risk. It becomes the duty of the *supervising teacher* (in this case Larry) to make an extra effort to protect pupils under such a situation.

What protections exist for the teacher? There are three types of protection available to most teachers. The first is governmental immunity. In the past it served as a protective umbrella for school employees. Given the tenor of recent court decisions, however, it is clear that individual teachers will be held responsible for their actions, particularly where negligence can be established.

A second line of defense for the teacher is the school district. In most districts, legal counsel will be provided (and paid for) where action is taken against a teacher. School districts may, however, be responsible only for the costs of legal counsel and not for payment of adverse judgments or other costs. State law in some states mandates that districts carry liability insurance, in which case district employees would be covered for settlement claims.

---

[8]A. Thiemich, "Tort Liability in Education" (St. Paul, Minn.: Minnesota Education Association, 1980), p. 2.

Perhaps the best form of protection for the individual teacher, however, is *employment liability insurance*. While the larger school districts often provide this, it may prove inadequate. Both the AFT and the NEA offer liability protection to teachers who belong to those organizations.

The preceding discussion illustrates the complexities of teachers' legal responsibilities. The National Education Association (NEA) has developed a code of educators' obligations to their students, to the public, and to the profession.

PROFESSIONAL RIGHTS

The responsibility of teachers toward individual students represents a sacred trust. Except for parents, few persons have such potential to influence young lives. But teachers, too, are individual human beings, and their rights must also be carefully guarded. Teacher rights may be divided into civil rights, rights of academic freedom, and contractural rights.

Civil Rights

As citizens, teachers have the same civil rights as everyone else. The American Federation of Teachers (AFT) has drafted a bill of rights that specifies the civil rights of teachers. This bill of rights is presented here.

Academic Freedom

The amount of control a teacher has over what is taught and how it is taught varies from school system to school system, and in fact, from school to school. For the most part, state or local governing bodies set up curriculum policy, select textbooks, and often even establish standards of minimum competency and/or administer achievement tests. Thus, in the public school system, there is little room for much deviation from the prescribed requirements of subject matter. However a teacher's own personal emphasis, or an administrator's leadership, for example, will affect what is taught.

Teaching styles vary as well. A teacher's philosophy of education may have to follow guidelines set up by a school board, but it is still that teacher's own philosophy. How the teacher presents material, handles classroom management and discipline, treats his or her students—these are all factors of teaching that will vary from person to person.

In some private schools, much more academic freedom exists than in public schools. Some private schools encourage teacher creativity and open education. In private schools, teachers are often responsible for developing the school programs and goals, whereas in public schools, such matters are often established by the school board. Throughout this book discussions of different types of school systems and different focuses on teaching will illuminate the many issues involved in teacher autonomy and academic freedom.

The rights and responsibilities of academic freedom are concerns of the professional teacher organizations (the NEA and the AFT) as well. By influencing local, state, and federal policy, the professional organizations play a role in what is taught. A later section discusses some of the goals of the teachers' organizations.

Contractual Rights

When a teacher takes a new teaching position, he or she signs a contract that specifies the terms of his or her professional agreement with the school board of that district. The terms of the contract include the number of days for which the teacher is expected to report for duty, the salary for the year, and specified legal holidays. Contracts are granted for one-year periods.

Other contractual elements include tenure and collective bargaining and the right to strike.

TENURE. Within the education profession, tenure is a status granted to a teacher after a trial period which protects him or her from dismissal without just cause.

In a legal sense, teachers are hired, rehired, or not rehired by the school board. In most cases, new teachers are hired for a probationary period, generally three years. During the probationary period a teacher's annual contract may or may not be renewed as the school board sees fit. If the board wishes not to rehire a probationary teacher, it must submit a written statement of the cause of the discharge at least thirty days prior to the effective date, and the teacher has no right of appeal.

After a teacher has served his or her probationary period, he or she is granted tenure. Tenure ensures that a teacher may not be discharged without a hearing. There are basically five grounds for the dismissal of a tenured teacher. Following are the five reasons from the document *Tenure for Minnesota Teachers in Cities of the First Class.*

> Subd. 4. (Grounds for discharge or demotion). *Causes for the discharge or demotion of a teacher either during or after the probationary period shall be:*
>
> 1. Immoral character, conduct unbecoming a teacher, or insubordination;
> 2. Failure without justifiable cause to teach without first securing the written release of the school board having the care, management, or control of the school in which the teacher is employed;
> 3. Inefficiency in teaching or in the management of a school;
> 4. Affliction with active tuberculosis or other communicable disease shall be considered as cause for removal or suspension while the teacher is suffering from such disability; or
> 5. Discontinuance of position or lack of pupils.

COLLECTIVE BARGAINING AND THE RIGHT TO STRIKE. A few short years ago, the idea of public school teachers on strike was virtually unthinkable. Mine workers, newspaper employees, and cabdrivers might strike, but not teachers. Teachers were professionals, and professionals do not strike. More than that, teachers were viewed as public servants much in the same way as police and firefighters were viewed. Calvin Coolidge, then Mayor of Boston, said about the 1919 attempted police strike, "There is no right to strike against the public safety."

The watershed years of the late 1960s and 1970s brought about new perceptions of the role of public servants. Alvin Toffler cited these changing role perceptions as a manifestation of future shock. Firefighters on strike. Police on strike. Teachers on strike.

Widespread opposition to unionism has disappeared among teachers in recent years. Both the NEA and the AFT have adopted an industrial model which includes collective bargaining and the right to strike as basic rights of the rank and file. Fifteen years ago, fewer than 100,000 public school teachers were serving under formal, written contracts. Today, virtually all public school teachers are covered by contractural agreements.

As each school year begins, thousands of teachers in districts across the land find themselves on strike. Teachers have joined organized labor.

CONDUCT CODES AND ETHICAL STANDARDS

A professional, by definition, aspires to conduct of the highest ethical standards. Whether that professional works in the field of law, medicine, education, or another profession, we expect of him or her an exemplary standard of conduct. The term "role model" is often applied to those in positions of leadership and public trust. We are saddened when a star athlete is sanctioned for drug abuse or gambling. We are shocked when a teacher has sexual relations with any student. The trust is broken, and fellow professionals suffer along with the offender. There is something implicit in the role of a teacher that calls for high moral character and positive social values.

In 1919 the Chicago White Sox stunned the sports world by "throwing" the World Series to their opponents. The star player of the White Sox, Shoeless Joe Jackson, was implicated in the scandal. As Jackson left the courtroom, a little boy is said to have looked up at his disgraced hero and said, "Say it ain't so, Joe." In more recent times, the alleged gambling connections of Pete Rose, the all-time Major League leader in base hits and in a number of other categories, resulted in his banishment from baseball.

Scandal, of course, comes sooner or later to all professions. It is a sad fact of human existence. The bad news makes headlines, while the positive efforts of so many professionals are taken for granted. The bad headlines cast shadows over the work of the professional athlete who visits children's wards in hospitals, spreading a little cheer. Lost in the furor over the teacher who broke the public trust are the quiet stories of the teacher who stayed late at school night after night to help a student catch up on his work after a serious illness, of the teacher who mobilized her class to collect food for the needy, of the teacher who takes papers home to grade night after night.

Violations of the Washington State Teachers' Code of Professional Conduct

- Sexual contact with any student enrolled in the teacher's district, with any former student under the age of 18, or with any student under the teacher's professional guidance, including students over 18 and those at a school-sponsored activity.
- Possession, use or consumption of hard drugs or of controlled drugs without a prescription.
- Consumption of alcohol on school premises or at a school activity if it is against the school's or district's policy.
- Falsification or misrepresentations in professional conduct, such as on applications for scholarships, jobs, grants or financial reports.
- Failure to file a complaint with the state superintendent's office when there is "reasonable suspicion" of unprofessional conduct; and failure to participate in an official inquiry by the superintendent's office.
- Use of a position for personal financial gain: for example, a sports coach who indirectly requires attendance at his private sports clinic, or a music teacher who pressures students to buy instruments only from his music store.
- Abandoning the general standards of the profession, such as harming students by failing to follow testing protocol, or a principal's failure to keep watch on school finances.

Over the last three years, while debate on education produced few results in the Legislature, the state Board of Education has approved extensive reforms of the teaching profession with little fanfare.

Among them were raising academic standards for teachers at private schools, requiring more training to teach specific subjects and increasing the amount of continuing education.

Source: *Seattle Post-Intelligencer*, December 8, 1989.

The purpose of a professional conduct code is to police the profession. In education, most conduct codes are written by the professionals themselves and approved by the particular state board of education. Violations of the code can result in various potential penalties, depending upon the severity of the violation, ranging from letters of reprimand to the outright revocation of a teacher's license. Beyond that, legal sanctions are also possible through the state criminal justice system.

In Washington state, for example, the Board of Education in 1989 approved a strict code of professional conduct for teachers. The code was written by teachers, administrators, and state officials. The new code encourages self-policing of the profession as opposed to the former procedure of allowing the state superintendent's office to revoke a teacher's certificate only following a criminal conviction. The new code clearly spells out the boundaries of professional conduct.

As we implied earlier, a true professional aspires to conduct of the highest ethical standards, shunning even the hint of impropriety. And we consider it a step in the right direction when the teaching profession comes to grips with sanctions for professional wrongdoing. Our criminal justice system sanctions the conduct of all citizens, but, for professionals, the profession itself must spell out its own set of standards in addition to those provided by legislation.

PROFESSIONAL ORGANIZATIONS

The two major professional organizations for teachers are the National Education Association (NEA) and the American Federation of Teachers (AFT). Membership in the NEA exceeds 1.7 million and that of the AFT is over 500,000. Slightly less than half of the 5.2 million-member teaching force of the United States belong to one or the other of the two organizations. The combined membership of the two organizations is greater than that of the Teamster's Union or the United Auto Workers.

The American Federation of Teachers (AFT)

The American Federation of Teachers (AFT) was established in 1916 and chartered that year by the American Federation of Labor. Present membership in the AFT is about 520,000. Interestingly, AFT card No. 1 was held by John Dewey.

The AFT claims to be both a union and a professional organization. In its capacity as a union, the AFT has led the fight for collective bargaining, higher salaries, and freedom from noninstructional chores. As a professional organization, the AFT has fought for involvement by teachers in educational policy decisions.

AFT membership is open to teachers but not to principals or other administrators. The AFT position is that a natural adversary relationship exists between teachers and those who are empowered to hire, fire, or discipline them.

The main working goals of the AFT include an increased level of federal support for education, federal assumption of state and local welfare costs in order to release more funds for schools, and federally mandated collective bargaining rights for all state and local employees.

Other AFT goals include the seeking of federal initiatives in the areas of early childhood education and adult (lifelong) education.

In addition to holding its annual meeting, the QUEST consortium (Quality Education Standards in Teaching), the AFT publishes a monthly newspaper, *American Teacher,* and a quarterly professional journal, *American Educator.*

Teachers who belong to the AFT also belong to state affiliates (for example, the New York Federation of Teachers [NYFT], or the Texas Federation of Teachers [TFT]) and local affiliates as well.

Code of Ethics of the Education Profession*

Preamble

The educator, believing in the worth and dignity of each human being, recognizes the supreme importance of the pursuit of truth, devotion to excellence, and the nurture of democratic principles. Essential to these goals is the protection of freedom to learn and to teach and the guarantee of equal educational opportunity for all. The educator accepts the responsibility to adhere to the highest ethical standards.

The educator recognizes the magnitude of the responsibility inherent in the teaching process. The desire for the respect and confidence of one's colleagues, of students, of parents, and of the members of the community provides the incentive to attain and maintain the highest possible degree of ethical conduct. The *Code of Ethics of the Education Profession* indicates the aspiration of all educators and provides standards by which to judge conduct.

The remedies specified by the NEA and/or its affiliates for the violation of any provision of this *Code* shall be exclusive and no such provision shall be enforceable in any form other than one specifically designated by the NEA or its affiliates.

Principle I: Commitment to the Student

The educator strives to help each student realize his or her potential as a worthy and effective member of society. The educator therefore works to stimulate the spirit of inquiry, the acquisition of knowledge and understanding, and the thoughtful formulation of worthy goals.

In fulfillment of the obligation to the student, the educator—

1. Shall not unreasonably restrain the student from independent action in the pursuit of learning.
2. Shall not unreasonably deny the student access to varying points of view.
3. Shall not deliberately suppress or distort subject matter relevant to the student's progress.
4. Shall make reasonable effort to protect the student from conditions harmful to learning or to health and safety.
5. Shall not intentionally expose the student to embarrassment or disparagement.
6. Shall not on the basis of race, color, creed, sex, national origin, marital status, political or religious beliefs, family, social or cultural background, or sexual orientation, unfairly—
   a. Exclude any student from participation in any program
   b. Deny benefits to any student

    c. Grant any advantage to any student.

7. Shall not use professional relationships with students for private advantage.

8. Shall not disclose information about students obtained in the course of professional service, unless disclosure serves a compelling purpose or is required by law.

Principle II: Commitment to the Profession

The education profession is vested by the public with a trust and responsibility requiring the highest ideals of professional service.

In the belief that the quality of the services of the education profession directly influences the nation and its citizens, the educator shall exert every effort to raise professional standards, to promote a climate that encourages the exercise of professional judgment, to achieve conditions which attract persons worthy of the trust to careers in education, and to assist in preventing the practice of the profession by unqualified persons.

In fulfillment of the obligation to the profession, the educator—

1. Shall not in an application for a professional position deliberately make a false statement or fail to disclose a material fact related to competency and qualifications.

2. Shall not misrepresent his/her professional qualifications.

3. Shall not assist any entry into the profession of a person known to be unqualified in respect to character, education, or other relevant attribute.

4. Shall not knowingly make a false statement concerning the qualifications of a candidate for a professional position.

5. Shall not assist a noneducator in the unauthorized practice of teaching.

6. Shall not disclose information about colleagues obtained in the course of professional service unless disclosure serves a compelling professional purpose or is required by law.

7. Shall not knowingly make false or malicious statements about a colleague.

8. Shall not accept any gratuity, gift, or favor that might impair or appear to influence professional decisions or action.

*Source: *NEA Handbook.*

The National Education Association (NEA)

The National Education Association (NEA), with its nearly 2 million members, is by far the larger of the two dominant professional organizations for teachers. The AFT's strength has traditionally been in the East and larger cities, while the NEA has held dominance in the Midwest, South, and West as well as in suburban and small-town districts throughout the country.

The NEA was founded in 1857 as the National Teachers Association. It later merged with the American Normal School Association and the National Association of School Superintendents.

In the past, the NEA resisted a union label, but in recent times its posture has become more militant. Increasingly, the NEA position on such issues as teacher strikes, sanctions, and collective bargaining has come to resemble that of the AFT.

Among the stated goals of the NEA are increased state and federal support for public education, teacher rights, and increased teacher salaries. The two overriding purposes of the NEA have traditionally been (1) to elevate the character and advance the interests of the profession of teaching, and (2) to promote the cause of education in the United States.

A tangible outcome of the NEA's goal structure has been the establishment of national Teacher Centers. The Teacher Centers have begun to provide leadership in the areas of teacher preparation and professional development. At the present time, more than 120 regional Teacher Centers exist in the United States.

The NEA holds a large (10,000 + attendance) convention yearly at which delegates deal with the pressing issues in the educational process. *Today's Education,* the official journal of the NEA, is published monthly. In addition, the NEA publishes numerous professional papers and booklets ranging from studies of research in teaching and learning to materials on teacher rights.

Two Organizations or One?

For years, there has been talk of a merger between the NEA and the AFT. To date, no serious plan is afoot to make such a merger. Of course, one large organization would have more visibility and influence than two smaller organizations.

One of the stumbling blocks to a merger is the question of membership. The AFT allows teachers only, while NEA membership is open to anyone in education, including principals and superintendents. To the AFT, principals and superintendents represent management while teachers represent labor; the NEA makes no such clear-cut distinction.

A final point to consider is that *more than half* of America's teaching force belongs to no professional organization.

SUMMARY

For the person who enters teaching with an understanding of the wider definition of education, there are many opportunities in the profession. Besides jobs in public and private schools, teaching positions exist in business, in government, in social services, and in the health professions. Factors influencing job availability include types of schools, specific subject areas, geographic location, level of teaching, nonschool positions, and teaching alternatives. Salaries vary according to teacher experience and education, as well as according to geography and types of schools. Most states have certification requirements for teachers; some states have competency standards and testing which must be fulfilled before certification is possible. Professional responsibilities of the teacher include an awareness of the rights of students; further, a teacher is liable for most of what goes on in the classroom although liability generally must be established by the court following a lawsuit. The teacher has professional rights; among these are civil rights and rights of academic freedom; in addition, he or she has contractual rights including tenure, the right of collective bargaining, and the right to strike. The professional organizations—the American Federation of Teachers (AFT) and the National Education Association (NEA)—establish standards of practice, professional codes of ethics, and guidelines for teachers' rights. These organizations are the principal bargaining agents in contract negotiations. They also function as lobby groups affecting federal, state, and local policy.

ACTIVITIES

1. List the factors influencing job availability. Next, determine what type of teaching position is in greatest demand in your area. Determine what type of position is in lowest demand. (You will need to do some investigating of the factors to respond to this problem.)

2. Investigate teachers' salaries in a school district near you. Compare this figure with the salaries of other occupations. (Choose at least two others.) How do you feel about the differences?

3. Make a list of rights that you feel you should have as a student. Now, make a list of rights you feel you should have when you are a teacher. Compare.

4. Examine the requirements for certification in your state. Compare these requirements with those of another state. Do the requirements seem fair? Does either state require preservice competency testing? What do you think of minimum competency tests for teachers?

5. In a school system where textbooks and curriculum are prescribed by the school board, how does a teacher maintain a degree of academic freedom? Is this an important issue to you?

6. Research the similarities and the differences between the AFT and the NEA. Which organization appeals to you more? Do you feel the organizations should merge?

SUGGESTED READINGS

BOLLES, RICHARD, *What Color Is Your Parachute?* Berkeley, Cal.: Ten Speed Press, 1991.

COMBS, ARTHUR, et al., *The Professional Education of Teachers.* Boston: Allyn & Bacon, 1974.

The Condition of Education, published yearly by the National Center for Educational Statistics.

Estimates of School Statistics, published yearly by the National Education Association.

PARKAY, F. W., and B. HARDCASTLE, *Becoming a Teacher.* Boston: Allyn & Bacon, 1990.

RUBIN, DAVID, and STEVEN GREENHOUSE, *The Rights of Teachers.* New York: American Civil Liberties Union, 1983.

RYAN, KEVIN, and JAMES COOPER, *Kaleidoscope: Readings in Education* (4th ed.). Boston: Houghton Mifflin, 1984.

Chapter 3

EDUCATIONAL REFORM
A Beginning . . .

EDUCATIONAL REFORM
>   Past and Present
>   The Issues

STATE VERSUS LOCAL CONTROL: THE SEARCH FOR BALANCE
>   The Answers(?)

EFFECTIVE SCHOOLS AND EFFECTIVE TEACHING

THE CONTRIBUTIONS OF RESEARCH TO EDUCATIONAL
REFORM

This textbook is intended as a clarifying experience. Our intent is to introduce the basic and abiding issues in education. We will present ideas, to paraphrase Alexander Pope, not as a maze, but as a map. Throughout the pages of this chapter, we will discuss a broad range of topics—from salaries to curriculum, from schooling to accountability—but at all times, our overview of education will be focused on education as it relates to you.

At the simplest level, for reform to take place knowledge must be transacted. Thus we will provide you with information to read and to consider. But in a deeper sense, reform depends upon the involvement of the professional. To that end, we will ask you to respond to our ideas from time to time. We will ask you to make judgments. We will ask you to create ideas for reform.

In this chapter, we will examine the current educational reform movement and the impact that the movement is having on education. We will look at some of the prescriptions for upgrading the schools. We will also examine the components of effective schools and effective teaching. Are you ready for "the challenge"?

EDUCATIONAL REFORM

Past and Present

The decade of the 1980s emerged as an era of intense scrutiny of the educational world. Commission after commission brought to bear its findings, which, in every instance, can be summarized by the simple conclusion: *the quality of our education system must be improved.* The clarion call to Excellence, an elusive quality at best, was sounded throughout the land by professionals, politicians, and the lay public.

The rhetoric of reform was strong. One report, headed by a former United States Commissioner of Education, stated that the nation was "at risk," that it was endangered by a "rising tide of mediocrity." Excellence and mediocrity are far apart on everyone's tide table.

In the autumn of 1957 the Soviet Union placed into Earth orbit the world's first artificial satellite, a grapefruit-sized sphere with a radio transmitter in it. It was called Sputnik. The United States had its own satellite in orbit within months of the Soviet launching, but the point had been made to millions of Americans that something was wrong. If we were not first in space, it followed logically that we were not first in a number of other arenas, most notably in the classrooms where present and future scientists were cultivated. Thus an outside event served as catalyst for an era of sustained attempts at educational reform. The launching of Sputnik coalesced public opinion, and it became reasonably easy to enact legislation that freed dollars toward efforts to change the education system. This became especially so as the society was mobilized behind efforts to provide equality of opportunity for children of all races. The reform era, which lasted through the 1960s and into the early 1970s, was primarily one dedicated to curriculum change: new math, new science, new social studies, and so on. There were also some attempts to change patterns of instruction leading to such innovations as team teaching and open schools. In short, it was a time of expansion—the student population reached new highs, creating more jobs for teachers—and of great experimentation.

In time, the revolution ran its course. It became the victim of a number of related societal forces, among them a primitive but powerful movement called "back to basics," which was essentially a call for a return to instruction as it had apparently existed prior to the curriculum revolution of the 1960s.

Our purpose here is not to offer a detailed account of the educational scene over the past thirty years, but merely to sketch the backdrop against which the current calls to reform exist. As ideas for the reformation of American public education are put forward in the closing years of the twentieth century, it is well to keep in mind several important factors: (1) for more than two decades there has been a steady decline in performance on most standardized tests of achievement by American students, (2) approximately one-fourth of our young people do not finish high school, (3) it has become increasingly difficult to recruit the ablest high school graduates into the teaching profession, and (4) basic skills testing of teacher education college graduates for certification as public school teachers in several states has shown failure rates of 30 percent and higher. These and other items, widely circulated as news stories by the popular press, have once again brought us to a watershed in American educational history.

A curious contrast is found between the prescribed reform measures of the 1960s and those of the 1980s. The earlier period saw the path to salvation in the form of the applications to school settings of the research findings of certain learning theories, particularly applications of the relatively new (to the schools) ideas of cognitive psychology and behavioralism, inquiry learning, behavioral objectives, behavior modification, and competency-based instruction.

Current reform measures represented a more modest, less expansive agenda. Few, if any, contained curriculum innovations or ideas for experimentation. They were, rather, a stern, no-nonsense call to higher standards: higher standards of achievement, of teacher training, of discipline. The ideas put forth ranged from lengthening the school day and school year (the "more is better" theory) to recruiting teachers directly from industry and/or subject matter areas, bypassing schools of education. In most instances the reform measures, unlike their 1960s counterparts, did not call for massive infusions of federal money for their development and implementation. In short, the earlier era was one of creative (often naive) energy devoted to program development, and the later era was one of emphasis on academic standards in a far narrower sense, based on the floodtide of legislation by the states.

The Issues

How did we arrive at this supposedly sorry state of affairs? The best answer seems to be that no one really knows. Possible reasons include an expansion of the career opportunities available to women (such as in law and business),

A National Goal Structure for Education

In 1990, President George Bush, acting in concert with the National Governor's Association, proposed the following national goals for education, to be achieved by the year 2000:

- All students "will start school ready to learn."
- The percentage of students graduating from high school will increase to at least 90 percent.
- Students will "demonstrate competency over challenging subject matter, including English, mathematics, science, history, and geography" in assessments in grades 4, 8, and 12.
- American students will "be first in the world" in achievement in science and mathematics.
- Every adult American will be literate and possess the skills "necessary to compete in a global economy and exercise the rights and responsibilities of citizenship."
- All schools will be free of drugs and violence and "offer a disciplined environment conducive to learning."

What is your response to these ambitious goals? How realistic and/or attainable are they? Do you agree with them? All of them? Some of them? What other goals do you think the President and the governors should have listed? What will it take to improve the condition of American education whether we subscribe to the goals listed above or another set of goals?

teaching salaries that have not kept pace with those of other professions, the general loss of prestige of teaching as a vocation, apathy on the part of students and parents, lack of sufficient funds, and so on.

The suggestions put forth as remedies by various groups include lures to bright students such as cash incentives, grants in aid, and forgivable loans. Other ideas include greatly increased teacher salaries and even differential salaries so that crucial areas such as math and science teaching could attract people from industry.

The other problem, that of upgrading the quality of teacher training, is equally troublesome. While it is possible that no school of education could reasonably be asked to perform miracles with the apparently less able group of students preparing for careers in education today, there does exist a widespread concern that much of what passes for teacher training is of questionable value. Certain states, notably New York, Georgia, and New Jersey, have instituted programs whereby college graduates with no pedagogical training are able to receive provisional certification to teach in the subject area of their academic degree. While the ostensible reason for such a move is to react quickly to fill the ranks in areas of teacher shortages, it is clear that there are those who value the content background of a teacher over the methodological training he/she might have received and that they are influential enough to persuade state certifying departments of their point over the objections of the teachers' unions and teacher training institutions.

The issue of teacher competency continues to grow, and schools of education find themselves increasingly under fire for producing essentially incompetent teachers. There is a certain irony to this in light of the fact that the vast majority of teacher competency tests are not tests of pedagogy but rather of the most basic skills of literacy and numeracy which should have been acquired not during teacher training, but prior to that time. It has long been assumed, wrongly perhaps, that anyone trained in methodology would already possess the skills of reading, spelling, writing, and computation. Now a whole new growth industry has emerged in education. Such businesses are peopled by those who operate remedial skills "labs," which service the victims of English and math tests and so on, and by those who develop, "validate," and administer teacher competency tests. No doubt, in time, the legal profession will become involved in the spate of litigation which will follow, as teachers and would-be teachers are rejected from the profession through testing.

The common argument of the National Education Association (NEA) and of many schools of education is that teaching competencies have less to do with knowledge of basic skills than with the ability to perform effectively in the classroom. The feeling is that while the two may be related, that is not necessarily the case. Regarding the testing of teachers and teaching candidates, the NEA's position is unequivocal:

> The NEA condemns any legislation which requires teachers, regardless of experience, to be tested in reading, writing, and mathematics, as well as their major fields of certification.
>
> The NEA opposes all testing of practicing teachers and must continue to monitor the development, implementation, and impact of testing on teaching candidates in order to ensure equity for all prospective teachers.

The two resolutions were adopted at the 1984 (The NEA's official position remains unchanged as of 1990) Representative Assembly in Minneapolis, along with a host of others, which included support for a Coors brewery boycott, the peace plan of the Democratic platform, the nuclear freeze, monitoring of day-care centers, protection of children from criminal abduction, expanded use of instructional technology, and higher wages for teachers.

In 1983, the National Commission on Excellence in Education published a remarkable document that called for educational reform in the schools of

America. The document was titled, *A Nation at Risk: The Imperative for Educational Reform. A Nation at Risk* became widely known for two key sentences, which were at the heart of the report's many recommendations:

> If an unfriendly foreign power had attempted to impose on America the mediocre educational performance that exists today, we might well have viewed it as an act of war.... We have, in effect, been commiting an act of unthinking, unilateral educational disarmament.[1]

Basically, the report said two things: (1) American education is mediocre at best, and (2) the purpose of education is to serve the national self-interest. These same two sentiments were expressed throughout the nation in 1957 when the Russian Sputnik came to symbolize the competitive edge the USSR's schools had presumably achieved over ours. In 1983, however, the competitive edge was presumably held not by the USSR but by Japan, an economic rather than a military competitor.

Thus did a *Nation at Risk* set the agenda for what was to become the list of problems which composed the educational debate of the 1980s. Those problems, though not surprising even in 1983, remain on the table for the educational reform movement of the 1990s. What are these problems and why have we not solved them in the past decade?

Foremost among the problems was the much lamented decline in literacy on the part of American students. Although this lack of literacy is discouraging, it is nothing new. In fact, the book *Why Johnny Can't Read*[2] was nearly 30 years old at the time the problem was noted once again in *A Nation at Risk*. What was surprising was the expansion of the literacy problem to include the recently coined term "cultural literacy." This concept, explored in great depth by E. D. Hirsch, Jr. in his book *Cultural Literacy*[3] and by Allan Bloom in *The Closing of the American Mind*,[4] raised the level of the debate from the chronically visited phonics/decoding skills arena to the search for a commonly held body of literature, history, and culture.

Another issue identified in the report included the disquieting number of students who drop out of public education prior to high school graduation, a figure variously estimated at 25 to 30 percent of students originally enrolled. Also cited in the report were the shortage of well-prepared, well-qualified teachers in such key areas of the curricula as math, physics, English, and special education; the "watered-down" nature of the school curricula itself (and its mainstay, the textbooks); the forecast of a society moving toward a large class of undereducated poor and a small class of comparatively well-educated elite; and the growing threat to education from disrupted home and family life, from drug and alcohol

---

[1] United States Department of Education, A Nation at Risk: The Imperative for Educational Reform, Washington, D.C., 1983.

[2] Flesch, Rudolph, *Why Johnny Can't Read*, New York: Harper and Row, 1956.

[3] Hirsch, E.D., Jr., *Cultural Literacy*, Boston: Houghton, Mifflin, 1987.

[4] Bloom, Allan, *The Closing of the American Mind*, New York: Simon and Schuster, 1987.

use among students, from discipline problems in classrooms, and from the lack of meaningful ways to address issues related to health and sexual education.

The problems addressed by *A Nation at Risk* were, and are, problems of great magnitude, and whether they are even "solvable" is problematic. Nevertheless, at least two distinctly different solutions were posed. The first attempt at a solution came in the form of a spate of legislation from each of the fifty state legislatures. Much of the legislation flowed directly from the recommendations set forth in *A Nation at Risk* and in the dozen or more other reports that called for similar reforms. Clearly, the legislative approach to school reform represented a top-down, centralized strategy. If the schools were not doing an adequate job of preparing our young people, then the solution was to pass laws, mandates, and regulations. These laundry lists of regulations, usually called initiatives, included proposals for longer school years, longer school days, stiffer graduation requirements, increased evaluation and testing of students, improved textbooks and materials, greater attention to and enforcement of school discipline, academic enrichment programs, specialized schools, improved teacher preparation, stiffer teacher certification requirements, and career ladder programs.

These early 1980s attempts at reform came, in the words of former National Education Association President Mary Hatwood Futrell, "not from the school-house, but from the statehouse."[5] In fact, the amount of school-directed legislative activity flowing from the fifty state legislatures was staggering. Upwards of 1,000 pieces of enacted legislation appeared, a veritable tidal wave of do's and don'ts washing over the schools. In short, the answer to school reform was thought to be found in the centralization of power and in increased bureaucratization. This was, of course, exactly the opposite path of that taken by the many successful corporate organizations around the world that were moving toward decentralization, deregulation, and away from top-down, enforced conformity.

It was a time in education characterized by research studies that showed that "effective schools" and "effective teachers" were those that used direct instruction, that taught the whole class together, and that enforced a high ratio of "time on task." Obviously, these are things you can tell teachers to do in the name of making them more effective. Thus, as Ernest Boyer, president of the Carnegie Foundation for the Advancement of Teaching, pointed out, teachers were being given "more responsibilities and less authority, less recognition, less empowerment. . . ."[6] Statewide regulation has, of course, been around for a long time in the form of credit requirements for graduation, textbook adoptions, length of school day and year, teacher certification, and so forth. What seems surprising in retrospect is the belief that achievement and satisfactions would improve by centralizing authority at the state (rather than the local) level and by mounting a frontal assault on the time-honored American educational tradition of local control.

[5] Futrell, Mary Hatwood, "Mission Possible: School Reform," *Phi Delta Kappan*, September 1989, p. 11.

[6] Boyer, Ernest, "An Imperiled Generation: Saving Urban Schools," Princeton: Carnegie Foundation for the Advancement of Teaching, 1988.

By the late 1980s, and now in the 1990s, a second wave of educational reform was ushered in. The top-down, centralized, bureaucratic approach to school improvement was widely attacked as lacking evidentiary credibility by such prestigious groups as the Carnegie Task Force on Teaching as a Profession, the National Governors' Association, the Education Commission of the States, the Holmes Group, and the Association for Supervision and Curriculum Development (ASCD). Even assuming that much of the research on effective schools was correct, the idea of telling local districts and schools what they must do in order to become better ran counter to the idea that the best way for a given school to improve is for that school to decide on its own goals and methods for achieving those goals. The shift to local control was on! As Theodore Sizer stated, "the decentralization of substantial authority to the persons closest to the students is essential."[7] Local control is a time-honored tenet of American education. And this time "teacher empowerment" lay at the heart of the matter.

Riding the crest of this second wave, every state developed legislation calling for proposals of "excellence" from local schools. The idea was, and is, to allow teachers to participate in "building-based management" and, as Mary Futrell wrote, to enact "the principle that effective reform must be defined, designed, and implemented by teachers at the local level, working in concert with the local community."[8] Thus, at least theoretically, excellence might vary widely from one locale to another. This represented a radical reversal of the first wave of reform, which stated that excellence could be spelled out and should be exported as a commodity to *all* schools. Such a remarkable shift from a centralized, "we'll tell you" position to a "you tell us" position in the space of a few years indicates just how shaky the ground of school reform really is. Whether our current decentralized mode of thinking about school reform is "better" is, again, problematic. Certainly, there is no reason to think that in order for schools to be excellent, they must be alike. Also, there is much to be said psychologically for allowing people to control their own destinies, particularly if those people are professionals. Thus the arguments for local control and diversity are compelling.

STATE VERSUS LOCAL CONTROL: THE SEARCH FOR BALANCE

As the balance of power in education continues its shift from a centralized to a decentralized locus, many inherent difficulties must be overcome, not the least of which is that, on average, a state's contribution to the funding base for schools is close to 50 percent. Such an enormous figure implies that states will not easily

[7]Sizer, Theodore, remarks to the Board of Directors of the National Education Association, 1986, quoted in Futrell, Mary Hatwood, "Mission Possible: School Reform," *Kappan*, September 1989.

[8]Futrell, Mary Hatwood, ibid., p. 14.

relinquish control to local school districts. Thus there is no easy answer to the question of whether or not or to what extent local control will emerge as the overwhelming approach to school reform that some have predicted for it. All the states are presently making attempts at school reform in such a way as to achieve an equitable balance of power between the particular state capital and its legislature and the local schools and school districts. One state, South Carolina, offers a good model. South Carolina takes what researchers Thomas Timar and David Kirp (1989) call an "interactive" approach to decision making, in which state and local control are brought into balance. The South Carolina model emphasizes balance between state accountability and local autonomy. As Timar and Kirp note, "the South Carolina experience also shows that authority and responsibility must be distributed across the entire system of education. . . . It is not enough simply to give schools more autonomy; encouragement and support must come from the state, as well" (1989, p. 510).

A list of selected topics from the South Carolina Education Improvement Act of 1984, as amended in 1985–89, illustrates that state's attempt to balance state and local authority. For example, the "Teacher Incentive Program" spells out clear state guidelines to reward teachers who demonstrate superior performance and productivity in their classrooms. But, to reinforce local authority, the guidelines state that "no teacher may receive funds under the incentive program unless he meets or exceeds all the eligibility standards set out in the district's program" (1989). Other topics address community involvement, parents as partners in their children's education, and broadening the participation of business and industry in the public schools. Thus we see in the case of one state, and others will undoubtedly follow, a sincere attempt to achieve a reasonable balance of power between the state and the individual locality.

The Answers(?)

The number of major reports which have been issued in the past several years is unprecedented. Never in the years of the republic has such widespread attention to American education been accompanied by so many prescriptions for improvement. Of the dozen or more major reports calling for reform of the nation's schools, several threads of commonality emerge. Of those threads we will use the next few pages to examine five prescriptions for upgrading the schools.

INCREASED CLASSROOM DISCIPLINE. A majority of the reports have called for an increased emphasis on classroom discipline, the prevailing feeling being that if teachers are not able to enforce rules, then all else is for naught. There is widespread professional and public belief that the screws must be tightened. The U.S. Department of Education's Commission on Excellence recommends "the development of firm and fair codes of student conduct that are enforced consistently"; and the Action for Excellence report of the Task Force of Education for Economic Growth calls for the creation of "firm, explicit, and demanding requirements regarding discipline, attendance, homework, and grades." A recent publication titled *Effective Schools and Classrooms: A Research-based Perspective* (Association for Supervision and Curriculum Development, 1984) begins a chapter titled, "Effective Schools: What the Research Says," by stating, "Pick a school you know and ask . . . does the school have an orderly environment?"

The report to the National Science Board, titled *Educating Americans for the 21st Century,* states that

> [the] breakdown of order in the classroom is one of the more disturbing manifestations of today's educational crisis. Discipline and, therefore, the ability on the part of the students to concentrate is too often absent in classrooms across the Nation. Such problems make it difficult for even knowledgeable, creative teachers to teach. The lack of disciplinary codes and the interpretation of the law often limit administrators and teachers from effectively dealing with discipline problems. Action that should be taken to maintain a classroom environment that is conducive to teaching and learning includes:
>
> - The adoption by schools of vigorous discipline policies which reflect goals and expectations.
> - Clear, written statements of the rules. These statements should be distributed to students and parents at the beginning of the school year. All rules should be applied consistently, fairly, and impartially.
> - Modification, where necessary, of state laws to permit effective discipline in the schools.
> - Greater support by parents of discipline in the school and classroom.

IMPROVED TEACHER TRAINING. The concern for the teacher as an improved product takes on two dimensions: (1) the quality of those who choose teaching as a career, and (2) the quality of their preparation—both professional and academic. Both issues are profound and difficult to treat. It is probably close to impossible to argue the validity of these concerns, but to remedy them poses a set of problems for which there exists no sure or agreed-upon cure.

The first issue, that of the quality of those who choose to become teachers, is vexing to say the least. The absolute number of graduating high school seniors who indicate a desire to become teachers has dropped dramatically in recent years. Only about 5 percent of current entering college freshmen indicate an intent to pursue an education major compared with about 20 percent a decade ago. This, of course, poses problems for schools of education because they are now forced to select applicants from a far smaller, often less talented pool of prospective students. Whereas a few years ago teacher-training screening committees were able to reject less promising applicants, that is seldom any longer the case. To compound the problem, which otherwise might merely be one of supply/demand ratios, those who do indicate a career preference for teaching are hardly the best and brightest. Emily Feistritzer of Feistritzer Associates, a consulting firm that, among other things, tries to make sense of educational statistics, writes,

> The level of student ability, as measured by Scholastic Aptitude Test (SAT) scores, of those choosing education as a profession is at an all-time low. Scores of

college-bound seniors planning to study education in 1982 were 32 points lower than all college-bound seniors on the verbal portion of the test and 48 points lower on the mathematics section. Compared to the 36 possible fields of study that a college-bound senior could select, those who chose education ranked 33rd on their SAT scores. Only seniors intending to major in home economics, ethnic studies, or trade and vocational fields had lower verbal and mathematics scores.[9]

One proposed remedy is to abolish undergraduate teacher training. Under this approach, suggested by the influential Holmes Group, only people with accredited degrees would be accepted by schools of education for training. This practice has gained favor around the country, particularly in the larger, more prestigious schools. Supposedly, people who already possess academic degrees will be better grounded in both the knowledge and the basic skills of literacy, numeracy, etc. The effect of the Holmes Group proposal has been a sweeping change from a prebaccalaureate method of teacher training to a postbaccalaureate approach. Like so many other educational innovations, it has been accomplished almost entirely on the basis of its seeming propriety rather than on any substantive evidence that this approach will indeed produce better teachers.

Teacher Salaries. There is a perception that teacher salaries, while not particularly high compared to the salaries of other professions, are adequate because teachers are typically assigned a work year of 180 days or 36 weeks, while the work year elsewhere in our society is generally considered 240 days or 48 weeks. The reasoning goes that it is quite logical to pay someone less who spends 25 percent less time on the job, especially when the source of funding is public money. The majority of the commission reports call for a longer year, not only for teachers but for students as well. The *Nation at Risk* report recommended a 200–220 day school year with 11-month teacher contracts, the difference between the 220 days and the 11 months being devoted by teachers to professional development and to programs for students with special needs. Signing teachers to contracts which call for more work days is, of course, a reason to raise their salaries.

Career Ladders. One of the problems that has plagued the teaching profession in good and bad times has been the absence of any kind of system of promotion. The beginning teacher holds essentially the same rank as the veteran of many years. All public (and many private) school systems reward years of service and credits earned beyond the bachelor's degree with pay raises, but there has been no corresponding method of granting the kinds of psychological advances found in college teaching, where it is possible to advance through various professional ranks, or in the system used by the federal government to advance civilian and military employees.

[9]C. Emily Feistritzer, *The American Teacher* (Washington, D.C.: Feistritzer Publications, 1983), p. 56.

The Policies of Accountability: Nine Necessary School Board Policies

Boards should ask their administrators to develop and present to them for review, revision, and approval a comprehensive set of policies that:

1. Recognize outstanding teaching performance through a system of promotions up a career ladder accompanied by appropriate salary increases.
2. Promote teacher inservice growth and improvement.
3. Identify and weed out teachers who do not perform well and would therefore be happier in other work.
4. Require student performance within limits of measurable standards.
5. Reward and motivate students to reach the outer limits of their ability.
6. Encourage public support and recognition of excellence in learning.
7. Protect time-on-task learning at school by limiting activities that cut into the same.
8. Require student mastery of a central core of very challenging academic subjects (such as the "new basics" recommended by the National Commission on Excellence in Education) that will produce highly literate, academically competent students.
9. Mandate the development of curricula that will motivate and challenge students on varying ability levels so that all may experience opportunity to reach the outer limits of learning capacity.

T. H. Bell, Secretary of Education, October 1983.

Critics of American education have pointed to the lack of personal incentive which permeates a system where rewards are basically unrelated to performance. A salary scale which recognizes only years of service and college credits earned beyond the Bachelor's Degree is hardly a screen for separating excellence from mediocrity. There is good reason to suppose that in a system of any kind where poor performance is rewarded in equal measure to good performance, good performance suffers. The argument is put forth that teaching is a complex act which is difficult to assess. The National Education Association is on record as stating that the Association believes that instructional performance pay schedules, such as merit pay, are inappropriate because of the complexity of the teaching-learning process.

The argument that the complexity of a process makes it inappropriate to judge performance is an intriguing one which may have a certain amount of validity. On the other hand, most processes that involve human interaction are fraught with intangibles, yet attempts are still made at assessment. To assess a baseball player's performance, the result of complex processes, one looks at certain statistics: batting average, fielding percentage, stolen bases, runs batted in, and so on. Still, the player is part of a team, and such intangible measures as leadership, cooperation, and so forth must also be taken into account.

One could not, of course, press the analogy too far between teaching and playing a game without raising an uproar. But if batting, fielding, base running, and pitching are basic skills of baseball—and can not only be identified but measured as well, in spite of the intricately complex processes involved in each—then might we not ask the question whether the teaching/learning process permits some identifiable measures of performance? An answer to that question is posed by the Florida Coalition for the Development of a Performance Evaluation System, a group representing school districts, the Florida Department of Education, and schools of education in Florida. The coalition has documented one hundred and twenty-one specific teacher behaviors that have been shown through research to be directly related to increased student achievement and improved classroom conduct.

What the Florida group has done is of some significance. They have identified two important outcomes of teaching and learning, namely *student achievement* and *classroom conduct,* and have translated the findings of literally hundreds of research studies into a "knowledge base for the measurement and development of teacher performance." The intent is to use this and seven other accompanying volumes as part of the meritorious teacher program created by the Florida Legislature.

At the present time, twenty-four states have adopted or are considering master teacher or career ladder programs, and six have pilot projects under way. In most cases, the career ladders have several rungs which incorporate both title and pay differentiation. Tennessee's Career Teacher Program includes a first-year Probationary Teacher rank and four "incentive steps" from Apprentice Teacher through Career Levels I, II, and III. Salary add-on ranges are from $500 to $7000, depending on the level and the length of the contract (for example, nine months versus ten months). The Career Teacher Program includes a requirement that teachers pass a recertification evaluation every five years. Teachers are evaluated at the local level for advancement up the first three rungs, but state teams will evaluate candidates for Career II and III levels.

MERIT PAY.   The theory of merit pay is exceptionally simple: Pay people who produce more or who produce better results more money than people who produce less or who produce inferior results. In other words, you begin with the premise that not everyone contracted to do the same job will give you the same results. Some will give you better results than will others. Businesses have, of course, used merit reward systems for years. There is nothing new here. In some areas of the work place, merit pay is automatically built in. For example, people who are engaged in sales and who work on commission are paid according to how much they sell. Such a system encourages industrious employees to spend more time and energy trying to make sales.

District A: Structural Model Career Ladder Program

Probationary Teacher (Nontenured)

- Frequent formative evaluations by Level II/III teachers
- Require or recommend completion of Fifth Year program before or during the first three years of employment
- Tenure determinations in conformity with state guidelines and district policies

Career Level I

- Annual evaluations as mandated by law for tenured teachers
- Additional coursework as required by the State Department of Education/District guidelines
- Nine-month contract
- Responsibilities similar to those of current classroom teachers with opportunities to demonstrate effectiveness with Level II professional tasks

Career Level II

- Two to three years of satisfactory evaluations as Level I teacher
- Teacher initiated
- Masters degree (possibly an equivalent in selective coursework)
- Flexible ten-month extended contract/equivalency (possibilities might include a tailored contract extension made up of evening/summer school teacher or summer contract time as determined by specific district or building needs); extended contract salary rate
- Supplementary payment of $3000
- Responsibilities to include supervision of student teachers, service as an instructional resource person for nontenured teachers, service as a resource person for program development and course piloting, participation in formative evaluations of probationary teachers

Career Level III

- Two–three years of satisfactory evaluation as Level II teacher
- Teacher initiated
- Masters Degree with additional coursework (possibly a Sixth Year program)

- Extended contract (11–12 months) with extended contract salary rate
- Supplementary payment of $5000
- Responsibilities to include supervision of student teachers, service as an instructional resource person for nontenured and career-level teachers, service as an instructional resource person for the district (including program development and piloting), curriculum writing, district resource person for workshops and inservice training, service as a formative evaluator of nontenured (and possibly career-level) teachers

Explanations

- Program participation limited to full-time classroom teachers
- Program participation is optional beyond Career Level I
- Participants in Level II/Level III should have open exit option
- Supplementary payments plan should include escalation provisions
- State funding of program costs
- Plan should be reviewed/revised annually
- Participation in the plan shall not be limited by quotas

The difficulty of merit pay in a profession such as teaching is found in the argument that good teaching is infinitely hard to measure. Students' test scores, achievement results, satisfaction with their learning, and so forth have been suggested as the basis for merit pay consideration for teachers. Proponents of merit pay state that excellence in the classroom should be rewarded. Opponents argue that there is essentially no satisfactory way in which to compare teachers because no two teaching situations are the same. We suggest you carefully compare the pros and cons of merit pay as listed in Table 3-1. What do you think? Is it possible for us to devise a system of merit pay that would be fair? What would a merit pay system do to teachers' morale? As we said earlier, the idea of merit pay has been around for a long time. Yet, it has failed up to this time to gain any widespread following within the education profession.

EFFECTIVE SCHOOLS AND EFFECTIVE TEACHING

A considerable amount of educational research has emerged in recent years around the concepts of effective teaching and effective schools. "Effective" in this context refers to the level of students' academic success, as measured by standardized tests, in the skills areas of reading and math. While one might argue that this is a narrow definition of success by students in a given classroom

Table 3-1   Pros and Cons of Merit Pay

PRO	CON
1. Amount of pay should vary according to excellence of teaching performance.	1. No consistent, reliable evaluation method has been developed.
2. School administrators and teachers can work out a merit pay program.	2. Merit pay is self-perpetuating: it is difficult to criticize a plan when one's salary is dependent upon it.
3. The fact that any merit plan will not be totally correct should not stop the use and improvement of such programs.	3. Evidences of excellent teaching are not immediately apparent nor measureable.
4. Teachers should be willing to study merit or experiment with it.	4. The majority of teachers do not want merit pay under present conditions.
5. Payment on the basis of college preparation and teaching experience preserves mediocrity. The mediocre teacher is opposed to merit pay.	5. The correlation between college prep or experience is as great or greater than that between good teaching and the ratings used in most merit systems.
6. Merit pay has proven successful in some school districts.	6. Many teachers in districts having a merit pay program do not like it because some staff members exhibit the kinds of behavior which appear important to raters.
7. Salary on the basis of efficiency, sales personnel, relations, invention, etc. has worked in business and industry.	7. There is greater opportunity for accurate measurement of efficiency in business and industry. Even so, there has been a steady decrease in the use of merit rating for salary purposes along with more inservice training.
8. Merit pay creates conditions more like those in other professions such as law, medicine, and dentistry where status and income depend upon ability, industry and competence.	8. Through proper preservice elimination and proper supervision of beginning teachers, the incompetents can be weeded out.
9. The public is more willing to support higher salary schedules and pay when they know good teachers are paid commensurate with their ability.	9. The public has demonstrated a willingness to pay more for teachers with greater amounts of college education and experience.
10. More money will provide a strong incentive for improvement of teaching and getting better qualified people to enter the profession.	10. Excellence of teaching cannot be purchased with extra money increments and may obscure important educational objectives.
11. Teachers are employed, retained, or dismissed on the basis of judgment of their effectiveness as teachers; they should be compensated on this basis.	11. Emphasis should be on helping all teachers to become better, rather than rewarding or punishing a few.
12. Teachers are constantly evaluating their pupils' achievements; why shouldn't they be evaluated by others?	12. Merit pay reduces staff morale and increases worry, nervous tension, and insecurity, especially at rating periods. It may also isolate administrators from teachers.

or school, it does address an issue of prime public concern, that of basic literacy.

The research showing that some teachers and schools are more effective than others is descriptive (as opposed to experimental) and *ad hoc* in nature. Specifically, test scores are compared either from teacher to teacher or from school to school and, when there are discrepancies between or among learning situations which should otherwise achieve similar outcomes (because of socioeconomic status, resources, etc.), then reasons for the differences are identified. It is as simple as that. Patterns invariably emerge which separate more effective teachers and schools from their less effective counterparts.

Richard Hersh[10] has identified a number of the key differences from which patterns emerge. He places the differences into two categories: a school's academic climate and its social climate.

With respect to academic matters, Hersh states that effective teachers and schools:

- Are more effective at achieving a match between curriculum goals and day-to-day teaching.
- Assign homework more often and follow through by evaluating it.
- Keep students at task achieving more time for instruction.
- Utilize a variety of teaching strategies.
- Consistently monitor student progress.
- Provide opportunities for student responsibility.

With regard to social organizations, Hersh says effective teachers and schools:

- Articulate clearly their academic and social behavior goals.
- Expect and enforce order and discipline.
- Hold high expectations of conduct and achievement from students.
- Demonstrate caring attitudes toward students.
- Provide public rewards and incentives for academic success.
- Are backed by administrators who provide leadership.
- Are supported by the community.

Effective teaching and schooling occur when all these forces are consistently brought to bear. The best learning conditions occur when teachers, students, administrators, and the public understand and agree to these high standards. There is little doubt that you will need to incorporate this list into your personal agenda as you look to your own career in teaching.

[10]Richard H. Hersh, "What Makes Some Schools and Teachers More Effective?" *Effective Schools and Classrooms* (Washington, D.C.: ASCD, 1983).

THE CONTRIBUTIONS OF RESEARCH TO EDUCATIONAL REFORM ⅃

One of the most lasting and perhaps least noticed elements of school reform is the systematic, gradual development of the research base in teaching. The fact is that in the 1990s we have a substantial body of research-based literature available to us. Politics, fads, societal momentum, etc. will always be major contributors to educational change and development. But we increasingly know more about what makes some teachers more successful than others. This information does not naively overlook the social construction of classrooms and the often unpredictable nature of classroom life. Rather it gives us a sense of direction.

The Institute for Research on Teaching at Michigan State University conducts and synthesizes research in the area of teaching and teacher effectiveness. The Institute is directed by researchers Andrew Porter and Jere Brophy. Porter and Brophy have put together a synthesis of the database that has accrued over the past decade, and several specific points emerge from their work. What they give us is a much sharper picture of effective teachers and effective teaching than we have had in the past.

Porter and Brophy describe the effective teacher as an involved, concerned professional who cares about his or her subject matter, students, and methods of teaching. The sketch that they provide is that of a complex, day-to-day operation run by a semiautonomous professional whose businesslike routine is the product of reflective thinking and thoughtful decision making about what is important and of lasting significance in teaching and learning.

Porter and Brophy offer the following research generalizations about effective teaching:

1. Good teachers are *clear about their instructional goals.* They have a sense of purpose regarding their task, and that purpose is well articulated. Such a sense begins with such simple questions as "What am I trying to accomplish with these students this year?" or "What are the key ideas that I want to teach these students?"

2. Good teachers are *knowledgeable about the content* they teach. This implies not only that they have a solid background of formal coursework in their disciplines but that they are interested in continuing reading and learning in the subjects they teach.

3. Porter and Brophy identify from the research literature that good teachers are *knowledgeable about a range of instructional strategies.* In order to reach all their students and offer some variety in the day-to-day routine, teachers need to have a command of a number of useful strategies that range from lecture to discussion to independent study.

4. Good teachers *communicate to their students what is expected of them—and why.* In the teaching/learning equation, the teacher is the designated

leader, and must use the position to tell students what they are expected to do and know. Of course, in a democratic society, it is good to let your followers know why you are doing what you do.

5. Good teachers are *knowledgeable about their students*. They may be teaching history, but are also teaching people, and it is necessary to get to know those people to adapt learning to their needs. Students in any situation will learn varied amounts, and the quality of what they learn will vary as well.

6. Good teachers *accept responsibility for student outcomes*. This is not to say that individuals are not responsible for the work they do; rather it is an admission of the joint responsibility for learning that a good teacher accepts, along with each of her or his students.

7. Research shows that good teachers *make expert use of existing instructional materials*. Textbooks, worksheets, etc., can become the entire social studies program in the hands of an uninspiring teacher. Skillful teachers see the text as a valuable resource but not as the key to the curriculum.

8. Effective teachers *teach students metacognitive strategies and give them the opportunity to use them*. Problem solving, critical thinking, and reflection on the things studied enable students to look more deeply into concepts and important issues than they otherwise might if they merely try to master content.

8. Good teachers *attempt to develop connections between their own subject area and other subject areas*. History, geography, economics, and the other social sciences are highly integrative disciplines that cry out for connections to literature, biology, mathematics, architecture, and other subjects. To deny or ignore the relationships that potentially can be cultivated is to diminish what is taught—to leave it poorer than it might have been.

9. Research in effective teaching tells us that good teachers *monitor student understanding by offering appropriate feedback*. Students, like everyone else, need and want to know what they are doing right and what needs correction.

10. Good teachers are *thoughtful and reflective about their practice*. They think about what they do and share it with others. And they try to profit from their experiences, good and bad.

This list of research generalizations is eminently practical. Each point represents something that teachers can implement within their own classrooms. Some are more difficult than others, and we do not presume to glibly suggest that these things will happen overnight merely because we present them in these pages. To the serious student of educational practice, this is a tangible goal structure for ongoing improvement of the teaching craft.

SUMMARY

Perhaps more so than in any other era in American history, there has recently developed a mood on the part of the public and professionals to raise the standards of the schools. The number of proposals and commission reports which have made recommendations for improvement is staggering. The last wave of educational reform, brought into focus by Sputnik, resulted in a myriad of new curricula. The current reform efforts focus on such concerns as school discipline, homework, time on task in instructional settings, and increased attention to math, English, and science teaching.

Teachers, as well as those who prepare teachers, have come under fire. Without a doubt, we will witness a raising of standards at both the preservice and inservice levels of teaching. The concerns range from competencies in the basic skills of reading, writing, and math to pedagogical competencies. These large-scale and wide-ranging attempts at reform will be implemented over perhaps a decade of time. The jury on our most recent efforts to upgrade the schools is still out.

ACTIVITIES

1. What evidence of school reform have you noticed over the past five years? Describe a scenario of what school will look like within the next five years, as a result of the public's response to the reform movement and reports such as *A Nation at Risk* and *The Nation Responds?*

2. Discuss with members of your class your feelings and concerns about schools. Do you agree or disagree with the findings of the major reports? Why or why not? Please be specific.

3. As a member of the education community, how would you respond to the following "Indicators of Risk" as outlined in *A Nation at Risk?*
   a. "Some 23 million American adults are functionally illiterate by the simplest tests of everyday reading, writing, and comprehension."
   b. "Both the number and proportion of students demonstrating superior achievement on the SAT's have dramatically declined."
   c. "Average tested achievement of students graduating from college is lower."
   d. "International comparisons of student achievement completed a decade ago reveal that on 19 academic tests, American students were never first or second and, in comparison with other industrialized nations, were last seven times."

4. What in your opinion is the difference between the Career Ladder concept and the Merit Pay concept? Which would you prefer? Why?

SUGGESTED READINGS

ADLER, MORTIMER, *The Paideia Proposal.* New York: Macmillan, 1982.

Annual Editions: Education. Guilford, Conn.: 1989/1990.

CARNEGIE TASK FORCE ON TEACHING AS A PROFESSION, *A Nation Prepared: Teachers for the 21st Century.* New York: Carnegie Forum on Education and the Economy, 1986.

CHANCE, WILLIAM, "... the Best of Educations." Denver, Col.: Education Commission of the States, 1988.

Educating Americans for the 21st Century: A Report to the American People and the National Science Board. The National Science Board Commission in Precollege Education in Mathematics, Science, and Technology, 1983.

FUTRELL, M. H., "Mission Not Accomplished: Education Reform in Retrospect," *Kappan* (September 1989), pp. 8–14.

GOODLAD, JOHN, *A Place Called School.* St. Louis, Mo.: McGraw-Hill, 1983.

A Nation at Risk: The Report of the National Commission on Excellence in Education. Washington, D.C.: U.S. Department of Education, 1983.

The Nation Responds: Recent Efforts to Improve Education. Washington, D.C.: U.S. Department of Education, 1984.

ORLICH, D. C., "Education Reforms: Mistakes, Misconceptions, Miscues," *Kappan* (March 1989), pp. 512–517.

SLAVIN, R. E., "PET and the Pendulum: Faddism in Education and How to Stop It," *Kappan* (June 1989), pp. 752–758.

South Carolina Education Improvement Act of 1984, As Amended, 1985–1988. South Carolina State Department of Education, 1989.

TIMAR, T. B., and D. L. KIRP, "Education Reform in the 1980's: Lessons from the States," *Kappan* (March 1989), pp. 504–513.

Tomorrow's Teachers: A Report of the Holmes Group. East Lansing, Mich.: Holmes Group, 1986.

Chapter 4

HISTORICAL PERSPECTIVES
Education in the Old World

THE GRECO-ROMAN TRADITION

    The Greek Philosophers

    Athenian Education

    Roman Influences

EDUCATION IN THE MEDIEVAL PERIOD

    Education: Authority

    The Medieval Universities

RENAISSANCE AND REFORMATION

    The Rebirth of Classical Traditions

    The Reformation

    The Development of Science and Reason

In the study of a subject, one is aided in making sense out of the present by first gaining an understanding of the past. The study of the development of education and schooling in the United States is no exception. In this chapter we shall begin to explore the roots of American education and schooling by taking a brief look at education prior to the colonization of America.

We will first view the intellectual climate of various periods and then focus upon important events and people who have contributed to important trends in contemporary schooling programs and educational practices. We will thread these trends through time and space in an effort to make our historical perspective both familiar and relevant.

Our study begins with an examination of the historical antecedents of modern education—Greco-Roman and Western European traditions. To become a knowledgeable educator, it is important to understand these developments, as well as their significance.

THE GRECO-ROMAN TRADITION

The Greek Philosophers

Many historical accounts of the development of American educational thought and schooling practice begin with the Colonial period. For some purposes this is sufficient. But if one is to truly understand the roots of educational thought and schooling practice in America, we must go back centuries earlier to the period of ancient Greece and Rome. For it is there that so much of what we do educationally in schools today really began. The contributions of the three great Greek philosphers—Socrates (469–399 B.C.), Plato (427–347 B.C.), and Aristotle (384–322 B.C.)—are the primary underpinnings of our educational thought.

SOCRATES.   Educators speak today about "inquiry" teaching as if it were some new-found instructional innovation. Yet 2,500 years ago, in the streets of Athens, Socrates engaged citizen and slave, young and old, in dialogue about issues of the day. He probed and questioned to uncover truth. Socrates believed that education and society were closely bonded. If education is successful and produces good citizens, then society will be strong and good. However, the failure of education yields a failed society as well, a society that is weak and whose workings are undermined.

Thus the discovery of what constituted education for good citizenship was a major theme of Socrates. Today, when educators list general purposes for education and schooling in America, citizenship education is always one of the first noted.

PLATO.   Plato was one of Socrates's students, and he was profoundly affected by his mentor. After Socrates's tragic death, Plato went into a period of exile during which he traveled and studied. He then returned to Athens to further the ideas of Socrates, whose work was not written down, and to develop and perpetuate his own principles of the ideal state.

Only the educated are free.

Plato

As a young man, Plato was an idealist who believed that the purpose of education was to mold people who would be capable of and devoted to serving the state; if the people were properly "molded," the state could be a utopian one. The key was that persons needed to be matched to their job in terms of their ability. Thus, some were destined to do physical labor while others would lead and govern. This philosophy is outlined in *The Republic*. As Plato matured in years, so did his thinking. His more realistic outlook on education and life is described in *Laws*. He later established his Academia, a school where young men from the entire civilized world came to study under his tutelage. But Plato did not see education as taking place only within the Academia. He believed that all the environmental stimuli the child encountered were part of education.

Plato saw education as serving the needs of the state, and thus felt that schooling should be under the control of the state. He also believed that all freeborn children should be educated and that great attention should be paid to individual differences. When these natural differences appeared, the children should then be directed into areas of study where their abilities would be developed to enable them to best serve the state. Plato believed that the state is best served when citizens are engaged in the particular endeavors which are meaningful to them; citizens who are happy in their work are citizens who have been properly educated to suit their needs and interests. Plato firmly believed that the quality of education in a society dictated the overall quality of the society as well.

ARISTOTLE.   Of the three philosophers, it was Aristotle who had the greatest impact upon the development of educational thought. He was a student of Plato's and spent some twenty years studying and teaching at the Academia. He had some very fundamental beliefs regarding education. First, he believed that education was so central to the preservation of the state that *only* the state should undertake the education of its citizens. Second, and directly related, he believed that there should be a common core of knowledge for all, a basic education for citizenship with a curriculum that would include reading, writing, music, and physical training. This second belief is embodied in American education and schooling today.

The very spring and root of honesty and virtue lie in good education.

Plutarch

Aristotle was the equal of his mentor. After Plato's death, Aristotle was called upon by King Philip II of Macedonia to educate his son, Alexander. Aristotle tutored the young prince for about three years and imparted his wisdom and knowledge to the future king. When he became a world ruler, Alexander the Great credited Aristotle for molding him into the person he was.

Aristotle returned to Athens and established a scientific university called the *Lyceum*. It was here that the groundwork for the fields we know today as biology, zoology, and botany was laid. With the help of Alexander the Great, specimens from all over the known world were acquired and brought to the Lyceum for study and analysis. Clearly, Aristotle's thinking and work laid the foundation for the classical humanist tradition in education. The "liberal arts" education still required in most colleges and universities has its roots in Aristotelian logic and educational practice.

Athenian Education

In Athens, students were generally educated in the classical sense, that is, in such topics as rhetoric, logic, ethics, and politics. It is important to note, however, that with few exceptions, only males were educated during the fifth-century "Golden Age" of Greece. In later periods, some girls did gain a general education, but for the most part, female children remained at home to be trained in the domestic arts by their mothers and by slaves. Male children of wealthy families were also tutored by highly educated slaves called *pedagogues*—hence the origin of the term used throughout the world today to refer to teachers.

In ancient Greece, education was a private matter; but with the unique development of the small city-state, discussion of any topic—certainly education—was a public matter. Greek citizens made a national pastime of discussing, debating, and playing with ideas. It is not surprising that most of their philosophic works are handed down to us in the form of dialogues.

In our discussion of Greek traditions of education, we should note that the model we are using is that of the city-state of Athens. There were sharp differences, of course, in educational ideals among the different city-states, most notably in Sparta where education was totally state-controlled and heavily slanted toward military skills.

Roman Influences

The Romans drew upon the Greeks for the development of their systems of education and schooling. As the Roman Republic expanded and brought Greece under its dominance, Greek scholars and teachers were brought to Rome to establish and direct schools. The well-educated Greek slaves, or pedagogues, were not used by Roman families to educate their children, but taught instead in schools. Before long, a system of Greek schools using the Greek language was functioning throughout Rome. The old adage, "Greece, conquered, conquers its conquerers," could not have been more true.

Perhaps the greatest contribution of the Romans to formal education was the development of the concept of the grammar school and the compendium of studies which set the pattern for what we, today, term a liberal arts education. These studies included logic, literature, music, geometry, architecture, grammar, rhetoric, history, and astronomy—the subjects that continue to be the underlying basis for liberal education. As the Empire matured, the Romans began to insist upon Latin as a citizen's first language rather than Greek. Latin

Quintilian's Qualities

Quintilian held that an educated person, an orator, should possess three qualities not easily developed.

1. The educated person must be of good moral character if he or she is to shape the moral conscience of the people.
2. The educated person must be a master of liberal studies if he or she is to speak with authority and conviction.
3. The educated person should be able to speak well.

These qualities probably sound familiar. Do they still apply to teachers today? Are there other important qualities? Perhaps at this time it would be useful for you to reflect on what you believe are the qualities or characteristics of a well-educated teacher. How many of these characteristics do you now possess?

then became the first language of both the schools of grammar and of rhetoric. The schools of rhetoric, established for the training of orators, might be considered Rome's equivalent of higher education.

QUINTILIAN. Quintilian (A.D. 35–95) contributed significantly to the direction of schooling both in the Roman period and ever since. He realized the importance of schooling during the early years and believed that children learn best when encouraged by praise and positive models. He bitterly opposed the harsh treatment used by some of his contemporaries. He strongly believed that the child's individual needs and interests should be taken into account when prescribing the curriculum for each individual.

EDUCATION IN THE MEDIEVAL PERIOD

The Western Roman Empire crumbled despite an occasional gifted emperor's efforts to hold it together. In A.D. 364, a second capital was firmly established in the East, at Constantinople, which flourished as a center of culture. It survived the early sweep of Islamic invaders and, along with the Arab centers of culture, became the repository of Western classical learning that would be rediscovered hundreds of years later by the Crusaders from Europe.

Lacking the stimulus of Roman cultural life and the protection of the Roman army, the West gradually modified institutions to fit existing needs. A practical social, political, and military system developed characterized by interlocking rights, privileges, services, and mutual protection. The system is called feudalism.

During this period, known as the Middle Ages or the medieval period (approx. A.D. 500–1500), education fell largely to a few monastic schools established by religious orders, where young boys, age ten and older, were taught to copy scrolls for their monastic libraries. The copying of these books was critical to the development of libraries, as printing had not yet been discovered in the West. Education outside of the monasteries was a private (and relatively unimportant) concern taken care of at home and in the manor house of the local lord. Literacy was almost exclusively the domain of the Church.

Education: Authority

Throughout history, students and teachers have relied on "authority" to resolve questions. But never, except during the Middle Ages, was it almost the exclusive practice. This is one of the central educational patterns that sets the medieval period off so clearly from the classical age before it and the Renaissance that followed.

THE CHURCH.   One of the legacies left to the West by the Romans was the formal recognition of Christianity. The Church soon established itself as one of the strongest stabilizing forces in medieval life. The Church saw its duty not to train fine orators for an earthly kingdom but to teach the moral and religious necessities of citizenship in the heavenly world to come. The authority of the Church in all matters, ecclesiastical and temporal, was unquestioned. Rather than attempt to solve a problem or discuss an issue by reason, a position was maintained on the basis of what earlier authorities had said.

CHARLEMAGNE.   Charlemagne (A.D. 742–814) was one of the few truly powerful medieval monarchs. Contrary to common practice, Charlemagne envisioned schooling as a state concern rather than a matter concerning the Church. He established a palace school under the direction of the most able scholars of the time, and often sat in on classes himself to improve his own education. There were undoubtedly other such experiments in the political patchwork that was Western Europe. But none of these schools thrived long enough to make a real impact. Ultimately, all schools would turn to the Church authorities in the case of any real questions.

The Medieval Universities

During the latter part of the medieval period, several great universities were established, each specializing in a particular field. Salerno (A.D. 1050) specialized in medicine; Bologna (A.D. 1113) in law; Paris (A.D. 1160) in theology; and Oxford (A.D. 1349) in liberal arts and theology. Programs were based upon the structure of the medieval guilds; students moved through the ranks from apprentice to journeyman and, upon defense of a thesis, to master. These universities thus developed professional scholars in the various fields of special-ization and promoted learning during an otherwise intellectually stagnant period. They laid the foundation for the intellectual rebirth which was about to take place.

RENAISSANCE AND REFORMATION

The Rebirth of Classical Traditions

The threads of the Renaissance are easily traceable from the tapestry of the Middle Ages. The crusaders who returned from the wars in the East brought back rich experiences from their contact with the Arab kingdoms and the Byzantine Empire. In the East were places and peoples infinitely richer materially and culturally, and in command of awesome literature and learning far surpassing anything available in the West. Italy, closest both to the classical Roman past and to the learned neighbors in the East, felt the impulses of those rediscoveries earliest and strongest. Classical literature, language, art, and science revitalized schooling throughout Italy.

Northern European scholars traveled south to study classical languages and literature. The north was affected by impulses of change through its many performers. Whereas the pagan ideas of ancient literature were an oblique challenge to the authority of the Church, the reformers of the north directed their criticism fully at practices sanctioned by the Church. Religious reform was frequently bound up with civil reform and with anti-Church power disputes.

As the pace of life quickened, the interaction of people and the collision of ideas brought out the complexities of issues that could not be resolved by simple authoritative statements. In emulation of classical practice, the Renaissance thinkers became more confident of humanity's ability to use reason to resolve problems.

The absolute authority of the Roman Church was broken. There was no longer a monopoly on who determined the right answer. A variety of schools were established to meet the needs of various groups. This diversity of thought and practice in education and schooling is with us today.

The Reformation

The Protestant Reformation had a considerable impact upon education in the fourteenth, fifteenth, and sixteenth centuries. While brewing for several centuries, the Reformation period finally burst upon the world in 1517, when Martin Luther published his Ninety-five Theses critical of the Roman Church. It was necessary, Luther believed, to be able to read and to interpret the Bible for oneself, rather than to simply accept the Church's position. Thus, formal education became very important in the development of literacy. Luther urged state control of education and supported compulsory education for both sexes. The Bible was translated into German, English, and French so that the common man could read it. The authority of the Roman Church was broken and the foundations for secularized education were established. A century later this had tremendous influence upon education in colonial America, and its impact is still felt today in the separation of church and state guaranteed by the United States Constitution.

Profile

Johann Comenius (Jan Amos Komensky), 1592–1670

The work of Comenius represents a departure from the traditional classic approach to teaching and learning; Comenius developed a philosophy that was nearly totally original, and upon which future educators would draw. Rousseau, Pestalozzi, and their American followers used Comenius's theories as a base for much of their philosophy.

Comenius was a bishop of the Moravian Brethren, a pietist sect characterized by a democratic spirit and dedication to equal rights. Fleeing the sect's persecution in Moravia during the Thirty Years' War, Comenius spent the later years of his life in Poland, Sweden, England, and Holland.

Perhaps Comenius's largest contribution to education was the fact that he was the first educator to propose a theory of growth and development in children. This was a revolutionary idea in his time. Comenius recognized stages of readiness for specific educational content and asserted that teachers must be aware of this progression of growth, in order that subject matter and methods coincide with cognitive functioning. To ensure that instruction paralleled appropriate stages of development, Comenius proposed four six-year periods of instruction: (1) infancy (informal education, usually based at home); (2) childhood (education in the formal school); (3) adolescence (education to include the study of Latin); and (4) youth (education at the university).

The teaching methods to be used in these stages were those that employed inductive reasoning and analysis of logical relationships. Comenius believed that all teaching should progress from the concrete to the abstract, and at the rate at which a child shows he or she is ready for new material. Education should have practical application and concepts should be taught with reference to the whole, seeing interconnections of parts en route. The emphasis Comenius placed on sensory learning and the effectiveness of added visual reinforcement through pictures grew with Rousseau and Pestalozzi and is still encouraged today.

The environment Comenius promoted was one of warmth and understanding, surprising in light of the popular acceptance of corporal punishment at the time and of the widely held belief that children werre inherently bad. Comenius saw corporal and psychological punishment as a brutalizing force that would tend to diminish learning rather than enhance it. Schools, he believed, should be joyful and pleasant places where the teacher patiently and gently "leads the child to use and to understand the world in which he lives."

Profile

Johann Pestalozzi, 1747–1827

Although he was Swiss, Pestalozzi's philosophy and methods are reflected in an important way in American education. His ideas were heeded in the construction of the American public education system in the early nineteenth century and in its reform in the late nineteenth and early twentieth centuries. His ideas surfaced again in the 1960s in reference to the education of the disadvantaged child.

Pestalozzi's philosophy was a particularly humanistic one. He believed that people were naturally good but could be manipulated by a corrupt society to behave otherwise. He thought traditional schooling was boring and called for reform to make it more relevant and interesting; he also viewed education as a way to initiate reform of a corrupt society.

Leonard and Gertrude, a novel he wrote in 1781, outlines his basic ideas of natural education: (1) evil originates in a corrupt social environment rather than in human nature; (2) education can bring about personal regeneration and social reform by developing the moral, intellectual, and physical powers of men and women; (3) the child's moral development begins at home as a response to motherly love; and (4) sensory and vocational instruction would produce economically self-sufficient individuals.

Pestalozzi wanted a child "to learn slowly, gradually, and cumulatively—understanding thoroughly that which he or she was studying,"* in an environment of emotional security. He stressed the importance of human emotions in learning and insisted that a teacher must be a person capable of loving children.

In 1801, Pestalozzi established an institution of education for children and for teacher preparation at Burgdorf. In 1804 he moved the institute to a castle at Yverdon, near Lausanne, where he taught for twenty years. During this time, educators came from throughout the world to study with him. Pestalozzi's philosophy and method continue to influence educators today. Many of his original terms, words such as *concrete, environmental education, sensory approach, the total child,* and *emotional security* all sound extremely familiar to Pestalozzi's professional counterparts of the 1990s.

*William H. Kilpatrick, *Johann Heinrich Pestalozzi: The Education of Man* (New York: Philosophical Library, 1951).

The brief Counter-Reformation by the Roman Church resulted in the formation of the Society of Jesus. The Jesuits established several fine secondary schools and universities throughout Europe, but perhaps their major contribution was to the training of teachers, through the practicum they established which emphasized teaching methods.

The Development of Science and Reason

The Renaissance and Reformation periods gave new life to intellectuals and stimulated them to explore scientific inquiry and reason as means to understanding the world and man's place in it. Once the dogma and superstition of the Church came under serious scrutiny, a number of intellectuals began to examine the world of nature. New methods of science based upon observation and inquiry were characteristic of the period.

A number of persons made significant contributions to education during this period. Most notable were: *Francis Bacon,* the English philosopher who developed the method of scientific inquiry still used by scholars today; *Johann Comenius,* a Moravian bishop who advocated universal education for both boys and girls and active use of sensory stimuli in learning experiences; *John Locke,* the English philosopher whose *tabula rasa* theory was the basis for modern behavior psychology; *Jean Jacques Rosseau,* who contributed to the theory of developmental psychology through his novel *Emile,* which describes the developmental nature of children; *Johann Pestalozzi,* a Swiss educator who tested Rousseau's ideas in his experimental schools through the use of "object lessons" designed to develop principles of teaching for the elementary school; *Friedrich Froebel,* who was a follower of Pestalozzi and who established the first kindergarten in 1837 which emphasized activity-based curricula and teaching methods; *Johann Herbart,* a German philosopher who developed a psychological theory of learning which resulted in five formal steps of instruction (preparation, presentation, association, generalization, and application); and *Charles Darwin,* whose theory of evolution as described in his book *The Origin of Species* is still a center of controversy today.

These persons, through their writings, were to have a profound impact upon education and schooling in the colonies of the new world. These antecedents are essential to understanding educational programs and practices in the New World.

SUMMARY

In this chapter we have traced the historical roots of schooling. We have looked at the contributions of the Greeks through the philosophers Socrates, Plato, and Aristotle, and traced the Roman influence through Quintilian. In the section on medieval education we looked at the birth and development of the great universities of Europe, and at the roles of authority, the Church, and the state in education.

The Renaissance meant the rebirth of the great classical tradition, and the Reformation brought with it the development of science and the age of reason. In the next chapter we will continue the story, focusing on the development of American schooling.

ACTIVITIES

1. How could the educational ideas and methods of Socrates, Plato, and Aristotle be made part of a modern school? Design a scenario of a hypothetical contemporary school in which the philosophies of these men are the basis of the school's purpose and methods.

2. Read one of the classic works of Aristotle or Plato. Compare the ideas with contemporary beliefs. Discuss which ideas would fit into your teaching career.

3. Imagine what problems a teacher in ancient Greece or Rome might have experienced. List these problems and compare them with teachers' problems today.

4. Research education in the Middle Ages and the Renaissance. Discuss whether or not American philosophies of education bear a resemblance to these ideas.

5. Read *Doctrines of the Great Educators* (noted in the Suggested Readings) for a better understanding of those mentioned but not profiled in this chapter.

SUGGESTED READINGS

BECK, ROBERT HOLMES, *A Social History of Education.* Englewood Cliffs, N.J.: Prentice-Hall, 1965.

BOYD, WILLIAM, AND EDMUND KING, *The History of Western Education.* London: A. and C. Black, 1972.

LEE, WINIFRED, *A Forest Full of Pencils: The Story of Schools Through the Ages.* Indianapolis, Ind.: Bobbs-Merrill, 1973.

RUSK, ROBERT, AND JAMES SCOTLAND, *Doctrines of the Great Educators.* New York: St. Martin's Press, 1979.

Chapter 5

HISTORICAL PERSPECTIVES
Education in America

Public education—free and equal for all persons—is so much a part of contemporary American life that it is easy to forget that such was not always the case. In the early days of this country, ideals and laws related to education differed from colony to colony. Even when the Constitution was adopted, no specific rulings regarding education were included. The principle of public education was a part of American culture that was left to develop according to public demands and the needs of the growing society. Yet this is a nation founded on democratic principles; and a society imbued with such ideals of democracy could not long survive without an educational system designed to perpetuate a citizenry that would understand and uphold its ideals.

Out of this necessity grew our ordinances and legislation regarding education. Today, education is an enormous part of our society; it is supported by state, local, and federal governments as well as by private sources. Its intent is to provide equal opportunity for all Americans, regardless of race, ethnic origin, or sex. It is regarded as vital to the future of our nation. In short, education is an inseparable, guaranteed part of American life.

In this chapter, we will view the development of American education and schooling, from the early colonial religious schools to the integrated public schools of today.

SCHOOLING IN COLONIAL AMERICA

Education and schooling were important to the early colonists settling the "new land." Colonial life was for the most part an extension of the European social, political, religious, and economic systems of the colonists' origin. Initially, the schools and processes of education mirrored European systems as well. Education in the colonies was dominated by three major elements: religion, literacy, and—for the wealthy only—classical studies.

Religion was one of the primary motives for the emigration of people to North America. The first schools were church-related. Education in these schools was primarily religious in character and content. Reading was taught through the Bible and strict moral codes of behavior based upon the Scripture were emphasized.

The first general schooling laws in the New World were passed by the Massachusetts Bay Colony. In 1642 the Massachusetts Bay Colony passed a law which mandated that parents ensure that their children could read and understand religious principles and the laws of the Colony. Parents who did not comply could be fined. This was followed in 1647 by the "Old Deluder Satan Law," which required that every community of 50 or more households provide a teacher to instruct the children in reading and writing. Townships of 100 or more families had to have a Latin grammar school.

New England Schools

As the colonies grew, so too did the need for more schools. The children of the wealthy continued to be educated in the classical tradition in Latin grammar schools. The oldest such school in this country was the Boston Latin Grammar

The Old Deluder Satan Law

The text of the Old Deluder Satan Law, as transcribed in modern spelling, is as follows:

> It being one chief object of that old deluder, Satan, to keep men from the knowledge of the Scriptures, as in former times by keeping them in an unknown tongue, so in these latter times by persuading from the use of tongues, that so at least the true sense and meaning of the original might be clouded by false glosses of saint-seeming deceivers, that learning might not be buried in the grave of our fathers in the Church, and Commonwealth, the Lord assisting our endeavors.

> It is therefore ordered, That every township in this jurisdiction, after the Lord hath increased them to the number of fifty householders, shall then forthwith appoint one within their town to teach all children as shall resort to him to write and read, whose wages shall be paid either by the parents or masters of such children, or by the inhabitants in general, by way of supply, as the major part of those that order the prudentials of the town shall appoint: *Provided,* Those that send their children be not oppressed by paying much more than they can have them taught for in other towns; and

> It is further ordered, That where any town shall increase to the number of one hundred families or householders, they shall set up a grammar school, the master thereof being able to instruct youth so far as they may be fitted for the university; *Provided,* That if any town neglect the performance hereof above one year, that every such town shall pay five pounds to the next school till they shall perform this order.

School, founded in 1635. Another popular type of school was the "dame" school. This was a school for very young children, rather like an elementary school. Classes were generally held in the kitchen or any other available room of some local housewife who collected a small fee from the parents for teaching the children their letters, spelling, and some arithmetic. She might also teach the children their catechism if all were from the same religious sect. The children who attended these schools generally then went on to apprenticeships or trade schools which specialized in practical subjects.

Another elementary-type school which developed in the Colonial period was generally referred to as the "common" school. This school served the masses of children. There were no rigid entrance requirements and students did not always attend on a regular basis. There were about twenty or thirty students to one teacher. Instruction was generally on an individual basis in the basic subjects: arithmetic, writing, spelling, and "ciphering." The hornbook, a type of primer, was a common instructional tool. Few students at the common schools ever went beyond an elementary education; most became tradesmen or clerks. These schools were paid for out of local taxes; this was the beginning of the concept of public support for education. The Massachusetts Bay Colony again led the way in 1693 with the first law giving towns the legal right to levy taxes to support schools.

A Day in the Life of a Colonial Schoolteacher

The schoolday for the colonial teacher would begin early in the morning when he would arrive at the small, usually one-room schoolhouse, polish and straighten the desks, sweep the floor, tend to the fire on cold days, and prepare for the arrival of the students. The colonial teacher was almost always male, and frequently ill-prepared for teaching—if prepared or trained at all. In fact, often indentured servants trained as craftsmen or household help would be released from their contracts and installed as teachers. Needless to say, teachers were not the most respected members of society.

When the dozen or so students arrived at the school, they would take their places on crude, backless wooden benches. The schoolmaster would take his place on a stool behind his desk and lessons would begin. When a student was unable to answer the master's questions, or when a student was unprepared for the lesson, punishment would be dealt out. Sometimes punishments took the form of beatings. More often, the offending student would be forced to sit on the dunce stool wearing a cone-shaped dunce cap, where he was subject to the teasing and criticisms of both the master and the other students; sometimes a degrading sign would be hung around the student's neck clearly identifying him as a clownish lout or a lazy simpleton.

Students of different ages would be mixed together in the one schoolroom, and the different classes would take turns reciting their lessons for the master. Reading, writing, arithmetic, and, of course, religion were the chief subjects to be learned. Methods and equipment were virtually nonexistent. Books, if they existed at all, would be the Bible, or a prayerbook, or a hornbook—a sheet of paper attached to a wooden paddle and covered by a transparent piece of animal horn. Usually, hornbooks were inscribed with the alphabet and the Lord's Prayer. In 1691, *The New England Primer* was introduced in many schools; it was the major school text for over a century.

At the end of the school day, the students would file out of the classroom and make their way home to their chores. The colonial teacher had chores as well; frequently he was required to serve various functions for the church or the local government. His duties ranged from ringing the church bell to digging graves. When his workday was over, he would return to his home—which usually consisted of a room or a portion of a room in someone's house. Payment to teachers by school boards often took the form of lodging and meals. The teacher's life was poor, difficult, and often ridiculed. It is no wonder that teacher cruelty was common in many schools.

Mid-Atlantic and Southern Schools

In the Middle Atlantic and Southern colonies, education differed from the New England tradition. In the Middle Atlantic colonies, the schools were religious in character but not dominated by one sect as was the case in New England. These colonies were representative of a variety of religious backgrounds. Each denomination thus established its own schools. The church rather than the state was responsible for formal education. This made it very difficult to establish the basis for a system of common public schooling.

The schools in the Southern colonies truly reflected the life of aristocratic landowners who had settled there. The children of these landowners received their elementary schooling from private tutors and then went to England to complete their education. The children of slaves were not educated, although some were tutored secretly by sympathetic owners' wives or children. Some church groups also attempted to teach slaves to read and write, but this generally met with strong opposition by the wealthy landowners and merchants. A few free schools were established for the children of poor white families; these were called "pauper" schools because the parents of those attending these schools had to declare themselves paupers.

Secondary and Higher Education

Secondary and higher education during the colonial period were reserved almost without exception for the children of the wealthy class. Secondary schooling took place in Latin or English grammar schools whose primary purpose was to prepare boys for college and/or the ministry. The curriculum consisted of Latin classics, grammar, religion, arithmetic, history, geography, and other selected subjects necessary for admission to Harvard (the first permanent college in the New World, founded in 1636) or to an appropriate college back in England. During the next hundred years, more colleges were founded in the colonies; William and Mary was established in 1693, Yale in 1701, and Princeton in 1746. The curriculum in all of these colleges followed the classical tradition. Only a select and usually wealthy few ever gained admission.

NEEDS OF A NEW NATION

The achievement of independence from England was not without its cost to education and schooling in the new nation. The war had seriously depleted the economic resources of the colonies, and education and schooling were not initially high-priority items as the nation began to seek its unifying characteristics.

Origin of Decentralized Education

The new Constitution made no specific provision for education. However, two of the ten amendments that are generally referred to as the Bill of Rights contained implications for education which remain intact today.

The First Amendment specifies that "Congress shall make no law respecting an establishment of religion or prohibiting the free exercise thereof." This has been consistently interpreted by the Supreme Court of the United States to mean church and state are separate. As this ruling thus applies to a system of *public* education, the inference is that the system should be a secular one. Even today this principle is tested in court by sectarian groups trying to gain government aid for the support of their schools and to reestablish prayer in the public schools. But the ruling of the high court has been consistent. This is a major distinguishing characteristic of our system.

The Tenth Amendment stipulates that "all powers not delegated to the United States by the Constitution, nor prohibited by it to the states, are reserved to the states respectively, or to the People." Thus, schooling in the United States has developed as a decentralized system in direct contrast with the centralized educational systems so prevalent throughout the rest of the world. The ability of this decentralized system to work toward national goals has never ceased to be a source of amazement and puzzlement to scholars and educators from countries with centralized systems. The significant contributions of this decentralized system to the development of the nation and the solving of many of its problems is a noble achievement. It represents one of the most visionary experiments in the history of humankind.

Franklin and Jefferson

Both Benjamin Franklin and Thomas Jefferson were visionaries who left their imprint on American educational thought and schooling practice. Franklin had long believed that the Latin schools did not serve the new nation's best needs for the development of the skills and abilities it required to grow. He favored instead a more practically oriented school patterned after the English academies. The academy he opened in Philadelphia offered courses in arithmetic, accounting, English grammar, bookkeeping, public speaking, penmanship, writing, drawing, navigation, and science—to name but a few. Instruction was in English to ensure that America would become a one-language nation. Of note, however, is that to this day the nation has no formal language policy. Unlike the grammar schools, Franklin's academy accepted girls as students. The school served as a model for other academies which soon began springing up throughout the nation. While these still were essentially private schools, charging tuition and thus limiting enrollment, they did begin to provide some hope for the rising American middle class, of which Franklin was a member.

In Virginia, Thomas Jefferson proposed the establishment of a system of state-supported, tuition-free schooling of three years duration that would be open to all *nonslave* children. Promising students from this elementary school would then be selected to attend a six-year grammar school, and the best of that group would be given scholarships to the College of William and Mary. Although his proposal was turned down by the Virginia legislature in 1779, it became a model for other states, and laid the groundwork nearly a century later for our system of free, public, universal schooling.

Education Ordinances

The period immediately following the American Revolution can be best described as one of stagnation in education and schooling. The nation had to first get on its feet with a sound economic and political base. However, two important land acts had a significant impact upon education: the Land Ordinance Act of 1785 and the Northwest Ordinance of 1787. These laws supported the concept of public land for educational purposes. Under these two acts, townships were divided into sections and Section 16 of each township was reserved to be used specifically for schools. This did a great deal to further the establishment of common schools, which would become a reality in the next century.

TOWARD UNIVERSAL SCHOOLING: 1800–1865

During the first half of the nineteenth century, increased attention was focused upon the need for some form of universal schooling if the nation was to become unified. Parents and educators alike began calling for equality for educational opportunity if the democratic promises of the United States were to be realized. They called for tuition-free schools to educate the children of laborers, farmers, and factory workers.

By 1865 public, tax-supported schooling for all children had gained widespread acceptance. Many states had enacted laws compelling local communities to levy taxes to support public elementary schools. Public secondary schools were still few in number, largely because the public objected to being taxed to support them. It was not until 1874 that the Michigan Supreme Court handed down its landmark decision that was to have far-reaching implications for the future of free public secondary schooling in this country.

> *It was in making education not only common to all, but in some sense compulsory on all, that the destiny of the free republics of America was practically settled.*
>
> *James Russell Lowell*

Public Support of Higher Education

In 1860 there were over 200 private and church-related colleges and universities, but only 17 publicly supported institutions of higher education across the nation. With the passing of the Morrill Land Grant Act in 1862, the doors of public higher education were opened to all qualified high school graduates. The law designated 30,000 acres of federal land for each congressman in the several states to be used for the creation of colleges for "liberal and practical education." The curriculum generally required instruction in agriculture, engineering, and mechanical arts (hence the term "A and M," for agricultural and mechanical colleges). Many of you reading this text are attending a college or university which was established under the Morrill Act.

Preparation of Teachers

As the number of schools at all levels grew, so too did the need for teachers. Because of earlier lack of demand, little attention had been given to the preparation of teachers. Those with any training at all had generally received it at one of the academies or grammar schools. Most elementary teachers had no more than an elementary schooling themselves. Some had no formal education at all.

The first state-supported normal school for the training of teachers was opened in 1839 in Lexington, Massachusetts, by the Secretary of the Massachusetts Board of Education, Horace Mann. The Reverend Samuel Hall had opened a private teacher-preparation academy in Vermont in 1823, but it was not until the establishment of the Lexington School that the individual states began to give any serious attention to the preparation of teachers for their schools. Soon normal schools began springing up in all of the states; the Oswego State Normal School in New York and the Illinois Normal University were among the exemplary institutions. Thus began the development of normal training of public school teachers in America. Over the years, these institutions have undergone several metamorphoses, from normal schools to state teachers' colleges to state colleges to (quite often) state universities.

The training programs in the normal schools were initially one year in duration, but gradually lengthened to two-, three-, and in several cases, four-year programs. The curriculum consisted of the subject matter of the "three R's" as well as instruction in the art and science of teaching and classroom management. Several of the more prominent normal schools provided model schools in which their students could do practice teaching. These were the forerunners of the laboratory schools which later accompanied nearly every teacher-training institution in the nation.

THE PERIOD OF EXPANSION: 1865–1920

The period following the Civil War was one of expansion for the Northern states and rebuilding for the South. The war had devastated the Southern school system and it took the better part of the next century to rebuild it. In the North, the rapid expansion of industrialization and increasing urbanization brought about the need for more schools and teachers to work in them. It was a period of massive immigration, and the children of these newcomers had to be acculturated into the mainstream of American life. One of the most efficient ways of doing this was through schooling.

Profile

Horace Mann, 1796–1859

Horace Mann is generally regarded as the Father of American public school education because of his vigorous support for a common school for all children. He received little formal education in his early years and was for the most part self-educated, except for a brief period spent studying law at Brown University. Though a lawyer by training, he soon became far more interested in the education and schooling of the new nation's future citizens. While serving in the Massachusetts legislature, he led a drive to establish a state board of education and became the board's first secretary in 1837. Mann used his office as a platform for his campaign for universal, publicly supported schooling and many other educational causes.

At the end of each year, Mann issued an annual report to the legislature describing current education practices and recommendations for improvement. These reports were circulated in other states as well and helped to achieve a number of educational goals throughout the nation.

His contributions included the following:

- He helped popularize the idea that education should be universal, free, and nonsectarian.
- He led the movement for the organization of schools into a state system.
- He succeeded in lengthening the school year by a month.
- He was instrumental in doubling appropriations for public schools.
- He succeeded in having teachers' salaries increased by more than 50 percent.
- He obtained the replacement of a great number of inadequate school buildings.
- He recommended compulsory attendance laws.
- He organized three normal schools in Massachusetts, which were the first in America.

Horace Mann left his indelible imprint on American schooling.

At this time, the need for free public secondary schooling became evident; however, the idea did not meet with universal approval. In the 1870s, a group of citizens in Kalamazoo, Michigan, challenged the right of the state to levy taxes to support their public high school. The Michigan State Supreme Court ruled that the city of Kalamazoo could levy taxes to support public secondary schools. This set a legal precedent for communities all over the United States to tax their citizens in support of public secondary education.

Accreditation

As the schools grew in number, educators became concerned about the problem of maintaining or improving standards to ensure quality educational programs in the schools at all levels. Thus, voluntary regional accrediting associations were established. Colleges and secondary schools were evaluated on a number of factors, including curriculum objectives, curricula used in the school, adequacy of library resources, student-teacher ratio, and school and administrative organization. The college or school under review was then issued a report which noted strengths as well as areas where improvement was needed. If the overall assessment was good, then the institution was listed in good standing. If not, the institution was expected to correct the deficiencies within a specified period of time. These accrediting associations function today in a continuing attempt to upgrade the quality of schooling across the nation.

Accreditation of schools led to the licensing or certification of teachers by the individual states. Each state department of education establishes standards for teacher-training programs under its jurisdiction. Teachers in training follow a prescribed course of study which, when successfully completed, leads to a teaching certificate awarded by the state. (You are now in the process of completing such a program.) This ensures some minimal control over the competence of those entering the profession. Teacher training and licensure standards have recently come under critical review as the American public seeks greater accountability from its teaching professionals.

American Educational Thought

This was also a period of major educational thought with respect to philosophy, psychology, and methodology in the schools. William T. Harris, Francis W. Parker, Emma Willard, William James, Mary McLeod Bethune, G. Stanley Hall, Prudence Crandall, Edward L. Thorndike, and George S. Counts were major figures. However, perhaps the most influential educational thinker was John Dewey.

These persons stimulated education in the United States with new ideas and innovative practices. They were instrumental in beginning to articulate a truly American philosophy of education and schooling.

Legislation: Impact on Schooling

DEPARTMENT OF EDUCATION.   During this period, three important legislative acts were passed that would have a lasting impact upon American schooling. In 1867, Congress established a Department of Education to collect and disseminate statistical data on the status of education in the various states and territories. This later became the U.S. Office of Education, under the Department of Health, Education and Welfare. Although the Constitution did not provide for

Profile

Mary McLeod Bethune, 1875–1955

Mary McLeod Bethune was born in Mayesville, South Carolina, in 1875, the seventeenth child in her family—and the first member not born a slave. When she was nine years old she began her education in a free school opened by missionaries near her home. Her first educational endeavors were those of teaching her family what she had learned. This was the beginning of her lifelong commitment to the bettering of education for blacks in America.

She continued her education at Scotia Seminary in Concord, North Carolina, with the assistance of a scholarship from a white Quaker seamstress from Colorado; following her graduation in 1893, she attended the Moody Bible Institute in Chicago. After completion of her studies she requested to be assigned as a missionary to Africa—a request that was denied.

Bethune decided to teach and turned her efforts to promoting educational opportunities for black girls who were victims of poverty. With meager funds, in 1904, she rented a rundown building in Daytona Beach, Florida, and started her own school, enrolling six students. The Daytona Normal and Industrial School for Negro Girls had tremendous financial difficulties and remained open only through the enormous efforts of Bethune and her students to raise funds through bake sales, concerts, and even begging for money. By 1912, Bethune's vital personality had gained the attention and support of James N. Gamble, son of one of the founders of the Proctor & Gamble Company, and of Thomas White, of the sewing machine company. Gamble and White became lifelong benefactors of the school that later became the coeducational Bethune-Cookman College. Bethune served as president of the college until 1942.

Mary Bethune was politically active and was an energetic spokesperson for human rights throughout her life. Among her many positions were: founder of the National Council of Negro Women (1935); director of the Division of Negro Affairs of the National Youth Administration (1936–1943); special assistant to the Secretary of War for the selection of officer candidates for the Women's Army Corps (during World War II); special advisor on minority affairs to President Franklin D. Roosevelt; and vice president of the NAACP. Besides her many foundation and government posts, Bethune held seven honorary doctorates and was a consultant for the drafting of the United Nations charter.

education at the federal level, the Congress determined that some measures were needed to assess what was happening educationally in the schools and thus established this federal-level office. The Office of Education was primarily concerned with carrying out these routine data-gathering functions until the mid-twentieth century, when federal legislation regarding education greatly expanded its role. In 1979, the Office of Education was given full cabinet status as the Department of Education. Today, it is a major bureaucratic agency responsible for education at the national level, administering millions of dollars in programs to improve curriculum and instructional methods in an effort to provide equality of educational opportunity for all the nation's children.

SMITH-HUGHES ACT.   The second piece of legislation during the expansion period was the passage of the Smith-Hughes act in 1917 which provided federal support for vocational education programs at the secondary level and for teacher-training institutions to prepare teachers for these schools. This, in turn, stimulated the development of comprehensive secondary schools whereas before there had been a single program that was largely college-preparatory in nature.

CHILD LABOR LAWS.   The third major area of legislation during this period dealt with child labor. This legislation was not the product of a single act but of a series of legal enactments throughout the various states which, during the first decades of the twentieth century, took children and youth out of the factories and placed them in the schools. Most of these were in the form of compulsory school attendance laws. These laws, coupled with the shift in the American population from a rural, agrarian one to an urban, industrial society, resulted in a marked increase in secondary-school enrollments. The schools, in turn, had to reassess the adequacy of their programs for this heterogeneous population. This combination of factors essentially realized Horace Mann's dream of common schooling for all.

Guidelines for Secondary Education

Toward the end of this period, in 1918, the National Education Association established the Commission on the Reorganization of Secondary Education, charged with examining the purposes and curriculum scope of the secondary school. Its report, entitled "The Cardinal Principles of Secondary Education," became a basic set of guidelines not only for the secondary schools but for the elementary schools and for institutions of higher education as well. The Commission suggested that a student should receive instruction in each of the following:

- civic education
- ethical character
- vocation
- health
- worthy home membership
- command of fundamental processes
- worthy use of leisure

These principles remained for decades as the guidelines for schooling in the United States.

I Promise Not To . . .

While education reformers were waging battles to provide universal public schooling, to improve methods of teaching, and to abolish child labor, conditions for the teachers did not always keep abreast of the reformers' humanistic improvements. As late as the mid-twentieth century, many school boards refused to allow female teachers to marry. Further, all throughout teaching history, loyalty oaths were required—some school systems required loyalty oaths well into the 1950s. Myron Brenton describes a typical teacher's contract in North Carolina during the 1920s, excerpts of which are as follows:

I promise to take a vital interest in all phases of Sunday school work, donating of my time, service, and money. . . .

I promise to abstain from dancing, immodest dressing, and any other conduct unbecoming a teacher and a lady.

I promise not to go out with any young man except as it may be necessary to stimulate Sunday school work.

I promise not to encourage or tolerate the least familiarity on the part of any of my boy pupils.

Myron Brenton, *What's Happened to Teacher?* (New York: Coward-McCann, 1970).

THE CONTEMPORARY PERIOD: 1920–PRESENT

The last sixty-five years of schooling history in the United States are characterized by four major developments: the progressive education movement; the 1954 United States Supreme Court decision declaring the "separate but equal" doctrine unconstitutional; the major role in school curriculum development assumed by the federal government as a result of the "space race"; and a call for a return to "excellence" in education in the 1980s and beyond.

The Progressive Movement

Although the Progressive Education Association was founded in 1919, its roots go back into the latter part of the nineteenth century, to Francis Parker's innovative programs in Quincy, Massachusetts, and to John Dewey's laboratory school at the University of Chicago.

The progressive movement focused increased attention upon the child-centered school and emphasized an activity-centered curriculum. The school program reflected both the needs and interests of the children. Teachers and their students planned learning activities together. Children were active learners. They initiated investigations and carried them out on their own with the probing stimulation of a caring teacher. This trend continued until the mid-twentieth century, when progressive schooling practices came under severe attack from both educators and lay people alike.

Brown v. The Board of Education

The second major development of the contemporary period was the landmark decision by the United States Supreme Court in 1954 regarding racial integration in the schools. Since 1849, most schools had been operating under the "separate but equal" doctrine which dictated that blacks could be forced to attend separate schools as long as their educational program was equal to that of schools that accepted only white children. In reality, this equality was seldom, if ever, defined or maintained. In 1954, in *Brown v. The Board of Education of Topeka,* the High Court ruled that the fundamental principle of discrimination on the basis of race in public schooling was unconstitutional. The states were accordingly ordered to racially integrate their public school systems.

The nation soon learned that enforcing the court ruling was a far more difficult matter. Many states and local boards refused to comply, and federal troops had to be sent in to enforce the order. Further, the Civil Rights Act of 1964 increased pressure for compliance by mandating that federal funds be cut off from any district or state that maintained a segregated school system.

Finally, when some districts continued to have high percentages of minority students in certain schools within a district, the Court again stepped in to order a racial balance within each school and to ensure that minority teachers were placed throughout the district. In some communities across the nation, school districts have had to bus children from their local school attendance area to another school in order to achieve the proper racial balance. This measure has frequently met with hostility.

Sputnik and American Education

The third major educational development during this period followed the launching of Sputnik by the Soviet Union in October 1957. American schools and the education they provided were sharply criticized for letting the Soviets forge ahead in the space race. Critics demanded that the child-centered, activity-oriented schools of the progressive era be abandoned and that the focus return to the content of the basic disciplines. Demands came for major curriculum reform. The perceived gap between schooling in the United States and that in the Soviet Union was seen as a possible threat to national security should the Soviets continue to make gains in the space race. Thus the federal government deemed it necessary to enter the picture and give assistance.

In 1958, Congress passed the National Defense Education Act (NDEA), which resulted in nearly $1 billion being granted over a four-year period to upgrade instruction in mathematics, the sciences, and foreign language. Supported by these funds, teachers attended summer institutes in their disciplines in order to strengthen their content background and to gain new techniques of instruction. College students were provided with loans in order to stimulate interest in these fields. Prospective teachers were also eligible for these loans, and when they began to repay them they were forgiven 10 percent for each year they taught up to a maximum of five years. Many of those teaching today were supported in large part by NDEA loans during their collegiate years.

The NDEA legislation stimulated further federal assistance to education. The Elementary and Secondary Education Act of 1965 provided $1.3 billion for upgrading public elementary and secondary schools throughout the country. High priority was given to the education of children from low-income families and to the purchase of educational books and materials for schools that needed them.

The United States Office of Education and the National Science Foundation also funded a multitude of curriculum development projects in the areas of mathematics, science, social studies, and foreign languages, to note a few. Scholars from the relevant disciplines and teacher educators were brought together on college and university campuses all over the nation to design and test new curriculum packages. These programs were then disseminated to school districts all over the country. The debate goes on as to whether the results merited the billions of dollars spent.

The 1970s

Educationally, the decade of the 1970s was both interesting and frustrating. The schools found themselves caught up in the social, political, and economic crises which were taking place in the larger society. The Vietnam War protests, counterculture politics, changing patterns of moral behavior, loss of respect for institutional authority, and many other trends and issues spilled over into the schools. Parents and students began to question school practices and programs. It was a period of intense restiveness in American society, and the schools felt the brunt of this. That an education was a worthwhile and necessary pursuit was no longer taken for granted; that the schools were good and were providing an adequate education for all students was seriously questioned.

Although these were very trying times for schools, teachers, students, parents, and public officials, much good also resulted. One result was a far greater concern for and attention to the educational needs of every learner. Bilingual education programs were designed to meet special needs of children whose first language was not English. The needs of handicapped children were given long-needed attention, and many "special" children were no longer segregated educationally but rather brought into the mainstream of the school environment and educational program. Parents began to demand more accountability from teachers and administrators regarding instructional programs and methods. Educational "alternative" programs sprang up all across the land providing, in some communities, a number of viable schooling options for parents. They ranged from the most basic, traditional school programs to the most avant garde, and everything in between. Teacher-training institutions were challenged to provide training in the many different teaching areas necessary to enable these schools to function effectively. Parents and the general public began taking a much greater interest in schools. Many volunteered to assist teachers in any way they could. It was in a way a decade of paradox—tremendous problems and crises facing the schools on the one hand, and excitement and renewed hope for better schooling in the years ahead on the other.

The 1980s

The educational innovations of the 1970s have been reexamined in the 1980s, along with a major review of the philosophy, methods, goals, and accomplishments of American public schooling. The 1980s will surely go down as the decade of the "great educational debate," as once again education became a primary topic of discussion throughout the nation. A number of factors stimulated this debate but none more than the report in 1983 from the National Commission on Excellence in Education, *A Nation at Risk.*[1]

> Our nation is at risk. Our once unchallenged preeminence in commerce, industry, science, and technological innovation is being overtaken by competitors throughout the world. This report is concerned with only one of the many causes and dimensions of the problem, but it is the one that undergirds American prosperity, security, and civility. We report to the American people that while we can take justifiable pride in what our schools and colleges have historically accomplished and contributed to the United States and the well-being of its people, the educational foundations of our society are presently being eroded by a rising tide of mediocrity that threatens our very future as a Nation and a people. What was unimaginable a generation ago has begun to occur—others are matching and surpassing our educational attainments.
>
> If an unfriendly foreign power had attempted to impose on America the mediocre educational performance that exists today, we might well have viewed it as an act of war. As it stands, we have allowed this to happen to ourselves. We have even squandered the gains in student achievement made in the wake of the Sputnik challenge. Moreover, we have dismantled essential support systems which helped make those gains possible. We have, in effect, been committing an act of unthinking, unilateral educational disarmament.
>
> Our society and its educational institutions seem to have lost sight of the basic purposes of schools, and the high expectations and disciplined effort needed to attain them.

This report was followed by a spate of others that were also generally very critical of the current state of schooling in America. Thirty years ago it was the Soviet breakthrough in space that generated a major reassessment of public elementary and secondary schooling in the United States. Today the demand for educational reform marks a response to the economic successes of Japan, and, more recently, to the prospect of a united European market in 1992. Firm in the belief that American public schools are not producing the trained, flexible work force needed to maintain the competitive edge in business and high technology, politicians have followed the lead of the public in calls for a return to "excellence" in education. In 1988 George Bush ran for president as a candidate who proclaimed his desire to be the "education president." The National Governors' Association produced a report in the spring of 1989 that emphasized the critical role of international education to help America compete in the global economic arena.

[1]National Commission on Excellence in Education, *A Nation at Risk* (Washington, D.C.: U.S. Department of Education, 1983), p. 5.

Proposed remedies for the public schools are wide-ranging, affecting educational finance, curricula, learning outcomes, teacher training, tenure, and salaries. The reform debate is being conducted in many arenas, as business leaders, politicians, and the general public clarify their own agendas for schooling. This discussion has inspired some new initiatives: business and corporate sectors have engaged in corporate/school "partnerships" to generate new materials and provide funding for innovative programs,[2] and the Holmes Group has been formed to restructure teacher education and make it a largely graduate-school profession.[3]

Recognizing the importance of teacher support for successful reform, educational leaders have joined the debate and generated their own ideas for school improvement. These include promoting better parent-teacher and community relationships as well as having more input with respect to both the content and management of schooling.

Innovations in education will always reflect the times that produce them. In the 1980s, as the American public addresses a host of critical social concerns ranging from the disintegration of the nuclear family to environmental awareness and economic interdependence, visions of the "essential" elementary and secondary education multiply: cultural literacy, multicultural education, global awareness, and ethics education represent some common variations on the theme of educating students for the twenty-first century.

The 1990s

The decade of the 1990s promises to be one of significant change in education. The teaching force at the elementary and secondary levels and the professoriate in higher education will experience a major generational shift, as nearly forty percent of each group will be retiring. This means there will be a substantial infusion of new people and ideas into schools, colleges, and universities—the first significant renewal of the profession in nearly thirty years. This change alone will produce many structural, contextual, and substantive changes in the way schooling is done and in the ways teachers are educated. Suffice it to say that if the reform momentum generated in the 1980s continues into the 1990s schooling in America is likely to be quite different at the beginning of the twenty-first century.

SUMMARY

We took up our history of schooling in this chapter with the establishment of the first schools in colonial America, and also took a look at secondary and higher education in the Colonial era.

After the American Revolution, the schools developed as decentralized systems—a phenomenon unique to this country. Men like Benjamin Franklin

---

[2]*Action for Excellence.* Report of the Task Force on Education for Economic Growth, 1983.
[3]*Tomorrow's Teachers: A Report of the Holmes Group* (East Lansing, Mich., 1986).

and Thomas Jefferson had a great influence on the system—Franklin in urging coeducational schools of practical orientation, and Jefferson in proposing a system of state-supported, tuition-free schooling.

After 1800, more and more attention was paid to the need for universal, tuition-free schooling. At the same time, public support was growing for some sort of higher education, and the first normal schools for training teachers were opened.

After the Civil War, the rapid expansion of industrialization, the growth of the cities, and the influx of vast numbers of immigrants from all over the world placed great demands on schools and teachers. This was also a time of major educational thought. Horace Mann and Mary McLeod Bethune, profiled in this chapter, were leaders in this area.

In the contemporary period, from 1920 to the present, we focused on four major developments: the progressive education movement, the 1954 Supreme Court decision declaring racial segregation unconstitutional, the role of the federal government in developing the school curriculum as a response to the space race, and the call for a return to "excellence" in education which resulted in a "great debate" on education and a call for reform and school improvement. The 1990s are likely to generate even more changes as teacher education reforms become more prominent and the teaching force undergoes a major generational shift.

ACTIVITIES

1. Analyze the "Old Deluder Satan Law." What positive effects did this law have on American education? What negative effects? Are any of its aspects part of American education today? Discuss.

2. Investigate the development of the United States Department of Education. Discuss whether or not you think education should be included in the president's cabinet.

3. Take one of the following positions and discuss: defend American public schooling as it exists now; defend the idea of public schools, but change them to suit contemporary needs; recommend viable alternatives to public schooling.

4. Throughout America's brief educational history, have the schools changed society, or have they adapted to the changing needs of society? Depending on how you responded, what does this say to you about the role of the school as an agent of social change?

5. Interview an elementary school student or a high school student. Find out what they think of public schools—and whether or not they think other choices are available. Compare these responses to your own attitudes. (Reflect on how you might have responded as a sixth-grader.)

6. Investigate the role of the courts in determining American educational policy. Discuss which decisions you support and which you do not support.

7. Discuss your views on the separation of church and state. Can you see any exceptions to this rule? Compare your opinions with those of another student.

8. Research the background of the higher education institution you are attending—was it established as a private college? an "A & M"? Describe its development over the years.

9. Read *A Nation at Risk,* the report of the National Commission on Excellence in Education, and then investigate how many of the recommendations have been acted upon since it was published.

SUGGESTED READINGS

BECK, ROBERT HOLMES, "A History of Issues in Secondary Education," in *NSSE Yearbook,* 1976, 30–64.

_____, *A Social History of Education.* Foundations of Education Series. Englewood Cliffs, N.J.: Prentice-Hall, 1965.

BOYD, WILLIAM, AND EDMUND J. KING, *The History of Western Education* (10th ed.). London: A. and C. Black, 1972.

BOYER, ERNEST L., *High School: A Report on Secondary Education in America.* Hagerstown, Md.: Harper & Row, 1983.

CHURCH, ROBERT L., AND MICHAEL W. SEDLAK, *Education in the U.S.: An Integrative History.* New York: Free Press, 1976.

COMMAGER, HENRY STEELE, *Our Schools Have Kept Us Free.* Washington, D.C.: National School Public Relations Association of the National Education Association, 1963.

CREMIN, LAWRENCE A., *American Education: The National Experience 1783–1876.* New York: Harper & Row.

GOODLAD, JOHN I., *A Place Called School.* New York: McGraw-Hill, 1983.

KRUG, EDWARD A., *The Shaping of the American High School.* Madison, Wis.: The University of Wisconsin Press, 1971.

LOEPER, JOHN J., *Going to School in 1776.* New York: Atheneum, 1973.

NATIONAL COMMISSION ON EXCELLENCE IN EDUCATION, *A Nation at Risk.* Washington, D.C.: U.S. Department of Education, 1983.

NATIONAL GOVERNORS' ASSOCIATION, *America in Transition: The International Frontier.* Washington, D.C.: 1989.

OTTO, H. J., "Historical Roots of Contemporary Elementary Education," in *NSSE Yearbook,* 1973, 31–59.

Phi Delta Kappan, 65 (November 1983). Contains a special section on educational reform in response to the national reports.

Phi Delta Kappan, 65 (April 1984). Contains a special section, "After the Great Debate," which reflects upon and critiques the educational reform movement one year after the national reports were issued.

RAVITCH, DIANE, *The Troubled Crusade.* New York: Basic Books, 1983.

Tomorrow's Teachers: A Report of the Holmes Group. East Lansing, Mich.: 1986.

Chapter 6

DEVELOPMENT OF EDUCATIONAL THOUGHT
Philosophical Perspectives

WHAT IS PHILOSOPHY OF EDUCATION?
>   Educational Philosophy: Sources

FIVE PHILOSOPHIES: AN OVERVIEW
>   Idealism
>   Realism
>   Neo-Thomism
>   Experimentalism/Pragmatism
>   Existentialism

EDUCATIONAL PHILOSOPHIES

TRADITIONAL SCHOOLS OF THOUGHT
>   Perennialism
>   Essentialism

CONTEMPORARY SCHOOLS OF THOUGHT
>   Progressivism
>   Reconstructionism
>   Existentialism

Each of us, at one time or another, has been asked what our philosophy of life is with respect to a certain issue or problem; or someone may comment on another's behavior by saying, "You certainly know what her or his philosophy is." Each of us has a personal philosophy which we apply, consciously or unconsciously, to our daily life. While some people are more informed than others, most people have established a basic framework within which to view life.

Similarly, each teacher has not only a personal philosophy of life but a philosophy of education as well. These two philosophies are quite closely related. A teacher's personal philosophy generally has a significant impact upon the educational philosophy he or she adopts. For example, how a teacher interacts with people in general will likely affect the way in which he or she chooses to interact with children and fellow colleagues in the teaching-learning environment. How the teacher views the importance of knowledge will affect that importance in the classroom. What the teacher values will affect the value patterns he or she models in the classroom. One builds upon the other. Your own personal philosophy toward life probably had a great deal to do with your decision to pursue teaching as a career.

Quite often, the term "philosophy" conjures up images of an abstract field of study pursued by those at the highest levels of academia. In many respects, philosophy is abstract. But it is also concrete, and as such it is with each of us at all times. In this sense, philosophy is the system of beliefs about life which each of us act out daily. It is one of the most important pieces of intellectual equipment that each of us has.

Philosophy pervades all aspects of education. It is the underlying basis for everything we do in the classroom. In this chapter, we will give you a brief sketch of the basic principles and underlying assumptions of five schools of philosophy which have, in turn, led to the development of a number of educational philosophies. While these are by no means the only schools of thought, they are the ones we consider to have had the most significant impact on education, both in the past and at present. In each case, we will briefly discuss the relationship of these philosophies of education in terms of their implications for the teaching-learning process. And finally, for each philosophy, we will present a brief profile of an educational philosopher who is generally identified with the particular school of thought. At the end of the chapter we will cite other readings which will give you a more in-depth perspective of the several schools of thought.

It is not our intent in this limited space to make educational philosophers out of you. The purpose of this section is to introduce you to the types of educational philosophies most prevalent in contemporary American schools. Also, we hope to convey to you the importance of a personal philosophy of education as you continue your professional training and enter the classroom. As you grow and develop both as a teacher and as an individual, you will need to study philosophy in more depth.

WHAT IS PHILOSOPHY OF EDUCATION?

Philosophy of education has its roots in classical philosophy. Philosophy is defined by Webster as "the love of wisdom," which is a literal translation of the Greek term. It is the study, through the use of the powers of reason, of the ultimate causes of things in the universe. It helps us to answer recurring questions—What is real? What is truth? What is of value? How do we know these things? It helps us to organize our personal system of beliefs in order to be able to apply them to our daily living. The study of philosophy helps us to better understand who we are, why we are here, and to some extent where we are headed.

> *What one knows is, in youth, of little moment; they know enough who know how to learn.*
>
> *Henry Adams*

Educational philosophy directs its attention to the same basic concerns as classical philosophy. But the philosophic probing of these concerns is directed toward the analysis and clarification of educational problems and issues. Just as one forms a general philosophy toward life, so too does one entering the teaching profession develop a philosophic position regarding education and schooling. There are numerous philosophic issues in education and schooling. A variety of philosophic issues in education confront the teacher almost daily. Some are major issues of broad import, while others are directly related to the daily teaching-learning process. Some of the more fundamental questions which philosophers and educators have been posing for ages are presented in the inventory. Underline the position you lean toward or support at this time for each of the ten items. At the end of the chapter, check back again and reflect on your original philosophical position; see if you would still make the same choices.

One of the goals of this chapter is to help you clarify where you stand with respect to your educational philosophy. Most of you are just entering the field of education, and will have time in the years ahead to develop and refine your educational philosophy. Classroom-teaching experiences and dealing with all kinds of educational problems and issues will provide more input for you, as will further study.

Your educational philosophy is closely tied to, indeed built upon, your general philosophy of life. Let us take a closer look at some of the sources of your developing educational philosophy.

Educational Philosophy: Sources

A general philosophy of life, as well as an educational philosophy, have many sources. Some of them are obvious; others are not.

Inventory

Your Philosophy of Education

You can begin to find out what your philosophy of education is by noting your responses to the following statements. Underline your choice of each of the ten opposing statements, and then see if your choices add up to a consistent attitude about education.

   I believe in education:

1. For all people/for some people
2. For intellectual development/for useful skills
3. For the individual/for all of society
4. For religious aims/for secular purposes
5. For private purposes/for public purposes
6. As an end in itself/as a means to an end
7. For discipline and control/for freedom of expression
8. For adult purposes/for children's needs
9. For training the mind/for applying the mind
10. For the status quo/for social reform

PEOPLE.   The multitude of people encountered during the process of maturing have a significant impact upon what one comes to believe; upon what one becomes. Parents, teachers, siblings, friends, members of one's extended family, clergy, neighbors, and other people in the community influence the development of an individual's thought and behavior. The kinds of relationships and experiences he or she has with these people helps to mold his or her attitudes and systems of beliefs.

SCHOOL.   The experiences the individual has in school are molding forces as well. The kind of school(s) one attends and the teachers in them are key sources of one's educational philosophy. Many of you have decided to enter the teaching profession because you enjoyed school and were influenced greatly by one or more teachers during the course of your schooling. Others of you have chosen to pursue teaching careers because you believe you can make schooling a better experience for tomorrow's children and youth than it was for you. There were things you did not like and want to change if you can. Your schooling has influenced, and will continue to influence, the development of your educational philosophy.

ENVIRONMENT.   The sociocultural environment the individual lives in and grows up in is another important source of his or her educational philosophy. If one grows up in a home environment and community that places a high value on education, this will influence his or her philosophy. If good books and other resources are available, these too will have an impact. Travel is also a factor.

These are the primary sources of one's philosophies of life and education. These sources and new ones will continue to have their effects as the individual continues to grow and develop.

FIVE PHILOSOPHIES: AN OVERVIEW

We will now take a brief look at each of the five major schools of philosophy that have influenced, and that continue to influence educational thought in the United States. These are not studies in depth, but rather short definitions designed to give you a general overview of each philosophy. These definitions will help you to better understand the five educational schools of thought that will be outlined following these definitions. The educational philosophies we will study later are all drawn from one or more of the philosophies briefly described here.

Idealism

Idealism is one of the oldest schools of philosophic thought. Plato, who is generally regarded as the father of idealism in the West, lived approximately 2,500 years ago; since then, the philosophy has been propounded, in various forms, by many others.

Idealism emphasizes moral and spiritual reality as the primary sources of explanation of the universe. Truth and values are seen as absolute and universal. Knowledge is in the mind, and needs only to be brought to the conscious level through introspection. To know is to rethink the latent ideas which are already present in the mind.

Realism

Realism is another of the classical schools of thought. Aristotle contributed a great deal to the development of this philosophy in ancient Greece. The realist sees the world in material terms. This world of things, which exists independently of the mind, can be revealed to the mind through sensory experience and the use of reason. The realist views reality in terms of the world of nature. Everything is derived from nature and is subject to its laws. Realism suggests that life in its physical, mental, moral, and spiritual sense is attributable to and explicable by the ordinary operations of the natural world. Realism is more concerned with things as they are than with things as they should be.

Neo-Thomism

This is one branch of the philosophy generally referred to as scholasticism. It was developed by Saint Thomas Aquinas in the mid-thirteenth century. This Christian philosopher integrated Christian thought with that of the early

Greeks, in an attempt to bridge the gap between the dualism of idealism and realism. Accordingly, humanity was viewed as having both mind and body. To the neo-Thomist, God is the creator of the universe and humans are His ultimate creation. Aquinas suggested that people need both reason and faith to understand God and the universe. Paradoxically, however, absolute truth is to be found in faith. This philosophy became the official doctrine of the Roman Catholic church during the late nineteenth century and is still influential today.

Experimentalism/Pragmatism

Experimentalism, also referred to as pragmatism, grew out of the work of the English philosopher Sir Francis Bacon and the German philosopher Immanuel Kant. Experimentalism/pragmatism views reality as constantly changing; thus, reality can be known only through experience. There is no absolute or permanent knowledge; only what can be observed and experienced are real. In order to deal with this world of change, humanity needs to develop a means for dealing with the problems caused by change. And just as knowledge is tentative, so too are values.

> *The whole art of teaching is only the art of awakening the natural curiosity of young minds for the purpose of satisfying it afterwards.*
>
> *Anatole France*

Existentialism

This modern school of philosophy grew out of the work of the Danish philosopher Sören Kierkegaard, who believed that the central problem facing humanity is the ability to cope with its own existence. Individual freedom is viewed as being of primary importance. Since there are no absolutes, the individual is what he or she determines to become. One must choose what is essential and meaningful for oneself in this life and accept the consequences of one's choices. And one must strive to live this individual life in a world that stresses conformity to group behavior.

EDUCATIONAL PHILOSOPHIES

Now let us turn our attention to the major focus of this chapter, the examination of five educational philosophies. These are perennialism, essentialism, progressivism, reconstructionism, and existentialism. In each case we will briefly sketch the significant assumptions and principles underlying each school of thought and then turn to an examination of the influence of these theories on educational purposes, curriculum, and method, and their effects on the role of the teacher and the role of the school. A profile of an educational philosopher who is clearly identified with each school of thought will also be presented.

Table 6-1 Overview of Educational Thought

EDUCATIONAL VIEWPOINT	PHILOSOPHIC BASE	ROLE OF TEACHER	PURPOSE
Perennialism	Idealism Realism	Teacher as an example of values and ideals	Absorption of ideas
Essentialism	Neo-Thomism	Teacher as mental disciplinarian and moral/spiritual leader	Absorption and mastery of facts and skills
Progressivism	Experimentalism/ Pragmatism	Teacher as challenger and inquiry leader	Problem solving and social experience
Reconstructionism	Experimentalism/ Pragmatism	Teacher as project director and research leader	Problem solving and rebuilding the social order
Existentialism	Existentialism	Teacher as noninterfering sounding board	Searching for self

From Van Cleve Morris, *Philosophy and the American School.* Copyright © 1961 by Houghton Mifflin Company. Used by permission of the publisher.

For purposes of organization, we have divided these five educational philosophies into two categories: (1) traditional schools of thought—perennialism and essentialism; and (2) contemporary schools of thought—progressivism, reconstructionism, and existentialism. We use the labels "traditional" and "contemporary" only to indicate the schools of thought which have been with us historically as opposed to those which are more recent in their development.

No one philosophy is right for all people. Each philosophy has its intelligent, informed, and thoughtful proponents as well as its ardent critics who are just as intelligent, informed, and thoughtful. Therefore, we will make no attempt to rank one philosophy as better than another—although our biases may show through from time to time. What is important is that you, as a future teacher, carefully examine each of these philosophies as you begin to define your own personal educational philosophy.

An educational philosophy is not just an abstract discipline to be studied and debated at the highest levels of academia. Rather it is a foundation, a life plan, a system of beliefs that we use daily. To work effectively with children and youth in the schools, a teacher must develop a philosophy in order to help students sort out what they believe.

TRADITIONAL SCHOOLS OF THOUGHT

Perennialism

Perennialism is an educational philosophy founded on the belief that that body of knowledge which has endured through time and space should form the basis for one's education. It contends that the basic principles of education are both timeless and recurring. Robert M. Hutchins, a longtime proponent of the perennialist school, summarizes education's task:[1]

> Education implies teaching. Teaching implies knowledge. Knowledge is truth. The truth is everywhere the same. Hence, education should be everywhere the same.

This school of thought developed out of the philosophical schools of realism and neo-Thomism described earlier. Perennialists view the individual as both a rational and a spiritual being. Let us now take a look at the perennialist position as it relates to specific areas of education.

A teacher affects eternity; he can never tell where his influence stops.

Henry Adams

PURPOSE.   The basic purpose of a perennialist education is to help the student uncover and internalize the lasting truths. Since these truths are universal and constant, it follows that they should be the goals of a genuine education. These truths are best uncovered through the careful training of the intellect in order to discipline the mind. Character training is also important as a means of developing one's spiritual being. The training of both the intellect and the spirit are central.

CURRICULUM AND METHOD   The curriculum of a perennialist education would be subject-centered and would draw heavily upon the disciplines of literature, mathematics, languages, and the humanities, including history. It would be what is commonly termed a "liberal" education. Hutchins suggests that the best means to attaining this enduring knowledge is through the study of the great books of western civilization. The method of study would be the reading and discussion of these great works which in turn disciplines the mind.

ROLE OF THE TEACHER.   The teacher, accordingly, must be one who has mastered a discipline, who is a master teacher in terms of guiding discussion which will enable the student to deduce the proper truths, and whose character is beyond reproach. The teacher is to be viewed as an authority in the field whose knowledge and expertise are not to be questioned.

ROLE OF THE SCHOOL.   The role of the school becomes one of training an intellectual elite who know truth and will one day be charged with passing this on to a new generation of learners. The school must prepare children and youth for life.

Essentialism

Essentialism is the second of the major traditional schools of educational thought. Although it has been the most predominant educational philosophy throughout history, the modern essentialist movement actually developed dur-

[1]Hutchins, Robert M., *The Higher Learning in America* (New Haven, Conn.: Yale University Press, 1936).

Profile

Robert M. Hutchins, 1899–1979

Hutchins was the primary spokesman for the perennialist philosophy in America and an important critic of educational practice (particularly in higher education) throughout the first half of the twentieth century. He felt that confusion in higher education is caused by three primary conditions in society: (1) the love of money, (2) a misconception of democracy, and (3) a mistaken idea of progress. He especially objected to the tendency to identify progress with the sheer accumulation of information. In such an approach, the reverence for facts leads logically to the teaching of facts—but, he argued, facts do not stay current, and in light of the rapid geometric generation of new facts, how do we propose to keep up? It made much more sense, he thought, to emphasize schooling in the classics and in intellectual thought, the power and importance of human reason.

While president of the University of Chicago from 1929 to 1945, a position he attained at the age of thirty, Hutchins did a great deal to promote the cause of liberal education. He abolished fraternities, football, compulsory attendance, and the course credit system. He felt that learning for learning's sake was being undermined by the concept of the university as existing only to prepare its students for work. This vocational emphasis greatly incensed him, because he saw it as a severe detraction from education. "To train a young person simply to do some servile task such as cosmetology, auto mechanics, or television repair, and this at the expense of an education, amounts purely and simply to the abasement of human nature."* He believed instead that the university should provide a liberal education and that practical training should take place in technical institutions.

In his presidency, writing, and lectures, Hutchins championed intellectual attainment and affirmed the need to preserve the scholarly traditions of Western thought.

*Max G. Wigo, *Philosophies of Education* (Boston: Heath, 1974), p. 244.

ing the early part of this century in response to the educational philosophy known as progressivism (which we will consider next in our discussion). Essentialism draws upon the philosophical schools of realism and idealism discussed earlier. The essentialist position relating to education was formulated by Professor William C. Bagley of Teachers College, Columbia University. Bagley, generally regarded as the father of the essentialist educational philosophy, believed that the major function of the school was to transmit the cultural and historical heritage to each new generation of learners.

Profile

William C. Bagley, 1874–1946

William Bagley led the essentialist movement in opposition to the progressive movement of John Dewey and William H. Kilpatrick. As an essentialist, he believed the schools should assist children in learning only the basic factual information (the essentials) necessary for them to adjust to and compete in a democratic society.

Born in Detroit, Michigan, in 1874, Bagley attended Michigan State College (now Michigan State University) and the University of Wisconsin and received his Ph.D. from Cornell University in 1900. After teaching in public and normal schools in Illinois and at the University of Illinois, in 1917 he came to Teachers College at Columbia University, where he taught for over twenty years, retiring in 1940. At various times in his career he also edited the *Journal of the National Education Association* and the periodical *School and Society,* and served as president of the NEA's National Council of Education.

Because Bagley saw education as the hard process of imparting facts, involving a relatively narrow range of studies that are essential to effective learning, he felt that there was no room for an elective course of study in the schools. The curriculum and the classroom environment should be structured by the teacher, with all time and energy directed to learning the essential curriculum.

The following, written a short time before his death, summarizes his essentialist philosophy:*

1. Gripping and enduring interests frequently grow out of initial learning efforts that are not intrinsically appealing or attractive.

2. The control, direction, and guidance of the immature by the mature is inherent in the prolonged period of infancy or necessary dependence peculiar to the human species.

3. While the capacity for self-discipline should be the goal, imposed discipline is a necessary means to this end. Among individuals, as among nations, true freedom is always a conquest, never a gift.

4. Essentialism provides a strong theory of education, its competing school (progressivism) offers a weak theory. If there has been a question in the past. as to the kind of educational theory that the few remaining democracies of the world needs, there can be no question today.

*William C. Bagley, "The Case for Essentialism in Education," *NEA Journal, 30,* 7 (1941), pp. 210–202.

PURPOSE.   The purpose of an essentialist education is to pass on the cultural and historical heritage through a core of accumulated knowledge which has persisted over time and thus is worthy of being known by all. This knowledge, along with the appropriate skills, attitudes, and values, embodies the essential elements of an education. The learner's task is to internalize these elements of an educated citizen.

CURRICULUM AND METHOD.   Like the perennialist curriculum, the curriculum of an essentialist education is subject-centered. The emphasis during the elementary school years is upon basic skills in reading, writing, and mathematics; in the secondary school, this is expanded to include a concentrated study of mathematics, science, the humanities, language, and literature. The mastery of these curricular areas is viewed as an essential foundation for the general education necessary to living a fulfilling life.

   The rigorous study of these disciplines will develop the learner's mind and at the same time make him or her aware of the surrounding physical world. Mastery of the basic facts and concepts of the essential disciplines is imperative.

ROLE OF THE TEACHER.   The role of the teacher following the essentialist philosophy is much like that of the teacher working under the perennialist position. The teacher is again viewed as a master of a particular subject field and as a model worthy of imitation. Teachers are to be respected as authorities in areas of knowledge and because of the high standards they hold. The classroom is very much under the teacher's influence and control.

ROLE OF THE SCHOOL.   The role of the school becomes one of conserving and transmitting to the current generation of learners the cultural and historical heritage through the accumulated wisdom and knowledge of the traditional disciplines. This is a school where each student will learn the knowledge, skills, attitudes, and values necessary to making him or her a contributing member of society.

CONTEMPORARY SCHOOLS OF THOUGHT

Progressivism

Progressivism, as an educational philosophy, grew out of the pragmatist philosophy of Charles S. Peirce, William James, and John Dewey. But it is primarily from the educational writings of Dewey that the general underlying principles of progressivism are drawn. In that sense, it is truly an American educational philosophy, designed to best meet the needs of those growing up and living in a democracy. Dewey viewed the school as a democratic society in miniature, where students could learn and practice the skills necessary to living in a democracy. It was through these experiences that the individual would be able to deal with a changing world. Since reality was constantly changing, Dewey saw no need to focus upon a fixed body of knowledge as did the perennialists and essentialists. Progressivism, instead, places emphasis upon *how* to think rather than *what* to think. The basic underlying principles of progressivism as summarized by Kneller are outlined below.[2]

1. Education should be life itself, not a preparation for living.
2. Learning should be directly related to the interests of the child.
3. Learning through problem solving should take precedence over the inculcating of subject matter.
4. The teacher's role is not to direct but to advise.
5. The school should encourage cooperation rather than competition.
6. Only democracy permits—indeed encourages—the free interplay of ideas and personalities that is a necessary condition of true growth.

PURPOSE. The purpose of progressive education is to give the individual the necessary skills and tools with which to interact with his or her environment—an environment which is in a constant process of change. These tools should include problem-solving skills which the individual can use to define, analyze, and solve problems of both a personal and a social nature. In addition, the learning process should focus upon cooperative behaviors and self-discipline, both of which are necessary for functioning in a democratic society.

CURRICULUM AND METHOD. A progressivist curriculum is generally built around the personal and social experiences of the students. It draws most often upon the social sciences as the core of the subject matter to be used in the students' problem-solving experiences and projects. But since problem solving involves communication skills, mathematical processes, and scientific inquiry, the curriculum is truly interdisciplinary in nature. Books are viewed as tools in the learning process rather than as sources of ultimate knowledge.

The methodology used is often difficult to distinguish from the curricular processes. The scientific methods of inquiry and problem solving are the generally accepted methods.

ROLE OF THE TEACHER. The teacher has a very different role to play when operating under the progressivist philosophy. This is a role in which many teachers are not at all comfortable. Because the students are viewed as learners who are capable of thinking and exploring their own needs and interests, the role of the teacher becomes that of a guide for the students in their problem-solving activities and projects. The progressivist teacher must help students define meaningful problems, locate relevant data sources, interpret and evaluate the accuracy of data, and formulate conclusions. This teacher must be able to recognize at what point a student needs instruction in a particular skill in order to proceed further in his or her inquiry. This requires a teacher who is patient, flexible, interdisciplinary, creative, and intelligent. It is not an easy role to fulfill.

ROLE OF THE SCHOOL. The progressive school is generally viewed as a microcosm of the large society. It is here that the young learner can study problems and issues faced by the community as a whole. The school becomes a living-learning laboratory, a working model of democracy.

[2]George F. Kneller, *Existentialism and Education* (New York: Wiley, 1958).

Profile

John Dewey, 1859–1952

No one person has had a more profound impact upon American education and schooling than John Dewey. Dewey, a native of Vermont, was one of this nation's intellectual giants and is considered the chief spokesman for the progressivist movement. Dewey's book *Democracy and Education* (1916) is perhaps the single most important book on education ever published in this country.

Perhaps it was pragmatist William James who influenced Dewey most intensely. Borrowing from James, Dewey saw education as a vital component of social reform. Further, Dewey strongly believed that education should be pragmatic and should be related to the life of the learner. As he said, "Education is life, not preparation for life." In his famous laboratory school at the University of Chicago, he developed a working model of his ideas. "The aim of education," he stressed, "should be to teach the child to think, not what to think."

Active in the progressive education movement in this country, Dewey was a social activist as well. He campaigned for democratic education and schooling, and for causes such as women's right to vote, welfare, and teachers' tenure. He was a firm believer in teachers' organizations. Dewey viewed the school as a microcosm of society and worked for the creation of schools in which different cultures and values could be preserved and respected.

He was a humanist who viewed the learner as the focal point of the educational process. The experiences of the individual student became the starting point in the school; direct investigation and solving of problems that mattered to the student became vital to the process. Dewey rejected the notion of authoritarian schooling and of fixed ends in learning; instead, he favored the use of achievements as the beginning of new investigations. He believed in continuous growth throughout a lifetime as the primary aim of education. In his view, each new educational experience should enable the learner to see some aspect of the world with new meaning.

Dewey was the primary exponent of reflective thought in his day, and his book *How We Think* (1910) is still widely used in education and philosophy classes.

John Dewey stands at the top of the ladder of this country's educational thinkers, past or present.

Reconstructionism

Reconstructionism, sometimes referred to also as social reconstructionism, grew out of the progressive movement in education. Reconstructionists generally contend that the progressivists do not go far enough in their efforts to improve society. They believe that progressivists are concerned only with the problems of society as it presently exists, when what is needed in this age of rapid technological advancement is the reconstruction of society and the creation of an entirely new world order. George S. Counts formulated the early thinking of this camp in 1932 with his classic work, *Dare the Schools Build a New Social Order?* (This work is "must" reading for any serious student of education.) Counts contended that the schools would not truly carry out their role until they became centers for the building of a totally new society committed to eradicating poverty, war, and racism. Counts states:[3]

> If the schools are to be really effective, they must become centers for the building, and not merely for the contemplation of our civilization. This does not mean that we should endeavor to promote particular reforms through the educational system. We should, however, give to our children a vision of the possibilities which lie ahead and endeavor to enlist their loyalties and enthusiasms in the realization of the vision. Also our social institutions and practices, all of them, should be critically examined in the light of such a vision.

Counts further contended that "to refuse to face the task of creating a vision of a future America immeasurably more just and noble and beautiful than the America of today, is to evade the most crucial, difficult, and important educational task." This challenge was issued by Counts in 1932; the statement is as contemporary now as then.

Theodore Brameld has also been an outspoken advocate of reconstructionist philosophy. He contends that although we have moved from an agrarian, rural society to a highly technological, information-oriented urban society, there exists a serious cultural lag in our ability to adapt to a technological society.

More recently, the historian Edwin O. Reischauer of Harvard University, a former United States Ambassador to Japan, has called for "a profound reshaping of education if mankind is to survive in the sort of world that is fast evolving."[4] Reischauer contends that unless we move quickly to bring about this reshaping of education, it will be too late.[5]

> Before long, humanity will face many grave difficulties that can only be solved on a global scale. For this there must be a much higher degree of understanding and a far greater capacity for cooperation between disparate peoples and nations than exist now. Education, however, as it is presently conducted in this country—and in every other country in the world, for that matter—is not moving rapidly enough in the right direction to produce the knowledge about the outside world and the attitudes toward other peoples that may be essential for human survival within a generation or two. This, I feel, is a much greater international problem than the military balance of power that absorbs so much of our attention today.

PURPOSE. The purpose of a reconstructionist education is to raise the consciousness of students regarding the social, economic, and political problems facing humankind on a global scale, and to instruct them in the necessary skills to solve these problems. The ultimate goal of a reconstructionist education is the creation of a new society, an interdependent global society.

[3]George S. Counts, *Dare the Schools Build a New Social Order?* (New York: John Day, 1932).
[4]Edwin O. Reischauer, *Toward the 21st Century: Education for a Changing World* (New York: Knopf, 1974), p. 3.
[5]Ibid., p. 4.

CURRICULUM AND METHOD.   The reconstructionist curriculum takes as its subject matter the multitude of social, political, and economic problems facing human-kind. This includes, as well, the social and personal problems of the students themselves. It uses the organizing structures of the social science disciplines and the processes of scientific inquiry as the methods for working toward the solution of these problems.

ROLE OF THE TEACHER.   The role of the teacher is very similar to the progressivist role. The teacher must make students aware of the problems facing humankind, help them identify problems they are committed to working on, and then ensure that they have the necessary skills to do so. Where they do not, it is the teacher's task to instruct them accordingly. The teacher must be skilled in helping students deal with controversy and change, for most of the problems to be solved are very controversial. The teacher must encourage divergent thinking as a means to creating potential alternative solutions to these problems. Further, the teacher must be well organized and capable of orchestrating many different learning activities simultaneously. It is a difficult role but a very challenging and stimulating one.

ROLE OF THE SCHOOL.   The reconstructionist school becomes the primary agency for social, political, and economic change in society. As such, it plays a very different role from that traditionally assigned to the school. Its task is to develop "social engineers," citizens whose purpose is to radically alter the face of contemporary and future society. How do you think contemporary American society, in general, would react to this kind of education philosophy put into practice?

Existentialism

The final school of thought which we will consider in this chapter is existential-ism. Existentialism is more difficult to describe in relation to schooling because, as a philosophy that stresses individualism and personal self-fulfillment, it generally runs counter to our group-normed system of education in the United States. In existentialism, each individual is viewed as being unique and uniquely responsible for his or her own fate. This theory is obviously the antithesis of reconstructionism.

PURPOSE.   The basic purpose of education as related to the existentialist position is to enable each individual to develop his or her fullest potential for self-fulfillment.

CURRICULUM AND METHOD.   Because each individual has specific needs and interests related to his or her self-fulfillment, there is no generally prescribed curriculum. Rather, the individual learner draws upon those experiences, subject-matter fields, and intellectual skills necessary to attain self-fulfillment. The processes of reflective thought are generally emphasized. The humanities and the arts are often viewed as appropriate subject areas which further the necessary introspec-tion and reflection. Students are encouraged to pursue projects that will help them develop needed skills and acquire requisite knowledge.

Profile

George S. Counts, 1889–1974

George S. Counts, a proponent of social reconstructionism, wrote: "Today a great gulf stands between many of the stubborn realities of our industrial civilization and our customs, loyalties, understandings and outlooks. The task of bringing our minds and our practices into harmony with the physical conditions of the new age is a gigantic and urgent educational undertaking. Indeed, we shall not know peace and serenity until this is accomplished" (*The Prospects of American Democracy*, 1938).

In 1922 Counts published *The Selective Character of American Secondary Education*, in which he accused the schools of perpetuating glaring inequalities along race, class, and ethnic lines. "At the present time," he maintained, "the public high schools are attended largely by the children of the more well-to-do classes. This affords us the spectacle of a privilege being extended at the public expense to those very classes that already occupy the privileged positions in modern society."*

During the Depression, Counts wrote perhaps his most famous work, *Dare the Schools Build a New Social Order?* The question, prompted by a society engulfed in economic difficulty and overwhelming social problems, challenged education to serve as an agent of social change and reconstruction rather than preserve the status quo with its inherent inequalities and problems. He encouraged the schools to ally with progressive forces of labor, women, farmers, and minority groups to bring about necessary change.

Counts criticized progressive education for having failed to generate any theory of social welfare, and he maintained that the "child-centered" approach was inadequate to ensure the necessary skills and knowledge of an education fitting to the twentieth century.

Counts spent the major portion of his professional career at Teachers College, Columbia University (1927–1956). He was an unsuccessful candidate for the United States Senate in 1952. Counts also was an active member of the National Committee of the American Civil Liberties Union from 1940 to 1973.

*Quoted in Lawrence A. Cremin, *The Transformation of School* (New York: Knopf, 1961), p. 225.

ROLE OF THE TEACHER.   The teacher's role is again similar to that of a progressivist or reconstructionist teacher, i.e., to guide the learner and gently stimulate reflective thought through probing questions. The teacher is, in a word, nondirective. The teacher presents the class with a variety of views in order to bring about a genuine discussion of the subject matter. While the teacher has read widely and can certainly set the subject before the class adequately, he or she instead *submits* the subject for discussion. After discussion, the teacher offers the class his or her

Profile

A. S. Neill, 1883–1973

Alexander Sutherland Neill was the son of a Scottish village schoolmaster. A poor student when he was a child, Neill became one of the most influential of the existentialist educators. As the founder of the famous experimental school Summerhill, Neill was a pioneer in education reform and is often described as a modern-day Pestalozzi.

Neill's poor schoolwork caused him to be the only of his parents' eight children not sent on to higher education. Instead, at the age of fourteen, he became a clerk in an Edinburgh factory; his later jobs included work as a draper's assistant. Finally, after disillusionment in the working world, he became an assistant in his father's school; this was the beginning of his teaching career, which was to take him from the rigidly disciplined schools of Scotland to the founding of his own student-governed Summerhill.

Neill's teaching experience caused him to come into contact with many students who would attend school sporadically, leaving the institution permanently at the age of fourteen to seek jobs on farms or as servants. Neill began to formulate his ideas about child education as he viewed his students' disinterest in school and their need to pursue employment; he noted that students learned only what they considered to be useful—the remainder of education was solely for the purpose of fitting into patterns and standards of expected adult behavior.

Neill's interest in Freudian psychology assisted him in formulating his ideas about the ideal education. His basic belief was in existential noninterference— freedom of choice and self-government; according to Neill, this was the best treatment for delinquency, for when faced with decisions, people choose what is best for them.

After World War I, and after a brief experience setting up an international school in Austria, Neill established Summerhill in England. The school was a fairly unusual one for 1924; it was coeducational, self-governing, and had a small student population—approximately fifty pupils ranging in age from five to sixteen. The students lived at Summerhill, created their own rules about classes, activities, and privileges, and were free to play or attend classes whenever they chose. Neill believed that the students would not abuse their freedom; rather, he felt that freedom was abused when it was cruelly withheld. Further, discipline and punishment at Summerhill were decided by the students themselves—and contrary to the apparently permissive atmosphere, the environment at Summerhill was fairly calm, responsible, and self-disciplined. What Neill viewed as hypocritical moralizing was absent from the curriculum—and to this Neill attributed Summerhill's success.

Neill's existential belief in noninterference was highly successful in educating young people. British education inspectors visiting the school were often astonished at the success of Neill's methods; further, they had praise for him as a "man of deep conviction and sincerity. His faith and patience must be inexhaustable." Further, Summerhill turned out traditionally "successful" students—students readily able to score well on Oxford examinations.

own view, formed after long reflection on the subject. The teacher asks the students to consider this view against their own experiences, including the knowledge they have gathered in this class and in previous ones.

Should the student reject the teacher's interpretation of the subject, it is the student's right to do so. Existentialism insists not that the teacher be "successful," but that the teacher be *honest*. Nevertheless, honesty leads to success, for if the teacher is honest with the pupil, trust is established. In an atmosphere of mutual trust the student knows that the teacher's interpretation of a subject is a wise one, and the teacher knows that the student will weigh this interpretation with the respect it deserves. Thus the dialogue that is education rests on trust between persons, a trust that the teacher must earn by integrity and create with skill.

ROLE OF THE SCHOOL.   The school should be a forum where students are able to engage in dialogue with other students and teachers to help them clarify their progress toward self-fulfillment.

SUMMARY

As stated at the outset of this chapter, we believe it is important for teachers to operate from a philosophical basis, to know and be able to put into practice what they believe about the process and content of education and schooling.

In this chapter we have attempted to expose you to several schools of philosophy: idealism, realism, neo-Thomism, experimentalism/pragmatism, and existentialism.

We divided the educational philosophies that grew out of these into two categories: traditional and contemporary. The traditional philosophies are perennialism and essentialism; the contemporary ones are progressivism, reconstructionism, and existentialism.

We have not tried to make educational philosophers out of you, but rather to give you the bases for developing your own educational philosophy. An educational philosophy is not just an abstract discipline to be studied and debated in a purely intellectual environment. Rather, it is a foundation, a life plan, a system of beliefs that you use daily. The following Profiles outline a few of the leaders involved in the various educational philosophies.

ACTIVITIES

1. Reflect on one of your former teachers—a teacher you thought to be a good instructor and with whom you had good learning experiences. Identify several elements of this teacher's methods and attempt to determine what the teacher's educational philosophy was. Discuss whether or not this philosophy is similar to yours.
2. Talk to a teacher who has been teaching for a number of years. Find out

what the teacher's philosophy of education was at the beginning of his or her career. Has the teacher's philosophy changed? Find out why or why not.

3. Read *Experience and Education* by Dewey and *Dare the School Build a New Social Order?* by Counts (both are very brief). Compare the philosophies of these two educators. Which position do you find more to your liking, and why?

4. Although you have been in this class only a short time, how would you classify the educational philosophy of your instructor? Explain.

5. Chart the educational philosophy(-ies) that you believe was most widely used by teachers in the various schools you attended. Discuss the possible reasons for these philosophies.

6. Often applications for employment ask a prospective teacher employee to explicate their philosophy of education. Write down how you would respond to this question.

SUGGESTED READINGS

BUTLER, J. DONALD, *Four Philosophies and Their Practice in Education and Religion.* New York: Harper & Row, 1968.

_____, *Idealism in Education.* New York: Harper & Row, 1969.

BRAMFELD, THEODORE, *Toward a Reconstructed Philosophy of Education* (2nd ed.). New York: Dryden Press, 1956.

COUNTS, GEORGE S., *Dare the Schools Build a New Social Order?* New York: John Day, 1932.

CREMIN, LAWRENCE A., *The Transformation of the School. Progressivism in American Education, 1876–1957.* New York: Knopf, 1961.

DEWEY, JOHN, *Democracy and Education.* New York: Macmillan, 1916.

_____, *Experience and Education.* Kappa Delta Pi Lecture Series, 1938.

GROSS, RONALD, ED., *The Teacher and the Taught.* New York: Dell, 1963.

HUTCHINS, ROBERT M., *Great Books: The Foundation of a Liberal Education.* New York: Simon & Schuster, 1954.

KNELLER, GEORGE F., *Introduction to the Philosophy of Education* (2nd ed.). New York: Wiley, 1971.

KUEHNER, QUINCY A., *Philosophy of Education Based on Sources.* Philadelphia: Century Bookbindery, 1984.

MARITAIN, JACQUES, *Education at the Crossroads.* New Haven: Yale University Press, 1943.

MORRIS, VAN CLEVE, *Existentialism and Education.* New York: Harper & Row, 1966.

NEILL, A. S., *Summerhill: A Radical Approach to Childrearing.* New York: Hart, 1963.

OKAFOR, FESTUS C., *Philosophy of Education and Third World Perspectives.* Lawrenceville, Va.: Brunswick, 1981.

POWER, EDWARD J., *Philosophy of Education: Studies in Philosophies, Schooling, and Educational Policies.* Englewood Cliffs, N.J.: Prentice-Hall, 1982.

WINGO, G. MAX, *Philosophies of Education: An Introduction.* Lexington, Mass.: Heath, 1974.

WINSING, MARIE, *Teaching and Philosophy: A Synthesis.* Boston: Houghton-Mifflin, 1972.

EDUCATION AND SCHOOLING

Monday morning: the traditional beginning of the school week. Teachers and students all over the United States pour into the nation's institutions of education, arriving via bicycle, school bus, motorcycle, auto, public transportation, pickup truck, and foot. Some attend public schools, some attend private schools. Some attend nongraded, multi–age-level classes; others are tracked by age and ability and post–high school goals. Some attend sprawling, campuslike schools surrounded by trees and playgrounds; others attend three-story structures in the middle of a city; still others attend classes in a schoolhouse with only a few rooms. Education and schooling have many faces in America.

Over the course of your career as a teacher, you may be involved in a number of different types of school settings and with different types of educational functions. And you will become acutely aware that the phrase "to get an education" is very different from the phrase "to go to school." The success or failure of some students' attempts at obtaining an education may have a lot to do with the nature of the school the student attends—or the teachers involved in that school.

In this chapter, we will sort out some of the differences and similarities relative to the concepts of education and schooling. Further we will take a brief look at the pros and cons of the possibility of deschooling society. We will also view the different types of schools that exist—and the different purposes of various types of schools.

EDUCATION VS. SCHOOLING

Drawing a distinction between education and schooling is difficult because people do not generally differentiate between the two. Most people view them as synonymous concepts.

> *Education is what you have left over after you have forgotten everything you have learned.*
>
> *Anonymous*

However, it is important to remember that schooling is only a part, albeit an important part, of one's education. Schooling is necessary to the continued development of a society. School is the place where a society's primary resource, its youth, can gain the common understandings and skills that will enable the society to continue to grow and develop. The degree to which schooling is done well will in large measure determine the future progress and direction of the society.

Education, on the other hand, is a much broader concept. Schooling is a part of it. But there are many other ways of learning than through the formal education of the school classrooms. Education in the broadest sense of the word, can occur anywhere. Still, in our society, when we speak of getting an education, we generally mean attending school. We believe this is too narrow a perspective for educators.

The following passage by John Laska may clarify this relationship between education and schooling.[1]

> It should be apparent that education is, in one sense, a much broader concept than schooling. Education is provided by many agencies in addition to the schools. The family, churches, the mass media, libraries, advertisers, the government, and many employers are all concerned with the educative process. Guided learning activities occur, moreover, in many informal situations that most persons encounter daily (such as conversations among friends). Educational experiences may also be obtained through various means of self-education (reading books to learn from them, for example).
>
> Thus the school system is only one of the several means of education available to a society. In fact, although every society has education, not every society has needed schools. Many so-called "primitive" societies have existed without a system of schools. The guided learning activities essential for the maintenance of these societies are provided by such educational agencies as the family, rather than schools.

It is important here to describe these concepts in terms of the way they will be used in this book. *Schooling* will be used to refer to the formal educational process which takes place in schools. *Education* will be used to refer to all learning experiences both in and out of school. In part, it is our hope that as teachers, each of you will encourage your students to look beyond their schooling to all the possible educational options which exist in the world around them.

What's the Difference?

The chart presented here depicts some basic distinctions between education and schooling. These are not absolute differences but general tendencies.

Education is . . .	Schooling is . . .
• lifelong	• time-bound
• open-ended	• structured
• all-encompassing	• content- and skill-oriented
• growth-oriented	• occupation-directed
• self-directed	• teacher-directed
• a variety of forms, settings and agents	
• both formal and informal	• formal
• life	• training for life
• random	• nonrandom

---

[1]John A. Laska, *Schooling and Education* (New York: Van Nostrand, 1976), p. 12.

WHAT IS EDUCATION?

Education is the sum total of one's learning experiences during a lifetime—not just organized formal learning experiences in schools, but all learning experiences. It is a process by which a person gains understanding of self, as well as the environment. Laska again provides a good view of education:[2]

> Education is one of the most important activities in which human beings engage. It is by means of the educative process and its role in transmitting the cultural heritage from one generation to the next that human societies are able to maintain their existence. But education does more than just help us to keep the kind of society we already have; it is also one of the major ways in which people try to change or improve their societies. . . .

> *Education is . . . hanging around until you've caught on.*
>
> *Robert Frost*

Education is a lifelong process. When only a few hours old, infants begin exploring their environment. The infants learn that a cry will bring the attention of another person to satisfy their needs. As a person grows, the process of education accelerates. The child learns how to respond to affection, how to examine things with the hands, how to manipulate objects and people. These are not taught; rather they are learned through inquiring about one's environment. All of us can recall childhood experiences which remain as vivid in our memories as if they had happened only yesterday. For example, we remember learning that the stove was hot by touching it (prior advice and warnings notwithstanding); and we recall learning to tie our shoes under the careful and patient tutelage of a parent, sibling, or teacher.

> *As I said before, man's education begins at birth; before he can speak or understand he is learning. Experience precedes instruction.*
>
> *Jean Jacques Rousseau*

Education is open-ended. It can take a variety of forms in a variety of settings with a variety of agents guiding the learning experience. It is an all-encompassing process. The classroom may be the home, the neighborhood playground, the street or alley, the woods on the family farm, the local discount store, or anywhere else. The agents of education come in many forms also—parents, grandparents, aunts, and uncles, siblings, playmates, television, books, records—to name a few.

[2]John A. Laska, *Schooling and Education* (New York: Van Nostrand, 1976), p. 3.

Education is both formal and nonformal. When we place education within a structured learning environment, we call it formal education. In our pluralistic society this usually takes place in a school, and we call it schooling. But there are other agencies that provide formal education experiences, among which are churches, YMCA-YWCA, community centers, FFA, 4-H, county extension service agents, scouting, and many others. Activities and learning experiences are structured to meet specific needs, and generally have formalized curricula.

Nonformal education, on the other hand, has few—if any—bounds. It is generally unstructured. It takes place in different settings and through different media—family gatherings, peer groups, street gangs, playgrounds, camp and travel experiences, places of work, and sports clubs. One of the most powerful, and generally nonformal, means of education is the mass media. Television is a particularly influential means of education. Although some excellent educational programming is now appearing on both the public and commercial networks, the majority of programs have no specific educational purpose. Yet they convey powerful images and stereotypes about our society. Children and young people watch many hours of television programs each week, and some educators believe this experience has a profound impact upon the watchers' intellectual, social, and attitudinal development. Business and industry spend millions of dollars in advertising directed at this lucrative young market. Sales figures indicate their efforts have paid off the initial investment many times over. Radio, popular literature, motion pictures, and rock concerts also contribute significantly to the education of children and youth, nonformal as their manner of presentation may be.

Education is an almost constant part of our development-change-being. It permeates everything we do.

WHAT IS SCHOOLING?

Schooling is a formalized educational process which takes place in institutions that we have generally labeled schools. Formal schooling came about when it was determined that the family and related social agencies, usually the church, could no longer prepare young people adequately to take their place in society.

In some schools students are required to follow a prescribed syllabus; in others they have choices. Because textbooks are among the primary tools of learning, verbal skills are highly valued. A variety of teachers with an equal variety of teaching styles and philosophies about schooling direct the learning activities. Examinations are among the most common means of testing what the student knows and does not know.

Schooling is timebound. The student is required by law to attend until a certain age, whether he or she wants to or not and even whether he or she is learning anything or not. Between the ages of five and seventeen, the student attends school five days a week for nine or more months each year and spends a sizable piece of the day there. Some schools are fun and exciting places to be; others are deadening.

Schooling is occupation-oriented. The focus of the curriculum, that is, the prescribed learning experiences, is upon specific areas of knowledge and skills which will prepare the student for the world of work. Some curricula are more specific in their orientation toward certain kinds of work; college-bound programs are an example. The constant in each curriculum is that the material will better prepare the student as a future citizen in the so-called "real" world.

SCHOOLING NON-RANDOMIZES LEARNING.   This is perhaps the most distinguishing characteristic of schooling. A curriculum is designed with specific goals in mind, and the learning experiences involved are planned and placed in sequence so that learning will have meaning. Rather than undergo a bombardment of random ideas and random activities, the student instead gains knowledge via a generally meaningful pattern of learning experiences.

Types of Schools

A school can fit into any number of different categories. For example, a school may be a *public school,* that is, a school supported by public funds and administered by a local Board of Education. Or, it may be a *private school,* in which financial support is provided by money from students' tuition as well as from contributions by citizens, corporations, religious groups, etc. Private schools can be secular and founded on some specific educational goal that differs from the goal of the public schools (for example, a "Montessori" school, a college-preparatory academy, a "free" school, or an "experimental" school); or they can be affiliated with a particular religious group and may incorporate religion into the curriculum.

Schools can be classified by age levels. *Preschool* or *nursery school* usually involves very young students (before kindergarten age); *kindergarten* is usually the first mandatory level of school—students are enrolled at age five, usually for half-day sessions; *elementary* or *primary school* usually involves grades one through six; *junior high school* precedes high school and can be either seventh and eighth, or seventh, eighth, and ninth grades; *middle school* can be the same grades as junior high school—or one or two grades may be added; *secondary* or *high school* consists of the last years of education before college or vocational school, either grades nine through twelve or ten through twelve, depending on the individual school system.

Schools can also be classified according to purpose: a school may be a technical or vocational school, that is, a school offering instruction in trades (such as business, industrial arts, etc.); it may be college preparatory; it may specialize in arts and music; or it may be a bilingual school geared to teaching a language other than English.

Types of schools, as well as traditional and alternative school patterns, are discussed in Chapter 9, "Contemporary Schooling Patterns."

TO SCHOOL OR NOT TO SCHOOL?

Education can occur without the existence of schools. Some people believe—and it is probably sometimes true—that schools can exist in which no education occurs. Unfortunately for the students involved, education and schooling do not always go hand in hand.

Not everyone agrees on the need for schooling in modern society. Since the launching of Sputnik in 1957, schooling in America has come increasingly under attack. Initially, the attack was caused by the fear of being overtaken by the Soviets in the space and arms races. Then the social upheavals of the Vietnam War period spread to the schools. In the 1970s, charges were brought that schools were inhumane. Proponents and opponents of schooling stated their cases. Some of the more outspoken critics of schooling in America during this period were John Holt and Ivan Illich.

Ivan Illich, a self-styled critic of schooling, was the leader of the contemporary movement to "deschool." Illich's book, *Deschooling Society,* sent a shock wave across the land. In his criticism of schooling, he defines a school as "the age-specific, teacher-related process requiring full-time attendance at an obligatory curriculum."[3]

Illich believes that schools are inherently unequal and only serve to alienate learners. Further, he believes that the purpose of *deschooling* would be to guarantee the learner his freedom "without guaranteeing to society what learning he will acquire and hold as his own. Each man must be guaranteed privacy in learning, with the hope that he will assume the obligation of helping others to grow into uniqueness."[4]

Illich contends that a good educational system should have three purposes: (1) to allow all persons free and easy access to resources at any time; (2) to enable all those who want to give their knowledge to others to be able to do so—and to allow those who want this knowledge to gain it; and (3) to guarantee public input regarding education.

Finally, Illich speaks to what is necessary for real learning to take place:[5]

> I believe that no more than four—possibly even three—distinct "channels" or learning exchanges could contain all the resources needed for real learning. The child grows up in a world of things, surrounded by people who serve as models for skills and values. He finds peers who challenge him to argue, to compete, to cooperate, and to understand; and if the child is lucky, he is exposed to confrontation or criticism by an experienced elder who really cares. Things, models, peers, and elders are four resources each of which requires a different type of arrangement to ensure that everybody has ample access to it.

Some persons are in complete agreement with Illich. Many others would agree that schools have problems and are in need of reform, but they do not believe in doing away with schooling. Still others totally disagree with Illich's position. An article by Arthur Pearl which strongly opposes Illich's standpoint appears in the box "The Case for Schooling America."

[3]Ivan Illich, *Deschooling Society* (New York: Harper & Row, 1971), p. 25.
[4]Ibid., p. 75.
[5]Ibid., p. 76.

Points of View

What Kind of School?

Home Education

A quiet rebellion against compulsory schooling is emerging today from the cities, suburbs, and backwater towns of America. Born as a rejection of impersonal, ineffectual, and, sometimes, downright destructive school systems, do-it-yourself education is in a sense one logical outgrowth of the often-invoked spirit of self-sufficiency. Home education is now seen by its practitioners as community control carried to the limits. To some parents, "deschooling" is an attempt to avoid the forced programming of their children through poor public-school systems into preordained slots in mainstream adult society. For others, the movement is aimed at fostering humanist priorities.

Literacy and the School

Compulsory education was introduced in Massachusetts as far back as the 1850s, but there was near universal literacy in this country by the early 1800s. The idea that schools produce literacy is sheer nonsense. Like so many others, one student told me that all this talk about deschooling or free schooling or whatever was only for rich white kids. She and other poor and black kids needed schools just as they were. I tried, without success, to say to this spirited and angry student that the school machine, if all went well, would someday stamp WINNER on her forehead, and perhaps give her the power to do something for black people. But this school machine at the same time would go on stamping LOSER on the foreheads of thousands or tens of thousands of other black kids. Doing so, it would rob them, above all in their own minds, of the power to help themselves.

Constitutional Rights: A Court Opinion

Parents have rights further than those explicit in the Constitution, among them, the right of parents to educate their children in the manner they choose.

Michael Harris, "Is Compulsory Education an Idea Whose Time Has Gone?" *Mother Jones Magazine,* April 1979.

John Holt, quoted in Michael Harris, "Is Compulsory Education an Idea Whose Time Has Gone?" *Mother Jones Magazine,* April 1979.

Franklin County (Massachusetts) Superior Court, 1978.

The Case for Schooling America*

Ivan Illich refuses to define his "desirable society" or to defend its feasibility. Instead of setting forth a set of goals and the logic for same, and a strategy that at least offers a promisory note for payoff, he parades before us metaphor and hyperbole that are—when analyzed—either contradictory or trivial. Any dream of a good life offered by a responsible critic should have at least: (1) its attributes sufficiently spelled out so that advocates and opponents know what they are arguing about; (2) its essence analyzed for ecological, political, psychological, and economic reality (which, of course, could then be debated); and (3) its political course laid out so that we are alerted to the tactics and strategy needed to get us from where we are to where we ought to be.

Illich doesn't come close. He is fuzzy about his "desirable society." He touches on freedom of the individual to learn whatever he desires to learn; he touches on the question of universal and unlimited access to the secrets and tools of the society. But he never discusses the feasibility of his good society. He believes that by the elimination of compulsory education, the good society will somehow emerge.

Illich never tells us how his improved society will function without institutions. Indeed, he in no way challenges my own belief that no steps toward what he and I might well agree are the goals of a "desirable society" can be taken without institutions. Public schools will be basic to this institutional infrastructure directed toward wide scale social benefits. Illich's call for deinstitutionalized schools in a deinstitutionalized society is nonsense, and dangerous to the extent that its simplicity is attractive.

> Deinstitutionalize a city and within a month that city will literally be buried in its garbage. To have a deinstitutionalized natural society in which man maintained himself through self-sufficient primitive hunting, fishing, or gathering would require that we reduce the world's population to something less than 200 million people.

It remains true, however, that although schools do not run society, they are more resistant to society's attempt to run them than are most other institutions. The fact is that our schools are not monolithic; people do not emerge from them as sausages out of a meatpacking plant.

True educational reform inside and outside schools is really possible, then, because the schools themselves do not have an already established or predetermined monopolistic role. They offer a variety of experiences and interests and provide a place for increasing numbers of "radical" teachers to function. It is, after all, only among persons with many years of compulsory education that Ivan Illich has any following—and that is not an accidental occurrence. Schools develop intellectual opponents to injustice not because they are designed to, but because once a group of inquiring youths are compelled to interact with each other, a percentage will begin to question the values and direction of their society. Thus it was the students and teachers in public institutions who first questioned the war in Vietnam; and efforts to restrict them, though powerful, cannot succeed.

Oh, for a Schooled Society!

It will not be easy to create schools with a democratically oriented leadership that convinces rather than coerces people to acknowledge the importance of education. And yet that challenge cannot be avoided either by the dehumanizing experts of education (B. F. Skinner and the like) or the humanely oriented romanticists (Illich and his buddies). Universal education is necessary and must be organized because the threats to man's existence are universal. What we have come to regard as human rights can be guaranteed only within an institutional structure—societies with primitive institutions never even considered individual rights.

The rights of students must be considered within a context of social responsibility. If the student chooses to be in a classroom rather than a library, laboratory, park, museum, home, or pool hall, he must justify that or the other choices within the context of the goals of a desirable society. He must make a case, with logic and evidence, that he has fulfilled his obligation to other human beings; he has equal rights to require that teachers and colleagues justify their actions to him.

But when Illich speaks with the voice of pure freedom, he masks a conservative message: ". . . protect the autonomy of the learner—his private initiative to decide what he will learn and his inalienable right to learn what he likes rather than what is useful to somebody else." To learn what one likes is to learn prejudices. If there is one thing we know about human beings it is that they don't want to know what they don't want to know. Erich Fromm tried to get that truth across to us twenty years ago in *Escape from Freedom*. The important truths of today are painful truths. People will do everything they can to avoid them. Important truths will require enormous changes in attitudes and lifestyle. Education self-selected will be no education—we have such education currently available to us (it comes to us on half a dozen simultaneous channels on television), and there we find a Gresham's law of culture: bad drives out good, and the frivolous outdraws the serious.

The institutional school has not, of course, been relevant to producing a "desirable world"; that is why it must be reformed. Schools must go beyond merely raising the problems; instead they must begin to suggest real solutions—describe models and plans for peace, a universal quality of life, and equal opportunity, within the context of lifestyles that are ecologically sane. Rather than eradicate the public school, then, Illich ought to be directing his fire against the powerful institutions—the ones C. Wright Mills identified as military, industrial, and political—that block the progressive potential of the schooling process.

The public schools are clearly in desperate shape. Reform won't come easily, and we have a long way to go. Illich and other critics provide a useful function when they hammer away at the schools' inhumanity; but they become counterproductive when they offer nonsolutions and lose sight of the Gideon's army of radical public-school leaders whose growing number has greatly contributed to the clamor to do something about war, racism, poverty, and the destruction of the earth during the past decade. Try to deinstitutionalize education as a symbol and the beginning of the deinstitutionalization of everything and you *reinstate the law of the jungle*—which quickly breaks down into a new set of oppressive institutions. The same unfortunate situation holds true for attaining any of the other goals of a desirable society. Politics learned at the hands of Richard Daley, culture picked up at the feet of Johnny Carson, and interpersonal relations gleaned from gropings in the street are the alternatives to school. That these alternatives are already too characteristic of contemporary American society is not a reason for removing schools, but for reforming them.

*Arthur Pearl, "The Case for Schooling America," in Alan Gartner, Colin Greer, and Frank Riessman, Eds., *After Deschooling, What?* (Perennial Library; Harper & Row Publishers, Inc.), pp. 112–117. Copyright © 1973 by Social Policy, Inc. Reprinted by permission.

Profile

Jane Addams, 1860–1935

Jane Addams was one of the most vocal and effective social leaders of her time. Her view of education involved moving education out into the community. The daughter of an Illinois banker and mill owner, her social conscience emerged when she was very young, and was deeply affected by the conditions in which her father's employees lived and worked. She decided as a child to do something to mitigate the problems of the people.

When Addams began her reform work in the last decades of the nineteenth century, New York, Chicago, Philadelphia, and Detroit were magnets for people seeking jobs, wealth, excitement, and a better life. When these people arrived, they were instead subjected to the ills of industrial civilization: poverty, squalor, and disease. Addams and other young reformers understood the complexity of poverty; they bluntly relegated a large share of the responsibility for the abominable conditions to the wealthy elite; they also exposed industrialism as the cause of the deterioration of the community—and ultimately of alienation and despondency. They spoke of regenerating the community and of humanizing industrial civilization, and they saw education as the primary means to that end.

In 1889, Jane Addams and a friend, Ellen Gates Starr, founded Hull House in Chicago. This settlement house was destined to become the most famous of American settlements. Addams remained there, exerting her will and positive spirit for the good of the community, until her death in 1935.

The settlement workers responded to immediate problems of the neighborhood. Their intent was to preserve the Old World culture while assimilating it into the New. In addition to dealing with immediate problems such as vermin infestation, street gangs, disease, unemployment, and child care, the settlement set up vocational and placement programs for adults and day care and kindergarten programs for children.

Addams was not a friend of the traditional educators of the time. She saw the settlement program of socialized education as, ultimately, a protest against the restricted view of the school as a place of purely formal education. She believed the school should be a force for social good, and that to do this it must be as aware of the community and its needs as the settlement houses themselves.

Politically, Addams was vocal and active throughout her lifetime, and lent valuable critical insight into the weaknesses of public education. She served for four years as a member of the Chicago Board of Education, constantly pressing for reform in education. In 1905 in an address to the National Education Association (NEA) she attacked the profession for not lending greater assistance in campaigns against child labor and called upon them to take a more militant stand in the future. Among her many other honors, she shared the Nobel Peace Prize with Nicholas Murray Butler in 1931.

SUMMARY

In this chapter we have tried to stimulate you to think about the concepts of education and schooling. We have tried to show that although they are related concepts, they each have distinct qualities, and we have attempted to define these concepts in terms of the way they will be used throughout this book. Finally, we have pointed out some of the controversy surrounding the concept of schooling, including Ivan Illich's program for "deschooling" society, and Pearl's argument for "reschooling" society.

ACTIVITIES

1. Describe the types of schools you have attended. In which of these schools did you feel most comfortable? In which of these schools, in your opinion, did you experience the best learning? Discuss what comprises the "successful" school experience—the teacher, the student, the type of school, the methods, a combination?
2. Invent a society in which there are no schools. Determine who would be educated and how. Discuss whether this system would be better, as good as, or worse than the system of public education we have now.

3. Choose one of the following educational theoreticians and investigate what he or she has to say about schooling. "Interview" one of these persons: Plato, Montaigne, Montessori, Rousseau, Skinner, Piaget.

4. Consider the education that you have received outside of school. What types of things did you learn? What were the methods of instruction?

5. Create your own definitions of education and schooling. Describe what you would consider to be the ideal setting and method for optimal education.

SUGGESTED READINGS

BEREITER, CARL,   *Must We Educate?* Englewood Cliffs, N.J.: Prentice-Hall, 1975.

BRANDWEIN, PAUL F.,   *Toward a Discipline of Responsible Consent.* New York: Harcourt, Brace & World, 1969.

GARTNER, ALAN, COLIN GREER, AND FRANK RIESSMAN, EDS.,   *After Deschooling, What?* New York: Harper & Row, 1973.

GRIBBLE, JAMES,   *Introduction to Philosophy of Education.* Boston: Allyn & Bacon, 1969. Excellent analysis of the concept of education.

HOLT, JOHN,   *Teach Your Own.* New York: Delacorte/ Seymour Lawrence, 1981.

ILLICH, IVAN,   *Deschooling Society.* New York: Harper & Row, 1971.

KELLEY, EARL C.,   *Education for What Is Real.* New York: Harper & Brothers, 1947.

LASKA, JOHN A.,   *Schooling and Education: Basic Concepts and Problems.* New York: Van Nostrand Company, 1976.

WHITEHEAD, ALFRED NORTH,   *The Aims of Education.* London: Williams & Norgate, 1932.

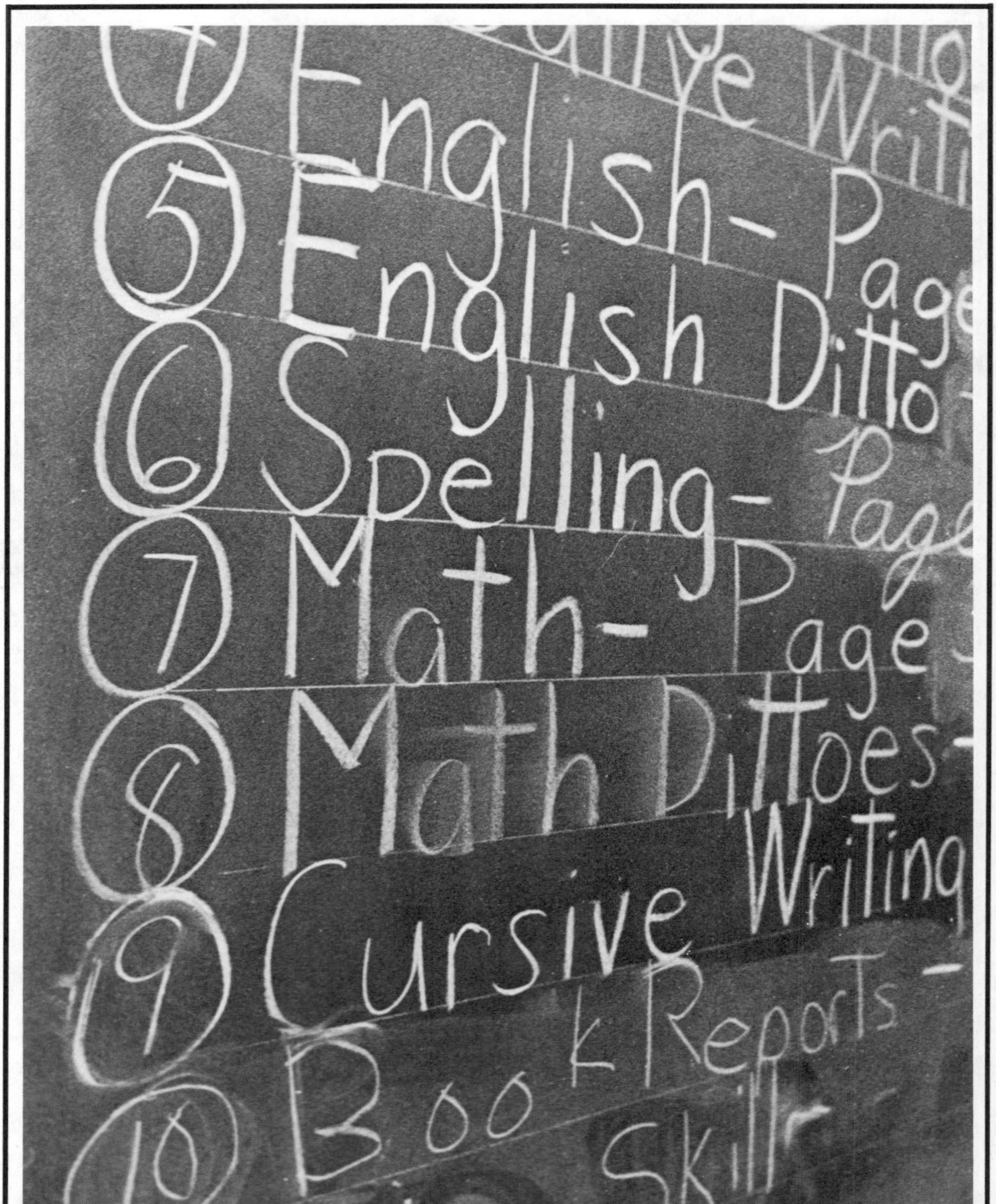

5 English- P
English Ditto
6 Spelling- Page
7 Math- Page
8 Math Dittoes-
9 Cursive Writing
Book Reports -
10 Skill

Chapter 8

SOCIETY'S EXPECTATIONS The Challenge to Education

In his excellent book, *Among School Children,* writer Tracy Kidder details a year in the working life of Chris Zajac, an elementary school teacher in Holyoke, Massachusetts, a rundown industrial town with an ethnically mixed population, including a large proportion of recent Puerto Rican immigrants. The book paints a portrait of a good, dedicated teacher who made a significant difference in the lives of her students. Kidder painstakingly details Chris Zajac's interaction with her students and her preparation at home. The reader is given a rare picture of a reflective, caring, sometimes feisty professional, who studies her pupils' characteristics closely, and who has daily to make difficult decisions about how best to help them.

Among School Children is a tribute to the ordinary, unsung virtues of attentiveness, caring, perseverance, support, and patience. Along the way the reader comes to learn that in Zajac's classroom, and probably in all classrooms, these virtues and improvisation are the stuff of good teaching. The wonder of the book is to be found in its message that we must learn to be satisfied with small victories and with the cumulative positive effect that a good teacher can have in the lives of children. As an almost perfect miniature, *Among School Children* stands in sharp relief to the multitude of reform reports that argue for legislative action and bureaucratic involvement.

As we consider society's expectations for its schools in this chapter, we would do well to begin with a consideration of life in classrooms. What are your own expectations about classroom life? What does the teacher do to set the tone for what happens there? What factors are beyond, or seemingly beyond, the teacher's control? What events are occurring in society that are changing the nature of classroom life and school life?

It is the end of a particularly difficult week of teaching and you find yourself alone in the teachers' lounge with a pile of papers, a stack of projects, and some serious questions. Every class discussion today seemed to turn into another argument about current events. And then there was your last class—half the students seem to have serious motivation problems. A colleague of yours had breezed on home an hour ago, pausing long enough to call out to you: "Relax. You're taking this much too seriously—just get your class primed for the achievement tests and forget about all this social responsibility nonsense. We're not parents; we're not the government; we're just teachers."

You are tired from the long work week and troubled by your colleague's remarks. To make matters worse, earlier in the day another teacher had complained: "Teaching is nothing but babysitting; kids today can't learn anything." Something is wrong here, and though you are discouraged, you decide to look for some solutions. You start rethinking why you wanted to teach in the first place; you start to ask questions about the purpose of education; you try to rediscover your role. Your search for answers kindles new enthusiasm: teaching is not a game or a business or a caretaking job and you know it. The purpose of education, the role of the teacher, and society's challenges all go hand in hand. To be a teacher is to be a very important person in the process of human and social development.

In this chapter, we will explore the many demands society places on the education process, on schools, and on teachers themselves. We will view the functions of education, and we will begin to discuss how well American education is doing with regard to these functions.

WHAT DOES SOCIETY EXPECT OF ITS SCHOOLS?

Schools and Culture

Preliterate or subsistence cultures furnish us with clearer insights to instructional processes than do highly formulated, technological cultures such as our own. In those cultures with simpler structures, the essential purpose of teaching centers around the process of cultural transmission. In such societies one's culture equals one's universe. Because these cultures are highly integrated and often static in their composition, a great deal of continuity accrues within them. Thus, rules or guidelines of authority and citizenship tend to be entrenched and unchanging over time. Coping skills such as hunting or subsistence farming and caring for children are central to the day-to-day functioning of the culture and therefore represent something crucial to be learned. Of course, the integrated nature of subsistence cultures means that religion, social responsibility, skills, etc., are all interrelated. The amount of knowledge is generally stable, and little expansion of new knowledge tends to occur. Thus, constant change related to technology, values, and skills is virtually nonexistent.

Most teaching in preliterate cultures takes on an informal but often highly ritualized style. Children learn by playing at and mimicking adult behavior. Later, they are included as helpers. They listen to stories told by old men and women. They attend and participate in ceremonies. Learning tends to be convergent, and the system of things essentially goes unchallenged. Those who teach are seldom professionals, although there are, in such societies, those who are looked upon as teachers in a broad sense, e.g., elders, shamans.

Thus, in these cultures with simpler structures, little or no distinction is made between formal and informal education. Enculturation, or the learning of one's culture, is the focus of the "educational" process. Children participate in the social processes toward the goal of citizenship in the group. The kinship group is the primary agent of learning. Formal education as we know it, with classrooms, paid teachers, supporting staffs, and instructional materials, is nonexistent.

In contrast, the nature of teaching in technologically oriented societies is much more formal. Teachers and students are expected to have non-kin rather than kinship relations (for example, popular advice is never to let your father teach you to drive a car). While most of the learning experiences in preliterate societies are natural, taking place in the context of day-to-day experiences, learning in technological cultures is often derived from contrived experiences (words, symbols, etc.) designed to prepare students for the future.

The universe of knowledge and ideas in such societies is vast, and decisions must be made about who learns what and when. Children are placed in learning categories, most often by age. A certain amount of work is then given to groups of students over a year's time, and those who complete it successfully move on to the next level. The schoolwork becomes increasingly abstract and formal with each succeeding year. As the curriculum becomes more difficult and as relationships between teachers and students become more distant, students drop out of school.[1] Those who drop out early often do so because they are motivated to have a job, but the best jobs are taken by those who stay in school longer.

Formal, contractual arrangements exist between teachers and school districts, and teachers are perceived by the public as paid professionals rather than as family or tribal elders whom one would naturally seek out for purposes of instruction. The teacher's role is thus institutionalized, and many students come to think (often wrongly) of the teacher as someone who is helping them learn merely because he or she (the teacher) is being paid for it.[2] Students who might quite naturally have thought in their early years that teachers taught simply because they wanted to, learn over time that teaching is a job.

Technological societies have gone to great lengths to ensure that the educational process is formalized and of long duration. This is so because of the complicated nature of the social functions of education which serve such societies. Among the demands that technological societies place on schools is the enormous responsibility of fulfilling the role of agents of socialization. (*Socialization* is the process by which persons acquire their habits, knowledge, customs, personality traits, social ideals, and other aspects of their culture.) In the past, socialization was considered to be the responsibility of the family; however, as society placed more demands upon individuals and institutions, "learning by doing," and "life experiences," which are key components in the socialization process, soon found their way into the schools. The next section will illustrate how the school's role is now complex, incorporating the teaching of skills and information with the teaching of ideas and values.

Social Functions of Education

While there are sharp differences between teaching and learning approaches in subsistence and technological cultures, a basic core of similarities may also be found. In all societies the teaching function encompasses certain basic attributes. Those attributes are to be found in the social functions of education. We shall discuss six of those functions: the transmission of culture, the transmission of skills, the transmission of values and beliefs, preparation for working life, the caretaking of youth, and the promotion of peer group relations.

[1] According to the national Center for Educational Statistics, about 72 percent of students who complete ninth grade finish high school.

[2] This is one of the arguments used by those who teach their children at home: parents who home-teach do not necessarily claim to know so much, but believe that since they care more, this outweighs mere knowledge or professional preparation.

THE TRANSMISSION OF CULTURE. Customs, mores, folkways, language, rules, and laws are the essence of a culture. In societies where culture change comes slowly and where a high degree of integration exists, learning one's culture is a relatively natural and well-defined task. In the United States and in a number of other countries such as Canada, Japan, Italy, and Great Britain, the 1960s, 1970s, and 1980s have been periods of great cultural change and cultural disintegration. The teacher attempting to transmit to students the diverse and complex culture of America in the 1980s finds this is a difficult task indeed. Interest groups, parents, principals, and other supervisors daily bring alternate and contradictory points of view to the classroom teacher. No wonder certain teachers, confused about whether a common core of culture even exists for them to teach, have retreated to the safer ground of emphasizing basic skills.

THE TRANSMISSION OF SKILLS. In every society, a certain array of skills must be acquired by individuals and groups in order for the society to function and maintain itself. Where the necessary skills tend to be general and in common use among the society's members, the teaching and learning of those skills tends to be naturalistic and informal. In a society such as ours, where development and acquisition of skills is increasingly specialized, the teaching of those skills is given over to non-kin, professional teachers whose instructional practices take on such formalities as having a set time and place. While the free school/open school movement which flourished in the 1970s was a reaction to the highly formalized teaching of skills to youth, the movement did not achieve wide acceptance. Attempts to abolish the trappings of formal education such as set classes, bells, textbooks, dress codes, etc., and to replace them by teaching broader life skills such as problem-solving and communication techniques served as an unwitting focal point in the public's reaction to declining test scores. However, to blame the "deformalizing" movement for low test scores is simplistic.

General agreement exists in the educational community that teachers do have an obligation to teach skills to students. Arguments continue, however, over which skills are most basic and therefore most crucial. Arthur Foshay notes four basic skills areas which he says represent fundamental obligations of teachers. He identifies these basics as (1) coping skills, such as mathematics, reading, and language; (2) character or social development skills; (3) citizenship or participatory skills; and (4) skills of private realization. Foshay distinguishes between the *formalist tradition* of education, which focuses upon skill development or questions of *how*, particularly skills of decoding, computation, and language usage; and the *academic tradition*, which focuses primarily upon meaning or questions of *why*. He suggests that those who merely know how will always be governed by those who know why.[3]

Another, broader, conception of the teacher's role as one who gives instruction in skill development calls upon teachers to account for skills of social interaction, emotional growth, physical awareness, aesthetic awareness, and spiritual response. Again, while most would agree readily with such a list of

[3] Arthur W. Foshay, "What's Basic About the Curriculum?" *Language Arts* (September 1977).

abstractions, there seems to be something less than consensus among Americans in the 1980s about the specifics of the teacher's role in skill development.

Education makes a people easy to lead, but difficult to drive; easy to govern, but impossible to enslave.

Lord Brougham Henry[4]

THE TRANSMISSION OF VALUES AND BELIEFS. Central to the teaching function is the task of teaching the young something of value. It is relatively easy to reach agreement on the need for instruction in values in the schools. It is relatively difficult to achieve agreement across a spectrum of American society regarding precisely which values ought to be taught and how teachers ought to go about teaching them. Obviously, for a society to remain intact, it must have a core of common beliefs. The task of discerning that core in a pluralistic society is often one of monumental proportion. This is particularly true where other value-teaching agencies, which are of equal or higher status in the minds of the students, such as the home, church, and neighborhood, present values that conflict with those of the school. In addition, the dualism which accrues with respect to certain cherished values renders the teacher's task in this area most troubling. How, for example, do teachers reconcile the differences between the value of individual personality with the demands for conformity, whether at the classroom or larger societal level? How do teachers reconcile the disparity between the right of parents to local control in a school setting and court edicts which call for quotas in school enrollments?

Robin Williams offers a summary classification of American values:[5]

1. Quasi values or gratifications: such as material comforts.
2. Instrumental interests or means values: such as wealth, power, work, and efficiency.
3. Formal universalistic values of western tradition: rationalism, impersonal justice, universalistic ethics, achievement, democracy, equality, freedom, certain religious values, and values of individual personality.
4. Particularistic, segmental, or localistic values: best exemplified in racist-ethnic superiority doctrines and in certain aspects of nationalism.

Williams's classification is helpful to the teacher perhaps as a starting point in examining his or her role as an agent in the transmission of values to students. The one inescapable fact that the teacher must face is that he or she *will* teach values. Whether this is done formally in the sense of offering actual instruction in values, or whether students merely "catch" values through observation of the teacher's day-to-day behavior, the teacher will teach values.

[4]From Lord Brougham Henry (1778–1868), in a speech at the House of Commons, January 29, 1828.

[5]Robin Williams, *American Society: A Sociological Interpretation* (New York: Knopf, 1960), pp. 468–469.

PREPARATION FOR WORKING LIFE.   Most Americans view the schools as having a "practical" as well as an academic function. Career education and vocational courses are manifestations of the phenomenon that asks more of the schools than a mere concentration of academic courses.

Almost all Americans agree that the school has a role in preparing students for working life. Most teachers and parents would say that an important purpose of "getting an education" is to ensure gainful employment in the future. A public service advertisement that ran for years on television advised would-be dropouts that "you can't get tomorrow's jobs with yesterday's skills." Stay in school, the message ran, so that you will be employed one day and therefore useful to society.

Education does make a difference. A study of 80,000 adults between the ages of 25 and 72 showed that the longer one stays in school the more he or she knows—throughout one's life. The study also showed that people from lower socioeconomic backgrounds who go to college are more successful in life than those from wealthy backgrounds who only complete high school.[6]

The argument, therefore, is not whether the schools should prepare students for working life—a widely supported cultural expectation. The argument, rather, is to what degree schools should prepare students for working life. There are many questions involved in this argument: Should vocations be emphasized in school? Should the school replace classes on poetry with classes on how to find a job? Should values and traits of the working world be applied to school situations? Is there any value in keeping unwilling students in school? Wouldn't an emphasis on the humanities assist a student in dealing with people at his or her future job—or are the humanities simply a waste of time? Does education really have anything to do with future earning power? How well do our schools prepare students for the future—any future?

Undoubtedly, the answers to these questions vary from person to person and from school to school. But the preparing of students for working life is an expectation of society; it is closely tied to the view that education is one of the keys to "getting ahead." American education is saddled with the task of dealing with this social demand.

THE CARETAKING OF YOUTH.   Every society must employ some method of caring for its children and youth. In all states of the United States, students are required by law to attend school from the first through twelfth grades, although the degree of enforcement may vary. A basic expectation in our culture is that the schools share an obligation to take care of the young. The conception of child and youth care as a school function varies from nursery-type early childhood programs, many of which include a day-care component, to the more formalized school programs which in addition to offering their students coursework, also offer lunch and breakfast.

The demand by parents for the schools to assume certain caretaking roles previously thought to be the domain of the home will apparently increase in scope. During the decade from 1970 to 1980, both the proportion and number of six- to seventeen-year-olds with working mothers increased. This was the case

[6]Harold L. Hodgkinson, "Education *Does* Make a Difference!" *Leadership* (December 1977), p. 223.

despite declines in the school-age population. The increased number of mothers in the labor force, coupled with the recent rise in the birth rate, will place additional demands for the caretaking of youth on the schools in years to come.

The family structure in the United States is changing. Single mothers, single fathers, divorced parents, and families in which both parents work are becoming more and more common. The public schools of America will continue to play the role of caretakers of youth. Perhaps in the near future that function will be extended to include even younger age levels than are presently enrolled. It is quite conceivable that three- and four-year-olds will be included in the formal school process. If such a step were taken, it would, of course, raise serious questions concerning the role of the home versus that of the school in the nurturing process. But in a very real sense, this step has already been taken in a random fashion through the establishment of private day-care and nursery schools. The question may ultimately become one of the right of every parent to publicly supported school experiences for the very young.

The caretaking of youth by the schools assumes more than the function of mere babysitting. In fact, as the nuclear family has replaced the extended family and as the nuclear family itself has diminished in size, causing the removal of a support system which met many social, intellectual, and emotional needs, the schools have been asked to undertake a much more inclusive set of responsibilities. Consider the fact that in recent years, the schools have been expected to increase the scope of subjects covered to include drug education, sex education, consumer education, career education, values and moral education, and computer education. This is, of course, in addition to such traditional responsibilities as the teaching of basic skills and related subjects. What was once the caretaking function of the home has become the caretaking function of the school. In many respects, the history of American education has been the gradual abdication of responsibilities by the home with the assumption that the schools will make these responsibilities their province.

THE PROMOTION OF PEER GROUP RELATIONS.   An oft-cited reason for the enrollment of three- and four-year-olds in early childhood programs is the perceived need by parents for additional socializing experiences for their children. All of us are aware of the powerful effect of the peer group in shaping our thoughts and in structuring our behavior. The effect of the peer group as a teaching/learning agent is generally perceived as a concomitant outcome in the learning process of education. Recently, attention has focused on ways to make constructive use of peer group relations as a more formal part of the goal structuring of classroom learning experiences.[7]

The peer group's presence and what the classroom teacher does with it educationally are of monumental importance to the intellectual, social, and emotional development of students. The inclusion of the peer group as a formal part of the learning process has been, until recently, relatively unexplored.

[7]See Johnson, David W. and Roger T. Johnson, *Circles of Learning* (ASCD, 1989).

Inventory

Schooling and Society

What responsibility do schools have to society? To see what your views are on this question, rate the following statements from 1 to 5, with 1 standing for Strongly Agree and 5 for Strongly Disagree.

_____ 1. One of the roles of education is to focus on understanding between different people with different backgrounds.

_____ 2. Understanding differences among people and learning how to work together fosters academic achievement.

_____ 3. Making social growth and cultural understanding part of the curriculum is to misconstrue the purpose of school and to overestimate what a teacher can do.

_____ 4. Schools must deal with moral and ethical questions as well as fundamentals of education.

_____ 5. Fundamental skills of literacy and communication need to be the focus of schools; other issues only confuse students.

_____ 6. The school is the place where students must be prepared for adult life and the working world, since parents often do not know how to cope with this responsibility.

_____ 7. A sense of self-motivation and self-discipline are among the most important concepts the teacher can instill in a child.

_____ 8. Most people never learn the meaning of work and self-discipline; discipline must be handed down from the teacher so that students will respect authority.

_____ 9. Decision making and problem solving are important processes that should be taught in schools.

_____ 10. Decision making and problem solving are best learned when they are used in the classroom as part of the learning experience.

_____ 11. Going through a subject step-by-step in a rote manner is the only way to really teach a subject.

_____ 12. A curriculum stressing social activism is a curriculum that fosters educated, responsive citizens.

_____ 13. Schools need not emphasize social activism; this is a natural instinct that comes with knowledge.

_____ 14. The most important function of the schools is to prepare students to hold productive jobs.

CHALLENGE TO EDUCATORS: AMERICA'S DEMANDS

Transmitting America's Heritage

In 1776, the Declaration of Independence proclaimed that all men "are endowed by their Creator with certain unalienable Rights" and that among them were the rights to "Life, Liberty and the pursuit of Happiness." This statement bears educational as well as political overtones because it is a commitment to opportunity, human values, and the dignity of each person. A free society cannot exist unless educators are willing to connect these basic principles with teaching practices.

In the transmission of America's cultural and historical heritage, several points must be considered. Among these are:

1. All Americans, including students, have a right to their own personal identity.
2. The American birthright carries with it freedom, rights, responsibilities, and opportunities.
3. America is a culturally diverse nation.

Students need to feel a sense of personal identity as well as integration into society as a whole. This sense can be developed through the education process in several ways. Among these are: giving students accurate and immediate feedback concerning their accomplishments; involving students in a wide range of experiences; assisting students to understand and to be understood.

The United States is an open society, a society that guarantees complete citizenship to all those who exercise their rights as well as their responsibilities. Though in an ideal sense there is equal opportunity in this country, in reality many Americans in the past and even today have been denied their full potential because of race, sex, age, or economic status. It is the job of the schools to insure that future citizens are aware of their freedoms and their responsibilities, that the important lesson of tolerance is learned, and that principles of justice are continued. Complete citizenship and equal opportunity should be long-range goals in which schools play a vital role.

Since we are living in a culturally diverse society, it is important that educators impart to their students a recognition, an understanding, and an acceptance of multiculturalism. In previous times it was considered "un-American" to allude to one's ethnic background. The melting-pot theory suggested that the United States offered everyone, regardless of origin, a new culture and a new way of life. However, some groups insist on maintaining their own customs, language, and religion.

It is important for the schools to reflect and perpetuate cultural diversity, as well as to teach a commitment to and a respect for values such as justice, equality, and human dignity. The schools can play a valuable role in fostering and guaranteeing the participation of all Americans from all cultural groups in the major policy decisions of the country.

The ultimate responsibility of education should be to restore peoples' sense of their own nobility. The goal of education, then, should be human freedom.

Developing Active Members of Society

Drastic changes are taking place in the schools' roles today. The real crisis is not necessarily in the area of reading or writing, but, as some psychologists point out, in attitudes, social relationships, and people's concern for each other. In the traditional period, the schools were viewed by society as a way to a successful and productive future. However, in recent times, due to mass media exposure, children learn a great deal before they enter school. The school has a new role of helping young people to become part of a productive society. To develop an educated citizenry, greater concern has been given to the affective aspect of the school curriculum. Problems within the school and the community are looked upon as important aspects of the school curriculum, and are used in problem solving. Examples of this might be a social studies class survey on why some students are continually absent, or a government class monitoring of school government. The feelings of the students can be externalized through art, music, creative writing, theater, and dance. A successful education depends greatly on the way pupils' attitudes toward school and schooling are formed. Active involvement and participation by students help to create good feelings about school. The student's lack of interest, or the idea of "just serving out the time" will be avoided when the student is actively involved and given a chance for self-expression. Educational experiences should prepare the individual in a creative fashion which will help him or her become a self-fulfilled member of society.

At the present time, as always, there has been a need for reform in American education. The United States is a dynamic society, and social changes must be accompanied by changes in course content and teaching techniques used in the school curriculum. There is a need to impress on our youth the understanding that in its relationships a free people must rely upon law and its institutions. The founding fathers of America assigned to public education a major political purpose: to promote the values, ideals, knowledge, and obligations required of citizens in a democratic society. It should then be the role of the schools to initiate new programs that will better prepare young people for citizenship.

Equal Opportunity

Education is the key to opportunity for all of us. Schools are instruments of society, and as such they are mirrors of that society. They serve the wishes of society and reflect prevailing aims and values.

In a totalitarian society where schools are instruments of the state, their tasks are clear—to represent the ideas of the prevailing party and to repress anything that is threatening to it. In a democracy, however, schools represent both the majority and the minority. They foster self-government and the goals of the community. America has been a work-oriented society and, accordingly, job skills and employability have received strong emphasis as reasons for schooling. However, American goals also call for a certain amount of constructive leisure time, a sense of dignity, respect for every individual, an awareness of and willingness to participate in events around us, and the development of rational thinkers.

Schools have further responsibilities to ensure survival and opportunity for all students. In order to survive, adaptability is an important asset, and continuing challenge is necessary for adaptability. When adaptability is lacking, society becomes inflexible and rigid, unable to respond to changing circumstances. The task of those who lead and teach is to find a balance between the security of conventional forms and the chaos which change sometimes brings. Schools can do much more than mirror the society they serve. They can help shape the society yet to be.

If schools are the shapers of a society to be, educational opportunity for all becomes a fundamental commitment of our society. Education is an entrance requirement to certain spheres of economic and social position.

In the nineteenth century, education became institutionalized. Because of this, education became public instead of private. As a public institution, the school became a place of occupational opportunity, and it became a central figure in the lives of all American children. The commitment to equality by our society became a matter of educational opportunity.

The commitment to education by American society is based on the theory of social benefit. This theory emphasizes the contributions of schooling to the overall improvement of society. The personal benefit theory, which educational progressivism introduced in the twentieth century, emphasized the importance of individuality and diversity. Acting on this theory, the schools have tried to address individual interests and individual potential.

The entire concept of equal educational opportunities is derived from judicially created law involving interpretation of the Fourteenth Amendment as it applies to public schools. Many educators have suggested that our schools are not yet proficient to educate the children of the poor, the nonwhite, and those from rural settings. These inequalities cannot be taken lightly. People from such different subcultures as the Hispanics, Native Americans, and blacks have insisted upon wider use of materials of an ethnic nature to which their children can relate. Spanish-speaking parents have asked for and achieved bilingual education in the schools. Previously standardized tests which were culturally biased and were of no advantage to minority students helped in forming inaccurate decisions about the intelligence of those students. "Culture-specific" tests of intelligence are an alternative to the solution of acculturation.

Public education is one of the ways in which all persons are given an opportunity to reach full potential. With educational opportunity, it is hoped that economic opportunity will follow—or that at least the deprivations of economics will not deny a person the chance to develop his or her intellectual powers. The schools can perpetuate democracy by preventing differences in economic status from undermining it. Public education is viewed as necessary for the achievement of productivity and for fighting the wars against poverty and crime.

Points of View

The Schools and Social Responsibility

Intellectual Despair

Citizenship education by the schools has long been a neglected area, but it now in a serious state of intellectual despair. In the elementary schools, it is an interdisciplinary subject that is frequently lost in the shuffle as society heaps more of its problems on the schools. The elementary schools are now expected to intervene in the national trend toward a new immorality by teaching courses on drugs, venereal disease, and sex.

From *NASSP Bulletin* (May 1975).

Balance of Rights

We have not paid sufficient attention to what we now realize is a very basic component of preparing our youth for lives of constructive participation in a changing society. We have failed to impress upon the very young how the law functions to protect individual rights—how it provides for orderly, democratic change; what the difference is between dissent and violent protest; why individual rights must be balanced with individual responsibility to the total society.

Leon Jaworski (Director of the Watergate Prosecution Force), "Leadership in Citizenship," *Today's Education* (January/February 1975).

Self-Perpetuating Greatness?

The French scholar and philosopher, de Tocqueville, in his prolonged studies of American democracy and our institutions, referred with unbounded admiration to the greatness and genius of our country. He concluded that America was great because America was good—especially in a sense of morality and in respecting laws and the rights of individuals. But this greatness is not self-perpetuating. It can vanish much faster than the time that it took to win it. Are these not truisms that need to be imparted to our young?

Otto H. Kerner, Ed., "Report of the President's Crime Commission" (Department of Health, Education and Welfare, 1968).

Effecting Social Change

Social change takes many forms in modern society and affects people in different ways. In the past, much of a person's satisfaction lay in occupation and work. The sources of satisfaction in our modern society are changing. People look for satisfaction outside of their work, often in the areas of leisure.

There are many social changes occurring in family life. There are more single-parent families and more families in which both parents work. More children are now placed in day care centers and nursery schools; these forms of preschool education are popular even in families in which the mother does not work and is the primary provider of child care. This development has greatly altered the social role of women in our society.

Major governmental decisions affect the lives of people by forcing upon them social change they may not wish or desire (e.g., the destruction of a house to build a federally aided project in its place). Individuals in this position are powerless. In order to prepare students for the many social changes that will take place in their future lives, the curriculum within the schools needs to focus on problems that are real, not contrived.

Many wonder if schools can bring about change in the social order. Dewey and Childs in the 1930s established a rationale for using the school for social change. They focused on what is done with children in the schools as a means of analyzing educational aims.

Educational aims vary according to the social purposes that are dominant in society. During the Colonial period, the role of the teacher was to indoctrinate pupils into a rigid class system where adherence to the status quo was favored. Education was seen as a way of protecting the existing hierarchy.

> In the span of 200 years the school was viewed as a bulwark of the status quo with an aim of protection as well as preservation of the best ideas of the race; then as an emerging institution designed to train technicians and leaders for fulfilling requirements of a growing industrial machine; and finally as a center of a pluralistic society requiring consensus and balance in achieving unity with diversity. Whatever the stated educational aims, it is clear all of the varied views of society are illustrated in today's educational practice.[8]

We have experienced great setbacks in the growth of both the school-age population and our resources. The symptoms of a transforming society have begun to appear: energy shortages, environmental pollution, proliferation of weapons of mass destruction, population explosion, and global starvation. Mario Fantini notes that:

> These symptoms clearly point to a society under severe strain, whose needs now fall clearly beyond any one institution and schooling. What is at stake is what statespersons have long forecast: humanity is in a race between education and catastrophe—between mere human existence and human potential. Societal forces seem to control us rather than the other way around. Education can help humanity regain its sense of fate control.[9]

It should be noted that the role of education is to help the individual become a self-actualizing citizen—one who can fit into and expand the roles society has established. Education should help to develop in each person those skills,

---

[8]Alfred North Whitehead, *The Aims of Education* (New York: New American Library, 1929), p. 55.
[9]Mario D. Fantini, "Toward a Redefinition of American Education," *Educational Leadership* (December 1977), p. 168.

Profile

Jesse Jackson, 1941–

"A civil rights activist in the sixties and a disciple of Martin Luther King, the Reverend Jesse L. Jackson today leads the nation's most effective movement for the fulfillment of the dreams of inner city blacks. The movement begins with education and will be realized, Jackson insists, only through student self-discipline and the work ethic."* This praise for Jesse Jackson was based on his work for Operation PUSH—People United to Save Humanity—an educational movement designed to assist blacks in urban environments. Jackson formulated his plans for PUSH in 1975 on Martin Luther King's birthday—January 15. Jackson, who was with King when he was assassinated, took on much of the leadership responsibility for continued efforts in the civil rights movement after King's death.

At a demonstration in Washington, D.C., Jackson was disturbed at seeing many young people "drunk or stoned, red-eyed, and out of control." Since then, Jackson has been working relentlessly to get the PUSH philosophy in operation within the schools.

The PUSH for Excellence philosophy is one of self-discipline and practice, calling upon all community members "to improve conditions in inner city neighborhoods through a concerted effort to root out or overcome forces which have made the inner city a difficult place in which to live and raise or teach children."**

Jackson contends, "Nobody can save us from us for us but us," and urges students to practice academics as much as they practice sports.

He believes that adults in the community—educators, politicians, the press, disc jockeys, the clergy, and other persons who influence children and youth—must provide adult supervision that includes motivation, care, discipline, and sometimes chastisement.

Much of the movement's success to date must be attributed to Jackson's charismatic leadership and dedication. PUSH has had profoundly positive results in many large cities, and its programs are being implemented throughout the country. Its faith in the people's ability to produce change is working. The community has taken up Jackson's charge: "Racism knocked you down: racism keeps you down and profits from your being down, so obviously it will not pick you up. The community must start the action to get up from the knockdown." If the community meets the challenge, a most important question then is: Will the educational institutions also rise to meet the challenge by improving instructional methodology and curriculum? Jackson believes they will.

In 1984 and again in 1988, Jackson became a candidate for president. He succeeded in winning more popular votes (in primaries) than any minority candidate in history.

*Cole, Robert W. "Black Moses: Jesse Jackson's PUSH for Excellence," *Phi Delta Kappan* (January 1977), p. 379.

**Eubanks, Eugene E., and Daniel U. Levine, "The PUSH Program for Excellence in Big City Schools," *Phi Delta Kappan* (January 1977), p. 384.

attributes, and talents which will be of benefit to him or her upon assumption of various social roles. We are a postindustrial, democratic society which requires an educated citizenry for political, economic, and social reasons. The school must be a structure that looks to the needs of the future rather than to those of the past.

In the past the schools have had a tendency to ignore social controversy. All members of a school community have the right to express in an open manner their points of view and in turn to listen to the views of others with regard to a topic that is of concern to them.

When controversy is dealt with in the spirit of inquiry, students will begin to understand and apply problem-solving techniques to their world of social problems and controversies. The effective use of inquiry techniques will help develop citizens who have learned to make reflective choices in a society where many choices are available. The schools will then produce individuals who are capable of functioning in society, who are willing to challenge established institutions, and who are willing to look for a variety of alternatives to resolve controversy in the society in which they live.

What Can Society Realistically Expect of its Schools?

Early critics of the schools looked at them as institutions of society which would foster a common culture. Some recent critics have looked at the schools as a destructive agency of society, an agency which molds and brainwashes its youth. Americans have lost faith in education, according to John Hope Franklin, the distinguished writer on black history. He urges that we help revive the "faith, courage, and foresight" which went into the foundation of our educational system.

Society *should* challenge the schools, should have expectations regarding the role education can play in improving our world. But society's challenge must be realistic. A summary of realistic social expectations was presented by Harry G. Miller:

- The school system shall endeavor to provide those learnings and activities which foster constructive membership in society.
- The development of vocational and avocational interests and capabilities are part of the total responsibilities of the school curriculum.
- It is a primary purpose of the total school program to teach basic learnings and skills.
- Understanding of and commitment to the values of our democratic society is a major function of the school program.[10]

SUMMARY

In this chapter we examined the whole question of what our society expects of its schools, and whether these expectations are realistic. Education serves a number of social functions in our society: the transmission of culture, skills,

[10]Harry G. Miller, "Do Schools Really Achieve the Goals of Education? How Do We Know?" *Kappa Delta Pi Record* (December 1976), p. 44.

values, and beliefs; the preparation for working life; the caretaking of our youth; and the promotion of peer group relations.

Beyond these functions, education in the United States is expected to serve other functions: to teach the basic principles of our heritage and to develop active citizens who can function in a democracy; to ensure that there is equal opportunity for all in our society; and to act as agents of social change.

Finally to look at the other side of the question, we discussed whether it was realistic for our society to make these demands on education, and settled on some expectations that could realistically be fulfilled.

ACTIVITIES

1. Discuss whether or not you think that many parents have abdicated some of their responsibilities and placed them on the schools. What do you think should be the role of the school?

2. List twenty ideas that are important to you. Ask yourself what effect these values and priorities will have on the students you teach. Discuss.

3. Discuss with another student the increasing role of the schools as caretakers of youth. Do you agree with this role? Disagree? What steps should be taken by the schools regarding this subject?

4. Observe a teacher at work (one of your own teachers, or a teacher in another class). Discuss whether or not any of the teacher's values seemed to be imparted to the students during the course of teaching.

5. Interview a person of a different race, sex, or ethnic background from your own. Compare school/education experiences. Discuss your own views of education as well as the other person's. Do either of you believe the United States is succeeding in educating its students? What changes should be made?

6. Investigate what Jefferson and the other early American theorists intended the role of the schools to be. Discuss whether or not we have strayed from their intentions—and whether this is good or bad.

SUGGESTED READINGS

COUNTS, GEORGE, *Dare the Schools Build a New Social Order?* New York: John Day, 1932.

DEWEY, JOHN, *Democracy and Education.* New York: Macmillan, 1916.

EISNER, ELLIOT, ED., *Learning and Teaching the Ways of Knowing.* Chicago: National Society for the Study of Education, 1985.

GLATTHORN, ALLAN, *Curriculum Leadership.* Glenview, Ill.: Scott, Foresman, 1987.

HIRSCH, E. D., JR., *Cultural Literacy.* New York: Houghton Mifflin, 1987.

KIDDER, TRACY, *Among School Children.* New York: Houghton Mifflin, 1989.

NICOLAS, ANTONIO, *Habits of Mind: An Introduction to the Philosophy of Education.* New York: Paragon House, 1989.

STANLEY, S. J., AND W. J. POPHAM, *Teacher Evaluation: Six Prescriptions for Success.* Washington, D.C.: Association for Supervision and Curriculum Development, 1988.

WEBB, R. B., AND R. R. SHERMAN, *Schooling and Society* (2nd ed.). New York: Macmillan, 1989.

Chapter 9

CONTEMPORARY SCHOOLING PATTERNS

TRADITIONAL PATTERNS
- Kindergarten
- Elementary School
- Junior High School/Middle School
- High School

ALTERNATIVE APPROACHES TO SCHOOLING
A CONTRAST IN CLASSROOMS AND CURRICULA
- Self-Contained Classroom
- An Informal or Open Classroom
- Curricular Alternatives (Historical) Perspective

In this chapter we will look at a variety of ways in which schools, and classrooms within schools, are organized. As students of education, you bring considerable experience to bear on this subject. While you have yet to embark on a teaching career, you have, in fact, lived in classrooms and schools of one type or another for more than a dozen years. Schools and classrooms are indeed familiar places. Recall these sounds for a minute: the buzz of thirty voices before the teacher called for attention; the long-awaited bell signaling the end of class; the furtive whisper of a friend at a closeby desk; the omnipresent voice of the teacher, giving directions, asking questions, sometimes providing soft private words of personal concern and other times showing justifiable anger with word-missiles directed straight for your desk. Remember these images in your mind's eye: rows of desks; hanging maps; blackboard exercises; the teacher's pet; the class clown; lines at the water fountain; mayhem in the lavatories; and in your locker the disarray of paper, pencils, erasers, and books scattered among assorted contraband. Can't you almost smell the ever-present chalk dust, newly sharp-ened pencils, orange peels in the wastebasket, freshly waxed hallways, and the collective aftermath of a sweat-inducing recess?

Take a minute or two and recall the most vivid memories from your days in elementary school, or from your experiences in high school. Do you think these memories of school might be similar for your parents or your grandpar-ents? Certainly there are many similarities, but your parents and grandparents might also recall other sights and sounds, such as the impact of a hickory stick, the sound of noisy radiators, a wood stove, a one- or two-room schoolhouse, daily recitations.

Doubtless, sharing such memories would reveal that certain common experiences in the classroom are timeless. Further, some basic differences in experience would exist not only between you and earlier generations, but also between you and your contemporaries. To understand and appreciate the diversity in contemporary patterns of schooling is in many respects to under-stand and appreciate the diversity of our great country and its people. For example, if a traveler from another country came here to visit and stayed in one location, whether in Los Angeles, upper Michigan, Washington, D.C., or Albuquerque, he or she obviously would have only a limited picture of our people and this country. However, if the visitor had the opportunity to travel widely, then he or she would be more likely to realize not only the commonality but also the diversity of our people and their values and customs.

It is our intent to take you on the grander tour, however brief. We wish to look at the diversity in schools as well as the commonality. In some regions, schools today are very much what they were for the parents—and even the grandparents—of the children who currently attend them. In other places, schools are likely to be considerably different.

There are a great many terms or labels which are used to communicate that a school has a specific focus. Terms such as "open," "nongraded," "year-round," "continuous progress," "fundamental," "school park," and "magnet," are used freely. It should be underscored that there is not always agreement on the definitions of types of schools. There are also times when a school employing a distinctive label in actuality differs little from most other schools. On the other hand, there is often considerable variation among schools and teachers who are not formally labeled as different or as presenting alternative approaches.

TRADITIONAL PATTERNS

An alternative generally is something which is presented as an *option* or a *choice* to something else. Therefore, before we examine some of the more common alternative forms of schooling, we should review briefly the more conventional forms of school against which these alternatives can be compared and contrasted. These are most likely the types of schools you attended for at least some portion of your career as a student. See Figure 9.1 for a sample traditional elementary school curriculum.

Kindergarten

Kindergarten education is available for the great majority of children today, especially in urban settings. A common admission requirement is that the student is five years old by the time the school term begins. About four out of five eligible five-year-olds attend kindergarten. Prior to kindergarten, a great many of these youngsters have also attended day care centers or nursery schools.

Early childhood is a critical time because of the rapid and critical phases of growth and development the child experiences. The kindergarten environment is commonly designed to introduce the child to new and expanded *social* relationships and cooperative work/play responsibilities which, in turn, enhance interpersonal development. A variety of aids and materials such as large building blocks, sand tables, toys, and costumes are used to facilitate large- and small-motor *physical* coordination. Various visual and auditory aids are employed to enhance *language development* and readiness for reading and writing. Kindergarten students usually attend school in half-day sessions either in the morning or afternoon. Class activities are quite independent from those of the rest of the student body in the elementary school. There are a few situations, however, where kindergarten students attend school for the entire day and where they interact more frequently in academic activities with other primary (K–3) students.

Whether youngsters attend full or half days, the typical kindergarten room is a beehive of activity. Physical fitness, social relations, science, performing arts, current events, the development of a positive self-concept, and constructive play are activities woven throughout the kindergarten curriculum. They support key foundational experiences which foster skills in reading, writing, and mathematics.

Elementary School

ORGANIZATION. The elementary school is commonly organized into grades, with students typically spending one academic year in each grade. Historically, most elementary schools were organized in a grade 1–8 pattern. Later kindergarten

Figure 9-1 The Program in Brief: A Plan for Kindergarten through Grade 8

SUBJECT	KINDERGARTEN THROUGH GRADE 3	GRADES 4 THROUGH 6	GRADES 7 AND 8
English	Introduction to Reading and Writing (phonics, silent and oral reading, basic rules of grammar and spelling, vocabulary, writing and penmanship, elementary composition, and library skills)	Introduction to Critical Reading (children's literature; independent reading and book reports; more advanced grammar, spelling and vocabulary; and composition skills)	Grade 7: Survey of Elementary Grammar and Composition Grade 8: Survey of Elementary Literary Analysis
Social Studies	Introduction to History, Geography, and Civics (significant Americans; explorers; native Americans; American holidays, customs, and symbols; citizenship; and landscape, climate, and mapwork)	Grade 4: U.S. History to Civil War Grade 5: U.S. History since 1865 Grade 6: World History to the Middle Ages	Grade 7: World History from the Middle Ages to 1900 Grade 8: World Geography and U.S. Constitutional Government
Mathematics	Introduction to Mathematics (numbers; basic operations; fractions and decimals; rounding; geometric shapes; measurement of length, area, and volume; bar graphs; and estimation and elementary statistics)	Intermediate Arithmetic and Geometry (number theory; negative numbers, percentages, and exponents; line graphs; the Pythagorean theorem; and basic probability)	General Math; Pre-Algebra; and Algebra *(Two from among the following one-year courses:)*
Science	Introduction to Science (plants and animals, the food chain, the solar system, rocks and minerals, weather, magnets, energy and motion, properties of matter, and simple experiments)	Grade 4: Earth Science and Other Topics Grade 5: Life Science and Other Topics Grade 6: Physical Science and Other Topics	Grade 7: Biology Grade 8: Chemistry and Physics
Foreign Language	[Optional]	Introduction to Foreign Language (basic vocabulary, grammar, reading, writing, conversation, and cultural material)	Formal Language Study *Two years strongly recommended*
Fine Arts	Music and Visual Art (songs, recordings, musical sounds and instruments, painting, craftmaking, and visual effects)	Music and Visual Art (great composers, musical styles and forms, elementary music theory, great painters, interpretation of art, and creative projects)	Music Appreciation and Art Appreciation *(One semester of each required)*
Physical Education/ Health	Physical Education and Health (body control; fitness; sports, games, and exercises; sportsmanship; safety; hygiene; nutrition; and drug prevention education)	Physical Education and Health (team and individual sports, first aid, drug prevention education, and appropriate sex education)	Physical Education and Health (strategy in team sports, gymnastics, aerobics, self-assessment for health, drug prevention education, and appropriate sex education)

Source: This sample elementary school curriculum is excerpted from *James Madison Elementary School: A Curriculum for American Students* (Washington, D.C.:

was added. This pattern is still common today in many rural areas or in private or parochial programs where often there are no separate facilities for a middle or junior high school program. However, in most elementary schools today, kindergarten through grade 6 is a more typical pattern. There are variations on this organizational scheme as well. In some instances, the children are transferred to a middle school in fourth or fifth grade, usually remaining there through the eighth or ninth grade. In many urban areas, elementary schools have been "paired" to meet desegregation guidelines. In these situations, more representative ratios of majority and minority populations are ensured by busing students of differing cultures to a K–3 or a 4–6 school depending on their grade placement.

PHYSICAL DESIGN. While the majority of schools today is still physically designed primarily for one teacher to teach about thirty students in one classroom (individual classroom teacher mode of organization), there is increasing diversity in school architecture as well. School facilities have moved from the more common square and rectangular patterns to a dazzling array of spheres, pentagons, even hexagons. In many situations, the once-familiar hardwood floor and institutional whites and grays have been replaced by carpeting and an aesthetically balanced spectrum of soft and relaxing or rich and exciting colors. Within the building there is often greater diversity in terms of instructional space: larger, more open areas to accommodate activities cooperatively taught and to facilitate ease of movement; and small, private spaces to accommodate personal forms of learning. Furniture and other instructional materials are frequently mobile. One can find an increased array of specialized facilities, even in elementary schools, for such activities as woodwork, pottery-making, film and photography, music and dance. Computer facilities are common in both elementary and secondary schools.

A typical elementary school building built during the growth boom of the 1950s and 1960s could accommodate three classrooms (of about twenty-five to thirty students) at each of seven grade levels (K–6). Thus, many of these schools were designed to accommodate between five hundred and six hundred students. Today, however, one can find considerable variation from this pattern. In urban areas and in some rural settings, larger, consolidated school "parks" or "complexes" have been designed to replace what were once two, three, or even four smaller schools. The assumption is that a greater variety of physical resources and on-site human services can be provided in this scheme. Also, youngsters have the opportunity to interact with a broad cross section of peers from a number of different races and cultures in this arrangement. Often "schools within a school," which offer some variation in program planning, exist in these large facilities. Programs which stress a good deal of independent learning, especially for more academically talented youngsters, are a common example of the school within the school notion at the secondary level.

On the other hand, many have argued for smaller schools. They desire to make the school more responsible to local community desires and more personalized in nature. The dramatic loss of student populations in the 1970s (primarily because of a greatly reduced birthrate) has contributed to smaller schools in some instances. However, the loss of operating physical plants is considerable, and often a school is closed in one neighborhood and students are bused to another to ensure maximum use of facilities and thus larger enrollments.

CURRICULUM. *The elementary school curriculum* is familiar to all of you and is examined in more detail in Chapters 14 and 15. Briefly, instruction in reading, writing (including spelling and grammar), and mathematics still constitutes the core of the elementary curriculum. This subject matter is complemented by the physical and social sciences. The application of the computer to these various subjects is increasingly common. The curriculum also includes some attention to the arts, music, and physical education. Instruction in these latter areas is often provided by teachers with specialized preparation who serve as resources to one or more schools.

FACULTY. In addition to the teaching faculty, the staff of an elementary school usually includes a principal and a librarian or media services specialist. In some situations, elementary school principals are either responsible for more than one school or assume some teaching responsibilities along with their administrative chores. A variety of resource personnel, such as a specialist in instrumental music, is often rotated among two or three elementary schools as well. There are frequently a number of other personnel resources available to most schools, especially in larger districts, and how these persons are organized and what functions they perform will be discussed later in more detail.

Junior High School/Middle School

CHANGES. The transition to *junior high school* (or in some cases middle school) is a major one and calls for rather major adjustments. While a few students may have encountered some departmentalization during elementary school, it is likely that the junior high school presents them with their first experience with changing classes and their first experience with a school calendar organized on quarters, trimesters, or semesters. They are also most probably confronted with higher academic standards and more out-of-class assignments or homework. There are other basic changes encountered in this move to junior high or middle school. First, the physical facility is usually much larger and has more specialized resources for subjects such as science, homemaking, and industrial arts. For the first time there are locker and shower facilities for physical education classes and formal athletic competition with other teams. The student has his or her first contact with a counselor to plan future studies. The student is presented with the concept of both basic, or core, courses—physical sciences, health, English, mathematics (algebra and geometry), physical education, and in some cases, a foreign language—and electives such as home economics, band, choir, graphics, art, and metalwork and woodwork. It is in the middle or junior high school that the student most likely attends his or her first study hall, pep rally, and school dance.

Curricular Excellence: A Profile*

Maryetta Elementary School
Stilwell, Oklahoma

The town of Stilwell is isolated in the rocky hills of eastern Oklahoma. Farming is difficult and industry is scarce. But as one real estate agent told principal Carthel Means, "It's easy to sell land in the area; everyone wants to send his kids to Maryetta."

In his 25 years at Maryetta Elementary School, Mr. Means has watched his school grow from a two-room building with just a few dozen students to a sprawling modern structure with nearly 400 students in kindergarten through 8th grade. Located at the very end of the "Trail of Tears"—the path taken by Cherokee Indians when they were forced to move from North Carolina 150 years ago—the school serves a student body that is almost 80 percent Native American. Most families in the area are poor, and virtually all Maryetta students participate in the school lunch and breakfast programs.

It's a special challenge to Mr. Means' faculty and staff. "One can't assume that these children go home to a house with a desk to work at or even adequate heating and electricity," he explains. But that doesn't mean lowered school expectations. Just the opposite, in fact; Maryetta offers a solid, ambitious curriculum, and teachers provide plenty of extra help to those who need it.

Because teachers noticed that many of their Cherokee-speaking students were shy and withdrawn in class, the school puts a special emphasis on language skills. "We don't just want students to hear us," Mr. Means says. "We want them to listen, to follow directions, and to comprehend." So Maryetta teaches a traditional English program that stresses oral and written communication, grammar, and correct usage, as well as a Cherokee language class where Indian and other students work side by side. Maryetta's other academic standouts include: a "hands-on" science curriculum that encourages understanding through observation; a rigorous math program that offers membership in a prestigious advanced math club to students in grades 7 and 8; and social studies lessons that include field trips to local historical sites.

As the school has grown, so has its reputation for excellence. The Stanford Achievement Tests show 80 percent of Maryetta students performing above the national average in reading and mathematics. Several years ago, Maryetta voluntarily lengthened the school day by 30 minutes, but nobody seems to mind. Daily student attendance is 97 percent. One recent Department of Education visitor noted that students come to the school every day with "obvious enjoyment." Their parents come, too; Mr. Means' open-door policy brings area adults into the school for frequent socials, student performances, and planning meetings. He listens to their suggestions and acts on them. "Maryetta Elementary is giving the people of this community what they want," says Mr. Means. "It's a school they are proud to send their children to."

*From *James Madison Elementary School: A Curriculum for American Students* (Washington, D.C.: U.S. Department of Education, 1987).

The chances are that the student is also introduced to a wider array of new friends and acquaintances, classmates who come from beyond the confines of what he or she had considered the "neighborhood." Also at some time in this period between the fifth and ninth grades, youngsters typically enter into that at once wondrous and frightening period known as adolescence. It is quite likely that for many students the memories of their first serious "crush" on someone, or their earliest experiments with cigarettes, pills, or alcohol, are more vivid than any recollections of their formal school experiences during this time.

MIDDLE SCHOOL.   It is a growing understanding of this special period of growth and development, and the implications of these changes in young people, that has given impetus to the concept of the middle school in many school districts. The middle school is a relatively recent phenomenon. In 1968, for example, only two states had established certification requirements for middle schools. Today there is a National Middle School Association, middle schools are in operation in all fifty states, and the development of certification guidelines for middle school teaching is commonplace.

CURRICULUM.   To illuminate why many have argued that a traditional junior high school with all the trappings of a high school does not accommodate well this special period of growth, we share with you some of the basic physical, social, and psychological characteristics of adolescents in the fifth through ninth grades (ten to fourteen years of age). We think you will recall many of the challenges you faced during this period of your life. Our discussion is intended as an aid in understanding the following points: (1) how the curriculum should be organized to meet the needs of the adolescent; (2) what types of teachers are needed for this type of school; and (3) whether this is the type of teaching role you might like to pursue eventually.

The characteristics of adolescents presented here are abstracted from a treatise by Fenwick on insights into the middle school years.[1]

1. The student experiences turbulent, shifting, and frequently conflicting emotions.

2. The student has a tendency to lack self-confidence, to appear moody and introspective; there is often an all-out quest for answers to the big question "Who am I?"

3. The opinions of one's peers are cause for either joy or dismay. The norm of conformity to peer behavior can result in intolerance of others' apparent differences, especially when these do not meet peer standards.

4. There is often an unpredictability in the student's response to adult affection, with a strong tendency to show either rejection or ambivalence.

5. The impact of rapid physical growth and accelerated hormone changes can produce skewed responses in individual student behavior patterns.

[1]James J. Fenwick, "Insights into the Middle Years," *Educational Leadership* (April 1977), pp. 528–535. Reprinted with permission of the Association for Supervision and Curriculum Development and James J. Fenwick. Copyright © 1977 by the Association for Supervision and Curriculum Development. All rights reserved.

6. Personal values and attitudes inculcated in the home or primary grades tend to be questioned and frequently rejected. "Other-imposed" values gradually give way to a self-imposed value system.
7. The student is able to grasp moral and ethical subtleties such as reality, truth, and goodness. There is a developing sense of social responsibility beyond that which involves self, family, and one's immediate peer group. The student can become fiercely idealistic.
8. The student establishes a clearly defined feminine or masculine sex role and ordinarily seeks meaning for that role in heterosexual settings. Hormonal changes, acceptance by peers, and influences of the mass media contribute heavily to the student's self-concept vis-à-vis his or her sex role.
9. The difficulties of this transition are often accentuated by value conflicts within our highly pluralistic society.

High School

The secondary school or high school is in many respects an enlarged version of junior high school. Originally the high school curriculum in this country reflected a strong academic, almost classic, course of studies. For example, the first year of high school study recommended by the Committee of Ten (a group set up by the National Education Association in 1892 to study the high school and its purposes) included English literature and composition, European history and geography, algebra, and both Latin and German. Since this benchmark Committee of Ten Report did much for the concept of high schools as preparation for college (if not much for the recognition of student interests and abilities or social conditions), it became increasingly necessary for a uniform system of allocating credits for high school studies as a basis for determining eligibility for college. Thus, in 1909 the Carnegie Foundation for the Advancement of Teaching proposed the "standard unit" as the common measure of time spent on a specific subject in high school.

The Carnegie Unit remains with us: the classical curriculum does not (with the exception of a few private and relatively exclusive preparatory schools). Today's *comprehensive* high school reflects considerable diversification in the curriculum. A cursory examination of the course offerings in one midwestern suburban high school illustrates the range of experiences available to many secondary students today.

Secondary Course Offerings

- English
- United States History
- World History
- Social Problems
- Mathematics
- Science
- Physical Education
- Health
- American Studies
- Biology
- World Cultures
- Humanities
- Chemistry
- Art (from sculpture through ceramics)

- Business Education (from typing to marketing and sales)
- Data Processing
- Reading
- Aviation Science
- Safety and Driver Education

- Foreign Languages (several are offered)
- Physical Education
- Family Living (from exploring childhood to effective consumerism)
- Woodwork
- Photography

- Lithography
- Architectural Drawing
- Metalwork
- Speech and Journalism
- Band, Choir, Orchestra
- Physical Education
- Physiology

Enough Time in the Day? Sample Student Schedules*

There are more than 15,000 public school districts in the United States. Roughly half of them organize secondary education around a six-period school day, which permits 48 semester-units of course work over four years. The other half follow a seven-period day, which permits 56 semester-units. Applied to either schedule, the 36 semester-units required by the *James Madison High School* program leave open at least 25 percent of available class time for supplemental, elective, or locally required study. That's a lot. It should be enough.

Consider the following sample student schedules, based on the more restrictive six-period day:

Student A

9th Grade

Introduction to Literature
Western Civilization
Algebra I
Spanish I
P.E./Health
Typing/Word Processing
    (*elective*)

10th Grade

American Literature
American History
Astronomy/Geology
Spanish II
P.E./Health
Bookkeeping (*elective*)

11th Grade

British Literature
Principles of American
    Democracy (*1 sem.*)
American Democracy and the
    World (*1 sem.*)
Plane and Solid Geometry
Biology
P.E./Health (*elective*)
Psychology (*elective*)

12th Grade

Introduction to World
    Literature
Algebra II and Trigonometry
Principles of Technology
Art History/Music History
Technical Writing (*elective*)
Graphic Arts (*elective*)

Student B

9th Grade

Introduction to Literature
Western Civilization
Algebra I
Astronomy/Geology
P.E./Health
Band *(elective)*

10th Grade

American Literature
American History
Plane and Solid Geometry
Biology
P.E./Health
Band *(elective)*

11th Grade

British Literature
Principles of American
Democracy *(1 sem.)*
American Democracy and the
World *(1 sem.)*
Algebra II and Trigonometry
Chemistry
French I
Band *(elective)*

12th Grade

Introduction to World
   Literature
Statistics and Probability
   (1 sem., elective)
Pre-calculus *(1 sem., elective)*
Physics *(elective)*
French II
Art History/Music History
Band *(elective)*

Student C

9th Grade

Introduction to Literature
Western Civilization
Plane and Solid Geometry
Astronomy/Geology
Latin I
P.E./Health

10th Grade

American Literature
American History
Algebra II and Trigonometry
Biology
Latin II
P.E./Health

11th Grade
British Literature
Principles of American
Democracy *(1 sem.)*
American Democracy and the
World *(1 sem.)*
Statistics and Probability *(1
sem.)*
Pre-calculus *(1 sem.)*
Chemistry
Latin III *(elective)*
Art History/Music History

12th Grade
Introduction to World
   Literature
Calculus AB *(elective)*
Physics *(elective)*
Latin IV *(elective)*
Computer Science *(elective)*
Painting and Drawing
(elective)

Each of these students fully satisfies *James Madison High School* requirements. In addition, Student A takes an extra year of physical education/health, and studies typing, word processing, bookkeeping, psychology, technical writing, and graphic arts. Student B takes an additional year of math and science and plays in the school band. Student C takes two extra years of a foreign language, a fourth year of math and science, a studio arts class, and computer science. The *James Madison High School* program prevents none of these students from fully pursuing individual interests, and it should also permit any school or school system substantial flexibility for course design and scheduling.

*Excerpted from *James Madison High School: A Curriculum for American Students* (Washington, D.C.: U.S. Dept. of Education, 1987).

In the mid-1980s, a number of major studies of high schools were conducted. These studies, in turn, resulted in a number of recommendations for change. The emphasis across the country was on upgrading the requirements for graduation and developing a more rigorous curriculum. The U.S. Department of Education's Commission on Excellence recommended that all students be required to take five basics: four years of English, three years of mathematics, three years of science, three years of social science, one-half year of computer science and, for college-bound students, at least two years of foreign language.

There are, of course, still many electives in the high school curriculum. Facilities and course offerings that were once offered only at the college level or in specialized trade schools are now commonly available to the high school student. Whereas only about 6 percent of the population graduated (at ages seventeen through nineteen) from high school at the turn of the century, today almost 80 percent of that age group will graduate.

In summary, today's high schools are designed to offer not only programs of academic preparation for college and specialized programs leading to vocational proficiency, but a good *general education* for everyone. They also provide multiple opportunities to explore individual interests in a host of curricular and extracurricular pursuits ranging from swimming to speech club.

ALTERNATIVE APPROACHES TO SCHOOLING

Having explored common patterns of organizing schools, we are going to spend a brief time examining how schools and classrooms at the same level might vary. This discussion should help you reflect upon the type of school or classroom you would prefer as a future teacher. Three major ways in which schools and classrooms are differentiated include: (1) the curriculum or subject matter; (2) the school environment—or how time, space, materials, and people are organized; and (3) the type or method of instruction employed.

THE PROGRAM IN BRIEF:
A Four-Year Plan

Subject	1st Year	2nd Year	3rd Year	4th Year
English	Introduction to Literature	American Literature	British Literature	Introduction to World Literature
Social Studies	Western Civilization	American History	Principles of American Democracy *(1 sem.)* and American Democracy & the World *(1 sem.)*	
Mathematics	Three Years Required From Among the Following Courses: Algebra I, Plane & Solid Geometry, Algebra II & Trigonometry, Statistics & Probability *(1 sem.)*, Pre-Calculus *(1 sem.)* and Calculus AB or BC			
Science	Three Years Required From Among the Following Courses: Astronomy/Geology, Biology, Chemistry, and Physics or Principles of Technology			
Foreign Language	Two Years Required in a Single Language From Among Offerings Determined by Local Jurisdictions			
Physical Education/ Health	Physical Education/ Health 9	Physical Education/ Health 10		
Fine arts	Art History *(1 sem.)* Music History *(1 sem.)*			

(Shaded area labeled ELECTIVES covers 4th Year column for Social Studies, Mathematics, Science; 3rd and 4th Years for Foreign Language and Physical Education/Health; and 2nd, 3rd, and 4th Years for Fine arts.)

Figure 9-2. The program: A Four-Year Plan

NOTE: This chart describes the *James Madison High School* curriculum. For each core subject it shows the number of years required and the names of courses that fulfill them. Each course is two semesters long, except as indicated.

In certain core subjects (English, social studies, and physical education/health), all students are obliged to take particular courses in a set sequence. In other core subjects (mathematics, science, foreign language, and fine arts), the selection of courses and/or their sequence is more flexible. This flexibility permits adjustments for individual student interests, needs, or abilities, and it provides room throughout the four-year program for elective, supplemental, or locally mandated study within or outside the seven core subjects.

The shaded area above represents room for such classes in a four-year schedule of seven-period days.

Source: this sample secondary school curriculum is excerpted from *James Madison High School: A Curriculum for American Students* (Washington, D.C.: U.S. Department of Education, 1987).

— Curricular Excellence: A Profile* —

Miller Junior High School
West San Jose, California

It's the morning after election day. None of the three presidential candidates has won a majority in the electoral college. A decision must be made—not by the U.S. House of Representatives, but by Ted Yanak's 8th-grade American history and government class at Miller Junior High.

Exploring the intricacies of the American electoral process is just one way in which students at this Silicon Valley school become familiar with American democracy. For its 715 6th-, 7th-, and 8th-graders, learning about our national heritage is an integral part of every school day.

Each morning at Miller begins with the Pledge of Allegiance and the announcement of "This Day in History," a short description of a significant event in the American past. Two of the school's most prestigious honors, the History Award and the Constitution Award, are presented to students with the highest scores on a series of oral and written examinations. The Harry S Truman History Club—Miller's largest student organization—regularly sponsors discussions with elected officials from the area. And schoolwide assemblies held throughout the year honor American leaders and traditions. Mr. Yanak, California's 1980 Teacher of the Year, frequently makes a guest appearance at these events dressed in a bright red jacket, blue pants, red-white-and-blue shoes, a flag-print tie, and a tricolor hat. "We are proud to be a flag-waving school," says principal Andrew Garrido.

Miller should also be proud of its challenging curriculum. Two years each of math, social studies, science, English, and physical education are required, and more than one-third of the student body is enrolled in foreign language classes. A full quarter of each day is devoted to English, and students do an extensive amount of writing throughout the entire curriculum. More than half of the students are enrolled in classes operating at least a year-and-a-half above grade level, and four out of five will go on to college. In 1986, the school received the California Distinguished School Award. And in 1987, its achievement on the California Assessment Program test placed it among the top 20 of 1,500 intermediate schools in the state. No wonder teachers hear former students complain that after they've left Miller, high school coursework seems "just too easy."

Mr. Garrido points to what he calls the "magic triangle"—motivated students, dedicated teachers, and supportive parents—as the key to Miller's success. And that triangle produces results: Miller's daily student attendance is 96 percent, its teachers rarely leave except to retire, and the results of district-wide surveys of parent satisfaction put the school in the 97th percentile. "These kids come here ready to learn," says principal Garrido. And the Miller staff keeps its part of the bargain, he adds. "This school owes those kids a good education."

*From *James Madison Elementary School: A Curriculum for American Students* (Washington, D.C.: U.S. Department of Education, 1988).

Curricular Excellence: A Profile*

Portland High School
Portland, Maine

Open since 1821, Portland High School is the second oldest secondary school in the United States. It is also one of the best. The school is located in the center of Maine's largest city, serving 1,150 students whom Assistant Principal Mary Jane McCalmon calls "a microcosm of the urban population." Some of Portland High's students come from affluent families and a large number are middle class, but nearly half qualify for the school lunch program. The student body is a mix of white, black, Hispanic, and Asian, and a number are recent refugees from various foreign countries.

Portland High School has earned national recognition for its excellence. In a businesslike atmosphere of quiet order and purpose, Portland High's administration and faculty provide their diverse students every educational opportunity. Daily attendance and graduation rates are better than 90 percent. An impressive number of students go on to college. "We are a proud school," says McCalmon. Portland High is especially proud of its curriculum. To graduate, all students must take four years of English, three years each of social studies and math, two years of science, one year each of physical education and fine arts, and a semester of classroom health instruction. Better than 99 percent of all students exceed these requirements before graduating. Honors or Advanced Placement classes are offered in all major subject areas, and about 20 percent of Portland students take one or more of them. Distinctive supplemental and elective courses abound, but the school has an especially strong foreign language program, with classes in French, Spanish, German, Chinese, Russian, Latin, and Greek.

Provision is made for the different abilities and interests of Portland's students by division of the curriculum into appropriate skill levels and programs. But placement is course-by-course and extremely flexible. On occasion, students may even enroll in more difficult courses than the school recommends. "We feel students have the right to try a more difficult course level," McCalmon says. "If a student wants to reach, we're not going to get in the way."

Whatever their abilities or future plans, all Portland students follow a program with one bottom line: content. All freshmen take an English class that introduces them to literature and gives them a strong dose of instruction and practice in writing. Similarly, all students take a three-year Western civilization and American history sequence, the goals of which closely parallel those of *James Madison High School*. Whoever they are, Portland students—including those in vocational training, whose studies may take them out of the school's main building for half the school day during their junior and senior years—must satisfy Portland High School's core requirements.

*From *James Madison High School: A Curriculum for American Students* (Washington, D.C.: U.S. Department of Education, 1987).

Schools frequently vary among one another along one of these three dimensions. Rarely do schools reflect major alternatives along all three dimensions. (See also Chapter 15 for a further discussion of curriculum, organization, and instruction.)

CURRICULUM. The most common changes made in schools are curricular in nature. For example, in the late 1960s and early 1970s there was increased attention to multicultural education, drug education, sex education, moral development, and sex-role stereotyping. In the late 1970s and early 1980s there was more of an emphasis, once again, on traditional core curriculum including science, mathematics, and foreign languages. Emphasis on different aspects of the curriculum tends to run in cycles. There are continuing philosophical and political debates over just who (home, church, school, or other social agency) is responsible for teaching what. Any time the school curriculum changes markedly, there is invariably a sector of the public who will demand a return to the former situation.

ORGANIZATION. The second type of change in schools has been in terms of organizational variables. Three familiar examples are "team teaching," where personnel—that is, teachers and students—are organized differently; "modular scheduling," where schedules are more variable; and "open space," where the physical facility itself is altered. The fact is, however, that organizational changes such as team teaching are rarely integrated with basic changes in the curriculum and/or teaching methods.

INSTRUCTIONAL METHODS. The most difficult type of change in schools appears to be that which is instructional in nature. Think about this for a minute. Certainly the text, such as this one, and the lecture or discussion which may accompany this reading, are the basic tools of instruction at every level of schooling. No doubt it is possible to identify other instructional methods and approaches as well, such as demonstrations, field trips, and laboratory experiments. Nonetheless, many teachers' repertoires of teaching skills are fairly limited. How many different approaches to teaching come readily to mind? The list is probably not long.

We are going to examine variations among each of these three dimensions (curricular, organizational, and instructional) by describing two different types of elementary classrooms. One classroom reflects a more traditional "self-contained" arrangement, and the other a more informal student-centered approach.

We educators seem to have the remarkable characteristic of being fascinated with what others are doing in other schools—and at the same time the capacity to generate inventive reasons why many of the good things others are doing are impossible in our particular setting.

Roland Barth[2]

[2]From Roland Barth, *A School for Everyone* (Cambridge, Mass.: Harvard University Press, 1980).

A CONTRAST IN CLASSROOMS AND CURRICULA

Self-Contained Classroom

Mr. Dillard teaches in a self-contained classroom in a K–3 graded elementary school in an urban setting. The school is located in a low socioeconomic neighborhood and at one time was a K–6 school with an almost totally black student population. Several years ago it was "paired" with a nearby school whose student population was largely representative of the white majority population. Some children from both neighborhoods are now bused. All K–3 (primary) students attend Mr. Dillard's school and all 4–6 (intermediate) students attend the other school. In this way, both schools now more nearly reflect the ratio of majority to minority persons in the city. Many students in Mr. Dillard's racially mixed class are from one-parent homes or from households with both parents employed outside the home. Each teacher in this school instructs his or her own class. Additional assistance in math and reading is provided by parent aides employed with federal monies provided to assist students from low-income homes. Specialists in physical education, art, and music each teach Mr. Dillard's class during one specified period each week. Additionally, Mr. Dillard often takes his class to the media center himself or arranges for individual students to go there.

Mr. Dillard is viewed as an outstanding teacher by his colleagues and is highly respected in the local community. He maintains a continuing dialogue with parents through monthly letters, home visits, and phone calls. He also encourages parents to stop in and visit his class during school hours, and many do this.

Learning to read is an important goal in Mr. Dillard's primary classroom. His reading groups are formed around a basal text approach. The texts are supplemented by phonics materials which are also studied by the entire class. Special drill and practice is available on two microcomputers in the class. English is a separate subject and is studied every day, with a major emphasis on grammar. Memorization is a basic priority for Mr. Dillard. Creative expression is also stressed. Thus, the children both write and recite poems. Other topics studied in Mr. Dillard's room include science and social studies with an emphasis on the local community. A specific time is set aside each day for these separate subjects, with the schedule and various assignments listed on the board.

Mr. Dillard provides considerable direction to each day's activity and frequently works with the class as a whole. The atmosphere in Mr. Dillard's class varies during the day from excitement to tranquility, often depending on the activity and the tone set by Mr. Dillard. "I try to make it [learning] as exciting as possible for them. I want to hear them actually cheering . . . enjoying what they're doing in here."

There are many advocates for teaching basic skills in early grades especially, much in the manner of Mr. Dillard. This form of instruction is commonly referred to as "active" or "direct" instruction and is characterized by the following:

- Lessons are structured through review and reteaching.
- Lessons proceed in small steps but at a brisk pace.
- The teacher provides many examples.
- The teacher asks a large number of questions and provides opportunities for practice.
- There is continuing feedback and corrections.
- Seatwork assignments tend to be short and focused.

Mr. Dillard's room is characterized by five rows of desks facing the front. This accommodates the several total group activities engaged in during the day by the entire class. There are tables and chairs in the back of the room. Near one table are shelves and storage space containing several reading and spelling games. Similar mathematics materials are organized near a second worktable. There are also two portable carts in the room, one containing a variety of science equipment and the second containing pictures and written materials focusing upon the history of blacks. Directions are available so that children can engage independently in "extra credit" assignments here. Mr. Dillard approves who can use these materials and when, and he employs both academic and social criteria to ensure that all children have frequent opportunities to engage in independent activities.

A look inside Mr. Dillard's classroom as the day begins provides us with a sense of the ebb and flow of the daily routine. All the buses have arrived. An outside bell has rung at 8:20 and, as the thirty or so children proceed to their desks, they either chat amiably with their classmates or gather around Mr. Dillard, who sits at his desk, listening to students and talking with them. One red-eyed, unhappy boy edges his way close to Mr. Dillard to complain of a toothache. A girl excitedly tells about her new puppy. Mr. Dillard comforts the ailing boy before sending him to the nurse, and attentively listens to the story of the puppy. A second bell rings at 8:30. Mr. Dillard stands and announces, "It is 8:30, time for socializing to stop."

Everyone stands at his desk, as the teacher signals Fran to display the flag; the class enthusiastically recites the pledge of allegiance, and follows this by singing, "Grand Old Flag." While still standing, the class next follows Mr. Dillard's lead in reciting from memory a poem written jointly by the class and the teacher.

Mr. Dillard switches off the lights as he moves to the back of the room. "Who has the news today?" he asks. Seven children approach the reading tables as Ricky steps to the front of the room and declares, "This is station KIDS reporting the morning news, weather, and sports." He follows by reading sections of newspaper articles about local and national events. As the class and Mr. Dillard applaud Ricky's presentation, he returns to his news group at the table. Similar presentations are made by other children in the class. Each child reads portions of articles dealing with sports and the weather and each describes some neighborhood activity as well. The rest of the class listens attentively at their desks, applauding after each announcer. This activity lasts exactly 15 minutes, at which time Mr. Dillard looks at the clock and announces, "Time for reading. I will meet with level 6. Levels 8 and 9, work in your workbooks and on skill sheets."

The seven children in level 6 scramble to the reading table with their textbooks, where Mr. Dillard meets with them. The session begins with vocabulary drill using teacher-made flash cards. Mr. Dillard had introduced the vocabulary yesterday before reading aloud a story from the basal text and had assigned the words to be studied as homework. The students anxiously respond to questions on vocabulary and their comprehension of yesterday's story. Most correct responses are followed by either approval from the group or a compliment from Mr. Dillard.

At the same time, each of the ten students in the level 8 reading group is working alone in his or her own workbook. Martin and Leroy are working at the microcomputer. Lisa is having problems, so she silently moves to Tom's unoccupied desk next to Mindy, who helps Lisa with her workbook question. After receiving assistance, Lisa remains in Tom's desk and continues alone on her assignment. This reading group has been assigned enough work to keep them quietly busy for about 20 minutes. Any questions they have are answered by fellow students. There is no interaction at this time between this level 8 group and Mr. Dillard, who is listening to the level 6 group read.

An Informal or Open Classroom

We are going to contrast the active-teaching, single-classroom, separate-subject approach with a more informal, less directive approach to teaching. Again, we selected an urban school to portray. The school is adjacent to a large, racially mixed, low-income housing project that contributes about half of the school's population. The balance of children are transported by bus from a middle-class, "professional" neighborhood. This school qualifies for state and federal support.

Approximately thirty children spanning three to five grade levels are assigned to each individual classroom in this school. So the first thing that we notice is that children in this situation are not assigned by age to a single grade and room. Individual teachers, in this case Mary Long, are responsible for the major portion of their learning experiences. However, in the middle of each day, for a period of an hour-and-a-half, optional activities are offered throughout the building in which children elect to participate. A new set of optional learning activities is offered every six weeks. This arrangement allows each child to participate in two options of their choice and to work with a variety of teachers. Teachers throughout the building are scheduled in various sequences during this period for lunch break, to teach one option, or to have some "prep time." Adults, as well as children, are addressed by their first names in this school. Mary Long's classroom has eighteen boys and eight girls from grades five through eight.

Study is often organized around themes which cut across separate subjects. The major theme emphasized during the fall is increasing the students' sense of their rights and responsibilities in a community. Mary Long chose this approach, "so we have a clear understanding of what needs to get done for ourselves and others." Ms. Long sees herself as a "facilitator of learning," encouraging children's interest in the broader outside world. As they investigate various problems and conditions, they begin to build their own themes of learning. She attempts to extend a child's or a group's learning through a continuing questioning process.

Children write weekly goals with specified daily expectations during individual and small-group planning sessions with their teacher. Parents are requested to be involved as much as possible in planning with their youngsters. At the close of the week, they compare their work with their goals and evaluate their accomplishments, again meeting with Mary who keeps a record on each child. Parents participate in long-range goal planning each trimester by filling out a goal sheet, at home, with their child. This helps serve as a guide for both the child and the teacher. Mary Long uses several record-keeping devices to assist children in this joint planning and assessment process. Each child, for example, has a list of the general competencies he or she is expected to achieve. These are reviewed periodically.

Reading skills are often refined and developed while reading library books which are selected by the student for both information and pleasure. Math skills are frequently stressed while working on the themes or projects, or in figuring out child/teacher-designed problems, but textbooks are also used. The teacher frequently discusses with the children how they might solve a particular problem. Children are also encouraged to cooperate on projects and to share what they have learned. Generally, groups form around common interests, involving children of varying ages and abilities. Mary Long also brings students together who need similar skill instruction. The entire class meets twice daily regularly for a "meeting," at which time the teacher usually teaches some concept directly which stimulates new directions and themes in the room. The "meeting" is also used for developing and practicing group skills and addressing various social problems which arise in the classroom. Primary responsibility for productive classroom behavior rests with the child. When disruptive behavior does occur, the children involved discuss the incident with the teacher and mutually decide on what the consequences should be. Mary Long explains: "A lot of discipline problems are caused by a lack of self-direction, not knowing what is needed to accomplish something for yourself in a positive way. So, sometimes I need to cut down the choices for kids; to reduce their realm of responsibility to a size that they can handle and which allows them to be successful. I approach discipline problems in a variety of ways, sometimes talking it through and at other times just saying 'Enough is enough.' It depends on the individuals and their mood that day because that's really relevant to how they're perceiving things. There is no one simple way to handle discipline problems which arise."

Let's briefly follow several activities inside Mary Long's room. School begins at 8:30 A.M., but there are no bells signifying the start of the day. Children begin to drift into the room prior to this time, quietly conversing with one another.

Mary does nothing special to indicate that it is time to begin. However, it is not long before the students begin to get their work out and settle down alone or in pairs. Perhaps surprisingly, the room has a quiet, calm atmosphere. The number of students, quite small initially, continues to grow as children arrive from finishing their school breakfast. Three children are gone for half the morning; two of them are participating in a special literature class that meets every morning, and the third child is taking part in a dance class sponsored by a dance troupe that is in its final week in residence at the school. Two additional children who are with a "learning problems" teacher return in about 30 minutes.

Around the room, the children are occupied in a variety of activities. The room is arranged and organized so that children can assume major responsibility for their daily activities. There is an emphasis on collaborative work in the room. Mark and Steve are conversing as they look for words on an animal word search that was designed by another child yesterday. Mary Long is listening to Sylvia read while correcting her own punctuation in a story she has written herself. Ed is computing problems from a math book. Dick and Kathy are discussing a book they are reading together. John is writing a science-fiction story in a bound book of blank pages that he has brought from home. The story has been in progress for several days and now covers almost thirty-five handwritten pages. He has designed his own cover and glued it over the original. Barb and Jane are working on the "hobbit hole," a project they are completing for the environmental theme. Allen is completing an exercise titled "Who Am I?" and now and then asks Dick and Kathy for help in spelling. Ted has created a "war" game where the players plot out the action. Three children are working at carrels with earphones and three more are at microcomputers. There are some who do not appear on task. For example, Dan is sitting at a desk alone with no visible work. Bob is poking holes in a crayon box with a pencil.

Curricular Alternatives (Historical) Perspective

Priorities in the curriculum and different approaches to instruction are obviously influenced by changing societal conditions. As was indicated earlier, the middle 1980s witnessed a major concern over the cognitive ability of youngsters graduating from high school—especially relative to other higher industrialized countries. It was not that long ago, however, that there was quite a different emphasis.

As so often happens in history, a variety of forces came together in the late 1960s and early 1970s to create a movement toward more alternative schools. The forces for change at that time included:

- A growing and general dissatisfaction with the Establishment, including schools (this attitude was escalated by our country's inability to disengage from a seemingly endless and futile war effort in Vietnam)
- A demonstrated ability, especially in urban areas, for grass-roots community groups to coalesce and exert coordinated pressures for change

- Heightened concern for civil rights and the essentiality of ethnic plurality, and what was viewed as an expanded responsibility of the schools to achieve these goals
- Several articulate, even passionate, contemporary school critics who were provided with considerable visibility through the media and who severely condemned many school practices
- A general social condition which fostered concern for mental health and individual well-being

The end result was a considerable concern for how to make the schools more humanistic, more responsive to individual needs and interests, and in many situations more socially conscious. The movement was, in many respects, tied to the noblest ideals of democratic society: freedom of choice and respect for the basic dignity of each individual.

What happened? Many "reformists," in their haste to make improvements, often relied more upon rhetoric than example. Also, some of the terminology employed, such as "open," "personalized," and "free," proved to be polemic. It implied to many teachers that they must be "closed," "impersonal," or "not free" if they were not part of this "new" education.

Yet, many teachers, as they do on a continuing basis, made changes in the classroom, but without adopting any labels and without any ballyhoo about alternatives. A few attempted to move to more radical instructional approaches. Some of these changes have survived, others have not. The harsh realities of a lack of needed knowledge to adopt new approaches, few qualified teacher educators to turn to, limited time and resources, relatively large numbers of students, lack of consensus on purpose (and, indeed, opposition from many, both within and without the profession), all worked against those who wished to make radical changes in the schools.

Other teachers opted for more structured approaches to achieve forms of individualization. Educational research and development agencies, as well as commercial publishers, devised curricula to assist teachers with continuing diagnosis in the basic skills; they then followed up their diagnostic literature with banks of materials and resources appropriate to responding to these diagnosed needs. The Multi-Unit, Individually Guided Education (IGE) approach, adopted by many schools, organized teachers into teams to accommodate this curricular scheme. Other well-known diagnostic-sequential programs are the Individually Prescribed Instruction (IPI) approach developed at Pittsburgh, and Westinghouse's PLAN, a computer-assisted curriculum scheme (see Chapter 15).

The social and political climate has changed considerably since the late 1960s and early 1970s. In the late 1970s, and well into the 1980s, the dominant trend across the nation was a movement toward more traditional values in many domains—schools included. "Back-to-the-basics" replaced "alternatives" as the media event in education. Again, there were several observable reasons for this shift: a very real and pervasive concern over depressed test scores; a perception that other highly industrialized countries had surpassed us in their educational endeavors; "tight money" and a corresponding unwillingness to put any more into schools for maintenance, let alone for experimentation until there was more evidence that schools were producing students with desired levels of skill and knowledge. As trends change and education patterns continue to evolve, what the 1990s will bring is still unclear.

We have attempted briefly to provide a recent perspective on the different approaches to schooling. Much of what the schools focus upon at any given time is a matter of values. Social conditions tend to reflect one set of attitudes more than another. Hopefully, both majority and minority values can continue to be reflected in different programs *at the same time,* in the same school system, and even in the same classroom. Mr. Dillard's classroom is different from Mary Long's classroom. There are basic differences in a direct versus an indirect approach to teaching. It is not a question of one *or* the other, of absolute rightness or wrongness. Rather, considering both empirical data and personal preference, it should be a question of which program is most desirable and best for which individuals—both teachers and students—and for which goals. It is hoped that options will exist at all times in our schools and teachers can employ a range of teaching methodologies and curriculum formats as needed and desired.

Regardless of how individual teachers approach their classroom, a number of research studies in recent years have contributed to distinguishing more effective schools from less effective ones. What happens at the district and school levels obviously enhances or constrains how effective individual teachers are. Effectiveness in these studies is generally defined in terms of students' cognitive achievement. These studies indicate that an academically effective school would be more likely to have explicit and agreed-upon goals relative to both student behavior and achievement. Expectations would be high but with strong conviction that the goals are attainable. There would be leadership exhibited to enhance instruction at the *building* level. The school staff would reflect a high degree of collaboration and collegiality. There would be good articulation and organization from teacher to teacher relative to how the curriculum is organized. There would also be strong leadership exhibited by the principal with a sense of order, discipline, and stability exhibited throughout the school. Time for learning academics would be maximized.

This brief portrait of some of the common elements of effective or successful schools clearly illustrates that teaching in many respects is a shared responsibility, calling for the cooperation of several professionals to maximize learning for youngsters. Although most actual teaching is an individual activity, planning and problem solving with one's colleagues can contribute very considerably to the success of that instruction. The ability and willingness of a teacher to work with her or his peers is essential.

SUMMARY

This chapter explored some of the different types of schools and how they are organized. The discussion included the basic patterns and levels of schooling: kindergarten, elementary (primary) school, junior high school (middle school), and secondary (high) school. The basic purpose of each of these levels varies, as do the educational needs of students at different ages. Across this large and culturally diverse country, many types of schools exist. The distinct approaches to instruction were reviewed briefly, and the set of conditions in society at different times in recent history which gave impetus to these variations was also traced. Characteristics associated with effective schools regardless of value orientation were also noted.

ACTIVITIES

1. Discuss the purpose of kindergarten with other members of the class. What types of goals should be emphasized in kindergarten? Should school begin at ages three or four? Why or why not?

2. Explore the organization of levels of schools in your community. For example, is it organized into elementary school, junior high school, high school? Or does it fit into another pattern? Investigate why the schools are organized as they are.

3. What type of instruction occurred in the schools you attended? Describe the schools and discuss whether or not the instruction from your vantage point seemed effective. What type of instructional pattern do you prefer? Why?

4. Given the glimpses of two different types of classrooms, reflect briefly upon the following questions: (1) What do the two approaches have in common? (2) What appear to be the basic differences between the two approaches? (3) What assumptions, implicit as well as explicit, are held about what motivates a child to learn; how is subject matter conceived of and organized; and how does the role and function of the teacher differ?

5. What makes a school "excellent"? Reflect on your own experience as a student. Can you recall some features of the schools you attended that would place them in a category of excellence? If you were to identify five or six criteria for school excellence, what would they be? How does your list compare to that developed by one or more of your fellow students?

SUGGESTED READINGS

COLLINS, MARVA, AND CIVIA TAMARKIN, *Marva Collins' Way*. Los Angeles: Tarcher, 1982.

ELLIS, A. K., MACKEY, J. A., AND A. D. GLENN, *The School Curriculum*. Boston: Allyn & Bacon, 1988.

GREENWOOD, G. E., AND F. W. PARKAY, *Case Studies for Teacher Decision Making*. New York: Random House, 1989.

GUTEK, GERALD, *Education in The United States: An Historical Perspective*, Englewood Cliffs, N.J.: Prentice-Hall, 1986.

MITCHELL, ANNE, "Old Baggage, New Visions: Shaping Policy for Early Childhood Programs, *Kappan* (May 1989), pp. 665–672.

PARKAY, F. W., AND B. HARDCASTLE, *Becoming a Teacher*. Boston: Allyn & Bacon, 1990.

SLAVIN, ROBERT, "Pet and the Pendulum: Faddism in Education and How to Stop It," *Kappan* (June 1989), pp. 752–758.

Chapter 10

MULTICULTURAL EDUCATION IN A PLURALISTIC SOCIETY

Multi-ethnic education is indeed at the crossroads. The future of this movement will influence how our children and their children will deal with racial problems and conflict. Without active and strong support from policy makers and opinion leaders in the government, in business, and in the education community, multi-ethnic education may fail in its central mission, and U.S. institutions, including schools and colleges, will retreat to doing business as usual. If this happens, muted ethnic tensions and frustrations will grow by leaps and bounds. This is a dismal prospect, but a distinct possibility.

James A. Banks
"Multi-ethnic Education at the Crossroads"

Sometimes, because of the many similarities we notice among people or because of what we see portrayed by the mass media, it is hard to remember that the United States is a multicultural nation. The population of this country is made up of people whose ancestries can be traced back to every nation on earth. With the exception of Native Americans (American Indians), each American family was founded by immigrants.

Though we tend to associate the word *immigrants* with the vast numbers of people who came to this country in the nineteenth century, it is important to remember that even the earliest colonists were people from other lands: England, France, Spain, the Netherlands, and Germany. Further, immigration to the United States is not an event of the past; each year, new American citizens are naturalized and continue to add to the layers of different cultures within our country.

The multicultural nature of the United States creates special problems in education and schooling. Picture this scene in a large urban high school. Li is just completing her first week in an American school. She arrived with her family from Southeast Asia just two months ago, and she is amazed at the size of American cities. Though she knows a little English, she does not feel comfortable answering questions or participating in class discussions. In her hometown many thousands of miles away, she was considered an excellent student, but now she fears that the teacher will think she is lazy or stupid if she answers in her halting English. She vows to sit silently and appear respectful—but she will not open her mouth until next year, perhaps, when her English is as good as that of Roberta, who sits next to her. Li glances around quickly at the other girls in the classroom, watching their movements, taking note of what they are wearing, so that she can learn how to behave and dress and, at long last, fit in. She is afraid the teacher or the students will criticize her if she does not.

In that same classroom is Luis, whose grandfather left Mexico to become a migrant farmworker. Luis's parents were both born in the United States and decided to raise their children in a city, where they could get solid educations, instead of on the migrant path, where education is sporadic. Luis's black, white, Asian, and Hispanic classmates all have different backgrounds, live in different areas of the city, have different attitudes about their families, and have different attitudes about the school and their teachers.

The teacher in a multicultural school must make special considerations when dealing with the students. Understanding that their backgrounds are diverse is only the beginning; with that understanding must come an awareness that different cultural groups have different values, different customs, different views of the role of education, different needs, and different goals.

MULTICULTURAL: WHAT DOES IT MEAN?

Israel Zangwill's play *The Melting Pot* portrayed America as a place where old customs would be left behind, where old languages would be forgotten, where ethnic and national differences would be melted in "God's crucible." Whatever the merits of this idea—and although the term "melting pot" is still tossed around—the fact of the matter is that it never really happened.

Figure 10–1. States with Percent Limited-English-Proficient above National Average

Source: National Center for Education Statistics.

Characteristics of Ethnic Groups

The National Council for the Social Studies (1976)* commissioned a Task Force on Ethnic Studies Curriculum Guidelines. The Task Force identified the following characteristics of ethnic groups:

1. Its origins preceded the creation of a nation state or were external to the nation state; for instance, immigrant groups or Native Americans.
2. It is an involuntary group, although individual identification with the group may be optional.
3. It has an ancestral tradition and its members share a sense of people-hood and an interdependence of fate.
4. It has some distinguishing value orientations, behavioral patterns, and interests (often political and economic).
5. The group's existence has an influence, in many cases substantial, on the lives of its members.
6. Membership in the group is influenced both by how members defined themselves and by how they are defined by others.

Task Force on Ethnic Studies Curriculum Guidelines (Washington, D.C.: National Council for the Social Studies, 1976).

Ethnicity and Culture

The ethnic and cultural differences among the population of the United States cannot be denied. And these ethnic and cultural differences affect the way different people interact socially, the way they vote, and the way they influence various aspects of society (including school programs!).

To assess your own perspectives about culture, try responding to the statements in the culture inventory. At the end of the chapter, return to the inventory and check your responses to see if they have changed.

To illuminate the terms *culture* and *ethnicity,* let us turn to definitions. *Culture* is the total of all the patterns of behavior, customs, and conditions that are characteristic of a particular group of people. *Ethnicity* is the sum of traits such as religion, language, ancestral heritage, and group identification characteristic of a particular group of people. As can be seen, these concepts are highly interrelated.

All of us belong to one—or more than one—ethnic or culture group. The idea that only people of certain minority backgrounds are members of ethnic groups represents a view that is not only highly restrictive, it is also false. Think about yourself in this regard. Your background is composed of your heredity and the cultural environment in which you were raised. Further, within these broad groupings of "ethnicity" and "culture" there are subcultures which are differentiated on the basis of various factors: religion, geographic background, sex, economic background, race, community background. More than you may know, these factors influence the way you look at life.

Your own ethnic-cultural profile is a product of your ancestry (for example, Afro-American, Polish-American, Native American, Anglo-American, Japanese-American) plus your religious affiliation (for example, Catholic, Protestant, Jewish, Moslem) plus all of your other cultural affiliations (for example, rural or urban, middle class or working class, male or female). These different life patterns overlap and create unique individuals with distinct ethnic-cultural backgrounds—and all these individuals are Americans.

The Great Migrations

In its earliest days, the United States was a paradise sheltering a vast agrarian dream. The great waves of immigration, beginning in the 1840s with Europeans victimized by famine, changed the profile of the United States from an essentially rural, Anglo-Saxon nation to that of an urban, multiethnic one. This immigration continued with the rise of industrialism, although the greatest influx of immigrants took place between 1840 and the end of World War I. Still, it is important to remember that immigration is a major part of America's cultural heritage; remember that of the fifty-six signers of the Declaration of Independence, eighteen of them were not of Anglo-Saxon extraction.

The vast majority of the immigrants were poor people who occupied the lowest strata of the societies from which they came; they arrived in this country full of hope, anxious to escape the poverty and famine they had known and to embrace a land of opportunity. They were eager to fit into American society; in many instances they anglicized their names as part of their zeal for citizenship.

Handicapped as they often were by language, cultural, and racial barriers, these new immigrants took the most menial jobs and found themselves once again occupying the lowest stratum of society. Strangers in a strange land, they were determined to make a better life for their children. This great migration and the wants of the immigrants enormously influenced education in the United States. The role of the schools had to change to respond to the immigrants' desires to be good citizens and to ensure their children's future.

The immigrants' desire to assimilate and their aims regarding the roles of the schools will be discussed in the next section, along with one other important point: while Anglo-Americans have been the dominant culture group in the United States since the founding of the nation, the accomplishments of this group are no longer considered the *only* ones worth studying. Studying the contributions of other groups and being attuned to the needs and wants of other groups is an important part of multicultural education.

THE MELTING POT: WHAT HAPPENED?

For immigrants, the hope for a better life rested on the educational system. The schools would do for the immigrants' children what they as parents could not do. In school, their children would acquire the tools necessary for a better life.

Role of the Schools

Thus, curiously, two related ideas about the purpose of schooling were born. These ideas have been so thoroughly subscribed to by so many for so long that it is difficult to realize that there are those who reject them as being inappropriate burdens for schools to carry.

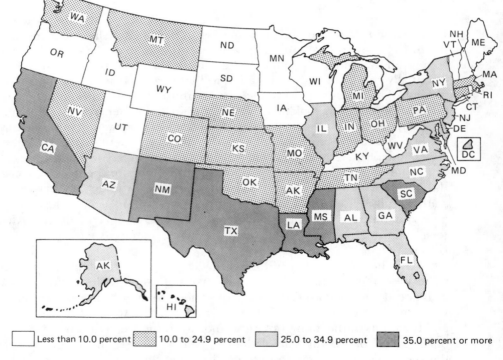

Less than 10.0 percent   10.0 to 24.9 percent   25.0 to 34.9 percent   35.0 percent or more

Figure 10–2.   Note: Percent minority enrollment in public elementary/ secondary schools was generally greatest in the Southern and Southwestern States and in California. The percent black enrollment was highest in the Southern States while the percent Hispanic enrollment was highest in New Mexico, Texas, California, and Arizona.

Source: National Center for Educational Statistics.

Inventory

Cultural Attitudes

What are your attitudes toward some of the following cultural issues in the schools? Rate each of the following statements from 1 to 5, with 1 standing for Strongly Agree and 5 for Strongly Disagree.

_____ 1. There is little reason for schools to try to change racist and sexist attitudes because the home environment is too powerful to overcome.

_____ 2. If a family of a different race moved in next door to me, I would feel somewhat apprehensive.

_____ 3. Insensitive teachers are a major cause of academic failure among minority group students.

_____ 4. Learning about cultures other than one's own is one way for students to develop positive attitudes toward other culture groups.

_____ 5. All teachers should be required to take classes which deal with racism and its causes.

_____ 6. If students are to study the contributions of different ethnic and culture groups, they should concentrate on the groups found in their own locale.

_____ 7. In addition to learning about minority contributions, students should also learn that in many cases certain groups have gone too far in asserting their rights.

_____ 8. It's time we all became Americans and forgot about all these ethnic and cultural differences.

_____ 9. Students should learn that institutions, including schools, often actually promote racism and sexism.

_____10. If emphasis is placed upon multicultural education, it could lead to the tearing down of American society.

_____11. Cultural diversity ought to be viewed as a strength rather than a weakness in our society.

Now join a group of four or five others who have completed this brief inventory and spend some time sharing your responses.

The first idea born of the immigration era is that of the school as an agent of socialization. To recent immigrants and to citizens who had failed to assimilate into the culture as they had hoped they would, the public schools represented the answer for their children. Here their children would learn to speak properly, learn to read and write English, learn modes of acceptable behavior, and, over time, become Americans. Although the schools accepted this task, it should be realized that from a historical perspective, such an incredibly difficult task had never before been attempted. The role of the school had expanded from that of an institution where students learned their culture.

A second idea about the purpose of schooling was the linkage of schooling to the job market. The notion was born that a basic purpose of schooling was to give students the skills and knowledge which would help them get better jobs than those their parents had. This idea became, in time, so pervasive that it came to apply to the linkage of schooling to the job market at all levels, both blue-collar and white-collar. Today the idea is so widely accepted that the few who challenge it are seen as academic snobs. Late-night television advertisements exhort would-be dropouts to stay in school not so that they might become better-educated people but because they will be locked out of the job market without a high school diploma.

Pluralism Versus Assimilation

The better life the immigrants hoped for rapidly became linked with American ideals, with patriotism, with citizenship. For a while, it looked as if Zangwill's idea of the melting pot was valid—and it is true that there are some values in this country which appear to be wholly American.

But on more careful analysis, despite some seemingly purely American ideals, it becomes apparent that we live in a *pluralistic* society, a society composed of many different and identifiable ethnic-cultural groups. Whether the identification can be made on the basis of physical characteristics, patterns of speech, the spelling of persons' names, or religion, it is still clear that the United States is composed of many different groups of people.

The concept of *assimilation* is the melting pot idea—the idea that cultural and ethnic differences should be melted into a larger "American" culture. This idea has been under attack for some time.

Advocates of a pluralistic society point out that no American archetype or model currently exists or ever has existed. Further, these advocates point out, not only do Americans encompass a range of peoples of great differences, but these differences are differences of value. Thus, the potential for conflict exists between advocates of cultural pluralism and those who believe that assimiliation of culture groups is a paramount goal of American society.

Past Mistakes

Indeed, the zeal for assimilation has contributed to many of the domestic problems of this country. These problems include cultural identity crises as well as others that are more damaging: negative stereotypes, racism, discrimination, and segregation.

Common Threads in a Pluralistic Society?

I had often seen people of the three races inhabiting North America brought together in the same place . . .

Alexis de Toqueville

More than 150 years ago, the Frenchman Alexis de Toqueville came to the United States on an assignment to study American prisons, then considered exemplary. The young aristocrat quickly became a student and anecdotal observer of the wider American culture. His observations led him in time to write the classic book, *Democracy in America.* The nation that de Toqueville saw in 1831 was far different from the America of today. But even in its infancy, the United States was far more pluralistic in its rural and ethnic makeup than was any other country of the time.

De Toqueville was taken by the differences he saw in people as his journeys took him to the Indian frontier and log cabins of Michigan, the Creole culture of New Orleans, the strangely separate but related black and white cultures of the South, and the industrializing eastern towns of Boston and New York where opulence and squalor lived side by side. But he also perceived some common-alities which he listed under the heading, "Causes of Social Condition and the Present Political Organization of America." Here is his list. How accurately does it portray the nation of today?

1. *Their origin,* fine starting point, intimate mixture of religion and spirit of liberty. Cold and reasoning race.
2. *Their geographical position.* No neighbors.
3. *Their activity,* commercial and industry. Even their vices are now helpful to them.
4. *The material happiness* which they enjoy.
5. *The religious spirit which reigns.* A Republican and egalitarian religion.
6. The diffusion of *useful* education.
7. *Very pure morals.*
8. *Their division into small states.* They are incapable of a great state.
9. *Their lack of a large capital* where everything is central. Care in avoiding such a large place.
10. *Communal and provincial activity,* which enables everyone to find employment at home.

CULTURAL IDENTITY. The underlying need of individuals to cling to group affiliations is part of their need for an affirmation of their sense of identity. The recent quest by so many to research their "roots" exemplifies this desire for ethnic, national, and cultural identification. In the past, the history of many ethnic peoples and the contribution of these peoples to American history was ignored, as were the contributions of women. Fortunately, the lack of cultural identity and history is being changed today; ethnic studies and women's studies are parts of a multicultural curriculum.

STEREOTYPES. A stereotype is an oversimplified opinion or attitude that is commonly held about a group of people. For the most part, stereotypes are negative and are the basis for prejudice and ethnic and racial hatred. Stereotypes generally arise because of a lack of knowledge and a limited understanding of different cultures. A typical stereotype is the characterization of Mexico as the land of tacos, lazy afternoon siestas, and continuous fiestas. This idea is inaccurate and tells us nothing about the Mexican people. Further, this stereotype can lead to a lack of understanding and a lack of tolerance for the Hispanics in the United States.

To avoid stereotyped information, the teacher must try to emphasize similarities as well as differences in culture, and to present information that is as accurate as possible. A good way to start is to display an awareness of the various ethnic backgrounds represented in a given class. Similarities and differences may be compared among the many cultures represented in the classroom.

RACISM, DISCRIMINATION, AND SEGREGATION. One of the ugliest chapters in American history is that of racism. Among the most dramatic and well-known examples of racism in our country was the enforced slavery of blacks. Another example was the enforced removal of various tribes of Native Americans from their native lands.

Yet blacks and Indians were not the only groups who suffered. Other ethnic and racial groups have also been victims of a racist point of view which renders the melting pot theory a cruel joke for them. Jewish-Americans, Mexican-Americans, Polish-Americans, Chinese-Americans, Italian-Americans, and many others have all experienced the frustration arising from the lack of tolerance shown them by others.

Furthermore, racism led to other negative effects. After the abolition of slavery, blacks still had to contend with segregation. This segregation ranged from enforced segregated neighborhoods to segregated restaurants to segregated schools. Since the Supreme Court's 1954 decision in *Brown v. The Board of Education of Topeka,* the schools have been involved in the long process of desegregation.

Discrimination is another form of injustice. People have been discriminated against (that is, treated unfairly and given unequal opportunity) not only on the basis of race and ethnicity, but also on the basis of sex. One of the main purposes of multicultural education is to strike a blow at discrimination of any kind.

INTRACULTURAL	*INTERCULTURAL*	*TRANSCULTURAL*
The "I" stage, characterized by a study of one's cultural heritage in immediate and personal terms; little transfer to other cultures; ethnocentric perspective	The "we" stage, characterized by the comparison of cultural universals from both contemporary and historical perspectives; the concept of interdependence is introduced	The "everybody" stage; global perspective; the concept of cultural relativism is developed; notions of world citizenship and membership in the human family are explored

Figure 10–3. Stages in the evolution of cultural pluralism

Source: "A Conceptual Model for an Integrated Curriculum" by Steven Jongewaard, Hamline University.

Cultural Pluralism: Implications

If people accept the arguments in favor of cultural pluralism, they are faced with the decision of how best to translate the concept into practice. Clearly the schools have a role to play in this implementation. One might argue that the schools, as a major socializing force, even have a responsibility to initiate the move toward a pluralistic society. And yet research has shown that the schools are woefully ill-equipped to handle such a charge. Some disturbing examples follow. (See also Figure 10-3 for a diagram of the evolution of cultural pluralism.)

In the late 1950s and early 1960s, studies were conducted to determine teacher awareness of sociocultural differences. It was concluded that "teachers, in general, are not sensitive to sociocultural differences."[1] While there was an awareness of obvious differences in language, customs, and experience, teachers were generally unaware of any of the underlying value conflicts which their students experienced. In addition, research indicated that in spite of any awareness that might exist, teachers were teaching essentially an undifferentiated curriculum geared to white, middle-class norms.[2]

It would be nice to think that the findings of these studies are no longer true. However, another study done in 1978 determined that the majority of teachers involved in inservice training in multicultural education did not significantly change their perceptions of minority children.[3] Not all the research is so negative. One authority suggests that the real problem is to gain a clear sense of cultural dynamics as they affect education.[4] Perhaps enough is not yet known in this area to isolate all of the critical variables and to do a consistent job of training culturally sensitive teachers.

[1] Miles V. Zintz, "The Indian Research Study," Final report. Section 1 of 2 sections. (Albuquerque, N.M.: College of Education, University of New Mexico [mimeo], 1957–1960), p. 106, as reported in Dolores E. Cross et al., "Minority Cultures and Education in the United States," *Education and Urban Society, 10,* 3 (May 1978).

[2] Horacio Ulibarri, "Teacher Awareness of Socio-Cultural Differences in Multi-Cultural Classrooms," Unpublished dissertation (Albuquerque, N.M.: University of New Mexico, 1960).

[3] D. E. Cross and J. Deslonde, "Inservice in Multicultural Education: Have We Scratched the Surface?" *Education Research Quarterly* (Spring 1978).

[4] Asa G. Hilliard, "Restructuring Teacher Education for Multicultural Imperatives," Educational Resources Information Center (ERIC), ED091380, 1974.

Looking at some of the work that had been done with students, one recent study is worth noting. The study, conducted to test the effects of the *Family of Man* social studies program on children's attitudes toward other nations and other peoples, yielded more optimistic results. Children in the experimental group did generally better than their control counterparts in overall social studies achievement. In addition, they exhibited a generally more positive attitude toward other nations and other people. Interestingly, children in the experimental group also showed a better grasp of facts and understanding about the United States.[5] This finding was of particular interest because it defuses the argument that time spent learning about other nations and other peoples will detract from learning about one's own heritage. It seems evident from these studies that *schools can play a positive role* in the development of the concept of cultural pluralism.

CURRENT SCHOOLS: FAILURES IN MULTICULTURAL EDUCATION. Unfortunately, there is multiple evidence to suggest that the net effect of schooling as it exists today leaves little room for optimism. It has been said that "the process of formal schooling is the struggle to substitute one kind of tradition for another within the mind of the child."[6] Here we get back to the thought mentioned earlier, that success within the system is frequently gained at the expense of many of one's own cultural and ethnic traditions and beliefs, and may result in serious value conflicts for the culturally different. From the first day of school, the locus of control begins to shift from an internal sense of learning, motivation, and self-appraisal to an external control imposed by the institution. This new control can strip the student of any intrinsic criteria for learning and replace it with extrinsic and therefore artificial criteria for performance, appraisal, and judgment of self-worth. This process is difficult for all students to some degree, but particularly so for those from nonmainstream, non–Anglo-Saxon traditions.

It is recognized that cultural pluralism should be a central and recurring theme throughout the entire curriculum. Yet it is also recognized that many school systems have as yet done little in this area. Several studies have concluded that "while the stated purpose of public schools is equal educational opportunity for all, public schools have been organized to deprive poor children of a quality education."[7] Two other findings bear mentioning. In a study conducted in the 1970s, the researchers included among their findings that "on the average, American education has not been a successful intervention strategy for the

[5]Charles L. Mitsakos, "FAMES Project: Final Report," published in cooperation with the Social Education Department of the School of Education, Boston University, 1977.

[6]Murray L. Wax and Rosalie H. Wax, "Great Tradition, Little Tradition, and Formal Education," mimeographed (National Conference on Anthropology and Education, American Anthropological Association, Washington, D.C., 1968); Murray L. Wax and Rosalie H. Wax, "Cultural Deprivation as an Educational Ideology," *Journal of American Indian Education,* 3, 2 (1964), pp. 15–18.

[7]M. Katz, *Class Bureaucracy and Schools* (New York: Praeger, 1971); M. Carnoy, *Education as Cultural Imperialism* (New York: David McKay, 1974); J. Spring, *The Sorting Machine—National Educational Policy Since 1945* (New York: David McKay, 1976), as reported in Dolores E. Cross, and others, "Minority Cultures and Education in the United States," *Education and Urban Society, 10,* 3 (May 1978).

upward mobility of children from poor families."[8] Finally, to complete this line of thinking, it has been shown that economic inequality is increasing in this country. In fact, the top fifth of American families receives 48 percent of all family income while the bottom fifth receives only 4 percent. Furthermore, the top 0.008 percent of all families in this country own as much as the bottom half.[9]

These facts are presented here because they represent the effects of an educational system that is anything but culturally pluralistic. There is no equal opportunity without equal access. And equal accessibility will not be forthcoming if the educational system in this country, consciously or otherwise, discriminates against large portions of the population. Biased standardized testing and the generally white, middle-class ethnocentricity of assessors and teachers have resulted in low expectations at the very least, and sometimes worse. For instance, there is a documented case of Chicago students in Riverside, California, being placed in EMR (educable mentally retarded) classes based on the use of an assessment instrument which was biased in terms of cultural content and language use.[10]

FUTURE HOPES.   Granted, we now live in a more enlightened era, but we also live in a time when the cry is for more emphasis on the basics. To many people, "back-to-basics" is the rallying call for a very real trend toward pulling back from the cutting edge of social equality and rebuilding the walls of prejudice and discrimination higher than ever.

The teaching profession, instead of leading the way toward a pluralistic society, may now be in a defensive and reactive posture. Teachers have been demoralized by tight budgets, declining enrollments, and an increasingly hostile public. School boards and curriculum committees have denounced "secular humanism" and have eliminated textbooks from the classroom. In 1979, J. D. Salinger's *Catcher in the Rye* was banned from the classrooms of a public school system in the state of Washington—this at a time when educators had thought censorship in the classroom was a thing of the past.

All of this is by way of saying that the road ahead is neither clear nor easy. For, in spite of what we know about how students learn, and regardless of our increasing awareness of domestic and international affairs which dictate the need for better cooperation among the peoples of the world, the time has not yet come when this cooperation will be embraced by all.

However, there is no need to give up efforts toward understanding. In this section we have considered some of the research that has been done on teachers, students, and the schools—research that has implications for the implementation of a culturally pluralistic curriculum. While the reviews are mixed, the evidence nevertheless supports the need for continued work with children toward

[8]S. Bowles and H. Gintis, "I.Q. in the U.S. Class Structure," *Social Policy* (January/February 1973); K. Kenniston, *All Our Children: The American Family under Pressure* (New York: Harcourt Brace Jovanovich, 1977).

[9]L. C. Thurow, "Problems without Solutions: Solutions without Problems," in N. F. Ashline et al. Eds., *Education, Inequality and National Policy* (Lexington, Mass.: Lexington Books, 1976).

[10]J. R. Mercer, *Labeling the Mentally Retarded* (Berkeley and Los Angeles: University of California Press, 1972).

eliminating prejudice and increasing multicultural understanding. The problems in our schools highlight the need for change. In the next section, we will consider some of the cultural elements a teacher should be aware of in students. This awareness of cultural patterns will aid understanding.

TOWARD CULTURAL UNDERSTANDING

Though past studies have concluded that many teachers are unaware of the value conflicts and cultural ideals of their students, it is also true that this is changing. Further, the profile of teachers is changing; many members of racial and ethnic minorities are now entering the teaching professions. Slowly, lack of understanding will evolve into increased understanding. There are many cultural factors the teacher must be aware of in dealing with students, in order that someday equal access to school buildings will also mean equal opportunity in education.

Factors of Culture

Different groups have different ideas about things; these ideas range from different preferences in food to different value systems. For diverse opinions and values to exist, it is not necessary to alter too many variables. For example, a teenager living on a farm will have different ideas about society than will a teenager from a large city.

Factors of culture include differences beyond race or ethnicity. These factors include sex, religious affiliation, geographic location, economics. We will explore some of these factors in this section.

RACE. The most obvious cultural factor is that of race. The United States is composed of people from every racial type. Since racial traits are usually so easy to see, racial differences are often very pronounced and racial discrimination is anything but subtle. It is important for the teacher to remember that all races have a deep sense of cultural pride; rather than cause problems, differences in the way people of various races live can be put to good advantage in the classroom. Students can learn from each other.

As more and more immigrants pour into this country, schools will have to deal with different types of racial problems than in the past. The black-white or white-red differences of the past are no longer the only racial differences. More and more Asians are entering our country, as are more and more persons from Latin America. The schools can be a forum for sharing among racial backgrounds, rather than a platform for increased tension.

ETHNIC BACKGROUND. The American people are unique in that, with the exception of Native Americans, they all can trace their ancestry to another country. After the influx of English, Dutch, French, German, and Spanish in the early days of our country, groups from other European countries followed: first the Irish, then Italians, Slavs, Scandinavians, and others. Africans, Asians, and South and

Central Americans are all included among this country's ethnic groups. Differences in customs, in food, in ideas about education and work, in ways of speaking, in family traditions all lend to the cultural diversity of the United States. The teacher must remember that different students from different backgrounds will have different attitudes about learning, about future job possibilities, about later education. Once again, a sharing within the classroom can ease tensions and provide a forum for ethnic identity and pride.

SEX.   The difference in views of male students and female students is partially due to what various cultures feel about the different sexes. To avoid discrimination, it is important for teachers to view both male and female students as equally important and as having equal potential. Both sexes will need to be encouraged to try areas of study and experience that they may not formerly have tried because of their sex.

RELIGIOUS AFFILIATION.   Just as this country has representatives from every race and every ethnic group, so, too, is every religious group represented in America. The major religions, Christian, Buddhist, Islamic, and Jewish, all have places of worship in America and are represented by many different sects and groups. Often, religious beliefs will be the determining factor in whether or not parents will send their children to public schools. Frequently, laws of diet or special holidays will have to be observed by certain students; problems with other students can arise because of these misunderstood differences. The teacher must be alert to religious differences and, once again, learn to use these differences as a starting point for understanding, rather than for intolerance.

GEOGRAPHIC LOCATION.   Urban life is certainly very different from rural life, and suburban life is different from both of these. Furthermore, students living in homes on tree-lined streets will be different from their fellow students who live in high-rises or housing projects or apartment buildings. Different levels of stress, different ways of coping with other people, different expectations about noise and crowds will all be elements to consider when teaching students from different types of neighborhoods. Transportation to school will be an added dimension, as will participation in extracurricular activities; the time spent at school and students' success with other students all relate to geographic location. Further, different geographic locations often have different ethnic mixes. For example, Hispanic people tend to live in the towns and cities of the Southwest or in large Eastern cities. The suburbs tend to be white. These combinations of factors affect schooling.

ECONOMIC STATUS.   As can be expected, economics is an important factor in understanding student differences. Different economic groups have different expectations about what the schools should provide. Working-class groups often expect the schools to provide awareness of future jobs, whereas middle-class or upper-class parents often expect more emphasis on literature and art. Parents from lower economic groups may expect the schools to assist their children in having a better future; or these parents may be disillusioned and may have no hope for the schools. Economics are important to consider when working toward understanding.

The Urban Educational Environment Today*

Data provided by Harold L. Hodgkinson in *All One System* (1985) gives us some sense of the conditions urban educators must deal with today:

- Since 1981, every day 2,000 children fall into poverty.
- Each year, almost 500,000 children are born to teenage mothers—twice the rate of any industrialized nation in the Western world.
- Every day, 40 teenagers give birth to their third child.
- By the year 2000, one-third of all Americans will be non-white; and the non-white school population will be above 50 percent.
- Beginning in 1983, 60% of the children born in this country will, by the age of 18, live in one-parent households. Growing up in a two-parent household is no longer the norm.
- Currently 45% of black children, 36% of Hispanic children, and 25% of all children live in poverty.
- There has been a 6,000% increase in drug use since 1960.
- Teenage homicides are up 200% since 1950, and delinquency is up 130% since 1960.
- Teenage unemployment rises every year.
- The dropout rate is more than 50% in many large cities.

Other studies show that of the more than 3,600,000 children who began school in September 1987, 25% were from poverty families; 15% were the children of teenagers; 15% were physically or mentally handicapped; 15% speak a language other than English; 25% will never finish high school; and 10% have illiterate parents. These data are nationwide. For urban schools, these percentages are even more staggering.

There are also statistics relative to current and anticipated teacher shortages in urban schools, which call for immediate action. In 1982 approximately 115,000 new teachers were hired in the United States. By 1992 the number of new teachers needed will be approximately 215,000. The total number of public school teachers is currently about 2.1 million. Of this total, about 10% are first-year teachers. These are national figures and do not begin to reflect the increasingly greater needs in urban areas. For example, 3,000 new teachers will be needed each year in Los Angeles and 2,000 in Houston.

Given the current and projected need for more teachers, it is troubling that there has been only a very modest increase in the number of college students who are entering teacher preparation programs. In 1985 only 4% of college students chose teaching as a profession. Today, this has increased to only 10% and is projected to remain at that level.

Although it is clear that there will be a shortage of teachers for urban schools, this is not likely to be true for rural, small town, and suburban schools except in math, science, and special areas. However, even in rural and suburban districts, fully one-half of the total teaching force leaves the profession and must be replaced in a five-year period. And the number leaving the profession is markedly higher in most urban school districts. Some argue that there is no teacher shortage, merely a distribution problem, and that the 1,297 teacher preparation institutions can meet the needs for the foreseeable future. Others contend that if we improve working conditions in urban schools, more teachers will stay and the shortage will be abated. The reality, however, is that there already is a shortage of urban teachers; and all signs indicate that the shortage will continue to increase.

Besides the shortage of teachers for urban schools, two other problems that must be addressed are: (1) Even successful teachers in urban schools report that their preservice teacher preparation program was not relevant to the kinds of problems they face in their day-to-day work. That they elect to stay in teaching under survival conditions has earned them the label of "strong insensitives." (2) There is growing evidence that the use of liberal arts graduates, who learn their professional skills on the job, is no panacea for the urban teacher shortage. For such programs to work requires one-on-one supervision from well-trained mentors. Few urban school systems use their most qualified staff for such assignments. However, it is possible to identify and train master teachers as on-site teacher educators. Local teacher associations welcome such career options because they give experienced teachers an opportunity to use their instructional expertise to help beginners.

A third and intensifying problem is attracting and retaining able minority teachers in urban schools. By the year 2000, it is projected that 50 percent of all urban school children will be from ethnic minority groups. At the same time, only 5 percent of *all* college students will be from ethnic minorities. Out of this small pool must come minorities preparing for all professions, not just teaching. Therefore, it seems totally unrealistic that we can expect to attract enough teachers from minority groups to develop anything close to a representative number for urban school classrooms—even if every minority group teacher candidate elected to teach in an urban school. Indeed, even if all minority group members in college became teachers, they would still not be adequately represented. Clearly, not enough teachers from ethnic minorities will be prepared unless new methods of recruitment and preparation are developed for untapped constituencies.

*Excerpt from Martin Haberman, *Preparing Teachers for Urban Schools* (Bloomington, Ind.: Phi Delta Kappa Educational Foundation, 1988), pp. 8–10. Used with permission.

A STEP BEYOND: TOWARD GLOBAL UNDERSTANDING

Besides aiding students in the understanding of people from our own country, a function of multicultural education is to aid students to understand people from a global perspective.

United Nations official Robert Muller recently noted that a child born today into a world of 4 billion people will, if he or she reaches the age of sixty, be sharing the earth with three times that many human beings. Muller goes on to say that "A child born today will be both an actor and a beneficiary or a victim in the total world fabric, and he may rightly ask: 'Why was I not warned? Why was I not better educated? Why did my teachers not tell me about these problems and indicate my behavior as a member of an interdependent human race?"[11]

Awareness of and Involvement in the World System

Individuals, and the groups to which they belong, are involved in the world system in a variety of very specific ways, and it may be useful to identify some of the basic dimensions of this very rich array of human experience.

As individuals, each of us is involved in the world system in the following ways:

- *Biologically*—because we are members of a single, common species and consequently share much in common with all humans.
- *Ecologically*—because we are a part of the earth's biosphere and thus inescapably linked to our planet's material and energetic structure.
- *Socioculturally*—because we are enmeshed in the human-created environment we call culture. In the modern world human cultures have become a global environment. (The technologies, institutions, languages, and beliefs which make up human culture link us, our communities, and our nation to people, communities, and nations elsewhere in the world. Through these cultural linkages we influence the lives of others and they, in turn, influence our lives.)
- *Historically*—because of the culture that surrounds us is an amalgam of technologies, languages, beliefs, and institutions initially created by humans who lived elsewhere in both space and time. Similarly, much of the culture surrounding others has been influenced by us or our ancestors.
- *Psychologically*—because we see the world beyond our borders through our perceptions, attitudes, and beliefs, just as our nation is viewed through perceptions, attitudes, and beliefs of others.

[11]EDCOM 84, Education Communications (November 1979), p. 207.

Profile

Prudence Crandall, 1803–1890

Prudence Crandall was a pioneer in the struggle to provide education for all people, regardless of their cultural background. Crandall campaigned for the education of women as well as the education of blacks. She was a Quaker and believed in the Quaker ideals of pacifism and human freedom, and was a part of the struggle for abolition of slavery, for temperance, and for the rights of women, particularly the right to vote.

Crandall had been a schoolteacher in Canterbury, Connecticut, where she established a boarding school for girls. Troubled by slavery in the South and the unjust and unequal plight of blacks in the North, Crandall began admitting only black students to her school in 1833. Her belief was that by providing education to young black girls, she would enable them to strive for better jobs, better living conditions, and ultimately racial equality. She was determined that her students learn reading and writing as well as other subjects which could enrich their lives.

But despite the fact that Canterbury was a Northern town and its black population was not enslaved, the townspeople still evidenced deep racial hatred. Outraged persons in the town attacked Crandall's school both through physical violence and legal action. Crandall's life was threatened, as were the lives of the schoolchildren. The drinking water was poisoned, supplies were not delivered or were destroyed, and the school was repeatedly vandalized.

Other abolitionists around the country rushed to Crandall's aid. Among those providing financial and moral support were William Lloyd Garrison, whose newspaper, *The Liberator*, published the ugly accounts of the attack on the Crandall school. Other newspapers took up the struggle, and Crandall and the students waged a valiant effort to keep the school in operation. Nevertheless, the violence and the mistreatment of students and Crandall herself finally became too much for the young Quaker to deal with. In 1834, the school that Crandall had so intensely worked for was forced to close.

Crandall's efforts in the campaign for human equality did not end, however. She continued to work for education of blacks, abolition of slavery, and equal opportunity for women. Her efforts for black education proved to be inspirations for other educators and reformers who were to open black schools, academies, and colleges. She was admired by feminists and abolitionists and was considered articulate and highly intelligent. She continued to improve her mind and her base of knowledge throughout her lifetime. Just before she died, it was reported that "in her 83rd year she is vigorous in mind and body, having been able to deliver the last 4th of July oration at Elk Falls, Kansas, where she now lives and advocates woman suffrage and temperance."

Though schools are now desegregated and though women have the right to vote, the struggle for equal opportunity and multicultural education representative of all is not over. However, the work of Crandall and others like her helped the struggle come this far—a long way from the injustices of the nineteenth century.

Two educators, Gilliom and Remy, suggest that middle childhood is an important time in children's international socialization. They write,

> Indeed, the period from about eight to thirteen years of age may well be unique in that it represents a time before too many stereotypically rigid perspectives dominate children's views of the world, and yet a time in which cognitive development is sufficiently advanced to make a diversity of viewpoints accessible.[12]

They conclude, in that spirit, that current research indicates a real need to introduce global education at the elementary level. We conclude that global education should continue beyond that point as well.

Recommendations for Global Education

Gilliom and Remy offer some worthwhile thoughts about the characteristics of a "fresh approach" to global education.[13]

1. *Global education should involve all areas of the curriculum.* Global education should touch on such other curricular areas as art, mathematics, music, and science.

2. *Global education should capitalize on the local community as a laboratory for studying international education.* Teachers should take advantage of the opportunities for exposing students to such global links as airports, banks, shipping firms, travel agencies, hotels, trade centers, and telephone facilities.

3. *Global education should look beyond the schools to other institutions as potential arenas of international learning for children.* Other institutions such as youth organizations, churches, ethnic associations, and scouting groups might well work in consortium with one another to further global concepts.

4. *Global education should involve learning for something rather than about something.* If interdependence is a key global concept, it should be *experienced,* not *taught* about. This is crucial to helping students develop skills which will enable them to cope with the consequences of interdependence in daily life.

5. *Global education should be infused throughout teacher education programs.* The necessity of viewing the earth as an interdependent system is as important to the teacher as is the need to communicate such an idea to his or her own students.

---

[12]M. Eugene Gilliom and R. C. Remy, "Needed: A New Approach to Global Educations," *Social Education* (October 1978), p. 501.
[13]Ibid., p. 502.

Ways to Improve Multicultural Understanding

Carlos Cortes* offers a useful model for thinking about ways to improve multicultural, multiethnic, and global understandings. He identifies four areas of "mutual interest" which exemplify the potential for partnerships between and among diverse peoples and groups: (1) the meaning of groups, (2) image formation, (3) perspectives, and (4) intercultural communication.

The Meaning of Groups

No person belongs to only one group. Each individual belongs simultaneously to many groups—involving such factors as gender, age, economic status, social class, region of residence, national origin, religion, and cultural or ethnic group affiliation, to name a few possibilities. At various times in each person's life, the fact of belonging to one or more of these groups may have a significant—sometimes a determining—influence on his or her values, attitudes, beliefs, goals, and behavior. Multiethnic and global education should help students recognize this fact and help them understand the differential impact of world trends and events on members of different groups. A knowledge of groups provides clues that help us better understand individuals. Awareness of the significance of groups—including ethnic groups—provides an important link between global concerns and individual ones.

Image Formation

How do group images—particularly stereotypes, which poison intergroup relations and impede global cooperation—develop? Both multiethnic and global education should address this important question. Students should be introduced to the ways in which group images are formed, the differences between stereotypes and generalizations about groups, and the pernicious effects of stereotyping. If students learn to understand the process of stereotyping, to detect stereotyping when it occurs, to avoid stereotypical thinking, and to use generalizations about groups as flexible clues rather than as mental straitjackets, they should become more thoughtful and sensitive citizens of the nation and of the world.

Perspective

People look at things from various perspectives—so do groups, whether small ones such as families, or massive groups such as the oil-producing nations. Both multiethnic and global education strive to help students understand what it means to see things from a particular point of view. Both kinds of programs also strive to help students learn to bridge points of view.

World events provide ideal situations for combining multiethnic and global thinking in analyzing the effects of differing perspectives.

Intercultural Communication

Both global and multiethnic education are deeply concerned with helping students learn to communicate across cultures, whether within the United States or around the world. Intercultural communication is not simply a matter of learning other languages. It also involves the skills of observing and interpreting nonverbal communication and knowledge of the different meanings that the same or similar words (albeit in different languages) have for members of other cultures.

Both multilingual and monolingual teachers can teach students about such aspects of intercultural communication as body language, gestures, personal space, conversational distance, and social customs.

*Quotes from Cortes, Carlos E. "Multiethnic and Global Education: Partners for the Eighties?" *Phi Delta Kappan* (April 1983), pp. 568–571.

SUMMARY

Because the United States is a country that is culturally diverse, a multicultural approach to education is vital in order to serve the needs of all students. Ethnicity and culture affect the ways people interact socially, as well as their personal ideas and goals. To be aware of some of the ways culture affects different beliefs is to broaden your view of the needs of students. In its earliest days, the United States was colonized primarily by British, Dutch, and German settlers; the colonial Americans lived in relative peace with the native American Indians. However, new groups arrived. Slavery was introduced to the country and, in the mid-1800s, waves of immigrants arrived in the United States from Ireland, Italy, and Eastern European countries. Their motivation for immigration was the political unrest in Europe as well as the economic difficulties in the world. At first, many theorists believed that the best way for these new Americans to become productive citizens was through the idea of the cultural melting pot; in other words, they would be assimilated into "American" culture. However, time and a careful appraisal of the situation have shown that cultural pluralism is a fairer and more realistic goal for our multicultural country. The melting pot theory and peoples' natural tendencies to distrust those who are different created problems of racism, discrimination, and segregation. It is the goal of multicultural education that these problems be eliminated. To achieve this goal, it is important to be aware of the factors of culture: sex, religious affiliation, geographic location, economics, race, and ethnicity. Each of these factors affects people's habits, their personal aims, their speech, and their attitudes toward schooling. Through gaining an understanding of the multicultural aspects of our own culture, we can go a step beyond: toward global understanding.

ACTIVITIES

1. Some people believe that assimilation of culture groups is a paramount goal of American society. Others believe cultural differences should be valued. What do you think?

2. Teaching children to become interdependent requires practice on their part. What are some activities that you as a teacher could create to help children feel the importance of interdependence?

3. Observe an integrated classroom. Watch how the children interact and record your observations. Were there any divisions in the class due to race, age, ability, or sex?

4. Describe your own cultural profile. Remember to include all the factors of culture in describing your background.

5. Do some research on the ethnic makeup of your community. What group appears to be the latest arrival? Does this group seem to have problems within the community?

6. Examine textbooks and learning materials used in your classes. Determine whether these materials are oriented toward a white, Anglo-Saxon, middle-class cultural profile, or whether they include women and minorities in the discussion.

7. What events occurring in society at this time (or recently) have had effects on education? Do you feel you are being prepared for a global perspective in teaching? Describe a program in global education.

SUGGESTED READINGS

BANKS, JAMES A., AND CHERRY M. BANKS, *Multicultural Education.* Boston: Allyn & Bacon, 1989.

BANKS, JAMES A., *Multiethnic Education: Theory and Practice.* (2nd ed.). Boston: Allyn & Bacon, 1987.

BANKS, JAMES A., ED., "Multi-ethnic Education at the Crossroads," *Phi Delta Kappan,* April 1983, pp. 559–585.

BROWN, LESTER R., *World without Borders.* New York: Random House, 1972.

GREER, R. G., AND W. L. HUSK, *Recruiting Minorities into Teaching.* Bloomington, Ind.: Phi Delta Kappa Educational Foundation, 1988.

GREER, COLIN, *The Great School Legend: A Revisionist Interpretation of American Public Education.* New York: Basic Books, 1972.

HABERMAN, MARTIN, *Preparing Teachers for Urban Schools.* Bloomington, Ind.: Phi Delta Kappa Educational Foundation, 1988.

HODGKINSON, H. L., *All One System: Demographics of Education.* Washington, D.C.: Institute for Educational Leadership, 1985.

JONES, ALAN, *Students/Do Not Push Your Teacher Down the Stairs on Friday.* New York: Quadrangle Books, 1972.

LYNCH, JAMES, *Multicultural Curriculum.* London: Batsford, 1983.

MARCUS, LAURENCE R., AND B. D. STICKNEY, *Race and Education: The Unending Controversy.* Springfield, Ill.: Thomas, 1981.

PETERS, WILLIAM, *A Class Divided.* New York: Doubleday and Co., 1971.

RAVITCH, DIANE, *The Troubled Crusade: American Education, 1945–80,* New York: Basic Books, 1983.

SAUNDERS, M., *Multicultural Teaching: A Guide for the Classroom.* New York: McGraw-Hill, 1983.

WOYACH, R. B., AND R. C. REMY, *Approaches to World Studies.* Boston: Allyn & Bacon, 1989.

Chapter 11

ACCOUNTABILITY
How Well Are We Doing?

Teachers are not wedded to status quo. Teachers seek serious and responsible change and are willing to make personal sacrifices and to take on more work themselves to make these changes successful. Perhaps the portrait is best summed up by an almost unanimous (96%–3%) majority who say 'I love to teach.' They want to do their job and are seeking excellence. A question can be raised whether the rest of the country—school administrators, parents, politicians, national leaders and others—is willing to take up the challenge laid down by teachers to meet new standards of excellence and accountability.

Pollster Lou Harris

Try to remember a time when you received a grade which took you somewhat by surprise. You may have been elated. You may have felt crushed. Whatever your emotional reaction, you may also have taken some time to attempt to deal with the issue of whether or not you "deserved" the grade which you received. Did you try to find out what was behind the surprise grade? Of course, age plays a role in one's ability and interest in questioning the validity of a grade. If you were in the fourth grade at the time you received your surprise grade, you may have had less of a tendency to question the validity than you would as a college student. Also, we often question the validity of surprise grades when they are low, but accept them as something we earned when they are high.

In any event, report card grades, or other marks which we receive, represent a judgment by someone about our progress. In that respect, two questions arise. The first question is, "How valid is the judgment?" The second question is, "How worthwhile is that which you are supposed to have learned?" These questions apply whether we are thinking about evaluating learning outcomes for an individual, for an entire class, for a school system, or for the education policy of a state or nation.

A typical instructional situation contains at least four components which can be considered for evaluative purposes: the teacher, the learner, the materials, and the context. We might agree quite easily that all four need to be evaluated in order to make a rational assessment of teaching/learning effectiveness. But can we necessarily agree on whether it is more important to evaluate the effectiveness of instruction than it is to evaluate learning outcomes? Can we agree that the two can be separated for evaluative purposes? While some will argue that the bottom line is that which the student learns, there are those who feel that assessing student outcomes places an unfair burden upon the teacher, who may be responsible for what and how he or she teaches but not for how well students learn. As Daniel Conable has observed:

> The question we must clarify in the minds of educators is whether they will judge themselves responsible for the *learning* assumed to have occurred (or *not* to have happened) within their institutions or, simply, for the *quality of* instruction they provide.[1]

[1] Daniel B. Conable, "Two Masters of the Sword: A Position Paper on Accountability," *Peabody Journal of Education* (July 1976), p. 233.

Pursuing the idea that instruction, not learning, ought to be the focus of accountability, Conable adds:

> I am convinced that educators who are persistent in trying to account for learning rather than inviting public questioning of the matter and style of their instruction (and, more basically, of the quality of life within their institutions) render a great disservice, both to those institutions and to the people who must use them.[2]

On the other hand, there are those who take the position that student performance, especially in terms of measurable outcomes, represents the most fruitful dimension for evaluation. The concept of behavioral objectives, developed by Ralph Tyler and popularized by Robert Mager in his book *Preparing Instructional Objectives*,[3] is based on the idea that the objectives of a program ought to be spelled out in terms of specific student performances that can be reduced to specific student behaviors. These behaviors are then measured by tests. Thus teachers, whatever their methods of instruction, are held responsible for student learning.

Clearly, the philosophical difference between the two preceding points of view lies in *who* ought to be evaluated: the teacher or the learner. What do you think?

ARE THE SCHOOLS RESPONSIBLE?

More than ever before, schools and the teachers who work in them are being held accountable for the job they are doing. The public thinks education is too expensive, and tax levies are continually voted down. The passage of Proposition 13 in California and similar measures in other states has signaled that the public has had enough of rising taxes, even if this means cutting back on essential services, including education. Parents are concerned about children who graduate from high school deficient in such basic skill areas as reading, writing, spelling, and math. There is a growing expression of concern by some about the lack of stress placed upon basic values of a democratic society—honesty, responsibility, respect for others, and respect for property. Some parents and members of the lay public feel that teachers are not performing their jobs as well as they once did. The result is that parents, the public-at-large, government, and concerned educators are demanding that schools and teachers be held more accountable for their performances. Ralph Tyler speaks to some of the developments which have led to this increased concern:

> Three recent developments appear to have influenced the current emphasis and concern with accountability: namely, the increasing proportion of the average family's income that is spent on taxes, the recognition that a considerable fraction

[2]Ibid., p. 234.

[3]Robert Mager, *Preparing Instructional Objectives* (Palo Alto, Calif.: Fearron Press, 1962).

of youth are failing to meet the standards of literacy now demanded for employment in civilian or military jobs, and the development of management procedures
by industry and defense that have increased the effectiveness and efficiency of
certain production organizations. These developments have occurred almost simultaneously, and each has focused public attention on the schools.[4]

Questioning the Effectiveness of Education

As we have discussed in other sections of this book, the public is placing more
and more responsibility for the socialization of its youth on the schools; parents
are assuming fewer and fewer of the duties of providing training, experience,
and values for their children. The public is making strong demands of the
schools and—going one step further—the public is holding the schools responsible for the failure of its children.

There are many questions involved in this debate. The first is a simple one:
Should the public question the effectiveness of the schools or should parents
question their own effectiveness? A related question is: Who determines what
the schools should teach? And when this is determined: How is the effectiveness
of the teaching measured? By standardized tests? By inspectors and evaluators in
the schools? By achievement and aptitude tests for both teachers and students?

The answers to these questions are not simple. Further, almost everyone—
educators, students, and the general public—has an opinion and it is usually a
strong one. For the most part, people tend to place blame with one group or
another, but perhaps a truer, more rational, more just response should be this:
We are all—parents, teachers, students, and members of the public—responsible
for what young people learn. Through the media, through schools, and through
community programs, we have a duty to ensure that skills and values are made
available to students. Teachers need to recognize the importance of teaching;
parents must participate; and students must use opportunities. We must find a
cooperative way to evaluate the results of our efforts—rather than abdicate
responsibility.

Accountability of the Teacher

Accountability is viewed by most teachers as a two-edged sword. On the one
hand, few, if any, responsible teachers would argue that they should not be held
accountable to some degree. The teacher is a professional who sees his or her
primary role as the development of the knowledge, skills, and attitudes in his or
her students which will enable them to become fully functioning and effective
citizens of a participatory democracy.

But on the other hand, nearly all of these same teachers would contend that
there are many pressures on today's students and schools over which they have
no control, and that these must be taken into consideration when the educational
goals for which they are to be held accountable are established. They note that

[4]Ralph W. Tyler, "Accountability in Perspective," in *Accountability in Education*, Ed. Leon M.
Lessinger and Ralph W. Tyler (Worthington, Ohio.: Charles A. Jones, 1971), p. 1.

many areas which used to be the responsibility of the home and other societal agencies have now been given over to the schools, either by conscious design or by default. Teachers believe that in order for accountability to work fairly for all parties concerned, they will need the full cooperation of parents, administrators, boards of education, and the students themselves.

This is a very important area of concern to all teachers. It cannot be taken lightly. The accountability movement is indicative of the fact that parents and the lay public are more knowledgeable and concerned about schooling and the education their children are receiving than at any other time in our nation's history. In many respects, this issue says much for the success of schooling in the United States—that is, we have developed a more intelligent and concerned citizenry.

We have only introduced the issue of accountability here, and we urge the teacher to read further and develop a personal position on how he or she will be accountable to the students' parents. One need look no further than the pages of the local newspaper for evidence of the accountability movement in any given area.

ASSESSMENT OF STUDENT LEARNING

Determining the accountability of the schools is inextricably linked to students' learning and achievement. In fact, some persons feel that the best way to measure whether or not the school is doing its job is by testing students to determine how much they know. Obviously, this starts the whole chain of questions again, for how does one determine fairly what a student has learned? Is it the fault of the schools or the teachers, or of the students if students fail at tests? What tests are fair—standardized tests? individualized tests? Do tests measure anything except a person's ability to take a test? This section will deal with some of the debate surrounding these questions as well as with some of the current public issues such as "truth in testing" laws and achievement test scores.

Priorities in Assessment and Evaluation

It is not easy to find teachers who are excited about testing. It is particularly difficult to find innovative teachers who feel that the active learning experiences which they promote are adequately reflected in pupil performance on paper-and-pencil examinations. Yet almost all who teach will at least grudgingly admit to the need for the assessment of learning outcomes. Assessment, like any other educational procedure, must be justified. The mere fact that "we have always tested students" is insufficient grounds for assessment. Let us attempt to place student assessment in a meaningful context by developing a rationale for its existence by examining some of the more important reasons for assessing student progress.

Inventory

Accountability

What are your views on the issue of teacher accountability? Rate the following statements from 1 to 5, with 1 standing for Strongly Agree and 5 for Strongly Disagree.

1. Teachers, whether they have tenure or not, should be periodically evaluated by skilled, independent evaluators.
2. Teachers should be held responsible for student performance, and that responsibility should be tied to pay increases.
3. Teachers should be able to give parents, evaluators, or other interested persons complete lists of behavioral objectives for the subjects they teach.
4. The most useful type of evaluation is done by an expert observing in a classroom, who then offers the teacher a critique of what he or she has observed.
5. Teachers are not really responsible for what their students learn because many students are unresponsive even to the best teaching.
6. It is virtually impossible to say that good or bad teaching is taking place in a given situation merely on the basis of scores on standardized tests.
7. Teaching is essentially an art form, and "scientific" attempts to evaluate its effectiveness will always fail.
8. The most important question a staff can pose about the effectiveness of its instruction is one of cost benefits or efficiency of money, time, and personnel.
9. Behavioral objectives are of little value as an instructional device because they tend to focus on specific details rather than on more lasting purposes of learning.
10. Evaluation, including feedback to students, is a necessary part of any meaningful instructional situation.

INSTRUCTIONAL PROGRAM GUIDANCE.   The best way to determine the success of a lesson or unit is to teach it. A sensitive teacher will want to assess the strengths and weaknesses of his or her teaching and make revisions in accordance with his or her perceptions of its effectiveness. Thus the assessment of teaching styles and program materials is an ongoing process.

INSTRUCTIONAL PROGRAM SUCCESS.   The newspapers are full of accounts of the success or failure of certain school programs. Reading scores and achievement test scores for states and school districts are regularly compared with national norms. Professional journals as well as the popular press carry feature articles which praise or criticize school programs.

Student Guidance.   Students need and want to know how well they are doing in school subjects. Parents want to know about their children's progress. Counselors and other interested school personnel need information in order to provide students with meaningful advice. It is an acknowledged fact that feedback is an integral part of the learning process. Evaluations provide information to students about their success in school.

Evaluation/Assessment Models

Although there is general agreement on the need to assess learning outcomes for students, there are still questions about *why* and *how* these assessments should be reached. And, of course, there is the additional question of what to do with the results obtained. Let us examine three models upon which assessment might be based. As will become apparent, each of the three models is based on different assumptions about the purpose of assessment.

The Information Diffusion Model.   The information diffusion model assumes that there is a passive target audience of consumers of evaluation information. This audience of consumers is composed of students, parents, and other interested persons. In this model, decisions about who will be tested, when, on which topics, and for what reasons are made by school personnel. Evaluation outcomes are perceived as products or end results of instruction. All students are judged by set criteria. Formal, standardized testing is emphasized because comparisons with other students and groups are made easier by the use of objective measures.

The Problem-Solving Model.   The problem-solving model starts with the individual student's needs. Diagnosis is the essential first step in the search for solutions. Each learner is treated as a unique case. The student's diagnostic profile is determined and his or her learning is assessed through a combination of standardized tests and other measures which may or may not be used by other students. The model assumes that a personalized diagnostic/evaluation procedure provides a high measure of self-motivation for the student. Emphasis is placed upon the extent to which the individual learns rather than upon comparisons with others.

The Social Interaction Model.   The social interaction model is based upon the assumption that the assessment of individuals is a misleading procedure because we tend to learn best in a social situation rather than in isolation. Thus, assessment ought to be considered in terms of: (1) group achievements, and (2) the individual's feelings and perceptions of his or her contributions to the group. This model assumes that it is irrational to expect students first to learn to interact with others in a cooperative way and then to be capriciously and arbitrarily subjected to unreal paper-and-pencil tests designed for individuals.

Criterion-Referenced and Norm-Referenced Evaluation

In 1953, Sir Edmund Hillary and Tenzing Norgay reached the summit of Mount Everest. They were able to achieve something that had never before been accomplished. As the word flashed around the world that the earth's highest mountain, 29,028 feet high, had at last been climbed, it became clear that a new standard had been set. No one can climb any higher, at least on earth. But to illustrate human kind's undeniable need to scale new heights and set new standards, a Japanese climber signed a contract with NASA to climb Olympus Mons on the planet Mars. At more than 90,000 feet, it is apparently the highest peak in the solar system.

In 1959, Henry "King" Tepsa of Clatskanie, Oregon, ate 115 smelt (a small fish) at one sitting. Although he had established a world record for smelt-eating, others claimed they would topple King Tepsa from his throne in subsequent contests. There seems to be no limit to the number of smelt a human being can eat: the next year someone else won the smelt-eating crown by eating 125 fish.

Mountain-climbing and smelt-eating contests provide examples of the differences between two types of evaluation: criterion-referenced evaluation and norm-referenced evaluation. Criterion-referenced evaluation represents *categorical* judgments in which a fixed set of standards are adopted and the achievement of each student is judged against these standards, e.g., climbing a mountain. Norm-referenced evaluation represents *comparative* judgments in which the performance of one student is compared with the performance of other students by ranking students in order of comparative excellence in academic achievements, e.g., who can eat the most smelt. In order for you to have survived the schooling process to this point, you have no doubt taken both kinds of tests many times. The passage below succinctly illustrates the distinction:

> Making a criterion-referenced judgment is judging what each student can and cannot do. If the criterion is for students to demonstrate ability to use propositional logic in solving a series of chemistry problems, then a teacher takes each student's answers and judges whether or not they have done so. Making a norm-referenced judgment is ranking the performance of students from high to low and judging where in comparison with peers the student's achievement falls.[5]

Every teacher must make decisions about some of the evaluation procedures he or she prescribes for learners. The teacher may also find that some evaluative decisions are beyond the scope of his or her authority, e.g., the administering of achievement tests to students at certain grade levels in a school district.

A pressing argument against norm-referenced evaluation is advanced by one authority who considers the competitive aspects of that approach to be potentially destructive.

[5]David W. Johnson, *Educational Psychology* (Englewood Cliffs, N.J.: Prentice-Hall, 1979), p. 452.

The average student enjoys few hours in which he is not judged by teachers, peers, family, and others. . . . At no other time in his career as a worker, member of a family, citizen, or person engaging in leisure activities will he be judged so frequently by others and, it is possible, by himself. . . . These judgments are made so frequently because schools have for so long stressed competition as a primary motivational technique.[6]

Indeed, as Edward B. Fiske notes,

The American kindergartener today can look forward to an alphabet-soup array of standardized tests, many originating in Princeton. There is the C.I.R.C.U.S. as you move from preschool into first grade; the S.T.E.P. to measure your progress in elementary school; the S.C.A.T. to measure your academic ability; the S.S.A.T. to get you into prep school; the P.S.A.T. to determine whether you will get a National Merit Scholarship; the S.A.T. to get you into college; the L.S.A.T. if you want to go to law school; and the M.S.B.E. if you want to pass the bar.[7]

NORM-REFERENCED EVALUATION.   Norm-referenced evaluation can be defined as grading the student as she or he ranks in some norm group, usually the student's classmates. Historically, norm-referencing for grading is a relatively new practice, but for many teachers it is considered the "traditional" method. Recently, norm-referenced evaluation has been criticized by many professionals including psychologists, educational researchers, and classroom teachers. Critics often cite the following:

- The norm-referenced grade represents *relative* rather than *absolute* learning.
- Class norming leads to significant year-to-year differences in the meaning of grades.
- Norm-referencing encourages undesired student behavior such as over-competitiveness and cheating.
- There is often an overemphasis on "winning," which can lead to a desire to see others "lose."
- Norm-grading can discourage those students who find themselves below the mean.
- Students who begin a class ranking low will remain low even if they progress as much as their classmates.

THE CRITERION-REFERENCED APPROACH.   A criterion-referenced evaluation system attempts to maximize the congruence among all components in the teaching-learning cycle and to increase communication among teacher, student, and parent regarding pupil progress and achievement.

Briefly stated, criterion-referencing means the establishment of specific, measurable performance standards which are shared with the student. These

---

[6]Benjamin Bloom, "Environment and Behavior," *American Psychological Association Psychology Monitor* (1976), p. 7.
[7]Edward B. Fiske, "Finding Fault with the Testers," *New York Times Magazine*, November 18, 1979, pp. 152–162.

goals, objectives, and/or performance standards are carefully developed by the instructor and introduced to the students in advance of any actual instruction. These *clearly specified, preestablished performance standards* are an essential component in the criterion-referenced system.

Another characteristic of this approach to evaluation and grading is that these are standards against which the individual's progress and achievement are measured. In this system, a given score or grade *is not dependent on any comparison to other students.* This distinction is perhaps the single most important factor setting criterion-referencing apart from norm-referenced evaluation.

Finally, under this approach there is a definite commitment to *maximizing student success.* The instructor implements a variety of techniques and skills which help to ensure the best possible performance from the largest number of students. A concerted effort is made to break down the teacher-student dichotomy and to establish a working relationship of trust and mutual respect within the context of a supportive and noncompetitive atmosphere.

Alternative Evaluation Models

E. R. House[8] describes several alternative evaluation models which examine, in turn, who will be evaluated, by what means evaluation should take place, and for whom the evaluation is intended. A brief summary of some of those models follows. As you read the descriptions of the evaluation models, try to clarify your own thoughts on: (1) the purposes of evaluation; (2) what should be evaluated; (3) who should be evaluated; (4) who ought to receive the results of evaluations; (5) what actions should be taken as consequences of evaluations.

Perhaps House's alternatives will assist you in clarifying your view of testing and evaluation. The models are:

1. *Behavioral Objectives.* The objectives of a program are spelled out in terms of specific student performances that can be reduced to specific student behaviors. These behaviors are measured by tests, either norm-referenced or criterion-referenced.
2. *Goal-Free.* The evaluator is not informed of any specified outcomes. Rather, the evaluator must search for all outcomes. Many outcome variables are considered.
3. *Art Criticism.* Evolving from the traditions of art and literary criticism is the model of an educational critic, one who is attuned, by experience and training, to judge the important facets of educational programs.
4. *Transaction.* This approach concentrates on the educational processes themselves: the classroom, the school, the program. It uses various informal methods of investigation and often employs the case study method.

[8]E. R. House, "Assumptions Underlying Evaluation Models," *Educational Researcher* (March 1978), pp. 4–12.

5. *Systems Analysis.* Questions of cost benefits and the efficiency of programs and instruction are central. Instruction and learning are based on an input-output model.

To clarify the application and intent of these five models, let us examine them in terms of their use in school settings. Imagine a hypothetical school in which one wants to determine the effectiveness of the instructional/materials/learning mix. The assumptions about what ought to be learned, how it ought to be taught, and the nature of its effects will certainly vary depending upon the evaluation model chosen. We will examine first the behavioral objectives model, then, in turn, the goal-free model, the art criticism model, the transaction model, and the systems analysis model.

EVALUATION BASED ON BEHAVIORAL OBJECTIVES.   The basic questions are those which relate to observable, measurable behaviors by students. These questions ask, in addition, what criteria should be applied to assess student behaviors. The objectives of the program must, therefore, be specific and readily understood. The written objectives must specify exactly what students will do and how they will be held accountable for learning. There must be no discrepancy among objectives, activities, and evaluation. Accountability, efficiency, and quality control are major concerns in this type of management model. Teachers are held accountable for student performance and in that respect the teacher, rather than the student him- or herself is responsible for student progress. For each behavioral objective the three crucial elements are: (1) identification of the expected student behavior, (2) definition of the condition in which the behavior will occur, and (3) identification of the criterion or standard for the expected student behavior.

Because of their specificity, behavioral objectives allow anyone concerned about student progress (teacher, student, parent, etc.) to determine exactly how well students are progressing. Accountability is based on tests and performance situations, and in many cases students are allowed to progress at their own rate.

Proponents of the behavioral objectives approach to evaluation cite its objectivity. Desired outcomes are clear and evaluator bias is virtually nonexistent. Judgments are based upon obvious evidence. Critics of this approach say that it is unfair to hold the teacher responsible for student outcomes when many students are indifferent to learning or incapable of attaining certain levels of achievement in spite of good teaching. Critics also point out that the very act of identifying specific behaviors trivializes learning because it places undue emphasis upon the mastery of a series of often unrelated tasks which seldom achieve synthesis.

GOAL-FREE EVALUATION.   Alternative and concomitant learning outcomes are often discovered through goal-free evaluation, because the evaluator is open to determining results, whatever they are. This does not mean that any outcome is deemed desirable regardless of whether it appears to be positive or negative. But an evaluator might discover that students using a simulation learning exercise not only learned certain skills and concepts, but enjoyed the learning experience as well. Or, an evaluator might find that even though students are learning their spelling words for the spelling tests, they are misspelling those same words in their written essays.

Goal-free evaluation is based on the premise that a strict behavioral prescription fails to take into account the wide range of learning outcomes that inevitably take place in a dynamic setting such as a classroom of twenty-five to thirty-five students. Goal-free evaluation is designed to accommodate the learner's needs and desires when someone else (the instructor or program) spells them out in advance on his or her behalf.

A misconception about goal-free evaluation is that the instructor has no learning outcome in mind for his or her students. It is important to bear in mind that the instructor may certainly plan on certain skills, concepts, and content being acquired, but would think it narrow, presumptuous, and unrealistic to assume that real learning can be reduced to several measurable statements (which tend to yield piecemeal results) developed before the learning experience itself has even taken place.

EVALUATION BY ART CRITICISM.   If the behavioral objectives approach to evaluation places a high premium upon objectivity in evaluation, then the art critic model values subjective judgment. Particularly valued is the judgment of an expert who has "arrived at his invariably plural principles by long training and experience. His taste has been refined so that he is an expert judge. Much of his expertise lies in how well he can intuitively balance the principles of judgment."[9]

Most beginning and untenured teachers find themselves being evaluated by means of the art critic model. This evaluation generally takes the form of a visit or visits by the building principal, who spends a certain amount of time observing and judging what he or she sees. What the observer looks for depends, for the most part, on what he or she feels is important in the instructional-learning process. Thus, two evaluators might come to somewhat different conclusions about the effectiveness of the same instructor. Of course, objectivity is lent to the evaluative process when (1) a given evaluator makes several observations, or (2) when more than one evaluator makes observations.

Philosophically, there is the feeling that teaching is basically a creative process and that ultimately the best judgments about creative work are rendered by experts in the particular field of creative endeavor. Thus behavioral objectives and their fulfillment in the instructional process are only as important in the teaching-learning process as they would be in the painting of a picture. Whether the objectives are met is relatively unimportant compared to the deeper question of their worth.

TRANSACTIONAL EVALUATION.   The transactional evaluation challenges the notion that educational outcomes exist primarily as products. Rather the educational process itself, or what happens to teachers and learners along the way, is the

[9]E. R. House, "Assumptions Underlying Evaluation Models," *Educational Researcher* (March 1978), pp. 5–6.

focus of attention. The transaction model of evaluation "focuses on events occurring in and around the program in context. It is based on perception and knowing as a transactional process."[10]

A great deal of subjective information is obtained through the transaction model. The subjective nature of the information limits its application to the particular situation being evaluated, and no attempt is made to generalize the results to other teaching-learning situations. This is so because the focus is upon specific, concrete individuals who are dealing with specific situations. Thus the case study approach, which examines the effectiveness of particular transactions between participants, is used. Perhaps a few more words about perception as a cornerstone of the transactional model are in order. The evaluator, in effect, participates in the transactional process because his or her presence affects and is affected by the teaching-learning situation itself. Thus, the separation which often exists between the evaluator and the evaluated is at least less distinct. A third point which House makes regarding the transaction model is that "each person creates his own psychological environment by attributing aspects of his experience to the environment.[11] This is a crucial point because it renders an instructional situation the product of perception by both teacher and learner rather than the cause of that situation. One would, therefore, have to allow for a variety of perceptions (and, therefore, learning outcomes), and the use of standardized tests to measure learning would have limited application.

SYSTEMS ANALYSIS EVALUATION.   Questions posed by the systems analysis evaluator run to notions of efficiency. Are the expected effects achieved? How much does the program cost in terms of money and time? Is there a more economical way to achieve similar or better results? Systems analysis has its roots in objectivity and bases its answers on quantifiable results.

Generally, test scores and the time, personnel, and money it takes to achieve them are the focus of attention. The United States Department of Education has taken this approach in recent years as a means of assessing programs. Efficiency in the production of educational services is a desired end result of this evaluative model. Learning outcomes become a function of educational inputs and outputs.

The systems analysis approach often makes use of experimental methods in order to make accurate assessment of the efficacy of one program over another. Thus if one method of teaching math were contrasted with another, the basic questions would be those of the cost benefits of each program. Ideally, the program that yielded higher test scores for less time and money would be the one chosen.

The systems analysis evaluator makes an attempt to exercise controls over an evaluative situation. Great emphasis is placed upon the development and refinement of evaluative techniques and instruments which can be applied with similar results to different situations.

[10]E. R. House, "Assumptions Underlying Evaluation Models," *Educational Researcher* (March 1978), p. 9.
[11]Ibid.

Factors Affecting Learning Outcomes: A Theory of Educational Productivity

Educational researcher Herbert Walberg offers a greatly expanded view of the factors which contribute to affective, behavioral, and cognitive learning. He suggests that a failure to take into account several often unexplored dimensions of the learning process restricts our ability to bring about optimal performance from students. Walberg* reviewed about 3000 studies of educational learning and distilled from those studies distinct factors, five of which he implies have been commonly examined and four of which have not. The factors fall into three categories. The first two categories, student aptitude and instruction, encompass the following five factors:

Student Aptitude

1. *Ability or prior achievement,* as measured by the usual standardized tests
2. *Development,* as indexed by chronological age or stage of maturation
3. *Motivation,* or self-concept, as indicated by personality tests on the student's willingness to persevere intensively on learning tasks

Instruction

4. *Amount of time* students engage in learning
5. *Quality* of instructional experience, including psychological and curricular aspects

Environment

6. *The home*
7. *The classroom* social group
8. *The peer group* outside the school
9. *Use of out-of-school time* (specifically, the amount of leisure-time television viewing)

Walberg concludes that teachers must do what they can to influence these factors in a positive direction. Obviously, some of the factors are more readily altered than others. He states that the most powerful teacher influencers of productive learning include (in order) reinforcement, acceleration, reading training, cues and feedback, graded homework, and cooperative learning.

*Herbert J. Walberg, "Improving the Productivity of America's Schools," *Educational Leadership* (May 1984), pp. 19–27.

Questions to Ask About Tests**

Here are some questions that the National Center for 'Improving Science Education* suggests that teachers and administrators ask when they evaluate the quality of a science test:

1. Are there problems that require students to think about and analyze situations?
2. Does the test feature sets of problems that call for more than one step in arriving at a solution?
3. Are problems with more than one correct solution included?
4. Are there opportunities for students to use their own data and create their own problems?
5. Are the students encouraged to use a variety of approaches to solve a problem?
6. Are there assessment exercises that encourage students to estimate their answers and to check their results?
7. Is the science information given in the story problem and elicited in the answer accurate?
8. Is there opportunity for assessing skills (both in the use of science tools and in science thinking) through some exercises that call for hands-on activities?
9. Are there exercises included in the overall assessment strategy that need to be carried out over time?
10. Are there problems with purposely missing or mistaken information that ask students to find errors or critique the way the problem is set up?
11. Are there opportunities for students to make up their own questions/ problems or designs?

**From S. A. Raizen, "Assessing Science Learning in Elementary School: Why, What, and How," *Kappan* (May 1989), p. 719.

PUBLIC PERSPECTIVE ON TESTING

As we have discussed many times, trends in education are continuously evolving. Trends are also cyclical in nature, and educational ideas and aims repeatedly go in and out of fashion.

The proper reward of learning is not that it pleases the teacher or the parents. . . . The proper reward is that we can now use what we have learned, can cross the barrier from learning into thinking. . . . Let us not judge our students simply on what they know. . . . This is the philosophy of the quiz program. Rather let them be judged on what they can generate from what they know.

Jerome Bruner

After the reform movements of the 1960s and early 1970s, in which educators called for humanization of the schools, a new trend followed: a concern with testing, a concern that students were no longer learning anything. The back-to-basics movement is based on the concern that the schools are teaching nothing. Naturally, in such an atmosphere, it is no wonder that the public is now concerned about achievement test scores and testing in general. Many fear that achievement test scores will continue to decline, and that this decrease in scoring means that American students are growing less educated. Accompanying this fear are the efforts of some reformers in some states to call for "truth in testing" laws. These laws call for analysis of achievement tests and college placement tests to determine the validity of the tests—and to achieve one extra purpose: to make test results and missed questions available to the student so that the student may challenge any errors on the part of the testing company.

Achievement Tests: Low Scores?

Cognitive development is one area of the school curriculum for which great concern exists. It is also perhaps the most easily measured area in terms of student performance. Widespread feelings of alarm have accompanied the publication of information which documents a recent overall decline in student performance on standardized tests of basic skills. These feelings are not confined to the United States. Recent studies show that performance on achievement tests is declining in other countries in certain areas of basic skills; among these countries is Australia.

For more than two decades, scores in the United States have generally declined for the following tests: Scholastic Aptitude Test, American College Test, Preliminary Scholastic Aptitude Test, Minnesota Scholastic Aptitude Test, Iowa Tests of Educational Development, Comprehensive Tests of Basic Skills, National Assessment of Educational Progress, Stanford-Binet, and Iowa Tests of Basic Skills. One attempted justification for low scores is that many students are attending school who would previously have dropped out, and the scores of these students lower the national averages. This argument was valid through the 1960s, but the fact is that enrollment percentages stabilized through the 1970s—and scores continue to decline, particularly scores of higher-level thinking.

Critics of standardized tests point to the narrow spectrum of skills which these tests measure, the fact that many teachers spend class time teaching material which is not found on these tests, and the accusation that many tests are biased either racially or culturally. Even such a well-known test and measurement authority as Oscar K. Buros has pointed out that "most standardized tests are poorly constructed, of questionable or unknown validity, pretentious in their claims, and likely to be misused more often than not.[12]

Perhaps the most quoted and widely disseminated nationally standardized tests in recent times are those of the National Assessment of Educational Progress. Developed for nine-, thirteen-, and seventeen-year-olds, they provide profiles of achievement for elementary, junior high, and senior high school students. One encouraging result of the test results has been the improvement in the last seven years of the reading and writing skills of nine-year-olds.

Truth in Testing

Some observers of the educational scene believe the fault in low scores lies not so much with the schools or the students, but with the testing companies. These observers believe that the tests do not provide valid assessment of student abilities and do not take into account factors such as economic status, race, and availability of opportunity. Further, some educators charge that the tests are simply badly written and that some of the "correct" answers on these tests are open to challenge. The testing companies, charge some educators, prepare tests that are inconsistent in content and questionable in validity. Further, computer error in scoring is possible and there are no checks and balances to guard against such error.

In the early 1980s, the first of these critics began to achieve some success in their campaign for "truth in testing" laws. These state laws demand several things. Although varying from state to state, the laws essentially call for: investigation of the testing companies; evaluation of the tests themselves; and the right of students to challenge their scores as well as the right to see their test results—including which questions they missed. This last demand would give students the ability to challenge answers they felt were incorrectly graded, guard against computer error, and also learn from mistakes.

Naturally, the testing companies are opposed to such laws and are challenging them. The companies cite the major expenses involved in such truth in testing. Not only would this complicate their bookkeeping, but new tests would have to be written each year. It remains to be seen what the outcome of truth in testing will be.

---

[12]D. K. Buros, "Fifty Years in Testing: Some Reminiscenses, Criticisms, and Suggestions," *Educational Researcher* (July/August 1977), pp. 9–15.

SUMMARY

Accountability is a major concern in schooling today. Not only are teachers accountable to principals and administrators, but the public is demanding that the schools be held accountable to them. Questions are being raised concerning the effectiveness of education and where the responsibility for education lies—with the schools or with the families. Assessment of student learning is of interest to students, teachers, and the public as well. Various models of assessment and evaluation exist. Some methods of evaluation, especially standardized testing, are criticized as being invalid means of assessing intelligence and achievement. The public perspective on testing focuses on two issues: low achievement test scores and "truth in testing" laws. The validity of testing itself is inextricably tied to these public concerns.

ACTIVITIES

1. What is your opinion of testing? What types of tests do you feel are most fair? What types of achievement or understanding do various tests evaluate?

2. Form a discussion group and discuss some of the things children learn that cannot be easily evaluated. How would you determine achievement in these areas?

3. Should the schools and teachers be accountable to the public? How should the public evaluate schools and the work of teachers?

4. Investigate the continuing problem of low achievement test scores. Discuss possible reasons for low scores. Do you consider achievement tests valid? How would you improve low scores?

5. Form a discussion group and decide what portion of education should be devoted to assisting students in passing achievement tests.

6. Prepare a debate on the "truth in testing" situation.

SUGGESTED READINGS

AMES, LOUIS BATES, CLYDE GILLESPIE, AND JOHN W. STREFF, *Stop School Failure*. New York: Harper & Row, 1972.

CHAMBERS, JOHN H., *The Achievement of Education*. New York: Harper & Row, 1983.

COVINGTON, MARTIN V., AND RICHARD G. BEERY, *Self-Worth and School Learning*. Principals of Educational Psychology Series. New York: Holt, Rinehart & Winston, 1976.

FLORIDA DEPARTMENT OF EDUCATION, *Florida Perfor-mance Measurement System*. Chipley, Fla.: Panhandle Educational Cooperative, 1984.

GRONLUND, NORMAN E., *Measurement and Evaluation in Teaching* (5th ed.). New York: Macmillan, 1985.

———, *Stating Behavioral Objectives for Classroom Instruction*. New York: Macmillan, 1970.

GUERIN, G. R., AND A. S. MAIER, *Informal Assessment in Education*. Palo Alto: Mayfield, 1983.

KIRSCHENBAUM, HOWARD, SIDNEY B. SIMON, AND ROBERT W. NAPIER, *Wad-Ja-Get? The Grading Game in*

American Education. New York: Hart, 1971.

MARTIN, JOHN HENRY, AND CHARLES HARRINGTON, *Free to Learn: Unlocking and Ungrading American Education.* Englewood Cliffs, N.J.: Prentice-Hall, 1972.

PURKEY, WILLIAM WATSON, *Inviting School Success: A Self-Concept Approach to Teaching and Learning* (2nd ed.). Belmont, Calif.: Wadsworth, 1984.

RAVITCH, DIANE, AND C. E. FINN, JR., *What Do Our 17-Year-Olds Know?* New York: Harper & Row, 1987.

ROGERS, VINCENT, "Assessing the Curriculum Experienced by Children," *Kappan* (May 1989), pp. 714–717.

SQUIRES, DAVID A., ET AL., *Effective Schools and Classrooms: A Research-Based Perspective.* Washington, D.C.: ASCD, 1984.

WIGGINS, GRANT, "A True Test: Toward More Authentic and Equitable Assessment," *Kappan* (May 1989), pp. 703–713.

Chapter 12

POLITICAL DIMENSIONS OF SCHOOLING
Federal, State, and Local

Federal, state, and local governments maintain diverse, often complex relationships with education and schooling. In this country there exists neither a hierarchical, federal-down-to-local form of educational policy making nor a situation of dominant local control. Rather, there is a blend of policy and practice which accommodates many different vested interests. In this chapter we will examine the roles played by federal, state, and local governments. Priorities in education change, and these changes are invariably influenced by government policy at one level or another. We will begin our discussion with the federal role in education.

The schools of the United States are among the most locally controlled in the world. From the early publicly supported schools of the seventeenth-century Massachusetts Bay Colony to the public schools of today on the verge of the twenty-first century, our schools have maintained a commitment to local control. However, as times have changed, particularly in the past three decades, the political control of the schools has not been that simple. The role of the federal government through the office of the U.S. Secretary of Education has expanded greatly since the Department of Education was created during the Carter Administration. It should also be noted that state revenues in all states exceed local revenues as a basis for school district funding. Given that the federal government provides nearly 10 percent of the funding, and that the states supply approximately 50 percent of the funding for public school districts, the time-honored precept of local control has shifted from an absolute doctrine to a relative one in which authority is shared by all three governmental jurisdictions.

In the 1990s, the federal government plays two crucial roles in the development of school policy. The first role is that of enacting, interpreting, and enforcing legislation. From the early federal legislation such as the Northwest Ordinances of 1785 and 1787, which were dedicated to the setting aside of public lands for schools, to the Entitlement Acts of the 1970s and 1980s, the most famous of which is Public Law 94-142, which provides federal funds to local school districts to provide free and appropriate school experiences for the nation's 8 million handicapped children, the national government has played a role in ensuring equity and equality of education throughout the land.

The second role played by the federal government has been that of provider of new ideas for public education. The many reform commission reports of the 1980s are examples. Among the better known of these are *A Nation at Risk, What Works: Research about Teaching and Learning, First Lessons: A Report on Elementary Education in America, James Madison Elementary School,* and *James Madison High School.* Each of these widely disseminated reports was designed to help local and state school systems with the never-ending process of school reform.

The shift in the balance of revenues from local dominance to state dominance occurred for the first time in our history during the 1980s. The pattern continues in the 1990s. State governments levy taxes and licence school personnel, two key ingredients when it comes to control. In addition, state governments establish standards that regulate the number and type of courses offered and required for graduation, school attendance, the length of school day and school year, and, in an increasing number of states, the testing of teachers for certification.

At the local level, districts do their own hiring of school personnel, set salary schedules, adopt curricular materials including textbooks, and set levies and bond issues for the building of schools. However, in the case of each of the foregoing matters, local districts must increasingly work in concert with state guidelines.

THE FEDERAL INFLUENCE

The federal government has a hand in making educational policy, but as we saw in our discussion of the history of American education, the Constitution did not set out specific directives regarding the government's participation in education. Nor did the Constitution set up a national school system.

Today, while the Secretary of Education is a member of the president's cabinet, there is still no national school system. Nor is there truly a single, coherent national education policy. Rather, federal involvement in education has evolved over time, as a response to needs and demands of certain groups and individuals. For example, the country's growing concern for equal education has resulted in the federal government taking measures to help ensure a better education for all. This section will examine some of the government's efforts.

Governmental Concerns

An examination of the various efforts of the federal government, especially its expanded involvement in the 1960s and 1970s, underscores two basic concerns. The first has been to enhance the quality of educational opportunity for those who have been disadvantaged in some way, either economically, physically, or through forms of social discrimination. Examples of this are numerous, ranging from the desegregation efforts in the 1960s to Head Start programs and compensatory assistance for the economically disadvantaged, to greatly increased opportunities for those with various physical and mental impairments, to the enactment of not one but a half-a-dozen sex equality bills which affect education and employment. The second major focus has been to support school improvement through a variety of research and development efforts, especially where progress has been limited by the lack of state and local resources. Efforts in this area include extensive federal investment in such ventures as Children's Television Workshop (which produces the popular education TV programs "Sesame Street" and "The Electric Company"), support for improved curriculum through agencies such as the National Science Foundation, and many research projects into what constitutes effective teaching and successful schools.

While major control of schools rests at the local district level and considerable financial support for elementary and secondary schools comes from state coffers—for the first time in this country's history, in 1984 state support of schools on the average exceeded local revenues, with the average aid per pupil at the state level being 49 percent of the total—federal expenditures are also very considerable. The 1990 budget for the Department of Education exceeded $18 billion, for example. Not all of those monies go for elementary and secondary schools.

The Secretary of Education presented this budget in three primary parts with almost half devoted to assistance for K–12 schools. Again, programs for which these funds are targeted either address equity concerns or assist states and local districts with projects designed to improve the quality of schools. A large second portion of the budget, almost $6.5 billion, is invested directly in students through college student aid programs. Finally, the third major emphasis of $1.6 billion, or about 10 percent of the budget, is devoted to vocational education.

Department of Education

There are also very considerable education-related expenditures in other agencies outside the purview of the Department of Education. These programs include: the GI Bill, administered by the Veterans' Administration; the many programs of research and development administered by the National Institute of Child Health and Human Development; the Bureau of Indian Affairs, administered by the Department of the Interior, which operates schools for Indian children; and numerous educational and exchange programs with other countries around the world administered by the Department of State or Department of Defense.

The Department of Education also has ten regional offices, which relate to over 90,000 school buildings, and is organized to serve a variety of constituent needs. One large bureau, for example, addresses the manifold needs of students in elementary and secondary schools. The Office of Special Education and Rehabilitative Services is concerned primarily with the needs of the special population of learners its title describes. Other offices or bureaus include the Office of Elementary and Secondary Education, Vocational and Adult Education, the Office of Postsecondary Education, the Office of Bilingual Education, and the Office of Educational Research and Improvement. The National Institute of Education (NIE) and the National Center for Education Statistics (NCES) are major parts of this latter office. NIE is a major source of monies needed to conduct research into such critical questions as what constitutes effective teaching or what differentiates a more effective from a less effective school. NCES is helpful in terms of providing a wealth of data about students, teachers, programs, and schools. It also provides projections of birthrates and future education needs.

Up until the late 1950s the role of the federal administration relative to education was largely one of gathering the type of data collected by NCES and disseminating it.

Legislative Efforts in Education

The federal government and its involvement in education was given considerable impetus under the Johnson Administration in the mid-1960s. While the National Defense Education Act (NDEA) of 1958 was of major consequence, it

A predominant social value of our era is that of freedom of choice. We have seen history-changing events taking place in the Soviet satellite states of Eastern Europe. The issue is freedom for people to choose their own destinies. Americans have always, at least in an ideal sense, subscribed to the idea that individuals ought to be able to live where they choose, do the kind of work they want to do, marry whomever they want, and so on. Now the idea has come in earnest to public education. Based on the theory that in our system people will shop around to find the best buy for a product or service, the schools of choice movement offers parents and their school-age children a similar plan.

In Minnesota, for example, the state legislature has decreed that parents can select any school in any school district in the state for their child to attend, and the state support money for that child will be designated to that selected school. The school must accept any applicant, the only legitimate reason for refusal being full enrollment. Further, students in grades eleven and twelve in Minnesota may enroll in college classes at state expense. Thus students who qualify are able to earn high school credit and college credit at the same time. At-risk secondary school students may choose from an array of alternative learning programs in order to help them successfully complete their high school education.

The idea is catching on in other quarters as well. Currently, the Chicago school system allows open enrollment, and many other districts in various states are presently considering moving toward this option.

On the surface, the schools of choice option seems like an idea whose time has come. But not everyone thinks it will result in an improved education for students. Some critics have called the schools of choice plan a smokescreen designed to focus attention away from real reform. These critics say that giving parents and students options will result in advertising and other gambits to lure students to schools that may or may not be better than the ones they left. Those who will be the real losers, critics predict, will be the poor, who lack transportation and even awareness of the options. Of interest, both critics and advocates see the encroachment of private education into the picture on the near horizon. Whether that is good or bad seems to depend on your point of view on just how numerous the choices should be.

Without question, the schools of choice issue is guaranteed to be the most discussed and controversial school issue since busing. Given a relatively free-market system of education, it is predictable that some schools will prosper (some are already at capacity with waiting lists) and some may suffer serious enrollment decline. Restaurants, clothing stores, and automobile companies must compete in an open marketplace for customers, but they represent the private sector. For public education to adopt such a model represents one of the most daring experiments in the history of schools. Only time will tell whether it also is a wise experiment.

What would you look for in a school if you found yourself in a position to choose one for your child? How important is geographic location? Would you want your child to attend school in his or her neighborhood? What if there were a "better" school several miles away? Would you be willing to drive your child well as men, they face the loss of federal funds in support of all programs in their schools. One of the most significant pieces of federal education legislation of the past fifteen years is Public Law 94-142, the Education for All Handicapped Children Act of 1975. Its passage signaled major changes in the ways handicapped children and youth were to be educated in the public schools of this nation. Some researchers have suggested that about 40 percent of all school children need specialized instructional assistance at some point in their academic experience. The legislative regulations are administered through the Office of Special Education.

Public Law 94-142 called for handicapped students to be placed in the "least restrictive environment"—or more commonly referred to as "the mainstream"—to have an Individual Education Plan written jointly by the school and the child's parents, to have an annual review of progress made toward long-term goals and objectives, and for parents to be notified of their due-process rights.

As you can tell, Public Law 94-142 has had and will continue to have an impact on the regular classroom teacher. The regular classroom teacher is not solely responsible for the education of the mainstreamed student, however. There are currently learning specialists who are hired by school districts to assist handicapped students and classroom teachers. The role of the learning specialist varies among the school programs and consulting models now in use. Specialists may perform diagnostic-prescriptive functions in which they make recommendations for improvement or changes in instruction. In a resource model, the teacher has the student leave the regular classroom for short amounts of time so he or she can provide remediation and direct instruction to the student. The learning specialist may do assessments, develop programs and materials, make instructional recommendations, provide direct instruction, and so on. The regular classroom teacher is still the major contributor to the child's program development and is a referral agent for problems that arise. Collaboration between the learning specialist and the regular classroom teacher cannot be overemphasized.

Obviously, this is a very important area in contemporary education and schooling and will continue to be so in the future. This law affects and will affect every teacher from the beginning of his or her teaching career.

SCHOOLS OF CHOICE: THE VOUCHER SYSTEM REVISITED

For years the idea of a voucher system in education has intrigued educators as a way of providing choices to parents and students. In brief, a voucher is a "check" for a certain amount of publicly funded support given to a student that can be used at any school. In the early 1990s, under the "schools of choice" plans cropping up in states around the country, the system is extended only to public schools. Whether private schools will in time enter the picture remains to be seen.

A predominant social value of our era is that of freedom of choice. We have seen history-changing events taking place in the Soviet satellite states of Eastern Europe. The issue is freedom for people, to choose their own destinies. Americans have always, at least in an ideal sense, subscribed to the idea that individuals ought to be able to live where they choose, do the kind of work they want to do, marry whomever they want, and so on. Now the idea has come in earnest to public education. Based on the theory that in our system people will shop around to find the best buy for a product or service, the schools of choice movement offers parents and their school-age children a similar plan.

In Minnesota, for example, the state legislature has decreed that parents can select any school in any school district in the state for their child to attend, and the state support money for that child will be designated to that selected school. The school must accept any applicant, the only legitimate reason for refusal being full enrollment. Further, students in grades eleven and twelve in Minnesota may enroll in college classes at state expense. Thus students who qualify are able to earn high school credit and college credit at the same time. At-risk secondary school students may choose from an array of alternative learning programs in order to help them successfully complete their high school education.

The idea is catching on in other quarters as well. Currently, the Chicago school system allows open enrollment, and many other districts in various states are presently considering moving toward this option.

On the surface, the schools of choice option seems like an idea whose time has come. But not everyone thinks it will result in an improved education for students. Some critics have called the schools of choice plan a smokescreen designed to focus attention away from real reform. These critics say that giving parents and students options will result in advertising and other gambits to lure students to schools that may or may not be better than the ones they left. Those who will be the real losers, critics predict, will be the poor, who lack transportation and even awareness of the options. Of interest, both critics and advocates see the encroachment of private education into the picture on the near horizon. Whether that is good or bad seems to depend on your point of view on just how numerous the choices should be.

Without question, the schools of choice issue is guaranteed to be the most discussed and controversial school issue since busing. Given a relatively free-market system of education, it is predictable that some schools will prosper (some are already at capacity with waiting lists) and some may suffer serious enrollment decline. Restaurants, clothing stores, and automobile companies must compete in an open marketplace for customers, but they represent the private sector. For public education to adopt such a model represents one of the most daring experiments in the history of schools. Only time will tell whether it also is a wise experiment.

What would you look for in a school if you found yourself in a position to choose one for your child? How important is geographic location? Would you want your child to attend school in his or her neighborhood? What if there were a "better" school several miles away? Would you be willing to drive your child across town? Could you? What if going to a "better" school meant adding an hour or two of driving time to your child's school day? Would your child's established friendships be a factor in where you sent your child to school?

Coincidental with the schools of choice phenomenon is the move toward decentralization of authority in the public schools. In the city of Chicago, not only may parents choose the schools they wish to send their children to, but also every school has its own school board vested with the authority to hire and fire school staff members. We find ourselves in times of great change in public education. Structures taken for granted only a short time ago are crumbling as the social issue of freedom of choice sweeps over the public school landscape.

Judicial Impact on Education

The judicial branch of the federal government has played an enormous role in influencing educational policy and programs. The Supreme Court has handed down many landmark rulings affecting areas from financing to equal opportunity. An example of this was its 1954 decision in *Brown v. The Board of Education of Topeka*. In this ruling, the United States Supreme Court dealt a major blow to the "separate but equal" doctrine and paved the way for school desegregation. Public schools, said the Court, must be open to all regardless of race, sex, or ethnic origin. This decision has paved the way for several subsequent rulings designed to provide access and equality for persons disadvantaged in one way or another.

FINANCE. An example of one of the more complex issues in education that has come before the courts is the financing of schools. It has been contended that a primary reliance upon local property taxes violates the equal protection clause of the Fourteenth Amendment. The concern voiced is that the quality of a child's education is dependent upon the wealth of his or her specific school district and not on that of the state as a whole. The argument is made that school finance systems should be fiscally neutral and should reflect the wealth of the state as a whole rather than be differentiated by the inherent, often dramatic economic differences which exist from district to district. While the Fourteenth Amendment itself cannot be cited as grounds for inequities in local school financing, lower courts have turned instead to equal protection clauses in state constitutions. Thus, intervention through the courts has had a major impact in terms of reexamining the traditional means of financing schools.

In *Serrano v. Priest* (1971), the California Supreme Court supported this fiscal neutrality theory. The court ruled that the California process for financing local districts was in violation of the Fourteenth Amendment (equal protection grounds), in part because of discrimination against the poor child, the quality of whose education was a function of the wealth (or lack of it) of his parents and neighbors. The court ruled in favor of the plaintiff and ordered statewide equalization of school district claims on wealth per student by 1980. There was at the time of this ruling considerable variation among districts in California in terms of their spending per pupil. The United States Supreme Court narrowly rejected a similar argument in *San Antonio School District v. Rodriquez* on the basis that there was no evidence that the poorest people were concentrated in the poorest districts. The majority opinion ruled that poverty could not be deduced as grounds that the system operated to the peculiar disadvantage of some "suspect class of people."

It has been said that the gavel of Judge Arthur Recht of West Virginia echoed resoundingly from coast to coast. Recht was the judge who issued the *Pauley v. Bailey* decision in 1982 in West Virginia. This case involved the plaintiff (Pauley) against the defendant (the state; Bailey was the State Treasurer) in a contention that the system of financing schools in West Virginia violated the state constitution by denying the Pauleys "a thorough and efficient system of free education." This contention was not that different from the well-publicized Rodriguez and Serrano cases in Texas and California, respectively, where the courts eventually decided in favor of those states.

In this instance, however, Judge Recht not only ruled that the system of financing schools in West Virginia was unconstitutional, but that to bring the public school system to conformity with the constitution, a master plan had to be developed which addressed all aspects of a *high-quality* system of education, including curriculum, personnel, facilities, materials, and equipment. His decision contained a list of specific, even detailed, standards that all schools had to meet. This ruling caused a great deal of controversy, especially regarding judicial intrusion into the administrative and legislative branches of government. Eventually, the court issued a supplemental order allowing the state superintendent and state board of education to develop the master plan mandated by the court.

This far-reaching, perhaps prototypical, master plan not only set forth conditions to ensure equity and excellence across that state, but even specified outcomes in all subjects at each grade level to be evaluated. It is important to note that the emphasis in this decision is not on the guarantee of minimal standards but rather on *high-quality* education.

THE STATE ROLE IN EDUCATION

The Tenth Amendment to the Constitution states that "the powers not delegated to the United States by the Constitution, nor prohibited by it to the states, are reserved to the states respectively or to the people." It would seem, then, that the state would logically be the primary source of policy for and influence over schools. Certainly, the decision by the Reagan Administration to move to a pattern of federal funding that flowed through state educational agencies, with far fewer strings attached at the federal level, contributes to the influence of state agencies. The amount of influence the states actually exert is highly debatable, however. Some would argue, for example, that while states have traditionally been responsible for general statutes guiding local educational agencies, in reality they rarely supervise what actually transpires at the local level.

There is, in fact, considerable variation among states with respect to the issue of state influence. For example, Hawaii, a small state, exerts considerable policy-making control, while in a large rural state such as Wyoming, local district control is much greater. States generally exert the most control in terms of such matters as certification of personnel, compulsory attendance, and requirements for keeping financial records. Their ultimate control is in matters of accreditation and program approval. (We will examine accreditation more fully in another chapter.) States also exert influence with respect to school calendars, revenue controls, type and amount of instructional content, and in some cases, textbook adoption. Both admission and graduation standards are set, and health requirements are established for the student while attending school. Finally, physical facility controls are established with respect to safety, transportation, and construction. It was clearly the case across the country in the middle 1980s that new legislation and revised regulations at the state level were commonly enacted in efforts to upgrade the quality of education.

Organization and Function

The implementation of new legislation falls under the aegis of a state education agency generally referred to as a State Education Department or State Department of Public Instruction. This department is generally administered by a chief state school officer referred to as a Commissioner of Education or State Superintendent of Schools. This person, in turn, is generally responsible to a State Board of Education for the execution of educational policy. In some states, the chief state school officer is elected; in others he or she is appointed by the governor of the state.

In many respects, the state department of education is similar to the bureaucracies described earlier at the federal level. It serves regulatory, supportive, and leadership functions. It is commonly responsible for accreditation of programs, certification of teachers, attendance, finance, and a variety of curriculum requirements. In addition, state departments commonly provide technical assistance and dissemination services to various local and intermediate units throughout the state. Yet another major role is the monitoring of several programs and the distribution of a variety of funds which the federal government channels through the state to local districts.

> *A society that neglects its children, its most valuable and vulnerable resource, also neglects its future.*[1]
>
> *Edward Zigler and Susan Hunsinger*

State Legislative Priorities

Influence or control of educational policy and practice at the state level, just as at the federal level, is exerted through the legislative, executive, and judicial branches. The state legislative branches are becoming increasingly involved in educational legislation.

[1]From Edward Zigler and Susan Hunsinger, "Look at the State of America's Children in the Year of the Child," *Childhood Education* (March 1979).

The mid 1980s especially saw legislative packages passed in many states which were intended to improve, even reform, schools. California is a good illustration of the type of legislation considered or passed. The California legislature in 1983 enacted a major education reform bill which included the following components:

Graduation Requirements: The legislation mandated graduation requirements effective in June 1987 of three years each of English and social studies, two years each of mathematics and science, one of fine arts or a foreign language, and two of physical education. The State requirements augmented those established by local districts. In separate action, the State Board of Education adopted in June 1983 model graduation requirements, including four years of English, three of mathematics, two each of science and foreign language, three of social studies, one of visual and performing arts, and one-half of computer studies.

Student Testing: The legislation instituted Golden State High School Achievement Tests for high school seniors to obtain honors at graduation and funded a pilot program to reward high schools for improving student academic achievement. Cash awards are available for improvement in student achievement relative to past performance. Criteria are being established for a pilot program to provide cash awards of up to $400 per pupil to schools that increase student achievement. The Department is studying ways to implement the honors program. The legislation adds tenth grade as a testing point in the State testing program. Tests are also being developed for grade eight, which was previously established as a testing point in the State Testing Program.

Textbooks: More money ($39.5 million) was provided for the schools to purchase textbooks and instructional materials for grades K–12. State funding was almost doubled in 1984. Schools may receive $14.40 per pupil for grades 9–12 and, for the first time, $21.40 for grades K–8. The State Superintendent has begun a campaign to upgrade textbooks in concert with other states.

School Day and Year: At the option of districts, the school year may be increased by 5 days to 180 days per year, and instructional time in the school day from 240 to 300 minutes in grades 4–8 and from 240 to 360 minutes in grades 9–12. Districts that add time will receive State funding. Per pupil payments range from $20 to $40 for incremental increases in time. (*A Nation Responds,* Washington, D.C.: Education Commission of the States, 1984.)

LOCAL SCHOOL DISTRICTS

Regardless of the types of policies developed at the state level and the degree of influence state agencies exert, local school districts generally have the most direct and immediate influence on what type of schools a community will have, what will be taught, and who will do the teaching. Specific budget priorities are established by the local school boards, and they hire the school superintendent, the chief administrator in the district. Principals and teachers have a certain amount of autonomy from school to school, but the degree of autonomy is established by the local level.

The Board of Education

Local school districts are governed by a body most commonly referred to as a board of education. This board is granted lawful authority by the state to establish local policies within the laws, statutes, and regulations established at the state level. School boards most typically have from five to nine members who are usually elected as at-large representatives (occasionally they are appointed) in districtwide elections. Their tenure in office can range anywhere between three and ten years with a three-year term being most typical. Even though individuals hold membership for several years, elections are frequently held for a portion of the board positions at least every other year to ensure both continuity (through overlapping terms) and, at the same time, responsiveness to current issues and problems.

A recent survey by the *American School Board Journal* yielded the following demographics about school board members: men are twice as likely as women to serve on local boards; the average age of board members is forty-seven years, but there is a considerable range among those who serve, from the minimal voting age of eighteen to well past seventy in some instances; reelection to office is common and the average length of board service is between seven and eight years; the most common occupation of school board members is local businessperson, followed by farmer, educator, and homemaker.

Citizens who accept this role must be highly interested in their schools and dedicated to donating considerable time and effort. School board members typically receive a minimal salary or no salary at all for the many hours of study they put in and the numerous meetings they attend. Thus, not everyone is willing or able to accept this challenging task. While a school board member can exert influence in a direct way toward what he or she believes to be desirable policy, the job is not without problems and pressures from various parties and persons in the community.

However difficult the role may be to assume, many concerned citizens continue to seek this office. School board election committees usually present several candidates for each spot. The positions these persons take and the policies they set obviously have considerable impact upon the role of the teacher.

Local Administration

We will now take a brief look at some of the key roles in the local district, especially that of the school superintendent and the school principal. However, before we do this, it maybe helpful to provide some picture of the human superstructure and diverse personnel resources which can be included in a school district. Schooling is big business. Many school districts assume responsibility not only for the instruction of young people, but the transportation, food, certain health services, professional counseling, and various forms of recreation. Educational and recreational services, under at least the partial sponsorship or supervision of the local school district, are often available year-round not only to the youth of a district, but to persons of all ages.

The variety of personnel in a school system, and their relative positions in terms of who is responsible to whom, is illustrated in Figure 12-1. The figure outlines what the organization of personnel looks like in a medium-sized district, one which has about a dozen elementary schools and three senior high schools. Organizational structures also exist below each of the seven directors. For example, the Director of Finance and Facilities has reporting to her coordinators for transportation, payroll, business, food, and building and grounds. Additionally, several accountants, purchasing agents, office staff, warehouse workers, custodians, and maintenance crews are under this person's authority.

Although teachers are commonly thought of as the key persons in education, it is obvious that many other persons make important contributions as well. It should also be apparent that there are opportunities other than teaching for those who receive a teaching credential, since teaching experience is often a prerequisite for many of the administrative and support positions such as those listed.

Role of the School Superintendent

The basic responsibility of the school superintendent is to ensure effective implementation of school board policy and of local, state, and federal laws, statutes, and regulations. Considering the array of state and federal guidelines, that can be a very considerable challenge. The magnitude of the task in turn demands considerable delegation of responsibilities, as illustrated in the figure below. While in the strict legal sense the school board decides policy and the superintendent is responsible for its implementation, these lines are often blurred. School boards commonly seek the advice and counsel of the superintendent's professional expertise and at other times it is difficult to separate policy formulation from policy implementation.

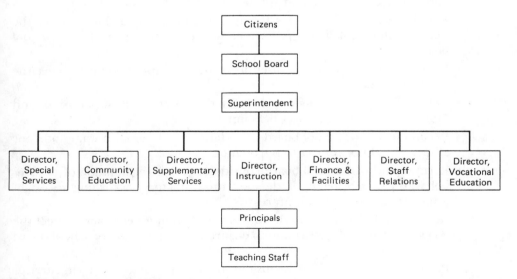

Figure 12-1. School organization chart

Superintendents commonly have had both extended educational experience and advanced study before assuming their responsibilities. A superintendent is probably in his or her forties, more likely male than female (although this is changing), has had experience as a principal or assistant superintendent of some type, has taught at one time, and holds a doctorate or specialist's degree in educational administration. It is not uncommon for the salary of a superintendent in a medium-sized school district to be $50,000 or more, and $75,000 and upwards in large urban districts. Relative to a teacher's salary, this is a considerable amount; relative to the salaries of high-level executives in business and industry, it is not.

A recent examination of the performance responsibilities outlined for a superintendent in a large suburban school district specified some fifty duties for this role; we have selected just a few of these to illustrate further the diverse responsibilities of this position:

- Assumes general administrative responsibility for all personnel, services, and programs of the school district.
- Develops and implements appropriate administrative procedures to ensure the implementation of school board policy and of local, state, and federal laws, statutes, and regulations.
- Establishes necessary procedures to ensure maximum coordination and cooperation with other agencies and governmental units concerned with education and youth, including social, health, and welfare services.
- Administers all negotiated agreements as they relate to school district personnel.
- Serves as executive officer and ex-officio member of the school board and attends all regular and special meetings of the board.
- Recruits, screens, nominates for appointment, assigns, and defines the duties of all school district personnel, subject to the approval of the school board.
- Develops and implements inservice programs appropriate to meet the needs of school district personnel.
- Designs and implements a system for the observation, supervision, and evaluation of school district personnel.
- Recommends for school board consideration salaries and wage rates for all personnel not subject to negotiation statutes.
- Recommends for school board consideration the termination of personnel whose performance is deemed unsatisfactory, according to established procedures of due process.
- Initiates and directs research studies and planning necessary to meet the goals of the school district and to ensure implementation of school board policy.
- Prepares, for school board consideration, major changes in the curriculum, instructional programs, or services of the school district.

- Prepares for school board consideration plans for alteration and reno-vation of buildings, new construction, and improvement of grounds and sites.
- Provides suitable instructions and regulations to govern the use of school facilities by community organizations.
- Assumes responsibility for the overall financial planning of the school district; prepares, for school board consideration, the district budget; and monitors the adopted budget for allocation of resources throughout the school district.

A common lament of the classroom teacher concerns the considerable demands that go with a teaching role. While few would deny that teaching is a challenging role, certainly the pressures and demands on the chief school administrator are also very considerable. The school superintendent is contin-ually in a position of mediating groups who hold conflicting positions. An examination of a few of the more common problems with which superintendents are confronted may help put the differences between the teaching role and the administrative role into perspective, and lead to a better appreciation of both. Common problems confronting the superintendent include:

- Shrinking tax revenues contrasted with inflationary rises in operating costs.
- The need to close neighborhood schools and reassign students in times of shrinking enrollments.
- The need to mediate between various factions, such as conservatives and liberals on the school board.
- The need to formally negotiate salaries and various conditions of employment of teachers.
- The need to be responsive to an increasing number of well-organized special-interest groups.
- The need to terminate employees for a variety of reasons.
- The need to satisfy a growing number of state and federal regulations and guidelines.
- The need to respond to growing litigation against school districts.

As one can see, therefore, the responsibilities of the school superinten-dent are far-reaching. The skills and knowledge required to be an effective administrator are not the same as those needed to be an effective teacher. There is no doubt, however, that effective classroom teachers possess traits and characteristics which, along with further training, are requisite to effective administration, and the opportunities for teachers to assume administrative responsibilities at the some point in their careers are always there.

The Principal*

Among a number of good ideas in the recent Carnegie report on teaching, I believe there was one flawed notion: the idea that schools should be run by committees of "lead teachers," with principals more or less officiating. On the contrary: As Study Group member Sandy Wisley observes, "You won't find an excellent school without a strong principal."

If a school is to function as a "working community," if all the parts are to mesh in an engine of achievement, the principal must act as catalyst. More than any other figure, the principal is able to create conditions for excellence—or what Study Group member Michael Joyce calls "an ethos of shared expectations." Says Professor James Guthrie of the University of California-Berkeley: "[If] you could only change one component of a school in order to make it more effective, finding a dynamic principal is the most important thing you can do."

There is a paradox at the heart of the principalship. Not only is the principal required to manage the business of the school; the successful principal also functions as an "instructional leader"—directing the actual teaching and learning process itself. This means working together with the teaching staff to implement academic goals; ensuring that order and discipline prevail; and making choices about materials and instructional strategies.

Every good principal develops his or her own version of instructional leadership. To Bruce Bernhardt, principal of Indiana's South Putnam Elementary School, it means supporting his veteran teaching staff—"finding 100 different ways to say 'good job.'" To Samuel Laitman, principal of P.S. 40 in Brooklyn's Bedford-Stuyvesant section, it means sending home "certificates of accomplishment" to parents who read with their children. To Jeremiah Kellett, of Woodland Elementary in Weston, Massachusetts, it means convening weekly staff conferences to discuss curricular and administrative issues.

A good elementary principal is ubiquitous, monitoring corridors, visiting classrooms, lunching with the children and staff. But in addition to duties within the school building, today's elementary school principal must occupy a position of visible leadership in the surrounding community. In the course of a week, a principal may be required to talk a local manufacturer into letting 50 fourth-graders tour his premises; testify before the school board as to why it should not eviscerate *Huckleberry Finn;* encourage the Chamber of Commerce to help buy new lab equipment; and give a talk to the Rotary about how the latest test scores turned out. And, as the National Association of Elementary School Principals notes, principals should "know how the media function, and make a point of becoming acquainted with education reporters who cover their school."

Principals' relationships with parents are multidimensional. Since parent involvement is critical to school success, principals go to great lengths to enlist their support. But parents may also come to school with concerns about a teacher's performance or behavior, or with conflicts over values and beliefs. (Of course, the latter set of dilemmas can more readily be resolved if the school is one the parents chose for their child in the first place—and if they have the option of choosing a different one.) The principal's task in mediating between parent and teacher may be exceedingly hard. To succeed in it, he must be a diplomat, a negotiator, and a judge, with the patience of Job and the wisdom of Solomon.

*Excerpted from William J. Bennett, *First Lessons: A Report on Elementary Education in America,* (Washington, D.C.: U.S. Department of Education, 1986).

Role of School Principal

The administrator with whom the teacher works most closely is the school or building principal. He or she is responsible for the implementation of policy and the administration of programs and personnel at the school level. The principal assumes several of the same responsibilities at the building level that the superintendent does at the district level. Principals, for example, assume a key responsibility in the selection and assignment of faculty, communication with the school community, administration of pupil services (enrollment, attendance, transfers, special programs for students), finance and business management, and communication with the various support services in the larger district. While they generally have ultimate responsibility for curricular changes and staff development in most schools, the great percentage of their time is given to administrative and coordinative functions. Thus, the former functions are increasingly delegated, with teachers assuming more and more responsibility for both program and staff development decisions. At the secondary level, such matters are often delegated to departmental chairpersons, and at the elementary level, teacher committees increasingly decide staff development agenda and work on curriculum changes.

Thus, the teacher is more likely to work with the principal in small working committees and in one-to-one consultation than to have him or her visit the classroom directly, an event that occurs only occasionally in many situations. Although there are districts where principals do engage in regular supervisory and teacher improvement schemes, in most cases most of the consultation and help given a beginning teacher is likely to be obtained from teaching colleagues or from district specialists in curriculum or teaching. Given the frenetic schedule of most principals, the beginning teacher is well advised to take considerable initiative with his or her school administrator in ascertaining the variety of services which are available, and in communicating what resources and assistance are desired.

In the Principal's Office

One way to get a feel for the role of principal is to interview one. This is what we have done, and we share some of this person's observations on the role here:

Parents expect a lot from principals. They expect that their children are in good hands. They want to see our school as a good place for them to be for learning, and feel something worthwhile is going on here. As they become more familiar with the school and personnel, their expectations tend to grow.

I feel these parent expectations are a constant invitation for me to grow as well . . . a chance for me to put *all* effort forth to provide the type of atmosphere they desire, within the framework of my own teaching and learning philosophy.

Time seems to be the big pressure; there is often not enough time to concentrate and *reflect* on the entire scene. The PR part of the job is also somewhat of a pressure . . . so many "publics" to interact with on so many different levels. And in order to ensure good communication, there has to be constant effort in this area. Conflicting values and differences in convictions can also exert a certain pressure, as I am involved with so many persons with different values and different priorities. It is really important to know firmly what your own educational values are, and to stand by those principles.

For my part, I try to emphasize certain traits in students. Our students' handbook states that self-discipline and personal responsibility are the aim of student conduct and behavior: "Respect and courtesy is expected and encouraged." These are broad, I realize, but they also encompass many aspects of the student's life that affect the atmosphere of the school. I ensure the participation of the Board of Education, teachers, Parent-Teacher guild, and students (through the advisory council) in setting these priorities.

I try to "accentuate the positive." The idea that "being and doing good pays off" is something I feel is important for students to learn—that is, within realistic limits . . . failure is also a part of the realistic, too. I issue commendation slips as well as probationary slips. Things are kept in proportion; nothing "big" is made of small incidents. Again, an attempt to be realistic.

A difficulty today is having truly dedicated teachers who are willing to reach out to students and their needs. I do not feel that effective teaching can go on without them . . . and they do need to be *dedicated.*

Now that you have "met" a principal, however briefly, here are a few questions to mull over. What did you learn about how this person sees the role that might not have been communicated in a formal job description? What characteristics and attitudes come through and how would these affect you as a teacher? Do you share the goals this administrator has for children? What recourse do you have when your values appear to conflict with your building principal's? In what ways could this principal be of assistance to you, a beginning teacher? What type of teacher-principal relationship do you think would be ideal?

Collective Bargaining

One cannot look at local policy formulation today without an examination of collective bargaining. During the 1960s, teachers began to negotiate in a formal and united manner, especially in urban areas, to achieve increased salaries, improved fringe benefits, and better working conditions. This was indeed a radical move. Negotiations went from a *one-to-one* bargaining procedure (individual teacher with the principal as representative of the school board) to *collective bargaining,* where representatives of *labor* (the teachers' associations) and *management* (the school board) negotiated mutually acceptable agreements concerning such matters as salaries and conditions of work. These written agreements, once they are signed by both parties, constitute a contract. This dramatic departure from prior practice developed most rapidly. For example, before 1962, there was not a single collective bargaining agreement in this country's 10,000 school districts. Today, the great majority of teachers are represented in collective bargaining procedures.

As a prospective teacher, you should be aware of (1) the basic principles of collective bargaining and (2) the types of issues which become the grist for negotiation.

PTA DEFINITIONS.   The National Parent Teacher Association prepared a paper for parents on the matter of collective bargaining. Their descriptions of this process are concise and accurate, and thus with their permission, some of these definitions are presented here.[2]

1. *Collective bargaining* is a process whereby representatives of management and labor meet to reach a mutually acceptable agreement concerning wages, hours, and conditions of work, with the written agreement signed by both parties constituting a contract.

2. If collective bargaining is to take place, the school board (the employer) must agree or may be required by statute to accept some individual group or organization as the *authorized representative* of two or more members of the professional staff (employees) for the purpose of negotiating conditions of employment. This action by the school board is called *recognition;* that is, the school board recognizes that the teachers' organization represents the teachers.

3. Where a majority of the teachers in the school district are members of an organization seeking representation rights, and no other organization makes a competing claim, the NEA and the AFT may agree that the majority organization should be granted *exclusive recognition* rights. In those instances where the claim to majority representation is challenged, the exclusive bargaining representative is chosen through either an election or other designation by the majority of the employees in the bargaining unit.

4. In a *union shop,* all employees are required by the collective agreement to become members of the union within a specified time after they are hired (typically 30 days) and to remain members of the union as a condition of continued employment.

[2]National Parent Teachers Association, *The Role of Collective Bargaining in Public Education* (Washington, D.C.: NPTA, 1979).

5. In a *modified union shop,* certain employees may be exempted from the requirement to belong to a union—those, for example, who were already employed at the time the provision was negotiated and had not yet joined the union.

6. In an *agency shop,* all employees in the negotiating union who do not join the exclusive representative are required by the collective agreement to pay a fixed amount monthly—usually the equivalent of organization dues—as a condition of employment.

7. *Dues checkoff* is the procedure whereby the employer, by agreement with the employment organization, regularly withholds organization dues from employees' salary payments and transmits these funds to the organization.

8. The *negotiating team* for the teachers' organization usually consists of several organization officers and a negotiating or executive committee. At times the organization employs attorneys or consultants to assist in negotiations.

9. Some teachers' organizations send the board a list of demands beforehand and expect the board to respond at the first *negotiating session.* Others simply indicate matters they want to discuss and then present their demands at the first meeting. In the largest school districts, subcommittees of the administration and the teachers' organization may study certain issues while negotiations proceed on others. When agreement is reached on a particular issue, it is put in writing and initialed by both sides.

10. If the school board and the teachers' organization cannot reach agreement on one or more issues, they have reached an *impasse.*

11. At this point, in an effort to create a contract acceptable to the union, the teachers' organization may call *a strike.*

12. *Mediation* is an attempt by a third party to help in negotiations or in the settlement of an employment dispute through suggestion, advice, or other methods of stimulating agreement, short of dictating its provisions. Most of the mediation in the United States is undertaken through federal and state mediation agencies.

13. A *fact-finding* board may be appointed (usually by an impartial agency) to investigate, assemble, and report the facts in an employment dispute. Sometimes the board is authorized to make recommendations for settlement.

14. *Arbitration* is a method of settling employment disputes through recourse to an impartial third party. Arbitration is voluntary when both parties agree to submit disputed issues to arbitration, and compulsory if required by law. In *binding arbitration,* the two parties agree to be bound by the decision of the third party; in some states,

state law provides for binding arbitration. In *advisory arbitration,* the decision of the third party is not binding. The parties usually agree in advance on the issues which the arbitrator is to decide.

Profile

Frederick Douglass, 1817–1895

Although not an educator in a traditional sense, Frederick Douglass laid the groundwork for the beginnings of racial equality in America and the means by which education could begin to further the realization of these goals. He was a spokesperson not only for abolition, emancipation, and suffrage of blacks, but was also dedicated to the premise that "the struggle of the black man was a phase of the larger, human struggle."* He was intricately involved in the women's movement from its inception and spoke for women's rights at a time when any man who did so was a target for ridicule. "Right is of no sex" characterized his stand on the subject. His life was one of unrelenting dedication to the above principles.

Douglass was born a slave in Maryland in 1817 and lived in several different slave situations until his escape to the North in 1838 at the age of 21. He learned to read as an adolescent through independent efforts and with the help of a woman who owned him; he would also barter food in exchange for impromptu reading lessons with young white boys in Baltimore. In 1841, he met the abolitionist William Lloyd Garrison at a meeting of the Massachusetts Anti-Slavery Society. With no advance warning, Douglass was called upon to speak and delivered an oration that captivated an audience of five hundred. From that event forward, Douglass began his successful efforts in educating the public to foster change.

After publication of a book, *Narrative of the Life of Frederick Douglass*, he traveled to England, speaking to large and sympathetic audiences, making friends, and gathering support for principles of equality from reform leaders there. Upon return to the United States Douglass had the $700 needed to buy his freedom and over $2000 to publish a weekly newspaper. In 1848 the first issue of the *North Star* was published; the newspaper gained a wide circulation and over the next fifteen years became a vehicle to present its publisher's views to a larger audience.

*Frederick Douglass, *Frederick Douglass: Great Lives Observed*, Ed. Benjamin Quarles (Englewood Cliffs, N.J.: Prentice-Hall, 1968), p. 9.

NEGOTIATIONS. Negotiations are the meetings in which both sides reach agreements and make arrangements and deals with each other, usually through discussions and compromise. Negotiations can cover literally hundreds of topics but are generally limited to matters of salaries, fringe benefits, and terms of employment. Several states have collective bargaining laws which specify which topics under "conditions of employment" are not negotiable. This is necessary because certain "conditions of work," such as duty-free lunches, class size, or length of school day, are often regulated by state law, as are certain benefits such as pension or retirement plans.

A typical listing of topics which have been negotiated between a local teachers' bargaining agent and a local school district include: length of school year, teachers' rights, grievances, school rules, and maternity leave policies, among others.

Obviously, teachers in a school district can effect a number of policies through collective bargaining in addition to negotiating what they believe to be equitable salaries. Policies with respect to length of school year and hours of daily service, numerous fringe benefits, maternity (and paternity) leaves, transfer from one school to another, and early retirement benefits have all been determined over time through negotiations. While, as we have noted, the classroom teacher can be subjected to a variety of pressures, it is obvious that the teacher in turn, through collective bargaining, is able to exert considerable influence as well.

SUMMARY

The role of the federal government in education has expanded in the last thirty years, especially in terms of (1) promoting needed research and development, and (2) assisting equal opportunity in education. While the cabinet-level Department of Education was established under the Carter Administration, under the Reagan Administration more monies were distributed and greater authority evolved again at the state and local levels. Legislative and judicial influences also considerably impacted education. The fifty states all make education policy as well, and the level of state influence varies from state to state. Local school boards have the most direct effect on schools in terms of administration and curriculum. They generally establish the working conditions and salaries of teachers. Collective bargaining is common in negotiating contracts between teachers and school boards and also is an important determinant of certain policies and practices.

After the Civil War, Douglass was a leader in the successful campaign to grant blacks the right to vote. He was appointed to various government positions. On this foundation was laid the black struggle for equality and equal opportunity.

ACTIVITIES

1. Investigate how the local schools in your area are administered. Interview a principal and/or a teacher about who and what is involved in the administration of a local school district.

2. What does the news report about recent involvement of your state government in education? What are current concerns? What curriculum area appears as a priority to the state government? Why?

3. How much impact does your state have on local schools? Research the priorities of your state. What type of autonomy do local school districts have?

4. Discuss federal involvement in education. In your opinion, does the federal government play too large or too small a role in education? What feelings do you have regarding a federal curriculum or national assessment of students?

5. Interview a member of the local board of education. On what issues did he or she base the campaign for election? What are his or her current ideas about the public schools?

6. With the creation of the Department of Education, has federal spending in education increased, decreased, or remained relatively stable? Discuss.

7. What is your view of collective bargaining? Can you describe another effective means for teachers to negotiate salary and working conditions?

SUGGESTED READINGS

ALEXANDER, KERN, AND M. D. ALEXANDER, *The Law of Schools, Students, and Teachers in a Nutshell.* St. Paul, Minn.: West, 1984.

BARR, R., AND R. DREEBEN, *How Schools Work.* Chicago: University of Chicago Press, 1983.

BLUMBERG, ARTHUR, AND WILLIAM GREENFIELD, *The Effective Principal.* Boston: Allyn & Bacon, 1986.

FINCH, L. W., "Choice: Claims of Success, Predictions of Failure," *American School Board Journal* (July 1989), pp. 31–37.

GREENWOOD, G. E., AND F. W. PARKAY, *Case Studies for Teacher Decision Making.* New York: Random House, 1989.

GUTEK, GERALD, *Education in the United States: An Historical Perspective.* Englewood Cliffs, N.J.: Prentice-Hall, 1986.

PAJAK, EDWARD, *The Central Office Supervisor of Curriculum and Instruction.* Boston: Allyn & Bacon, 1989.

RIST, M. C., "Should Parents Choose Their Child's School?" *Executive Educator* (March 1989), pp. 24–26, 32.

Chapter 13

FINANCE
Who Pays the Bills?

Financing public schools is possibly the most difficult challenge that faces educators. There are many factors influencing the funding of schools, which include economic, legislative, and judicial developments at the local, state, and national levels. The total expenditures of public elementary and secondary schools in the United States rose from $28 billion in 1967 to $93 billion in 1987, an increase of over 200 percent.[1] Education is big business in the United States. Yet many school districts are having difficulty paying the bills.

The individual who is about to embark upon a teaching career may wonder what this has to do with him or her. It is the teacher's job to teach—not to administer the financial program of the school. School finances are the responsibility of the superintendent and other district administrators. Thirty years ago this response might have sufficed, but not today. Today's teachers are increasingly involved in the financial processes of schooling, and it is essential that those planning teaching careers understand the causes of the financial problems faced by schools and be aware of possible solutions to these problems. There is a growing movement toward site based management in which teachers actually help decide how the budget will be organized and spent.

This chapter will provide an outline of the economics of schooling, including historical precedents, sources of support, traditional allocation procedures, and some proposed solutions for the financing of educational opportunity for all. It will provide a brief overview of educational finance. You should consult the Suggested Readings at the end of the chapter for more depth. Your instructor will, no doubt, add to this as well.

AN ECONOMIC PROBLEM

The financing of public education and schooling in the United States represents the basic economic problem faced by all people and all societies—scarcity. Scarcity is an outgrowth of the fact that societies have unlimited desires and only limited resources available for fulfilling those desires. For this reason, an understanding by educational leaders of the close relationship between economics and schooling is essential if the complex problems of educational financing are to be solved.

There are several factors which create unpredictable economic conditions. High inflation levels, high interest rates, tenuous foreign relations, trade deficits, and unemployment are just a few conditions which affect the supply of money at the local, state, and federal levels. For example, high unemployment rates reduce the federal tax revenues and, at the same time, place a demand on the federally funded social programs. The funding for education actually comes from the same pool of funding that helps the unemployed, the elderly, minorities, and so on. Therefore, when the economy slows down, the funding pool shrinks at a time when money is most needed by all groups.

[1]National Center for Educational Statistics, Statistics of Trends in Education, 1966–67 to 1986–87 (Washington, D.C.: U.S. Government Printing Office, 1978).

Where the financing of public education is concerned, economics is primarily concerned with the allocation of scarce resources (money) to competing consumers (social institutions, including schools). The ongoing debate in this area centers on the issues of equity versus excellence. During the 1970s the focus was on equity; in the 1980s attention was shifted to excellence. The Phi Delta Kappa Commission on Alternative Designs for Funding Education noted the benefits which accrue to society as a result of the expenditure of public funds for education.

> The justification for expenditure of public funds for education goes much deeper than a mere common desire to possess knowledge. Mass public education can be justified on the more basic grounds that it creates and perpetuates the culture, promotes social equality, and enhances economic development. Each of these alone may be ample reason for government to finance education, but to view them in combination leaves little doubt as to the importance of education. . . . The commission believes that investment in public education is abundantly justified on any or all of the above grounds. However, public education must finally be encouraged on the grounds that education removes the individual from the "tyranny of ignorance." Every human being has a right to develop his individual abilities to their fullest through education, and the state has the responsibility to finance education in appropriate ways to allow each person to realize this goal.[2]

Where Does the Money Come from?

The condition of national economics directly affects state and local finances in numerous ways. When there is a recession, states and local communities feel the effects through unemployment, loss of business, and lower tax receipts because of decreased consumer spending. This loss of state revenue directly affects public schools because of their dependence on state aid. The greatest threats to public schools, however, are the restrictions on property taxes, upon which public schools rely heavily, and the direct action of legislatures to keep expenditures at a minimum. Since responsibility for providing for education is a function of each state and local community, there is no overall formula for financing education. Each state and local community decides its own method of organizing and financing its schools. Table 13-1 shows the distribution of revenues by source.

STATE. State revenues now comprise about 50 percent of the financing for schools. Sales and income taxes comprise the two major sources of state revenue for schools.

Nearly all of the states currently levy some type of sales tax, generally ranging between 2 and 8 percent. Sales taxes based on gross receipts are easy to collect but they have two major shortcomings. First, the revenue generated is totally dependent upon business conditions. In periods of good economic growth revenues are high; in periods of economic recession revenues can fall off substantially. Second, sales taxes, like property taxes, are regressive, since low- and middle-income level consumers spend proportionally more of their incomes than do wealthy individuals.

---

[2]*Financing the Public Schools: A Search for Equality* (Bloomington, Ind.: Phi Delta Kappa Commission on Alternative Designs for Funding Education, 1973), pp. 6–7.

Table 13–1 Distribution of Revenues by Source

SCHOOL YEAR ENDING	STATE	LOCAL	FEDERAL
1970	39.9%	52.1%	8.0%
1975	42.2	48.8	9.0
1980	46.8	43.4	9.8
1981	47.4	43.4	9.2
1982	47.6	45.0	7.4
1983	47.9	45.0	7.1
1984	47.8	45.4	6.8
1985	48.9	44.4	6.6
1986	49.5	43.9	6.7
1987	50.0	43.8	6.2

Source: U.S. Department of Education, National Center for Education Statistics, *The Condition of Education, Vol. 1: Elementary and Secondary Education* (1988), p. 94.

The personal income tax is a second major source of revenue in most states. The percentage varies from state to state but is generally progressive, i.e., the greater the income, the higher the rate of taxation. But the income tax, like the sales tax, is subject to the rate of economic growth.

While there are numerous other taxes collected at the state level—liquor and tobacco, licenses, gasoline, utility, and many others, they generally contribute very little revenue directly to the schools.

There are increasing demands in both educational and governmental circles for state revenues to assume a larger share of the burden for funding education. In fact, during the last decade, the percentage contributed by the states has been on the increase, while the percentage of local revenues has been declining.

Property taxes make up the major share of local revenues for education. This form of taxation goes back to our traditional agrarian economy when wealth was determined by the amount of property owned. Despite the nation's transition to an urban, industrial society, the property tax has remained as a major source of revenue for schools in many states. While this is a stable form of revenue, it is increasingly regressive, resulting in a situation where persons of low- and middle-income levels pay a greater proportion of tax than those who have considerable wealth. Those on fixed incomes also suffer under this form of taxation. Taxpayers across the nation are signaling that property taxes have risen beyond the point of being reasonable. More and more frequently, school-operating levies based upon increases in property tax are being voted down. Increased attention is being given to other, more equitable forms of taxation. A number of states have passed referendums limiting the percentage of property tax which can be levied.

Some states have attempted to ease tax burdens through methods other than reducing or freezing property taxes. By exempting food or medicine from the state sales tax, the lower-income families, who spend a higher proportion of their income on those items, get some relief. Other states have experimented with a concept known as "indexing," or adjusting income tax brackets according to the inflation rate. There are some creative ways to ease inequitable property taxation, such as homestead exemptions and circuit-breaker provisions. Some of these revisions offer relief to taxpayers and minimize the damage to state and local government revenues.

But in spite of these several shortcomings, the property tax is likely to remain as a major source of revenue for the schools because it does provide a steady income. The trend, however, appears to be toward demands that the state assume a greater share of the burden.

FEDERAL. Revenue at the federal level continues to decline—about 6.2 percent. This comes from revenue generated by the federal income tax which, like most state income taxes, is progressive in that the rate of taxation increases with income. Federal financial support for schooling is generally aimed at specific educational needs and is initiated by congressional legislation. It is not the general form of aid provided by local and state revenues. One of the major thrusts of federal programs has been to equalize educational opportunity for all children and youth, for example, through educational funding for the handicapped.

The major change at the federal level came during the second year of the Reagan Administration. Chapter Two of the Education Consolidation and Improvement Act (ECIA) of 1981 replaced the categorical funding for forty-three separate programs with one block grant which state and local education agencies could use for a broad range of educational purposes to improve elementary and secondary education. This move resulted in a 40 percent reduction in aid.[3] The consequences of this consolidation are yet to be fully understood, but a body of opinion is beginning to form.

> There is little doubt that Chapter Two has removed many of the constraints imposed on local school districts, has made federal funds more accessible for less work, and has maximized both administrative and programmatic discretion at the local level. But . . . deregulation has not been achieved without cost. Perhaps most important, we do not yet know if "snipping the strings" works for or against the development of well-planned and innovative solutions to local educational problems.[4]

This major piece of legislation embodied the Reagan Administration's philosophy on the federal role in education and deserves close scrutiny in the remainder of this decade.

Local, state, and federal monies represent the major sources of revenue for schooling. The larger proportion comes from state and local sources, where the control also rests. During the 1970s there was a gradual shift away from local support, which is based almost solely on the property tax, to increased state funding, which draws primarily on income and sales taxes toward which the public shows less resistance. Increased funding at the state level also has the potential for equalizing funding from district to district, which in turn equalizes

---

[3]Deborah A. Verstegen and Patricia Anthony, "Is There a Federal Role in Education Reform," *Journal of Education Finance, 14,* 1 (Summer 1988), p. 46.

[4]Anne H. Hastings, "Snipping the Strings: Local and State Administrators Discuss Chapter 2," *Phi Delta Kappan, 65,* 3 (November 1983), p. 198.

educational opportunity. However, there has been less rapid movement in this direction during the 1980s. We will now examine the ways in which revenue has traditionally been allocated to school districts.

Allocation Systems: How Does the Money Get to the Schools?

The allocation of revenue generated through the several kinds of taxes discussed above takes place in one or more ways: local district funding, flat grants, and foundation equalization programs. Since each state is responsible for determining how allocation will take place, a variety of systems are used. Let us briefly examine each of the three allocation models listed above.

LOCAL DISTRICT FUNDING. This is the oldest model. Because the costs of education have risen far beyond what most local communities can support, and because this method does little to provide equality of educational opportunity, it is seldom used today. Under this model, where one lived during his or her school years largely determined the kind of education he or she received. In wealthy communities, financial support for schooling was generally very good; in poor communities, the quality of education was likely to suffer. More recently, local district funding has been replaced in most instances by some sort of state grant or foundation program, which may be supplemented by local taxes.

FLAT GRANTS. As education costs increased and other community agencies demanded a greater share of local taxes, school districts turned to state governments for financial aid. This movement really gained its momentum at the turn of the century. One of the earliest forms of state funding was through grants which were designed to provide relief to local taxpayers. Under this model, each school district in a state receives a flat grant from the state, generally based upon the number of pupils enrolled in the district. While this eases the burden on local taxpayers, it does little to reduce inequities between poor and wealthy districts, because the local district is still free to supplement its revenue through local taxes. The basic assumption under this model is that the grants ensure a minimum standard of education for all children and youth. But how the minimum standard is to be determined is the larger issue. As one group of researchers point out:

> The principal difficulty is that there is no way of knowing how much education is minimally necessary. Consequently, there is no way to determine how much it costs. Instead, the size of the flat grant is determined by the political process, and, because there are many other demands on the state treasury it is inevitably lower than the level at which even flat grant proponents believe a minimal education can be purchased. Another problem . . . is that the flat grant typically lacks consideration of the special needs of atypical children. Nor does it account for the fact that it costs more to provide a minimally adequate education in some districts than in others.[5]

No state today depends exclusively upon the flat grant to finance the state's share of educational costs, largely because this model does not provide for equity between districts, as illustrated in Figure 13-1.

[5]James W. Guthrie, Walter J. Garms, and Lawrence C. Pierce, *School Finance: The Economics and Politics of Public Education*, 2nd ed. (Englewood Cliffs, N.J.: Prentice-Hall, 1988), p. 189.

Ranked high to low,
by weighted mean expenditures:

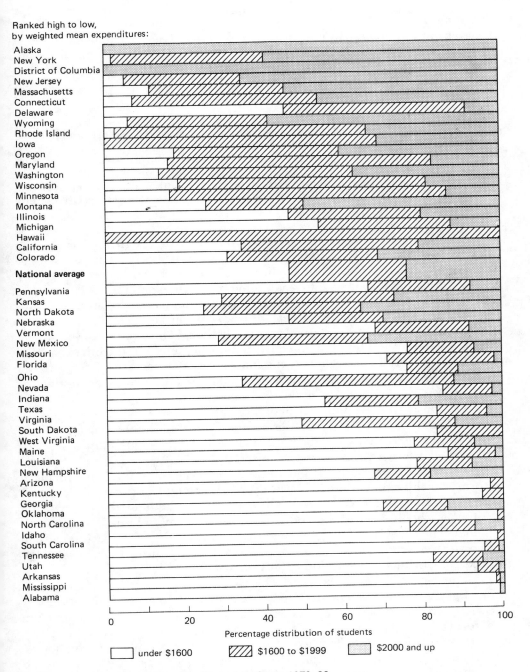

Figure 13-1. Core Expenditures Per Student by State, 1979–80.

Note: In school year 1979–80 core expenditures per student varied from
under $1000 (in districts representing 3 percent of students) to over $2900
(in districts representing 5 percent of students), with the majority of students enrolled in districts spending over $1600 per student.

Source: National Center for Education Statistics, 1983.

FOUNDATION EQUALIZATION PROGRAMS. Most states today use some form of foundation program in an attempt to ensure equity. Like the flat grant model, under a foundation program the state designates the dollar amount per pupil allotted to each district to support a basic instructional program that will guarantee a minimal level of education for all students. Here is how this allocation system works.

> The state computes each district's contribution at a fixed tax and provides only the difference between the amount computed and the guaranteed expenditure level. Thus, a property-poor district will raise very little with the tax at the specified rate, and the state will provide generously. A district richer in property will raise almost as much as the dollar guarantee and will receive very little equalization aid from the state. A very rich district will raise more than the guarantee and will receive nothing from the state.[6]

As a further supplement, some states allow districts a degree of local leeway with excess local taxes. A wealthier district could thus use its taxes in excess of the foundation level to try innovative educational practices. The degree of leeway varies a great deal from state to state, some of which allow substantial margins while others impose considerable restrictions. But this leeway has its drawbacks. Those states which allow a great deal of leeway encourage wealthier districts to further widen their gap between poorer districts. This runs counter to the primary intent of the foundation equalization programs. On the other hand, it is in the wealthier districts that new and innovative programs are piloted with the additional funds. Allowing no leeway would greatly curtail the testing of innovative ideas. Equalization is clearly a dilemma.

Obviously, the evolution of allocation systems has been directed toward providing more equity. However, this has not been easy and the task is far from being finished. Problems and inequities exist with all the models just described, and further alternatives are yet to be offered.

Perhaps the most significant decision in terms of stimulating financial reform was the ruling handed down by the Supreme Court of California on August 30, 1971, in *Serrano* v. *Priest*. The court ruled that the system of financing California schools violated the Fourteenth Amendment and thus was unconstitutional. The court decision demanded that educational spending within a state be equal from school district to school district, thereby ensuring the availability of the same quality of education to all students.

The consequences of the *Serrano* decision have been significant. Six weeks after the California ruling, the Minnesota system of financing education was declared unconstitutional by a federal district court judge who accepted the California ruling as being equally applicable in Minnesota. Several other states had their financing systems rejected by court decisions and numerous other states began studying and revising their financial programs. The future of the property tax as the primary means of financing school programs was seriously

[6]Walter J. Garms, James W. Guthrie, and Lawrence C. Pierce, *School Finance: The Economics and Politics of Public Education* (Englewood Cliffs, N.J.: Prentice-Hall, 1978), p. 190.

questioned and studies were undertaken to explore other means of financing programs. Some of the more important studies were the National Education Association's National Educational Finance Project, the Phi Delta Kappa Commission on Alternative Designs for Funding Education, and the Fleischmann Commission Study in New York State. These studies all recommended new approaches to school finance. Let us examine some of these approaches.

Alternative Models

As noted at the outset of this chapter, the goal of any proposed reform in education finance has been traditionally to establish both equity and excellence within the context of schooling. In the past few years, however, the question of efficiency has also been drawn into the discussion. As the cost of schooling continues to rise, taxpayers are demanding more accountability for each dollar spent. They want equitable and high-quality programs for the least amount of money possible. In part, this is due to increased demands on tax dollars to fund additional educational and social services, e.g., AIDS education, prenatal care for teenage mothers, and programs for at-risk students. But in the main, the public is concerned with wastage in the process of schooling. As programs of educational reform are implemented, taxpayers want assurance that they are getting maximum value for every dollar spent.

In order to improve both excellence and equity, a number of financing alternatives have been suggested.

EDUCATIONAL VOUCHERS.   Under a voucher plan, parents have the freedom to send their children to the school of their choice. Parents would receive annual credit vouchers for each child, redeemable for a specified sum of public funds, to be spent on any approved educational service, public or private. However, this still does not ensure equity, as parents are permitted to supplement the voucher to secure additional educational services. There are both assets and liabilities of the educational voucher as noted in the following paragraph.

> Parents would be allowed to place their children in schools of their choice, instead of being forced to use schools and teachers for which they had no enthusiasm. The injection of a greater amount of private enterprise would make schools more efficient and promote a healthy variety. Salaries of teachers would become more responsive to market forces. On the other hand there would clearly be more segregation by economic class, and probably also by race, than at present. The few public schools that remained might become the dumping ground for pupils private schools were unwilling to accept.[7]

The voucher plan has not gained complete acceptance as an alternative. Some believe the voucher system would seriously weaken the concept of universal public schooling. The plan has never really been fully implemented with both public and private sector schools competing for students. In 1989–90, Minnesota will implement a program of choice whereby any child may attend

[7]Walter J. Garms, James W. Guthrie, and Lawrence C. Pierce, *School Finance: The Economics and Politics of Public Education* (Englewood Cliffs, N.J.: Prentice-Hall, 1978), p. 222.

any *public* school in the state that will accept her or him. This program will be closely watched nationally in terms of equity, excellence, and efficiency.

DISTRICT POWER EQUALIZATION (DPE).   One alternative to the voucher plan is district power equalization. As one writer defines DPE: "The basic principle behind a DPE plan is that at any specified tax rate, every school district in a state, regardless of wealth . . . has the same dollar resource level per pupil as any other district."[8] Although the plan was first advocated some sixty years ago, only recently has it gained any support, and then largely due to court decisions such as *Serrano*.

Under DPE, the state determines a floor or minimum spending level for school districts in order to maintain a standard level of education throughout the state. Each district in turn has the right to tax itself beyond this minimum level to provide an even higher standard of education. This assures a degree of local control over schooling decisions. However, most DPE plans also have some kind of ceiling or maximum beyond which districts are not permitted to spend, in order to reduce frivolous spending which would produce only marginal returns on the investment. The ceiling also gives the state some notion of what its share of the cost of schooling will be in a given year, since lack of a maximum could result in a great deal of fiscal uncertainty for a state.

However, reform of educational finance is no easy task. Even programs such as DPE, which reduce or eliminate many of the inequities of pre-*Serrano* plans, contain a different set of problems, including inequities in taxation. But let us turn to a third major reform alternative, full state funding.

FULL STATE FUNDING (FSF).   A full state funding plan for financing education is another acceptable alternative response to the principles of the *Serrano* decision. Under this plan, the state government becomes the sole agency responsible for funding schooling. To many this seems only logical, since according to the United States Constitution the state is the level of government responsible for education. Others, however, claim that under FSF local control of educational programs will be seriously jeopardized if not eliminated. Arguments for FSF include the idea that revenues could be equalized throughout the state and competition for state funds could be eliminated. Arguments against FSF include a possible loss of local influence in the education program and a curtailment of innovative, but expensive, programs. In achieving equalization, some school boards fear a decrease in their own quality.

WHAT IS JUST?   Of the three reform plans described above, the full state funding plan would seem to provide the best means of providing for equity in educational opportunity for children while at the same time allowing for excellence. There are no perfect plans. Each has its assets and its limitations. But the benefits of the full state funding plan would appear to outweigh its shortcomings. The basic thrust of the *Serrano* decision was that children were being deprived of equality of educational opportunity because of inequities in the financing of school programs. The decision mandated that the educational

[8]James W. Guthrie, *Equity in School Financing: District Power Equalizing* (Bloomington, Ind.: Phi Delta Kappa Educational Foundation, 1975), p. 7.

needs of children take priority over the desires for tax relief. Michelson summarizes this argument very well:

> Justice in the allocation of school resources is most likely to be achieved if the distribution question is separated from questions pertaining to revenue (in the local district), thus eliminating the potential for decisions based on the desires of adult taxpayers. Accordingly, the needs of children themselves will probably be more determinative when finance decisions are made by a unit of government that is less responsive to direct parental pressure than is the school district.[9]

Where Does the Money Go?

Figure 13-2 shows how each dollar of revenue for schooling is spent. The largest amount goes for instructional costs, and the greatest share of that goes for teacher salaries. Relatively small amounts are designated for administration and plant maintenance. It is the instructional costs which are coming under more careful scrutiny by the public. As noted earlier, taxpayers are demanding accountability for every dollar spent. They question whether the cost of instruction really needs to be as high as it currently is and whether they are really getting any more productivity from teachers as salaries continue to rise. They are not questioning the value of an education but rather trying to ensure that they get the best possible return out of each dollar spent.

In response to these queries many school systems have gone to a planning-programming-budgeting system (PPBS), to tie educational goals directly to the school budgeting process. The primary purpose of PPBS is to replace broad and generally stated objectives with specific, measurable ones so that both schooling

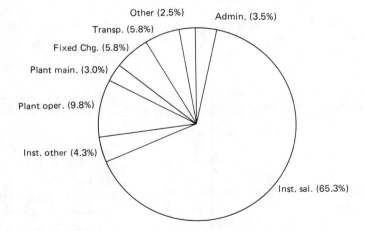

Figure 13-2. The School Dollar and How It Is Spent

Source: *Financial Summaries: Idaho School Districts,* State Department of Education, 1990.

[9]Michelson, "What is a 'Just' System for Financing Schools? An Evaluation of Alternative Reforms," *Law and Contemporary Problems, 38,* 3 (Winter/Spring 1974), p. 442.

personnel and the supporting public can see what kind of return they are getting on their money. The PPBS planning cycle includes:

1. Establishing objective goals.
2. Determining the financial cost of an alternative plan for reaching the objectives.
3. Evaluating the results.
4. Improving the objectives.
5. Adding to and improving the alternative plans to reach the revised objectives.[10]

Simply speaking, PPBS is the application of long-established management techniques to the school planning and budgetary process. As in the economic world, taxpayers (like consumers) are demanding a closer relationship between input and output. This helps school personnel make better use of the limited tax dollars available for supporting the schools.

Recently, PPBS is being integrated with another growing school reform, called "site-based management," to improve both management and efficiency. Site-based management is based upon the principle of shared decision making. Teachers take a very active role in this process.

> The theory is that those closest to children should be making crucial decisions in schools. Giving teachers more power will make them feel better about their jobs, make them better teachers and improve schools . . . Site-based management isn't easy. Some principals have difficulty giving up authority; teachers must learn to make decisions and take responsibility for them.[11]

Many feel this is part of a long-term change in American education that can lead to greater efficiency in the process. This innovation will bear close watching in the final decade of this century.

THE PROBLEM: HOW TO FINANCE FOR EQUAL OPPORTUNITY AND MAINTAIN QUALITY

Our discussion thus far has repeatedly focused upon the major problem facing the area of school finance: How to provide for equity in financing to ensure equality of educational opportunity while at the same time providing excellence in educational programs. As we have noted several times, the courts are playing an increasingly important role in determining solutions to this problem. The box "Historical Precedents" lists some of the important court decisions during this century that have affected school finance.

[10]Percy E. Burrup, *Financing Education in a Climate of Change*, 2nd ed. (Boston: Allyn & Bacon, 1977), p. 228.
[11]Mary Jane Smetanka, "Some Teachers Move to Head of Class Past Principal," *Minneapolis Star-Tribune*, August 13, 1989, p. 1B.

Historical Precedents

To really understand the current financial problems faced by the schools, a brief historical review is needed. What were the historical precedents for the concept of public financing of schooling? We touched upon a number of these in a previous chapter, when we reviewed the development of schooling in America from a historical perspective. The following are highlights of important precedents related to school finance:

1693	Massachusetts Bay Colony gives towns the legal right to levy taxes to support elementary schools of a "common" nature.
1785–1787	Northwest Ordinances provide public land for educational purposes—first federal aid to education.
1795	University of North Carolina opens as first state-supported university; Pennsylvania and New York establish state aid for schools.
1839	State-supported normal school for the training of teachers opens in Lexington, Massachusetts.
1832	Morrill Land Grant Act creates federally supported land-grant colleges.
1874	Michigan Supreme Court upholds the right of Kalamazoo to levy taxes to support public secondary schools—a landmark precedent for communities across the nation.
1917	Smith-Hughes Act provides federal funds for the support of vocational education programs.
1944	Congress passes GI Bill to provide for the education of veterans.
1946	Congress passes National School Lunch Act.
1958	Congress passes National Defense Education Act in response to Soviet gains in space race, thus initiating an era of large-scale federal aid to education.
1964	Civil Rights Act provides for the removal of federal support from school districts practicing racial or religious segregation.
1965	Elementary and Secondary Education Act provides federal support for educational programs and materials for children of low-income families; Teacher Corps Program provides federal support for the training of teachers for impoverished areas; Head Start Program initiated for preschool children of low-income families.
1967	Education Professions Development Act provides funds for the training and retraining of teachers.
1968	Bilingual Education Act provides funds to establish bilingual education programs for Spanish-speaking children.
1970	Elementary and Secondary Education Act extended.

1971	U.S. Supreme Court rules direct aid to private and parochial schools unconstitutional; in *Serrano* v. *Priest*, California Supreme Court rules that quality of education cannot be dependent upon the wealth of individual school districts.
1972	State and Local Assistance Act is passed to provide federal support for schools through revenue sharing.
1975	Comprehensive Employment and Training Act (CETA) is passed to create jobs and opportunities.
1978	California passes Proposition 13—a call for reform in government spending; soon other states follow.
1981	The Education Consolidation Improvement Act (ECIA) replaces forty-three separate programs with block grants to the states.
1983	The Supreme Court upholds the constitutionality of Minnesota taxpayers who send their children to parochial schools to deduct expenses incurred in providing tuition, transportation, and textbooks for their children's education.

Parochaid: A Legal and Financial Controversy

The question of direct public funding for nonpublic schools has been debated in this country for more than a century. The controversy becomes even more heated in periods of severe financial problems for the schools. This is both a legal and a financial problem. The legal issue is the crucial one. The First Amendment to the United States Constitution makes quite clear the separation of church and state: "Congress shall make no law respecting an establishment of religion or prohibiting the free exercise thereof." This principle has been tested again and again in court hearings throughout our 200-year history, and the result is generally the same— direct aid to nonpublic schools is ruled unconstitutional.

Those who support the claims of the private schools to public funds argue that without aid they will be forced to close their door thereby laying on the public schools the serious burden of providing an education for these children. Some states have attempted to provide some type of direct aid for non-public education based upon the belief that private schools provide a viable educational alternative for some children. A number of states have attempted to enact legislation to provide support for private and parochial schools. When these statutes were tested in court, they were struck down under the provisions of the First Amendment.

Proponents of direct aid argue that the courts guarantee parents a choice in educating their children. They cite the case of *Pierce* v. *Society of Sisters* (268 U.S. 510) as a guarantee of such choice. Said the court: "The fundamental theory of liberty under which all governments in this union repose excludes any general power of the state to standardize its children by forcing them to accept instruction from public teachers only." They further argue that nonpublic schools aid the public by decreasing the amount of money needed to operate schools for all children. Figure 13-3 illustrates private school enrollment.

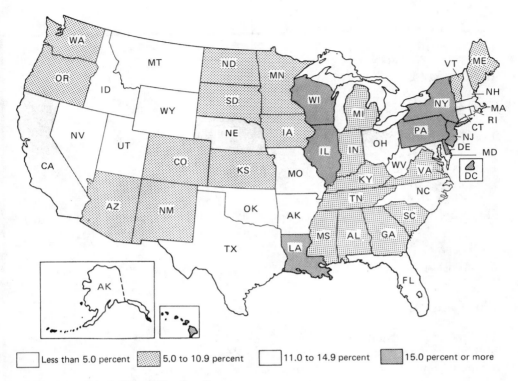

Figure 13-3. Private School Enrollment

Note: About 5 million or nearly 11 percent of elementary/secondary school students were enrolled in private schools in 1980. Private school enrollment made up more than 15 percent of total enrollment in Delaware, Hawaii, Illinois, Louisiana, New Jersey, New York, Pennsylvania, Rhode Island, Wisconsin, and the District of Columbia.

Opponents of direct aid argue that aid to nonpublic schools violates the First Amendment and does not enforce the separation of church and state or doctrines of nondiscrimination.

The controversy centers largely around the question of direct aid to nonpublic schools. Some indirect aid has been approved by the courts, however, in areas such as lunch program funding, textbook lending, and transportation of children to parochial schools.

In April of 1983, the Minnesota taxpayers brought action against the Commissioner of Revenue and taxpayers who had taken tax deductions for their children's expenses (tuition, textbooks, and transportation) while they were attending parochial schools. In this case called *Mueller* v. *Allen,* the Supreme Court held that the Minnesota statute did not violate the establishment clause by providing financial assistance to sectarian institutions. Justice Rehnquist stated that

Unlike a tax credit, which may wholly subsidize the cost of religious education if the size of the credit is sufficiently large, or a tax deduction of an arbitrary sum, a

Points of View

Tuition Tax Credits

The Case For . . .

Tax credits are a particularly appealing form of financial assistance for they do not require an individual to come as a supplicant to the federal bureaucracy asking to be declared suitably needy. All the tax credits do is allow individuals and families to retain a bit more of their own income during that period of their lives when they are singularly oppressed by college costs. No complex procedures are involved and no new forms. It is simple; it is direct; it is reasonable; and it maintains an exemplary relationship between the citizen and his government.

Senator Daniel Patrick Moynihan, "The Case for Tuition Tax Credits," *Phi Delta Kappan*, (December 1978).

The Case Against . . .

As a parent, a citizen and an officeholder, I have always believed that public education is the best investment a nation can make. It develops a diversity, a competitiveness, a competence that is nowhere else available. . . . No private school can boast this kind of diversity . . . Our public schools are and must remain the cornerstone of America's education system. This is not to deny or deprive private education, which can and should remain a vital part of our nation's education. But we are being asked now to discriminate in favor of the private, and what is left alone and unfunded is public education.

Senator Ernest F. Hollings, "The Case against Tuition Tax Credits," *Phi Delta Kappan*, (December 1978).

deduction of tuition payments from adjusted gross income can never provide a basis . . . for *complete subsidization of . . .* religious schools.[12]

Still, as the financial pressures build upon both public and nonpublic schools, the controversy promises to become even more intense. The use of tuition tax credits is the most current proposal to be put forth as a remedy. (This idea is discussed in the box, "Tuition Tax Credits.")

Another option is that of offering greater choice for students but within the system of public education. Magnet schools, with strengths in given areas, provide a modified form of choice. But the most wide-ranging experiment of this kind is taking place in Minnesota, as noted earlier,

[12]*Mueller v. Allen*, U.S., 103 S.CT. 3062 (1983). This case is probably the most controversial of the public aid cases reviewed by the Supreme Court because it has far-reaching fiscal implications for public education.

where students across the state may attend any public school of their choice if the school is willing to accept them. This does not include the option to attend private schools at taxpayer expense. This initiative builds upon Minnesota's program of postsecondary options whereby high school students may attend nearby colleges or universities when classes they desire are not offered within their own school district and if they qualify for admission. These students receive both high school and college credit in most instances.

Proponents of these programs say that this gives students and their parents the widest degree of choice (equity) while at the same time strengthening the public schools (excellence). Detractors claim that it will result in an all-out competitive war for students, thus strengthening some districts while destroying others. This program is being watched closely by other states in terms of the issues of equity, excellence, and efficiency.

Obviously, the issues are intense and often very emotional. The controversy will no doubt continue. More court litigation will be common as proponents and opponents of public aid to nonpublic education seek to further their cause to achieve some resolution to this very complex issue. (See article by Thackery in Suggested Readings.)

Financing Educational Reform

The publication of the report of the National Commission on Excellence in Education, *A Nation at Risk,* in the spring of 1983 clearly brought education back into the national limelight. Education was visible once again, a visibility that carried over into the 1984 and 1988 presidential election campaigns. A host of other reports critical of the status quo and calling for major reform followed close behind. "Excellence" became the watchword. Many states quickly moved to upgrade their systems—Arkansas, Florida, California, South Carolina, Utah, Tennessee, and Texas led the way, and others were preparing to follow.

Elements of educational reform cited frequently by state officials included:

1. New programs for teacher compensation
2. Longer school days and school years
3. Smaller classes and addition of support staff
4. Stiffer requirements for high school graduation
5. More student-testing programs
6. Prekindergarten programs for disadvantaged children
7. School improvement initiatives
8. Merit school plans
9. School finance reforms[13]

[13]Allan Odden and Van Dougherty, *Education Finance in the States: 1984* (Denver, Col.: Education Commission of the States, 1984), p. 12.

With school reform came new school finance issues. The major issue once again was how to fund programs which focused both upon equity and excellence. There are differing opinions as to whether the balance is being maintained as evidenced by the following two quotes:

> Adequacy of funding and the distribution of state aid to core educational programs, traditional equity programs, or new excellence programs are all important issues. . . . There does not seem to be a trend toward allocating most new funds to excellence initiatives without increasing aid to other programs. In fact, the reverse is true: excellence initiatives in most states are small, categorical programs, receive relatively small allocations, and most state aid increases are allocated to the school finance formula and traditional categorical programs (e.g., state compensatory, bilingual, and special education programs). Nevertheless, since the funding of traditional equity programs has received relatively little publicity, it would seem prudent for states to maintain a record of how funds are allocated among programs, if only to demonstrate that progress is being made toward equity as well as excellence.[14]

> [W]e are deeply troubled that a reform movement launched to upgrade the education of *all* students is irrelevant to many children—largely black and Hispanic—in our urban schools. In almost every big city, dropout rates are high, morale is low, facilities often are old and unattractive, and school leadership is crippled by a web of regulations. There is, in short, a disturbing gap between reform rhetoric and results.[15]

Traditional sources of revenue are under increasingly heavy pressure these days to fund reform programs. As a result, schools have begun to explore new sources of funds. During the late 1970s and early 1980s the use of local and state taxes found increasing restrictions placed upon their use for education. Thus, other sources are emerging, many of them private.

One of the new sources is a local educational foundation. These foundations provide supplemental funding for school districts. Several states have also set up education foundations to stimulate the development of innovative programs. But these foundations have remained small and their development bears watching.

A second new source is a fee-for-services practice. These are generally levied for activities not considered to be part of a school's core curriculum, for example, summer computer camps, day care, and preschool programs. Although these fees provide schools and teachers with additional revenue, "their role in the financing and governance of public schools may need to be scrutinized more closely."[16]

One of the most interesting of the new financing possibilities is school/business partnerships. A number of states have begun to investigate these partnerships.

> Business/school partnerships supply anything from free tutoring to equipment for computer labs, summer jobs for students and teachers, salary supplements for

---

[14]Ibid., p. 22.

[15]The Carnegie Foundation for the Advancement of Teaching, *An Imperiled Generation, Saving Urban Schools* (Princeton, N.J.: The Carnegie Foundation for the Advancement of Schools, 1988), p. ix.

[16]Ibid., p. 23.

Table 13-2 A Decade of Rating the Public Schools

GRADE GIVEN TO PUBLIC SCHOOLS	1978	1980	1982	1984	1986	1988
A	9%	10%	8%	10%	11%	9%
B	27	25	29	32	30	31
C	30	29	33	35	28	34
D	11	12	14	11	11	10
F	8	6	5	4	5	4
DON'T KNOW	15	18	11	8	15	12

Source: George Gallup, "The 20th Annual Gallup Poll of the Public's Attitudes Toward the Schools, *Phi Delta Kappan* (September 1988), pp. 33–46.

mathematics and science teachers and outright financial grants. These also expand participation in the governance of the schools, either formally or informally. The positive short-run political effect of partnerships has been to involve the business community in the schools and help to redefine its stake in the future of public education.[17]

States and local districts will be forced to continue looking for new sources of revenue, especially as the pressure mounts for dramatic increases in teachers' salaries in an attempt to hold the best already in the profession as well as attract highly qualified new teachers. Teacher salaries now comprise a major portion of school districts' budgets, and the kinds of compensation being recommended would greatly increase those costs. Even with the public's rating of the public schools once again showing a gradual upward trend (see Table 13-2), schools will have increasing difficulty generating the kind of monies necessary to carry out major reforms.

Noteworthy, however, is the fact that 64 percent of the public favors raising taxes to improve education.[18] The area of educational finance will bear close watching in the near future as major developments are likely if the educational reform packages being proposed are to be carried out.

IMPACT UPON THE TEACHER

The teacher or future teacher may still wonder what all this has to do with him or her. Under site-management programs, teachers are increasingly involved in developing the school budget. Thus, how the school district decides to spend the revenue available to it will greatly affect the teacher.

School Budgets and Teachers

Teachers are no longer content just to take what the board of education gives them. Rather, a large percentage of teachers in this country now engage in some

[17]Ibid., p. 23.

[18]George Gallup, "The 20th Annual Poll of the Public's Attitudes toward the Public Schools," *Phi Delta Kappan* (September 1988), p. 33–46.

Profile

Emma Willard, 1787–1870

Emma Willard was a reformer who believed that money should not be a consideration in educating people, but that all persons, rich and poor, male and female, had a right to a strong, free education. Willard believed that the key to providing this equal opportunity in education was through public support of the schools. She stressed that relying on private funding created huge discrepancies in educational opportunity as well as the quality of education.

In 1821, Willard took educational matters into her own hands and founded a seminary for women at Troy, New York (later known as the Emma Willard School). She defied the traditional restrictions of curriculum normally placed on women's education. Instead of receiving instruction only in subjects like singing and sewing, students at Emma Willard's academy were taught academic subjects, including astronomy, physics, and physiology. Willard sought out a well-qualified faculty—unique in its day since many teachers were ill-trained and inexperienced. Another of her innovations was the emphasis on the applied sciences, at a time when the science taught in American schools was almost purely theoretical.

Willard encountered problems in obtaining suitable texts for her students; at times, the school did not have the funds for materials. She dealt with these problems by writing the necessary books, many of which became the standard texts of the day.

Willard was a figure of great inspiration to students and other educators alike. Her efforts in campaigning for equality of women were intense and continuous. One of her pupils, the nineteenth-century feminist Elizabeth Cady Stanton, wrote in her memoirs that Emma Willard "was a splendid looking woman . . . and I doubt whether any royal personage in the old world could have received her worshippers with more grace and dignity than did this far-famed daughter of the Republic . . ."

The chains of economic inequality were detestable to Willard. Her academy admitted rich and poor pupils alike, and many of these students were given scholarships by Willard herself. Her campaigns for state support of education and her personal commitment to providing quality education are important landmarks in the history of public funding of schools.

form of collective bargaining with their hiring board through their teachers' union or professional association. And the bargaining involves much more than salary, although that is still generally the key item to be negotiated.

SALARIES. Teachers' salaries are generally determined by two factors: (1) level of educational preparation, and (2) years of classroom teaching experience. If the teacher assumes other duties in addition to classroom teaching responsibilities, he or she is also likely to receive additional pay. Some examples of nonclassroom duties are athletic coach, club sponsor, advisor on journalism activities (school paper or yearbook), band director, drama coach, curriculum writer.

More recently, with calls for educational reform, new programs for teacher compensation have been suggested. These generally center around programs of merit pay, master teacher plans, or career ladders. The National Education Association, a major teacher organization, has gone on record in opposition to these plans, especially merit pay, while the vast majority of the American public favors such plans.[19]

RELATED BENEFITS.   Most collective bargaining negotiations now result in a "master contract" between the district and its teaching staff. In addition to salary, the contract usually provides for a number of fringe benefits. These include items such as health insurance, retirement benefits, income protection, and opportunities to buy additional tax-sheltered annuities for one's retirement period. Who pays for these related benefits and in what proportion varies greatly from district to district. In some instances employer and employee share the costs while in others the district pays the full cost. Increasingly, these related benefits are becoming seriously negotiated items as district boards attempt to keep down salary costs.

In addition to these benefits, teachers are negotiating items such as class size, released time for instructional planning, provisions for inservice training and further education, and released time for professional meetings and workshops. All of these items affect the amount of money needed to operate schools. The negotiating process often becomes long and intense and when agreement cannot be reached it is not uncommon for teachers to go out on strike to make their demands known to the public. Usually, at that point, the two sides compromise and agreement is reached. But the message is clear: times have changed in teacher–school board negotiations and, directly or indirectly, money is clearly an issue.

THE 1990s

The struggle between equity and excellence in schooling will continue throughout the last decade of this century as related to education finance. Berne notes several trends to monitor:

> [First], issues of choice . . . are being debated in several states. The equity issues of students crossing school district boundaries as well as moving between the public and private sectors are complex but will probably become part of the continuing debate. A second trend over the past several years is the increased recognition of differences in educational needs among different children. Need variables have not been merged with equity concepts on a regular basis and this presents both an opportunity and a challenge.

[19]Ibid., p. 44.

Public Inventory

Paying for Schools

Use this survey to test the attitudes of people in your community. To provide a variety of respondents, gather your data in at least three different places in the community; for example, on a busy street corner, in a shopping mall, at a factory exit, at a school, in front of a bank, at a fast food restaurant, or in a residential neighborhood.

Survey

1. Occupation
2. Age
3. Sex
4. Do you have children in school now?
5. Are they in public school or private school?
6. Do you think the cost of running the schools is: too much/about right/too little?
7. It has been suggested that state taxes should be increased for everyone so that the state government would pay more of the expense of running the schools and thus reduce local property taxes. Would you favor an increase in state taxes so that local real estate taxes could be lowered?
8. Do you believe that only those who have children in school should pay the total cost of schooling?
9. Do you believe that the same amount should be provided for each child's schooling whether they live in a wealthy or poor area?
10. Do you believe the federal government should contribute more money to the states for running the schools?
11. Do you believe that public funds should be used for support of private schools?
12. Do you believe that in relation to other professional groups teachers' salaries are: too high/about right/too low?

Lastly, as the nation pays more attention to policies for young children, the equity concerns for child care are bound to interact with education equity concerns. Similarly, as children and schools become the focal point for the delivery of a range of social services, notions of equity will have to be redesigned to capture the equity aspects of these expanded services.

And finally, equity issues will continue to play a role as policymakers explore ways to link finance and performance.[20]

SUMMARY

Certainly how to provide for the greatest possible equality of educational opportunity for all children through quality programs while at the same time attempting to provide for equity for the taxpaying public is one of the most important issues currently facing education. As we have seen, vouchers, tuition tax credits, district power equalization, full state funding, and increased opportunities for choice are possibilities. But there are no simple solutions. The nation continues to be strongly committed to providing a quality program of schooling for all its children. The courts have continually mandated that every child receive an equal opportunity for education and that the states find a way to ensure that this is realized. The financing of education has a great impact upon the teacher; it is an area of concern and importance from the moment of signing the first contract through retirement.

ACTIVITIES

1. Some educators and lawmakers have stated that there is no truly equitable way to design a financial formula that will provide complete equality of educational opportunity; i.e., wealthier districts will always have better educational programs. Based upon your reading of this chapter, do you agree or disagree with this belief? Why?

2. Many parents who elect to send their children to private schools believe they are discriminated against financially. They contend that they still must pay taxes which go to support the public schools, besides paying tuition for their child's private or parochial education, and thus are paying twice. Do you find this argument valid or is it specious? State your reasons.

3. You will often hear parents complain that teachers are overpaid: "They only teach thirty to forty weeks per year, get all those holidays and vacations, and don't teach in the summer." How would you respond if a parent said this to you?

4. Some educators and lawmakers believe that wealthier school districts should be encouraged to tax far above the "foundation level" in order to try out innovative ideas. Others contend this only widens the gap between the quality of education in these districts and in those districts which are less financially able. Which view would you take and why?

---

[20]Robert Berne, "Equity Issues in School Finance," *Journal of Education Finance, 14,* 2 (Fall 1988), pp. 179–180.

5. Some suggest that a federal-level equalization program is the only way to solve the funding crisis in public education. How does this proposal interface with the fact that currently the control of public education is left to the individual states? Do you think increased funding for education at the federal level necessarily leads to increased federal control? State your reasons.

6. Visit a local school board meeting. What percentage of the meeting time is given to agenda items or discussion concerning matters of finance?

7. Invite a state legislator, a superintendent, and a school board member to your class to discuss the financing of public education. Based upon your reading in this chapter, what kinds of questions would you ask them?

8. Invite an educational representative from the local Roman Catholic archdiocese and a member of the local (public) school board to debate or discuss public funding of nonpublic schools. Based upon your reading in this chapter, what kinds of questions would you ask?

9. Use the survey form ("Public Inventory: Paying for Schools") to gain an understanding of a cross section of people in your community regarding issues related to the financing of education. Share the results with your classmates.

10. Profile someone who, like Emma Willard, has made a major contribution to the improvement of financing education.

SUGGESTED READINGS

BENSON, CHARLES S., *Education Finance in the Coming Decade*. Bloomington, Ind.: Phi Delta Kappa, 1975.

BERNE, ROBERT, "Equity Issues in School Finance," *Journal of Education Finance, 14* (Fall 1988), pp. 159–180.

BURRUP, PERCY E., *Financing Education in a Climate of Change* (2nd ed.). Boston: Allyn & Bacon, 1977.

CALDWELL, RICHARD, "An Equitable Framework for Corporate Participation in the Public Schools." Denver, Col.: Education Commission of the States, 1983.

CAMBRON-MCCABE, NELDA H., "The Changing School Finance Scene: Local, State, and Federal Issues," in *School Law Update . . . Preventative School Law*, Ch. 10, pp. 106–123. Washington D.C.: National Organization on Legal Problems of Education, 1984.

GARMS, WALTER I., JAMES W. GUTHRIE, AND LAWRENCE C.

PIERCE, *School Finance*, Englewood Cliffs, N.J.: Prentice-Hall, 1978.

KEMMERER, FRANCES, AND ALAN P. WAGNER, "The Economics of Educational Reform," *Economics of Education Review, 4,* 2 (1985), pp. 111–121.

ODDEN, ALLAN, AND VAN DOUGHERTY, *Education Finance in the States: 1984*. Denver, Col.: Education Commission of the States, 1983.

ODDEN, ALLAN, ET AL., *School Finance Reform in the States: 1983*. Denver, Col.: Education Commission of the States, January 1983.

ODDEN, ALLAN, AND DEAN L. WEBB, *School Finance and School Improvement: Linkages for the 1980's*. Fourth Annual Yearbook of the American Finance Association.

PHI DELTA KAPPA COMMISSION ON ALTERNATIVE DESIGNS FOR FUNDING EDUCATION, *Financing the Public Schools*. Bloomington, Ind.: Phi Delta Kappa, 1973.

Phi Delta Kappan, 65, 3 (November 1983). This issue contains an excellent series of articles on "Cutting the Strings: A New Federal Role in Education."

Research Memo, "School Finance in the 1980's," National Education Association, *Research Memo,* Washington, D.C.: NEA, 1980.

THACKERY, RUSSELL I., "Some Things You May Want to Know about Tuition Tax Credits." Bloomington, Ind. *Phi Delta Kappan, 66,* 1 (September 1984).

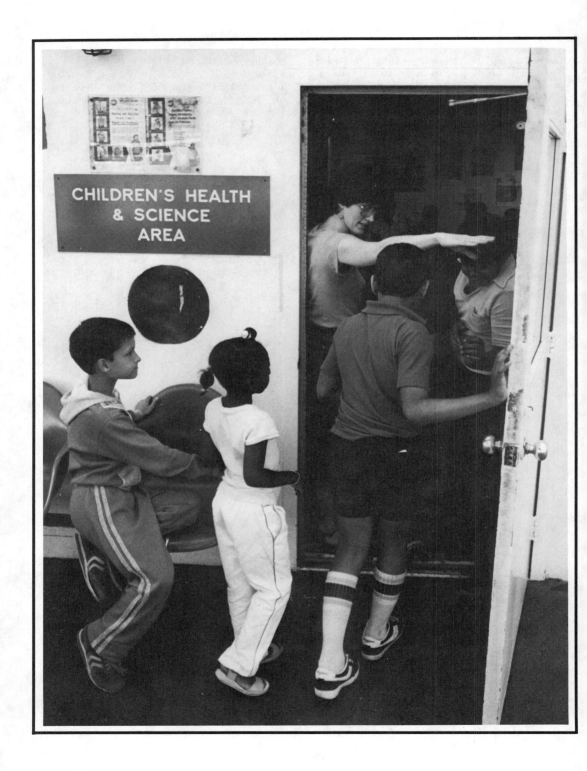

Chapter 14

SOURCES OF INFLUENCE

Education decision making in our democracy has not, historically, been a highly centralized or federalized process. We do not have prescriptive curricula for all schools and all teachers, as is the situation in many countries. While all three branches of the federal government—executive, legislative, and judicial—do at times exert considerable influence over the schools, primary authority for education rests with the states, who in turn have traditionally honored a considerable degree of local control. The result is a complex set of interrelationships where at different points in time, different legal and political agencies and levels of government have exerted varying degrees of influence on the schools.

The federal government, at one point in history, intervened to eliminate de facto segregation. Subsequent to that, the unnecessary separation from the mainstream of persons with various forms of physical and mental disabilities became a concern at the federal level. In both instances these problems had not been adequately addressed at the local level. However, government is not the only influence in making educational policy.

While both state and federal governments have intervened at different times to influence curriculum changes in the schools, dedicated parents and teachers at the local school level spend countless hours to ensure that policies and practices suited to their own particular needs and interests are enacted as well. In the final analysis, the classroom teacher is confronted with the daily challenge of what to do to meet the needs of several youngsters for between six and seven hours each day.

Daily planning is not a simple process of drafting "lesson plans" that meet "legal" requirements. Many forces shape the teacher's daily decisions about what to do in the classroom. Some are subtle and some not so subtle. Some are altruistic in intent and some are self-serving. Some can be readily accommodated and some not. Some will present minimal problems and others may create considerable soul-searching. Others will call for personal courage and professional risk-taking on the part of the teacher.

In this chapter, we examine some of these potential sources of influence and determinants of curriculum. We have classified these sources of influence into seven basic categories:

1. Individuals involved in the local school community.
2. Organized special interest groups.
3. Commercial interests.
4. Developers of new information and ideas.
5. Changing economic and social conditions.
6. Professional organizations and learned societies.
7. External evaluation and accreditation.

Abandon the notion of subject-matter as something fixed and ready-made in itself, outside the child's experience; cease thinking of the child's experience as something hard and fast; see it as something fluent, embryonic, vital; and we realize that the child and the curriculum are simply two limits which define a single process.

John Dewey

INDIVIDUALS AS A SOURCE OF INFLUENCE

A number of persons are able to exert considerable influence in terms of what is taught in our schools. Students, parents, the general public, the teacher and his or her colleagues, all have ideas about what should be taught in school and what is important in terms of knowledge, skills, and values. In this section, we will discuss some of the ways these people influence curriculum.

The Student as a Source of Influence

We have organized this chapter to examine factors influencing curriculum; the factors are ranked in order of the frequency with which the teacher is likely to confront them. Thus, we start first with the students themselves.

Any teacher who works with a large group of students (twenty-five to thirty-five children or adolescents together at one time is a large group) is confronted with a basic problem: how to adequately accommodate each individual's needs and interests. What a teacher accomplishes on a daily basis is obviously dictated, to a large degree, by what various students can or cannot, will or will not do. The degree to which teachers desire, on the one hand, and are able, on the other, to incorporate student input into decisions about the whats, hows, and whens of the classroom varies considerably. Nonetheless, these student needs—as well as parental desires—are undoubtedly the most pervasive influence on a teacher. *What distinguishes one classroom and one teacher from the next—as much as anything—is the degree of influence, both formal and informal, both planned and unplanned, which students exert in terms of what is done.*

Our purpose here is not to place a value on the extent to which students should or should not be involved in decisions about their school curriculum. The age and ability of the students are obvious factors which must be considered in such decisions. Rather, we underscore that this is a matter which warrants considerable thought and reflection on the part of the teacher. It is a matter that will be decided over time as the teacher acquires experience and examines and experiments with the variety of means which have been developed to involve students in classroom decisions. Local norms and expectations will also influence, perhaps even direct the teacher, in this matter. There is a variety of classroom meeting formats and student advisory models which might be explored. Our intent at this time is simply to underscore that any discussion of what influences curriculum must consider how the basic teacher-student relationship is viewed and practiced.

STUDENT RIGHTS. Certainly the concept of student rights in general has been considerably advanced in recent history. Title III of the Civil Rights Act of 1964 was intended to ensure equal opportunity for an education to all persons regardless of sex, race, color, religion, creed, national origin, or marital status. Title IX of the Education Amendments of 1972 was intended to ensure, among other things, comparable athletic opportunities for women as well as men. Public Law 94-142, which went into effect in 1978, was designed to ensure the "least restrictive educational environment" for students with varying degrees of physical, emotional, or mental disabilities; the law calls for *individual* education plans (IEPs) for these students, to be made up in consultation with the teacher, the student (if possible), and the parents. These efforts have advanced the concepts of equal education opportunity and individual student rights.

As a prospective teacher you should also be aware that many schools and school districts have adopted formal policy statements and procedures about such matters as student discipline, student rights, and equal opportunity.

Teachers in training may not give much thought to the concept of student rights. They may not know what rights they themselves have as a student. But this concept should be borne in mind in the course of preparing for a career in teaching. Students obviously exert influence in the classroom in both formal and informal ways, and the teacher should be as familiar as possible with means of effectively involving students in the classroom and with the rights which are accorded to them. Enabling students to take increasing responsibility for their learning is, of course, a major educational goal.

Parents as a Source of Influence

Do individual parents exert influence? Imagine you are in your first assignment as a teacher. After ten weeks or so, you meet formally with the parents of each of your students. Along with many compliments and a great deal of support (surveys show that generally parents are not nearly as critical of schools and teachers as one might be led to believe), you will also probably hear comments such as these:

- Jennifer used that same reading text last year when she was placed in a special "accelerated" program. We were hoping she wouldn't have to go over this material again.
- I have always thought that reading and math were taught very well in this school. This school has always had the highest standards. All six of my older children have benefited. But I have to believe that some of the things around this school now—repairing small engines, "creative" movement, a course on TV—are basically trivia. I hope as a newcomer you'll be able to help turn around what I see as a most unfortunate trend.

- Given John's level of ability, I really think he will have to put little if any time in your math program as you have it organized now.
- I couldn't believe it when I saw they still have these outdated French texts for you to use.
- Not that I want to be critical, but I teach in the College of Education at the University and I suggest . . .
- Sex education should be the responsibility of the parents. Any kind of morality, religious training, sex education, that is not strictly an objective situation, should not be taught in the schools. I don't think teachers can entirely avoid those issues if they come up in class, but I don't believe they should elaborate on them, and certainly not hold classes on these topics. I'm shocked they would put this in the curriculum.

Enough said. While there may be situations in which the parents appear apathetic, most parents are indeed concerned about the education of their children. Parents are involved as members of advisory councils and the Parent-Teacher Association. Parents serve as room parents, science fair judges, general classroom aides, and chaperones and supervisors for field trips. In addition, parents are represented on numerous ad hoc and standing committees ranging from textbook adoption for elementary reading to student discipline.

PTA. While there are a variety of local school organizations which involve parents and the community in the affairs of the school, the National Parent-Teacher Association represents by far the most common and most powerful *collective* voice of parents in education matters. Local PTAs and PTSAs (Parent/ Teacher/Student Association) can be found in all parts of the country. Some of the major goals of the National PTA include:

- Promoting the welfare of children and youth in home, school, community, and place of worship.
- Raising the standards of home life.
- Securing adequate laws for the care and protection of children and youth.
- Bringing into closer relation the home and the school, that parents and teachers may cooperate intelligently in the education of children and youth.
- Developing between educators and the general public such united efforts as will secure for all children and youth the highest advantages in physical, mental, social, and spiritual education.

Other issues that the PTA has identified as important priorities include quality education for the handicapped; needs of the single-parent family; ensuring health and welfare services for children, youth and families; and supporting research focusing on the needs of children and families.

Points of View

Schools vs. Parents

Is A War Going On?

Public schoolpeople in America generally take a jaundiced view of parents' motives, concerns with the school, and interest in their own children. They have even questioned seriously the right or ability of parents to rear their offspring. They have fought efforts to buy the different kinds of training and nurturing parents sometimes desire for their children.

In the history of the educators' undeclared war on families, parents have served two main purposes for the school: They produce the clientele and they pay for the system. When parents have demonstrated an understandable lack of enthusiasm for this limited and "specialized" participation, educators describe them as apathetic. Now, with the decline in birthrate and increasing disapproval of the system (as registered in failing bond issues), "apathy" has apparently turned to hostility.

Dwight Roper in "Parents as the Natural Enemy of the School System," *Phi Delta Kappan,* (December 1977).

The Right Way: Which Way?

Having performed the miracle of mass education, we are now confronted with the results of our labors: an adult population of parents who are knowledgeable, questioning, and restive.

What this new, highly informed breed of parents—and perhaps especially the young parents of the postwar baby boom generation—is in the midst of discovering is that there is no single, uniform, widely agreed-upon, indisputably "right" way to educate all children.

Evans Clinchy and Elisabeth Allen Cody in "If Not Public Choice, Then Private Escape," *Phi Delta Kappan* (December 1978).

The National Parent Teacher Association (PTA) has been in existence now for close to a hundred years and is one of the few organized groups that represents the lay public as well as the professional educator in matters that affect the welfare and education of children. Not only does it attempt to exert influence at the local school level, but it also has representatives commonly testify at state legislative committee hearings and nationally at congressional hearings on education. It also provides representatives to serve on committees and advisory boards sponsored by such federal agencies as the National Institute of Education.

ORGANIZED SPECIAL INTEREST GROUPS AS A SOURCE OF INFLUENCE

Public schooling is obviously a very political enterprise. Various groups that are not directly involved with education try to influence educational policy, as do various groups within the field itself. For example, in 1976, the National Education Association, for the first time in its history, endorsed a presidential candidate, Jimmy Carter, and saw him elected. As a result, the NEA's concern for a separate, cabinet-level Department of Education was given priority and was established by the Carter Administration. Candidates at the state and local level have long received the political endorsement and financial support of various education groups. Spokespersons from numerous educational organizations testify at congressional subcommittees that affect education legislation. The number of lobbyists listed with any Ethical Practices Board, and who have vested interests with respect to educational legislation, is considerable.

The number and diversity of lobbyists involved in education matters should underscore once again that education is a very political enterprise. It is not only squarely in the public domain, it is big business as well. Education-related legislation affects a wide variety of individuals and businesses. Parents, students, and teachers are not the only ones regularly affected by such legislation; suppliers of goods and services such as school bus owners and operators or those who supply food and nutritional services to schools are also involved. Representatives of special subpopulations affected by general education decisions, such as Native Americans or mentally retarded individuals, also lobby or testify for their special needs and interests on a regular basis. Finally, the education professions themselves represent a multiplicity of role groups in addition to teachers; these include state education personnel, professors, researchers, superintendents, leaders of professional organizations, and such specialized personnel as vocational educators and curriculum specialists.

External pressure groups often focus their efforts on local school or school district policies and practices. During the 1960s and early 1970s many liberal reformists were concerned that school conditions become more "personalized," "humane," and "open," that the schools assume a greater role in examining moral and ethical problems. Then, beginning in the late 1970s, the general posture of the country became more conservative in terms of school curriculum. Attempts at censorship of school materials and activities grew in intensity at this time and still exist today, especially among ultraconservative groups. For example, in Kanawha County, West Virginia, in 1974, controversy over textbooks led to months of upheaval and violence. Any efforts by the schools that might lead a student to examine and possibly change his or her values met with great resistance.

Coalition within the local community can, of course, arise from both sides of the political spectrum. The influence of advocates for more student-centered schools in one community or at one time can be as substantial as that of back-to-basics advocates in another place or another time. Still other groups, such as the League of Women Voters, often exert pressure to resolve conditions which might deny equal educational opportunity to any person or any group. One of the basic League principles states:

> The League of Women Voters believes that every citizen should be protected in the right to vote; that every person should have access to free public education which provides equal opportunity for all; and that no person or group should suffer legal, economic or administrative discrimination.[1]

As a result, this organization has put considerable energy into enforcing standards which would correct racial imbalance and ensure equalization of aid across the school district.

COMMERCIAL INTERESTS AS A SOURCE OF INFLUENCE

Testing

The National Center for Fair and Open Testing (FairTest) estimated that U.S. public schools administered 105 million standardized tests to 39.8 million students during the 1986–87 school year. Such a figure computes to an average of 2.5 standardized tests per student per year and to a figure of 30 standardized tests by the time of high school graduation. At least half of these tests were given in order to fulfill state and local mandates. A third or more of the tests were administered to students in compensatory and special education programs. Other standardized tests include those used for kindergarten and prekindergarten screening and those used to rank high school students for college admission and placement. In short, the test industry in America is a growth industry that shows no signs of abating.

The use of standardized tests of intelligence, aptitude, and achievement is widespread and endemic. Using tests has become a matter of course in the schooling process. Obviously it represents a huge investment of time and money. The use and interpretation of so many tests is often a controversial, even volatile, matter. Neil and Medina challenge the worth of standardized tests for large sectors of our student population, particularly minority students:

> Test makers claim that the lower test scores of racial and ethnic minorities and of students from low-income families simply reflect the biases and inequities that exist in American schools and American society. Biases and inequities certainly exist—but standardized tests do not merely reflect their impact; they compound them.[2]

[1]*League of Women Voters Program for Action* (St. Paul, Minn.: League of Women Voters, 1979), p. 4.

[2]D. M. Neill and N. J. Medina, "Standardized Testing: Harmful to Educational Health," *Kappan* (May 1989), p. 691.

Fred Hechinger, formerly education editor of the *New York Times,* represents the opposing view in this statement:

> There is today something like a last-ditch battle being waged which attacks everything that permits schools and colleges to be subjected to comparisons. In this battle, tests are not sniped at primarily because they are foolish tests (which some of them are) or because youngsters are scared (which fewer of them are than many of their teachers think); tests are attacked because they test the school, the community, and the state and thereby violate the fundamental freedom of American education—the local option to be as comfortable as the local school board, superintendent or college dean think good. I hear time and again . . . the warning that national tests and such commissions as the College Board on English and Mathematics "put the American education in a straitjacket" and "dictate the curriculum." I would rather use a different kind of image—that of the importance of a skeleton, a brain, and a heart to make American education more than a formless mass.[3]

Our task at this point is not to argue the merits or limitations in standardized forms of testing, but rather to underscore that they are an obvious source of influence on the curriculum. What is common to both of the opposing perspectives above is that standardized tests are common and indeed give direction to the curriculum. As future teachers, you need to be familiar with various tests, testing procedures, and test interpretation; in the context of this discussion, it is most essential that you examine the validity of the content of these tests in terms of how congruent the information is with your instructional goals. The fundamental question of influence, at least in terms of standardized *achievement* testing, comes when an adopted standardized test does *not* measure what the teacher is attempting to achieve and the teacher changes the curriculum to accommodate the test. If the test measures something else, then the teacher must consider whether or not that something else should become a part of his or her curriculum, or whether different assessment is needed. At least an accurate interpretation of the test in light of his or her curriculum should be provided.

Textbooks

If testing is big business, the creation of textbooks and related curricular materials is even bigger. We are all quite familiar with the text as a basic tool. This text itself is one of hundreds used over the years in the course of a student's career. Texts, like tests, are not likely to undergo diminishing use, although increasingly they may be translated to software for the microcomputer. The rapid accumulation of information and transmittal of ideas demands that the teacher rely upon organized data sources other than his or her experience alone. Elementary school preparation for a variety of subjects would be an extremely arduous task without the help of well-prepared commercial texts and curriculum materials. The key, as with tests, is the congruence of these materials with the

[3]Fred M. Hechinger, "The All-American Picnic Is Over," *New England Association Review* (January 1961).

needs and interests manifested in the classroom. In this regard, then, the selection of texts and other teaching materials becomes a critical task. One of the most common, yet critical, decisions that confronts the teacher is the selection of appropriate and helpful curriculum materials.

Reflect for a moment on the attributes of a text that give it the most appeal for a learner. A text, such as this one, is merely a tool or resource to be employed in teaching. Thus, any decisions by the teacher about what he or she wants in a textbook or other curricular material depends to a large extent on how he or she eventually plans to use them. Obviously, texts and the other related materials used by the teacher directly influence what is finally learned in the classroom. The extent to which this type of influence is placed in proper perspective is greatly related to the extent to which the teacher exercises informed judgment in its selection and use.

RESEARCH AND DEVELOPMENT AS A SOURCE OF INFLUENCE

Knowledge *is* power. Research data does and should influence what is done in the classroom. Educational research should be something that is not only understood by teachers but in basic and applied terms also undertaken by them from time to time.

You, the Researcher

Perhaps the best way to appreciate research data is actually to become somewhat of a researcher. The National Institute of Education has as a basic priority the support of more teachers as researchers on what actually transpires in their classrooms. Many effective teachers adopt an experimental approach to teaching, right from the beginning of their careers. The process starts with an inquiring mind and a willingness to examine systematically just what happens in schools and classrooms. The effective teacher will continually gather data on the efficacy of various teaching approaches or different curriculum materials. (A good portion of Chapter 15 is devoted to examining ways in which the teacher can assume an experimental posture in the classroom.) Thus, we suggest that early in your career, you acquire the tools to at least understand, if not conduct some basic experiments yourself. We also suggest that throughout your career you keep informed about the latest research through journal subscriptions and occasional courses or seminars with scholars who are working in areas of particular interest to you. There is nothing more persuasive in an argument for a certain course of action than generalizable data. Thus, research data is another source of influence on school practice and policy.

AN EXAMPLE OF RESEARCH. A beginning teacher might wonder how directive as opposed to more informal he or she is while interacting with youngsters in a classroom. Is it possible for research to shed any light on how direct or indirect various teachers are, and what difference these strategies make? Certainly, effective teachers employ direct methods at some times and indirect approaches at other times. Researchers have conducted literally hundreds of studies of what occurs in the classroom between teacher and students. One person who has studied the extent of influence teachers appear to exert in the classroom is Dr. Ned A. Flanders.[4] Flanders developed a widely used observation guide for systematically observing and recording teacher and student verbal behavior in the classroom. This guide is referred to as a category system. Every ten seconds, trained observer-recorders note who, if anyone, is talking in a classroom, and then classify that talk as falling into one of the ten categories in the Flanders Interaction Analysis Category System (FIAC). These codings of verbal discourse over time can provide a teacher with information about how he or she tends to interact with students. Classroom patterns such as who initiates discourse, who answers questions, who talks to whom, how much discussion is devoted to academic content and how much discussion to personnel needs or ideas, can be ascertained in this way. The teacher can then decide whether to alter his or her teaching pattern or style to provide more structure, or to solicit more student involvement. This is one form of practical research in which teachers can easily engage.

Additionally, there have been a number of studies of classroom interaction which can provide guidance to teachers in terms of how they might achieve different types of educational goals or the efficacy of different approaches to teaching. A teacher, like other professionals, has an obligation to keep abreast of recent research and development. When teachers have empirical data to support their preferred classroom practices, they are better able to defend them to those who might disagree.

THE INTERPRETATION OF RESEARCH.   There often are basic disagreements about the validity of the reported data. Further, it is important to know about the design of the studies from which the information is gathered. For example, it is important that a research study shares such information as:

- How many teachers or how many students were involved in the study.
- What type of socioeconomic setting the students were from.
- What age level or area of curriculum they were working in.
- What part of the school day or school year the recordings were made in.

It is also necessary to know what specific statistical analyses were conducted, in order to see whether the information collected could be generalized to other populations or predictive of future behaviors on the part of students and teachers. Properly used, research can assist teachers in making decisions about what and how they will teach.

[4]N. A. Flanders, *Analyzing Teaching Behavior* (Reading, Mass.: Addison-Wesley, 1970), p. 34.

ECONOMIC AND SOCIAL CONDITIONS AS A SOURCE OF INFLUENCE

We have noted that among other things, commercially prepared curriculum materials and research studies are likely to influence the teacher's curriculum. Both quality texts and quality research, however, take considerable time to design and develop. They commonly communicate information which to some extent carries the test of time. What these data sources cannot always do adequately is speak to contemporary issues which have the power to dramatically affect the lives of the teacher and his or her students.

Sometimes it is difficult to spend much time on topical issues. The elementary school teacher, however, may find it fairly easy to incorporate whatever issues and concerns are currently relevant into his or her curriculum. The newspaper daily provides evidence of social concerns and economic conditions which might affect the curriculum.

Contemporary conditions, and major world problems, influence the curriculum both directly and indirectly. Students may be directly affected by their socioeconomic conditions and the hardships they encounter outside the schools, and it may be necessary to adjust the curriculum accordingly. Conversely, some students, who do not feel these pressures themselves, may exhibit dangerously distant attitudes toward the life-and-death plight of others. Both conditions call for skillful manipulation of the curriculum to accommodate not only the needs of the individual but the individual's responsibility to society as well.

Economic conditions can radically alter attitudes and behavior toward health, leisure time, travel, and geography. Wars and threats of wars are very real even to younger children. No sensitive and caring teacher can totally ignore contemporary conditions and close them off from the classroom. Current social conditions considerably impact the school curriculum.

A tangible example within the school curriculum of the influence of changing social conditions is the emergence of health as a serious subject of study. The health curriculum, nonexistent in years past, has become taken for granted today. The topics of survival skills, refusal skills, AIDS education, drug and alcohol education, teenage depression and suicide, and a host of others are seen by the community as crucial. Teenage pregnancies, abortion, sexually transmitted diseases, and mental and emotional health are considered by the public as issues of the highest priority, as polls continually remind us. Let us examine a half dozen emerging trends in the teaching of health in the school curriculum. As you read the list of topics, bear in mind that they did not even exist as serious curricular topics a generation ago. Now, changing social conditions dictate their inclusion. Because the health curriculum is inherently interdisciplinary, health issues (social, mental, emotional, physical, and moral) appear not only in health classes but also in science, social studies, and other areas of the curriculum as well.

1. *AIDS and other sexually transmitted diseases.* It is estimated that there will be 50 million known cases of AIDS worldwide by the year 2000 (source: World Health Organization). Other sexually transmitted diseases, such as syphilis, gonorrhea, and chlamydia are also reaching epidemic proportions. The prevention of sexually transmitted disease can happen only through acting on a knowledge of appropriate sexual behavior.

2. *Child abuse.* Even the most casual reading of the daily newspaper makes us aware of the dimensions of this problem in our society. Sexual abuse, mental abuse, physical abuse, etc. of children has grown beyond the stage of isolated incidents. The teacher's role in identifying and referring cases is crucial as is the teacher's role in conveying information to children and adolescents of their rights in cases of abuse.

3. *Interpersonal skills.* Children come increasingly from homes in which both parents work or from homes where a single parent works. Terms such as "latch-key orphans," "shopping-mall orphans," etc., enter our vocabulary and are taken for granted. U.S. Census data show that the average American home has 2.62 people living in it. This means that, in many instances, students come from homes where there is virtually no one with whom to interact socially. The give and take found in larger families of the past is no longer possible. Social behavior must be taught, practiced, and guided. Classrooms do provide us with a large enough "critical mass" of people in order to create situations where cooperative behaviors can be practiced.

4. *Drug and substance abuse.* It is no longer unusual for high school teachers to report that their students are suffering from the obvious effects of alcohol, marijuana, and other drugs. One high school (in Shoreline, Washington) initiated Breathalyser tests to be administered to students suspected of being under the influence of alcohol during school hours. Although civil liberties groups quickly challenged the propriety of such a procedure, the point nevertheless is made that the situation is in many cases a desperate one.

5. *Coping skills and survival skills.* Programs such as "Here's Looking at You" are curricular programs designed to deal with such issues as assertiveness in the face of peer pressures to use drugs and to participate in illegal activities. Natural Helpers Programs have sprung up across the country as a way of enlisting students within the peer group to help their fellow students cope with depression, drugs, etc.

The list, of course, could go on. But we see here the influence of society in shaping school curricula. Some people have termed this effect the "add-on curriculum" meaning that we take our social problems and dump them on the schools to solve. Whatever the case, the schools can hardly refuse to take on these issues because the support system based on churches, clubs, neighborhoods, and the homes has been considerably weakened.

THE ORGANIZED PROFESSIONS AS A SOURCE OF INFLUENCE

As may be recalled from our review of the concept of collective bargaining, many of the concerns of teacher organizations have to do with working conditions in the classroom. However, both the National Education Association (NEA) and the American Federation of Teachers (AFT), the two largest organized teacher groups, attempt to influence the school curriculum in positive ways. In addition to holding membership in one of these two teacher groups, many teachers also belong to at least one other professional organization which provides them, through publications and meetings, with current materials and ideas about a specific area of the curriculum or a specific type of student. Examples of this would be the International Reading Association, the National Council for Social Studies, or the Association for Early Childhood Education. As you pursue studies in the various content areas of the school curriculum, you will become more familiar with these different professional organizations, the information and services they can generate, and the positions which they take on curricular issues and problems. For now, however, we will examine briefly the two major teacher organizations and where they choose to exert influence on what happens in classrooms.

National Education Association

The National Education Association is by far the larger of the two organizations. In addition to teachers, the NEA has over 1.7 million members. The NEA has affiliates at the state level in every state, and local associations in the majority of school districts. It maintains standing committees on, among other things, human relations, instruction and professional development, international relations, legislative and financial support for public education, and civil rights. The NEA president also appoints eight individuals to the National Council for Accreditation of Teacher Education (the recognized national agency for approval of teacher education programs such as the one you are now in). Some of NEA's continuing legislative concerns include:

> *Bilingual, ESL, and LEP Education.* Bilingual, English as a Second Language, and Limited-English-Proficiency programs are unique and necessary to achieve functional proficiency in English and so should be funded sufficiently to be available to all students not proficient in English. The educational program should reflect the cultural diversity and heritage of the children within the district, including, but not limited to, Chicano and Spanish-speaking children, Haitian children, Asian/Pacific Island children, Native Hawaiian children, American Indian/Alaskan Native children.
>
> *Child Care.* The federal government should assist states and local communities in improving and expanding child care services, including childhood development programs, and should strengthen and endorse existing standards.

Computers in the Schools. The U.S. tax code should be revised to provide for equitable donations of computer equipment only if such donations include software and provisions for classroom-user training along with limitations of use to classroom instructional purposes.

Education of Children of Noncitizens. The federal government shall provide funds to school districts for the education of children of undocumented workers, refugees, and members of the diplomatic community.

Guidance and Counseling for Elementary Students. Legislation should be enacted to provide comprehensive guidance and counseling programs for elementary students through state and local education agencies.

Materials for Classroom Use. Access to copyrighted materials and off-air recording of commercial and public television for not-for-profit classroom use should be assured. A portion of cable television (CATV) capacity should be reserved for educational uses.

Optimum Class Size. Federal programs should include incentives for local districts to provide for optimum class size.

Testing. Standardized tests should not be used to deny students full access to equal educational opportunity or to evaluate teachers or students on a single national or state basis. Truth-in-testing legislation should be passed.

American Federation of Teachers

The American Federation of Teachers is also a nationwide organization, in this case both a professional organization and a union. While it has fewer members than the NEA, it is affiliated with the very large and powerful AFL-CIO. Thus, nationally, at state levels, and in some 2,000 locals, the AFT also exerts considerable influence. Both the national and state organizations of AFT maintain special task forces to keep abreast of major issues, trends, and problems in education. Like the NEA, they also draw upon the skills and talents of hundreds of classroom professionals.

The AFT nationally is committed to a much higher level of federal support for education, to a federal assumption of state and local welfare costs to release more funds for schools, and to federally mandated collective bargaining rights for all state and local employees so that public employees will enjoy the same rights private sector employees have enjoyed since 1935. In addition, the AFT seeks federal initiatives in the areas of early childhood education and lifelong-learning opportunities so as to make more adequate use of school space and personnel and meet the nation's very great education needs.

As can be seen, professional organizations influence curriculum in a variety of ways. While goals such as those stated above will change over time, our purpose in listing them here is simply to illustrate that the "collective voice" of the classroom teacher is increasingly influential in educational decision making generally and is a definite factor in the direction in which school curriculum proceeds.

Effective Schools*

Research Finding

The most important characteristics of effective schools are strong instructional leadership, a safe and orderly climate, school-wide emphasis on basic skills, high teacher expectations for student achievement, and continuous assessment of pupil progress.

Comment

One of the most important achievements of education research in the last 20 years has been identifying the factors that characterize effective schools, in particular the schools that have been especially successful in teaching basic skills to children from low-income families. Analysts first uncovered these characteristics when comparing the achievement levels of students from different urban schools. They labeled the schools with the highest achievement as "effective schools."

Schools with high student achievement and morale show certain characteristics:

- vigorous instructional leadership,
- a principal who makes clear, consistent, and fair decisions,
- an emphasis on discipline and a safe and orderly environment,
- instructional practices that focus on basic skills and academic achievement,
- collegiality among teachers in support of student achievement,
- teachers with high expectations that all their students can and will learn, and
- frequent review of student progress.

Effective schools are places where principals, teachers, students, and parents agree on the goals, methods, and content of schooling. They are united in recognizing the importance of a coherent curriculum, public recognition for students who succeed, promoting a sense of school pride, and protecting school time for learning.

Bossert, S. (May 1985). "Effective Elementary Schools." In R. Kyle (Ed.), *Reaching for Excellence: An Effective Schools Sourcebook*, (pp. 39-53). Washington, D.C.: U.S. Government Printing Office.

Corcoran, T. (May 1985). "Effective Secondary Schools." In R. Kyle (Ed.), *Reaching for Excellence: An Effective Schools Sourcebook*, (pp. 71-97). Washington, D.C.: U.S. Government Printing Office.

Doyle, W. (May 1985). "Effective Secondary School Practices." In R. Kyle (Ed.), *Reaching for Excellence: An Effective Schools Sourcebook* (pp. 55-70). Washington, D.C.: U.S. Government Printing Office.

Finn, C. E., Jr. (April 1984). "Toward Strategic Independence: Nine Commandments for Enhancing School Effectiveness." *Phi Delta Kappan*, Vol. 65, No. 8, pp. 513-524.

Purkey, S. C., and Smith, M. S. (March 1983). "Effective Schools: A Review." *The Elementary School Journal*, Vol. 83, No. 4, pp. 427-452.

*Source: *What Works: Research about Teaching and Learning*, Washington: U.S. Department of Education, 1986, p. 45.

ACCREDITATION AS A SOURCE OF INFLUENCE

The final source of influence on the curriculum reviewed in this chapter is that of accreditation. The Commission on Schools has established standards which all schools are expected to meet. Standards have been established with respect to: (1) the purposes of the school; (2) the school climate; (3) organization and administration; (4) professional staff; (5) the curriculum; (6) instruction and pupil evaluation; (7) media; (8) pupil services; (9) school-community relationships; (10) physical facilities; and (11) financial support.

The six regional associations which accredit schools (from elementary through college) collectively cover all geographic regions of the country. The largest of these voluntary associations is the North Central Association, which covers a nineteen-state area and has been in existence since 1895. To be eligible for membership, a school must meet the minimum standards for accreditation. NCA is a regional, nongovernmental association of schools which are committed to (1) meet minimal accreditation standards established by the Association, and (2) conduct comprehensive, periodical evaluations of their educational programs. Its basic purpose is to improve education.

Accreditation, then, is determined by a school's ability to meet and maintain a set of discrete threshold standards. It is intended to provide assurance to the public or the consumer that desired standards are met. One of the standards for accreditation is that schools conduct periodic evaluations. NCA has established the following criteria for conducting these evaluations:[5]

- The evaluation is a comprehensive one involving the total faculty and, ideally, students and community members as well. It is conducted in three phases: self-evaluation, review by a team from outside the district, and implementation.
- A school's evaluation is based on its own statement of goals and objectives.
- The statement of goals is derived from a study of the school community.
- A school's goals are adopted by its faculty and the board of education.
- The school uses an evaluation instrument previously approved by the Commission on Schools—or a self-developed instrument which has the approval of the state committee.
- The evaluation includes objective and subjective measures as well as professional and consumer opinions.
- A team of educators from outside the district validates the self-evaluation.
- The self-study report and on-site validation report are then used to generate a school improvement plan.

---

[5]*Policies and Standards for the Approval of Elementary Schools, 1978–1979* (Boulder, Col.: North Central Association of Colleges and Schools, 1979).

Individual teachers are asked to serve on one or more subcommittees during the self-study. A teacher engaged in such a review might be asked, among other things, to gather information on various aspects of the school, the students, and the school curriculum. In order to evaluate existing programs and procedures in the school, the teacher would have to determine both the most notable strengths of the school's program and those aspects most in need of improvement. Once areas of concern have been identified, the teacher would help frame specific recommendations and proposals for the improvement of the school. Finally, he or she would be asked to help implement those changes which the school evaluation process has suggested as vital for the continued vigor of the school.

For a school to be accredited, specific guidelines must be followed. Accreditation does not preclude new directions and experimentation in the schools, but it is intended essentially to guarantee that various basic conditions and goals are met regardless of any philosophical or organizational variation in a school. Thus, the accreditation process exerts a pervasive influence on how schools are organized and operated.

SUMMARY

This chapter identified a number of sources of influence and factors which determine what finally occurs in the classroom. A teacher, for example, routinely confronts the needs and concerns of students and their parents. Textbooks and other curriculum materials, however they may vary, are everyday tools of the trade. Testing occurs at relatively frequent intervals in most school systems. The self-renewing teacher has multiple opportunities to not only review recent research and development in education, but to engage in it. Other forces for change are more evident at different times and to different degrees. As pointed out, changing social and economic conditions can have profound influences. Special interest groups will also exert varying degrees of influence at different times. The priorities of the organized professions themselves will change, and this will have an impact on classroom practice. New legislation will mandate changes, and periodic internal evaluation or external review such as accreditation will suggest yet other alterations. Thus, there is little doubt that the curriculum will continue to change in a variety of ways over time. The teacher who understands and can anticipate those forces that promote change is the one most likely to adapt classroom practice in appropriate ways. We hope this brief review will assist the new teacher in anticipating some of the forces for change that he or she will eventually encounter.

ACTIVITIES

1. Describe how you, as a student, might have influenced curriculum in the past. How can you influence it now?

2. Reflect on your parents' involvement in your schooling and in your schools' curriculum. What kind of influence did they exert on your teachers? What do you think of parental involvement in school curricula?

3. Testing companies and textbook companies influence curriculum. In what other ways do commercial interests affect curriculum? Discuss.

4. List some of the major economic and social events of the past year. Did you find these events cropping up in the your classes? Did any of these events directly or indirectly affect your own education?

SUGGESTED READINGS

"CONTEMPORARY ISSUES: CORPORATE INFLUENCE ON SCHOOLS," *Educational Leadership* (December 1989/January 1990), pp. 68–86.

DUCKETT, WILLARD, "Using Criterion-Referenced Tests to Drive Instruction," *Kappan* (April 1988), pp. 605–608.

ELLIS, A. K., MACKEY, J. A., AND A. D. GLENN, *The School Curriculum*. Boston: Allyn & Bacon, 1988.

FINSTERBUSCH, K., AND G. MCKENNA, *Taking Sides: Clashing Views on Controversial Issues* (5th ed.).

Guilford, Conn.: Dushkin, 1988.

GUTEK, GERALD, *Education in the United States: An Historical Perspective*. Englewood Cliffs, N.J.: Prentice-Hall, 1986.

TYSON-BERNSTEIN, HARRIET, "The Academy's Contribution to the Impoverishment of America's Textbooks," *Kappan* (November 1988), pp. 192–198.

VALENTE, W. D., *Law in the Schools* (2nd ed.). Columbus, Ohio: Merrill, 1987.

Chapter 15

CURRICULUM Purpose, Patterns, and Technology

Curriculum is most commonly defined as the scope and sequence of courses offered in a school's program. The most important curriculum decisions have to do with deciding goals and objectives, developing and organizing activities to achieve those goals, and developing means of assessing the effectiveness of both these plans for instruction and the actual instruction. In this chapter, we will explore purposes and patterns of curriculum, and corresponding-instruction.

In the preceding chapter a number of potential sources of influence on what is done in the classroom—that is, on the curriculum—were reviewed. We suggested that different people, events, and processes come together, in different ways at different times, that may affect school policy and the actions of the teacher. The teacher may be confronted both with informal, individual expectations and with formal, institutional directives. Both can have impact. The concerns of an individual parent, expressed only once, might have as much influence on some aspect of classroom operation as a full-blown accreditation process. A shift in the makeup of a school's student population because of a new busing policy might have more far-reaching implications for change than any new textbook adoption. If, as has been said many times, there is one thing that remains constant, it is change itself.

At certain times, pressures exerted by local, national, and even international conditions may become especially strong. For example, in the late 1950s and early 1960s, when this country perceived the Soviet Union to be making more rapid and significant technological advances than we were, federal legislation (through the National Defense Education Act) promulgated a very discipline-centered curriculum. Scholars in major universities and research centers became more involved in the development of curriculum materials. Emphasis was placed upon methods of scientific inquiry and the need to understand the different life goals. In such school systems, there are high schools emphasizing preparation for college, high schools emphasizing vocational training, and specialized high schools emphasizing art or music or theatrical performance. Still other school systems are organized to include all of these types of programs within one building. Yet other school systems provide for an integration of academic and vocational skills for all students, regardless of the individual student's stated future goals.

No matter how school systems are organized, schools provide a link between the learning process and the experience of the world. Maturity and knowledge are aims in all kinds of learning situations. The teacher is responsible for assisting students with achieving their life goals. Whether the curriculum tends to be vocationally oriented or precollege, preparation for the future is an underlying dimension in teaching.

The term *curriculum* is a Latin word that translates roughly as "running course." The metaphor of a running course or a race track is, in some ways, appropriate. Young children set out on the course at the tender age of five or six, and those who stay the course are awarded a high school diploma at the end of the race. But in our day the term curriculum has come to have more subtle shades of meaning than the image of a race track might suggest.

There are a number of ways to think about the curriculum. Perhaps the most commonly held definition of the curriculum is one that refers to the subjects studied at school. Although the average child is probably unfamiliar with the term curriculum, he or she could in all likelihood quickly tell you the names of the school subjects: English, math, science, social studies, music, etc. Such a basic definition of curriculum is a useful place to start because it provides us with a sense of the priorities in American public schools. Surveys of what is taught (Goodlad, 1983) give us a sense of the curricular dominance of English and math, for example, and of the relatively low priority given to the fine arts in our schools. Whether one considers the present state of curricular balance (or imbalance) appropriate is a matter for debate, but the facts are that some subjects are considered by the public, students, and professionals to be more "basic" than others.

Another way to consider the school curriculum is to think about it in an ideological sense. Thus, while everyone seems to agree that reading should be a subject taught in the primary grades curriculum, a great chasm divides those who espouse a phonics-based delivery system and those who advocate a whole-language approach to reading. In brief, the phonics method uses basal readers, and teachers emphasize the word attack skills of decoding. The whole-language approach, on the other hand, is based on literature and experience. Of course, our description here is oversimplified, but it serves to illustrate our point that any given child's experience may vary considerably from one reading curriculum to another, depending on whether that curriculum is phonics oriented or whole-language oriented. To focus this issue a little more clearly, imagine the plight of a slow reader who moves from one town to another (and perhaps from a phonics-based to a whole-language approach) in the middle of the first grade school year!

To a great extent, the most visible differences in the ideological debate about curriculum occur between what is advocated in the "ivory tower" of the methods courses in schools of education where teachers are trained and in the "real world" of the school where teachers actually teach. Methods courses tend to advocate activity-based, inquiry/discovery, "hands-on" learning in such subjects as math, science, and social studies, while teachers in classrooms tend to emphasize textbooks, worksheets, and rote, passive learning. There are exceptions to this dichotomy, of course, but overwhelming evidence points to the fact that it is real.

Closely related to this ongoing controversy is the issue of whether curricular subjects ought to be approached from a "process" or "product" point of view. Advocates of the process approach tend to stress experiential learning and the conduct of inquiry by students, while advocates of the product approach tend to stress the outcomes of knowledge with the idea in mind that if students are not exposed to the products of knowledge they certainly will never discover them on their own. Two very influential educators give us a good insight into the issue. They are Jerome Bruner, an advocate of the process approach to the curriculum, and Lynne Cheyney, who argues for the product-centered approach. Take a few moments to read the two brief excerpts which follow. After you have read them both, take a position on one side or the other, or somewhere in between the two. We will allow some space for you to express yourself on this difficult issue.

Knowledge as a Process

. . . a theory of instruction seeks to take account of the fact that a curriculum reflects not only the nature of knowledge itself—the specific capabilities—but also the nature of the knower and of the knowledge-getting process. It is the enterprise par excellence where the line between the subject matter and the method grows necessarily indistinct. A body of knowledge, enshrined in a university faculty, and embodied in a series of authoritative volumes is the result of much prior intellectual activity. To instruct someone in these disciplines is not a matter of getting him to commit results to mind; rather, it is to teach him to participate in the process that makes possible the establishment of knowledge. We teach a subject, not to produce little living libraries from that subject, but rather to get a student to think mathematically for himself, to consider matters as a historian does, to take part in the process of knowledge-getting. Knowledge is a process, not a product.

Jerome Bruner, *The Process of Education*, (1960).

HELPING THE STUDENT LEARN

A major purpose of teaching is sharing knowledge in such a way that a student is able to learn. There are several means to this end. Among them are: creating a positive learning environment; being aware of parental, peer, and social demands; and understanding the students' individual needs.

In the following sections, we will explore the viewpoints of several educational theorists and will examine their ideas about creating a positive learning setting, awareness of demands, and students' (human) needs.

JEROME BRUNER. Jerome Bruner became widely known in the field of curriculum development through his controversial elementary social studies program, *Man: A Course of Study* (MACOS). Bruner's instructional model is based on four key concepts: structure, readiness, intuition, and motivation. (These concepts are developed in detail in Bruner's classic book, *The Process of Education*.)

The concept of the *structure* of a discipline is not new. It is certainly as old as Aristotle, who made the case for learning significant ideas as opposed to mere facts. Bruner defines the structure of a discipline as its basic concepts and methods. The structure of anthropology, for example, is composed of its organizing concepts, such as culture, beliefs, customs, and symbols. Its methods of investigation include direct observation and case studies.

Knowledge as a Product

"A refusal to remember," according to Nobel Prize poet Czeslaw Milosz, is a primary characteristic of our age. Certainly there is abundant evidence that it is a primary characteristic of our nation. Teachers tell of students who do not know that George Washington led American forces in the Revolutionary War; that there was a World War I; that Spanish, not Latin, is the principal language in Latin America. Nationwide polls show startling gaps in knowledge. In a recent survey done for the Hearst Corporation, 45 percent of those polled thought that Karl Marx's phrase "from each according to his ability, to each according to his need" is in the U.S. Constitution.

Cultural memory flourishes or declines for many reasons, but among the most important is what happens in our schools. Long relied upon to transmit knowledge of the past to upcoming generations, our schools today appear to be about a different task. Instead of preserving the past, they more often disregard it, sometimes in the name of "progress"—the idea that today has little to learn from yesterday. But usually the culprit is "process"—the belief that we can teach our children *how* to think without troubling them to learn anything worth thinking about, the belief that we can teach them *how* to understand the world in which they live without conveying to them the events and ideas that have brought it into existence.

To be sure, countless people within our schools resist this approach. I have met school administrators who are convinced that education should be about mastery of knowledge. I have met teachers who, deeply knowledgeable themselves about the roots of our culture, are passionate about wanting their students to be.

Lynne Cheney, *American Memory*, (1987).

Bruner suggests that teaching students the structure of a discipline as they study particular content leads to greater active involvement on their part as they discover basic principles for themselves. This, of course, is very different from more traditional approaches which suggest that students ought to be receivers rather than developers of information. Bruner states that learning the *structure* of knowledge in a given discipline or subject area, rather than endless sets of facts, facilitates comprehension, memory, and learning transfer.

The idea of structure in learning leads naturally to the process approach, where the very process of learning (or *how* one learns) becomes as important as the content of learning (or *what* one learns). This position, misunderstood by many, has been the focus of considerable controversy, and it is important to keep in mind that Bruner never claimed that content was trivial. The false dichotomy between process and content need not exist. Bruner writes:

Your Position: Process versus Product

_____

_____

_____

_____

The best way to create interest in a subject is to render it worth knowing, which means to make the knowledge gained usable in one's thinking beyond the situation in which the learning has occurred. . . . An unconnected set of facts has a pitiably short half-life in memory. Organizing facts in terms of principles and ideas from which they may be inferred is the only known way of reducing the quick rate of loss of human memory.[1]

In terms of *readiness* for learning, Bruner believes that any subject can be taught effectively in some intellectually honest form to children at various stages in development. Obviously an important determinant of readiness for learning is intellectual development, or how a child views the world. Throughout Bruner's writing is the notion that the key to readiness is a rich and meaningful learning environment coupled with an exciting teacher who involves children in learning as a process that creates its own excitement.

Bruner clearly values *intuition* or intuitive thinking as a learning style. He feels that it has been generally overlooked and undervalued as a legitimate tool for learning in classrooms. Real problems, particularly those with an interdisciplinary focus, seldom lend themselves to the neat, lock-step approach found in textbooks.

Motivation is another important concept in Bruner's instructional model. Why someone wants or does not want to learn something is often very difficult to ascertain. But, Bruner suggests that intrinsic motivation—the idea of learning as its own reward—is an essential key to effective learning. John Dewey wrote of "the teachable moment," when motivation and information come together. A teacher who is curious, who values reflective thinking, and who accepts the student's childlike attempts at intellectual reaching-out will have a motivating presence. Whatever a teacher can do to enhance a child's desire to learn is valuable.

JEROME KAGAN.   Kagan is among the psychologists who have challenged the traditional assumption that early experiences are crucial to later development. He develops two basic themes about the development of the child. The first theme is that of the impact of recent experience; the second is a cognitive interpretation of child development.

[1]Jerome Bruner, *The Process of Education* (New York: Vintage Books, 1963), pp. 31–32.

Kagan believes that the *most recent experiences* of children are often more important than the earliest ones. He points to the impact of remedial efforts which have led to dramatic growth in social and intellectual functioning by children from deprived backgrounds. He stresses the value of rich experiences as an important source of continuity in development. And perhaps most important of all in this respect is the stability of the child's learning environment. Thus, a goal of teachers is to create a stable, positive learning environment.

Positive recent experience, a rich environment, and stability are conditions that a teacher can develop regardless of a child's previous background. In this regard, Kagan presents us with an optimistic view of the potential impact of an effective, caring teacher. Kagan disdains the notion of "traits" as predictors. He notes, for example, that an infant's social class (as indicated by parental education, employment, etc.) is a better predictor of temperament and intellectual functioning during childhood than are measures of the infant's own intellectual functioning. Thus he makes a strong case for environmental influences.

Kagan promotes the idea that a child's *rate* of development varies considerably with experience but that final outcomes tend to be similar across wide ranges of experiences. Rate of development, of course, deals with what Piaget has called the "American question," that is, how can we speed up the process?

Using the analogies of the first automobiles, which were made to look like motorized buggies even though there was no reason why they had to, and of artificial turf on football fields, which is green only because grass is green, Kagan is of the opinion that we are all too often guided by past experience—both the child's and the teacher's.

In his theories of *cognitive interpretations of child development,* Kagan states that children prefer to deal with learning environments (both social and intellectual) which exhibit a "moderate discrepancy" from their existing views of the world. He argues that the "resolution of certainty" by a learner is emotionally satisfying. He thus makes a strong case for discovery learning in which the resolution of a conflict or discrepant event is the goal.

Effective learning in children proceeds from a sense of involvement in problems. Skills are taught naturally in this context and their use is seen immediately as that of effective tools in the development of key concepts. Kagan's views on development are thought-provoking in that they represent an alternate position to that often taken by Head Start groups and other early interventionists. Since he is a psychologist and not a curriculum developer, his thoughts on curriculum must be inferred, but they obviously tend toward an enriched, exploratory environment and the type of facilitative teaching and materials that are supportive of children's intellectual reaching.

JEAN PIAGET.   According to the late Jean Piaget, the two fundamental characteristics of a child's learning and cognitive development are *organization* and *adaptation. Organization* is the systematizing of information into meaningful patterns or structures. A learner uses these structures or patterns which he or she has developed to organize new information and events so that they do not appear random or chaotic. Piaget's perception of humans is that they are born as active, exploratory, curious information processors. They have an innate need to classify, categorize, and assimilate information.

Adaptation is the process through which a person copes with the integration of new information into existing patterns and perceptions. Thus, adaptation becomes an ongoing process of assimilating and accommodating new ideas into existing ideas about the world. Adaptation, of course, is a lifelong process for all of us.

Piaget argues that a definition of intelligence follows from one's ability to organize and adapt. He views intelligence not as a fixed trait but rather as the ability to organize and adapt to the environment. Piaget's concept of the learner's organization of and adaptation to the environment is a dynamic one in which continual adjustments and modifications of perceptions are required. Thus adaptive behavior, or intelligence, results.

Piaget's position that children are not merely miniature adults is widely held. He states that their thinking is *qualitatively* different; children think in ways which adults can no longer remember. Piaget describes stages of cognitive development through which children typically progress. He emphasizes that while the stages are age-related, they are not age-determined. Therefore, differential rates of progress through the stages will occur.

For the person teaching children of elementary school age, Piaget's description of *developmental stages* is particularly important. A knowledge of these stages is useful in determining not only the content of a program in particular subjects, but sequencing as well. In addition, certain teaching strategies which would be appropriate at one level may be inappropriate at another.

The *sensorimotor* stage covers the period from birth to two years. From the initial reaching, grasping, and sucking behaviors a child proceeds to more highly organized activities and the development of oral language. During this stage, children depend heavily upon trial-and-error methods of mastering their environment.

The *preoperational* stage covers the years from two to seven. It is usually divided into two substages: preconceptual (two to four years) and intuitive (four to seven years). The *preconceptual* substage is characterized by dramatic growth in language development. By age three, most children are speaking in full and often complex sentences. Experience and modeling are the keys to cognitive development at this stage.

Children from ages four to seven are considered by Piaget to be at an *intuitive* stage of development. Their judgments are incomplete and inconsistent. They do not think in terms of formal categories. Piaget defines intuition as something that is grasped by the mind immediately without the intervention of any deliberate, rational thought process. Children of this age group are just beginning to bring a semblance of order to their sense of space, direction, size, number, and distance. Thus, a three-year-old may have little difficulty with the idea that airplanes and the people inside them obviously become smaller as they fly higher into the sky.

The years from seven to twelve cover the stage of *concrete operations*. Systematic, logical thought begins to supersede the impressionistic thinking of the preoperational stage. Apparent discrepancies and differences no longer fool children at this stage. They are able to count, measure, weigh, calculate, and test problems. Children at this stage begin to see the world without necessarily perceiving themselves as its center. The attention span increases. Rules become more acceptable. A clear sense of time emerges. Children at this stage, however, remain unconvinced of the virtues of delayed gratification—they are essentially now-centered.

The stage of *formal operations*, beginning at about age twelve, is a time at which children begin to think hypothetically and abstractly. Verbal associations often take the place of direct, concrete experiences. Reasoning takes on a time dimension of past, present, and future. Ideal and abstract concepts become attractive. It should be noted, however, that even when a person has "entered" the stage of formal operations, he or she often reverts to the employment of earlier-stage behaviors in coping with and adapting to the environment. The extent to which one employs formal operations in adapting and organizing is a measure of one's success in growth and development.

DAVID AUSUBEL.   Ausubel distinguishes between reception learning and discovery learning. In reception learning, students learn content as product. Students are required to internalize material so that they can give it back (e.g., on a test) at a later date. Discovery learning is based on the idea that content is not given to learners in finished form; rather, it is discovered by learners before they can internalize it. Thus in discovery learning, the learner's major task is to discover something and not merely to learn some content. Put rather simply, the difference lies in emphasizing *product* in learning rather than *process* in learning.

Ausubel points out that the distinction between reception and discovery is not identical to the distinction between triviality and meaningfulness. This is a misconception often conveyed by well-intentioned advocates of discovery learning. Ausubel writes:

> Actually, each distinction constitutes an entirely independent dimension of learning. Thus reception and discovery can each be rote or meaningful, depending on the conditions under which learning occurs. In *both* instances meaningful learning takes place if the learning task is related in a nonarbitrary and nonverbatim fashion to the learner's existing structure of knowledge. This presupposes (1) that the learner manifests *a meaningful learning set*, that is, a disposition to relate the new learning task nonarbitrarily and substantively to what he already knows, and (2) that the *learning task is potentially meaningful to him*, namely relatable to his structure of knowledge on a non-arbitrary and nonverbatim basis.[2]

Ausubel contends that the best balance between reception learning and discovery learning is one that favors more reception than discovery. Of course, such a balance presupposes meaningfulness of instruction, regardless of the method used. The power of discovery learning lies in the fact that the learner actually generates the knowledge to be learned and is thus able to see how

---

[2]David P. Ausubel, "The Facilitation of Meaningful Verbal Learning in the Classroom," *Educational Psychologist, 12* (1977), pp. 162–163.

information comes into existence. The limiting factor in the discovery approach is that it is often an inefficient means of conveying important information.

ABRAHAM MASLOW.   As a psychologist, Maslow focused on counseling, and in that regard, he was concerned with basic human needs which are manifest in an educational environment. Maslow's theories of humanism are based on his hierarchy of needs. Beginning with basic needs such as food and shelter, a person progresses through the needs of security, needs of love and affection, needs of self-esteem, and finally needs of self-actualization.

Maslow believed these needs to be important for education as well as for life in general. He stated that effective learning in children incorporated over time the concepts of freedom, knowledge, self-actualization, creativity, motivation, and esteem.

Maslow advocated reasonable degrees of freedom for children. Maslow saw the role of the teacher as that of helper, or (as he called it) "helpful let-be." He believed that good helpers are the most fully human persons—compassionate and caring. The best way to become a better helper (teacher) is to become a better person; and one becomes a better person by helping others.

Maslow felt that an effective, helping teacher is one who recognizes that growth has two components—the urge of a healthy organism to stretch, to venture out, and the polar urge to remain in the safe and familiar. In this context, Maslow envisioned the teacher's primary responsibility as that of establishing the right conditions for growth. Thus a teacher becomes a supportive individual who sets conditions which will allow risk-taking by students to happen. While such ideas may seem obvious and even trivial in print, this combination of support and risk-taking is not always easy to achieve nor even consistent with the values of all educators.

Maslow was of the opinion that education at its best deals with the real and often serious problems of life. Maslow stated that an affirmative response to life (to one's self and to one's environment) is the overriding goal of education.

It is well to examine Maslow's concept of knowledge. Maslow felt that we can know only that which we are worthy of knowing. In that respect, self-knowledge must precede knowledge of a wider world. As Francis Bacon wrote centuries ago, "Be so true to thyself, as thou be not false to others." Maslow pressed the case for a balance between objective and subjective knowledge. If an imbalance exists, it is certainly not in favor of the subjective and experiential. Rather, "objectivity" and abstraction are all too often presented to children in the name of knowing and knowledge.

What is Maslow's message to the teacher? If the authors may venture a guess, it is that the teacher should make his or her first priority one of deep concern for the children he or she works with. Difficult as it may be, the teacher must develop an atmosphere of acceptance and love for his or her students, bearing in mind that learning about ideas and about people must begin with the real issues already present in the classroom. From there, a hands-on, experiential base will form a foundation for the accumulation and ordering of knowledge. In such an atmosphere, love and knowledge become natural companions.

Inventory

Elements of Teaching

There are many different styles of teaching—have you begun to think about how you will conduct yourself as a teacher? Here are some questions that will help you begin to plan for teaching:

1. What basic sources will I draw on as a teacher?
   a. my personal experience
   b. a current issue or concern
   c. organized information, such as a textbook
   d. the students' needs and interests
2. What types of goals will I focus on in class?
   a. knowledge development
   b. attitude development
   c. skill development
   d. a combination of these
3. What degree of student involvement do I want?
   a. verbal communication
   b. written application
   c. simulated activity or role-playing
   d. application outside of school
4. What type of thinking do I want to stimulate in students?
   a. recall or interpretative
   b. analytic
   c. evaluative
   d. projective
5. What type of social interaction will I encourage?
   a. students work independently of one another
   b. students share and cooperate in their work
   c. students carry on structured dialogue in class
   d. students debate or resolve conflicts with one another
6. What kind of information will I use in the lessons?
   a. facts, empirically derived data
   b. conventional wisdom or consensus of opinion
   c. contested data, opinions
   d. attempt to generate new information
7. How much will I focus on experiences and events from:
   a. the past
   b. the present
   c. the future
   d. on-going, timeless

8. To what extent will the student be in the role of:
   a. receiver of information
   b. sharer of information
   c. seeker of information
   d. user of information

PATTERNS AND VARIATIONS

Naturally, the development of patterns of school curricula was influenced by the purposes of education. In this section, we will examine some of the elements pertaining to the teacher in relation to developing a curriculum. We will investigate teaching styles and explore some of the objectives of different curriculum patterns. Further, we will examine patterns of organization (and variations), as well as patterns of instruction (and variations).

TEACHING STYLE: HOW WE TEACH.   Teaching style treats the matter of *how* we teach and is therefore a function of personality, values, experience, and training. It is the most personal element affecting patterns of curriculum. Teachers are invariably provided with structure and guidelines in terms of the content or subject matter they are to address, especially teachers of specific subjects at the secondary level. There tends to be greater latitude in terms of the type of teaching style or teaching approaches one employs, although the task of teaching several young-sters in several subjects often constrains against desired experimentation and development of different instructional approaches.

> *The teacher . . . must give substance and structure and style to his teaching. His is a way of giving the child experience—not random experience, which is endless, but experience that is in search of meaning. . . .*
>
> *Paul Brandwein*

In fashioning a teaching style, the teacher can borrow from the thinking of the theorists discussed earlier in this chapter: Bruner, Kagan, Ausubel, Piaget, and Maslow. Determination of a teaching style must take into account several points: discipline and classroom management; learning environment; desired relationship with students; and the choice of whether to use an inquiry and discovery (problem-solving) mode of teaching, a didactic or fact-oriented mode, or to stress interpersonal relationships.

Further, the teacher must examine the types of goals and attitudes he or she expects to instill in the students. Goal structuring is a pervasive element of teacher style. Goal structure is defined as the amount of interdependence existing among students.[3] The classroom teacher generally establishes, either consciously or unconsciously, the type of goal structure to which his or her students are exposed.

Johnson and Johnson[4] have identified three goal structures for classroom teaching. A *cooperative* goal structure exists when student performance is interdependent, that is, when students must work together toward a common goal. Committee assignments are based on the assumption that a group of students will work together to complete a task that would have been difficult to complete alone. A *competitive* goal structure exists when students perceive that their success lies in achieving that goal. Grading individuals on a curve is an example of a competitive goal structure. An *individualistic* goal structure is one where the achievement of learning goals by one student is unrelated to the achievement of those goals by other students. In an individualistic goal structure, a minimum amount of student interaction takes place.

All three types of social dynamics are appropriate in the classroom. There are certain activities more suited to cooperation, and others are more suited to competition. Caution must be taken that a classroom doesn't fall into a single pattern, especially one that fosters continuing competition only. Learning to work and play harmoniously with others is a critical skill and attitude. We continue to learn more about how these can be fostered in the classroom, while at the same time acquiring needed academic knowledge and skills.

CURRICULUM DEVELOPMENT. There are at least four major sources of influence or information which can be drawn upon in developing a curriculum. These are (1) information organized for study (that is, texts, curriculum guides, reference materials); (2) topical events which are external to the school (matters of interest, crosscutting problems, unresolved issues); (3) the learner (his or her interests, needs, moods, and behaviors); and (4) the teacher (his or her experience, interest, needs). At one time or another all of these sources for deciding curriculum are used. At different times there will be distinct pressures for the teacher to employ one source more than another. These different sources for curriculum call for different ways of organizing the curriculum. Approaches to organizing the curriculum include the *separate subjects* curriculum; the *unified* and the *correlated* schemes, which rely primarily on information organized across traditional disciplines; or the *core* and *persistent problems* approaches, which emphasize keeping abreast of current societal problems. At the elementary level there are *child-centered* and *integrated day* approaches, which demand more dialogue and goalsetting with the learner. While it may take a good bit of teaching experience to become competent and comfortable in integrating ideas from each of these data sources into classroom activities, the teacher should at least be aware of these ways of organizing curriculum, and how they can contribute to achieving different types of goals.

[3]D. W. Johnson and R. T. Johnson, *Learning Together and Alone* (Englewood Cliffs, N.J.: Prentice-Hall, 1975), p. 7.
[4]Johnson, D. W., and R. T. Johnson, *Cooperation and Competition: Theory and Research*. Edina, Minn.: Interaction Book, 1989.

Basic Elements of Cooperative Learning*

Positive Interdependence

Students must feel that they need each other in order to complete the group's task, that they "sink or swim" together. Some ways to create this feeling are through establishing mutual goals (students must learn the material and make certain group members learn the material), joint rewards (if all group members achieve above a certain percentage on the test, each will receive bonus points), shared materials and information (one paper for each group or each member receives only part of the information needed to do the assignment), and assigned roles (summarizer, encourager of participation, elaborator).

Face-to-Face Interaction

No magic exists in positive interdependence in and of itself. Beneficial educational outcomes are due to the interaction patterns and verbal exchanges that take place among students in carefully structured cooperative learning groups. Oral summarizing, giving and receiving explanations, and elaborating (relating what is being learned to previous learning) are important types of verbal interchanges.

Individual Accountability

Cooperative learning groups are not successful until every member has learned the material or has helped with and understood the assignment. Thus, it is important to frequently stress and assess individual learning so that group members can appropriately support and help each other. Some ways of structuring individual accountability are by giving each group member an individual exam or by randomly selecting one member to give an answer for the entire group.

Interpersonal and Small Group Skills

Students do not come to school with the social skills they need to collaborate effectively with others. So teachers need to teach the appropriate communication, leadership, trust, decision making, and conflict management skills to students and provide the motivation to use these skills in order for groups to function effectively.

Group Processing

Processing means giving students the time and procedures to analyze how well their groups are functioning and how well they are using the necessary social skills. This processing helps all group members achieve while maintaining effective working relationships among members. Feedback from the teacher and/or student observers on how well they observed the groups working may help processing effectiveness.

*From D. W. Johnson, R. T. Johnson, and Edythe Johnson Holubec, *Circles of Learning: Cooperation in the Classroom*, rev. ed. (Englewood Cliffs, N.J.: Prentice-Hall, 1986).

Patterns of Organization

SEPARATE SUBJECT CURRICULUM. Most teachers rely primarily on a *separate subject* curriculum. In this approach, each discipline is addressed separately in terms of how it appears to structure itself best for learning. The teaching of mathematics may be approached one way, English in quite another way.

UNIFIED CURRICULUM. At some times, the effective teacher might approach curriculum employing a *unified* curriculum design. Here the teacher draws upon a variety of related disciplines. The "social studies" curriculum, for example, could build upon themes or key ideas and concepts which cut across economics, history, sociology, and anthropology. There is no attempt to maintain discrete subject areas in this approach.

CORRELATED CURRICULUM. At other times, a teacher might approach each of the subject areas above separately but examine common concepts across each subject. This strategy is commonly referred to as a *correlated* curriculum design. In this way of organizing curriculum, the concept of interdependence, for example, might be examined through illustrations in music, in science, or in mathematics—but music, mathematics, and science would still be treated as separate subjects.

CORE CURRICULUM. Perhaps the most radical approach to curriculum a teacher can take is a *crosscutting-problems* approach. Addressing the problem of child pornography would be an example. This concern becomes the total focus for a given period of time and specific subjects are not generally scheduled. The assumption is that the issue has the power to pull students into desired subject matter. This approach or design is referred to as a *core* curriculum or a *"persistent problems"* approach, because a core issue or concern becomes the hub of the curriculum to which different subject matter is brought to bear.

INTEGRATED CURRICULUM. In a somewhat similar vein, the *child-centered* or *integrated* curricula found in elementary schools stress the *application* of skills and information as the vehicle for moving the interests of children into other topics and projects, and towards the acquisition of further skills. Knowledge of weights and measures are used to construct a playhouse, for example. In this approach, teachers try, whenever possible, to employ the current interests and skills of the child as a starting point, gradually showing the child where further skill learning or information will be necessary if those interests are to be pursued successfully.

COMBINING DESIGNS. The competent teacher will approach curriculum from a variety of perspectives. If it seems most appropriate that time be given over to intensive study of a major social crisis, this can be done with desired content and skills incorporated into the approach. On the other hand, if it's more efficient and effective to concentrate on one specific discipline at a given time, that can be done as well. The effective teacher can organize and present material to the students, or he or she can organize the curriculum so that students have to take more initiative themselves. The teacher who is best able to cope with and accommodate the various pressures noted in the preceding chapter, is the teacher who can skillfully alter his or her approach to the curriculum as these conditions require.

ORGANIZING STUDENTS FOR PLANNING.   Certainly the most constant and pervasive force for making a variety of at least minor changes in the curriculum are the students themselves. The degree of ownership or involvement in what is being studied is often related to the student's degree of interest. The question is how can students be effectively involved, and to what extent at different stages of their school career?

Not everyone agrees upon the degree and extent of student involvement, but there is little disagreement that there are aspects of schooling in which students can be involved. There are several options for soliciting and using student input. Included in these options are the power model, the input model, the management team model, and the delegated authority model. Each of these approaches is reviewed briefly.

In the *power model,* the teacher makes the great majority of decisions with little discussion or consultation with the students. Accountability is clear, and this model tends to be efficient in terms of time. On the other hand, its detrimental aspect in terms of lack of student involvement in subsequent activity must be considered.

In the *input model,* a representative group of students, such as class leaders or class officers, are periodically consulted, especially before major decisions are made. The teacher, however, assumes responsibility for the final decision. In this model, accountability once again is clear, and decision making is relatively efficient in terms of time. This approach does expand the range of decision options for the teacher. It can, however, be self-limiting in that as students acquire skill in the decision-making process, they often desire more responsibility than this model actually provides. This model also places pressure on the teacher to follow the advice given, in order to ensure continued and effective student participation.

In the *management team,* a representative group of students, together with the teacher, form a team which collectively makes decisions. The types of decisions which are jointly made can, of course, be differentiated from those which the teacher makes alone. This model tends to motivate the students and usually has more students desiring to "buy into" the decision-making process. However, accountability is at times unclear, and this model requires a longer time to make decisions. Especially difficult are those decisions which must be made immediately. The management team model also demands extra time of the students, as well as the teacher.

In the *delegated authority model,* authority for many decisions is delegated, with the teacher performing a consulting/advising role. This approach can be highly motivating for students. It calls for maximum student creativity and can assist in developing latent leadership talents. It also often produces the most widely supported decisions. This model places the teacher in a maximum risk-taking role, as he or she is still ultimately accountable for the action of the class. It also requires the greatest amount of time for planning, coordinating, and communicating.

TRACKING VERSUS HETEROGENEOUS GROUPING.   Besides organizing students for planning purposes, students are also organized for learning purposes. Common ways of doing this are through *tracking* and *grouping.* In tracking, students of similar abilities (usually determined on the basis of testing or past grades) are grouped together in a single class. Thus, a teacher can focus on educational goals geared to the students' abilities. However, critics of tracking believe it attaches a stigma to the students in the "lower" tracks. Further, many educators believe that because there is no precise way of determining students' abilities, frequently they will become underachievers if they are labeled as such. The alternative is *heterogeneous grouping,* in which students of varying abilities and interests are mixed within a single classroom, thereby learning with and from each other.

MULTIAGE GROUPING.   In multiage classrooms, students are grouped randomly. This practice is usually confined to elementary schools. In each classroom, students may vary in age by three or four years. Learning experiences are geared both to the entire group as well as to individual age groups and single students. In some instances, for example, a reading group might consist of a combination of eight-, nine-, and ten-year-olds. A younger student may participate in a project with an older student. No stigma is attached to the mixing of ages, nor are achievement expectations designated according to age.

NONGRADED SCHOOLING.   In nongraded or continuous progress arrangement, employed most frequently in an elementary school, students proceed through the curriculum at their own pace rather than moving from one grade to the next on a year-by-year basis. This scheme necessitates the multiage group described above. In this design, no student would have to repeat another year in a given grade with the stigma of failure so often attached to such a retention process. Rather, the student is likely to spend from two to four years with either a primary (1–3) or intermediate (4–6) cluster of students, often working with a team of teachers throughout this period of time.

MODULAR/FLEXIBLE SCHEDULING.   This is an organization pattern frequently used in secondary schools. Students attend classes on rotating shifts. Classes may not always meet at the same time (therefore, for example, a teacher will not always have the same group of students for a class held during the last—and often most tiring—period of the day). Modular/flexible scheduling allows more room for electives in coursework; however, it has been criticized by some theorists on the basis of the lack of continuity it involves.

TEAM TEACHING.   Teachers also can be organized differently than the traditional one-teacher–one-classroom mode. One of the more common variations has been

Cultural Literacy*

Research Finding

Students read more fluently and with greater understanding if they have background knowledge of the past and present. Such knowledge and understanding is called cultural literacy.

Comment

Students' background knowledge determines how well they grasp the meaning of what they read. For example, students read passages more deftly when the passages describe events, people, and places of which the students have some prior knowledge. The more culturally literate students are, the better prepared they will be to read and understand serious books, magazines, and other challenging material.

Most school teachers, college professors, journalists, and social commentators agree that the general background knowledge of American students is too low and getting lower. Surveys document great gaps in students' basic knowledge of geography, history, literature, politics, and democratic principles. Teaching is hindered if teachers cannot count on their students sharing a body of knowledge, references, and symbols.

Every society maintains formal and informal mechanisms to transmit understanding of its history, literature, and political institutions from one generation to the next. A shared knowledge of these elements of our past helps foster social cohesion and a sense of national community and pride.

In the United States, the national community comprises diverse groups and traditions; together they have created a rich cultural heritage. Cultural literacy not only enables students to read better and gain new knowledge; it enables them to understand the shared heritage, institutions, and values that draw Americans together.

Anderson, R. C., Soiro, R. J., and Montague, W. (1977). *Schooling and the Acquisition of Knowledge.* Hillsdale, NJ: Erlbaum Associates.

Finn, C. E., Jr., Ravitch, D., and Roberts, P. (Eds.) (1985). *Challenges to the Humanities.* New York: Holmes and Meier.

Hirsch, E. D., Jr. (Spring 1983). "Cultural Literacy." *The American Scholar,* Vol. 52, pp. 159-169.

Hirsch, E. D., Jr. (Summer 1985). "Cultural Literacy and the Schools." *American Educator,* Vol. 9, No. 2, pp. 8-15.

Levine, A. (1980). *When Dreams and Heroes Died: A Portrait of Today's College Student.* San Francisco: Jossey-Bass, Inc.

Resnick, D. B., and Resnick, L. B. (August 1977). "The Nature of Literacy: An Historical Exploration." *Harvard Educational Review,* Vol. 47, No. 5, pp. 370-385.

*Source: *What Works: Research about Teaching and Learning,* Washington: U.S. Department of Education, 1986, p. 53.

some form of team or cooperative teaching. Team teaching is commonly defined as an arrangement where two or more teachers jointly assume responsibility for the planning of instruction, actual instruction itself, and evaluation of that instruction. Thus, instead of each teacher instructing thirty youngsters alone, three teachers working together would plan for ninety youngsters.

The following are some of the commonly cited advantages and disadvantages of team teaching.

Potential Advantages:

1. There is more effective division of labor. Teachers can complement one another with their strengths and offset each other's limitations or lack of interest in one aspect of the curriculum or one type of teaching style.
2. Teachers are able to model different teaching methods for one another, jointly solve problems, give one another feedback on their teaching, and contribute an esprit de corps. Team teaching can also be a basic form of continuing education for teachers through sharing and feedback.
3. A student is seen from several different perspectives. He or she is unlikely to be unfairly or inaccurately judged. Also, the student has a better opportunity to relate in a significant way with at least one teacher. If the student has only one teacher, the chances for a positive relationship are reduced.
4. Several teachers can offer a more diverse and richer array of options for students in this type of arrangement.

Potential Disadvantages:

1. Research shows that teachers are usually very much alike in their backgrounds and training. They tend to duplicate rather than complement one another and thus spend considerable time (the most precious of commodities) in trying to make decisions one person could make just as well alone.
2. Working closely together with others on a daily basis is not easy. Planning more diverse instruction for more students takes considerably more time and energy. Jointly planning instruction for students, let alone helping one another with teaching demands a great deal of extra time and energy.
3. Students tend to get lost in the shuffle. With larger numbers of students, it is more difficult to know anyone very well. The validity of student evaluation depends to a large degree on how well one person knows the student.
4. The consistent structure of one teacher and one classroom is helpful to most students.

Patterns of Instruction

Earlier in this chapter we discussed how teachers employ various models of instruction to convey ideas and information. The *didactic model* is one that relies on lectures and textbooks to convey information. The *problem-solving* or *inquiry/discovery model* is one in which the teacher assumes the role of "project director" or facilitator and guides the student through a search for knowledge. The *interpersonal learning model* emphasizes affective, as well as cognitive goals, and calls for more student collaboration.

Obviously, a teacher will want to combine these elements for the most effective approach to teaching. The teacher will want to encourage creative thinking and intuition as well as a firm understanding of the basics of education.

There are many other means of presenting knowledge to students. The following sections discuss some additional patterns of instruction.

DEMONSTRATION/EXPERIMENTS.   One means of assisting students in understanding basic concepts is through demonstration and experimentation. This need not be confined to the sciences. Students may demonstrate principles of mathematics, or art, or social problems; they may conduct experiments in ideas in current events as well as in principles of chemistry; they may organize research projects in poetry or history. Demonstration and experiments are "how-to" or "show-and-tell" ways of making information clear. Another type of demonstration is *role playing,* in which students discover solutions to problems through acting out hypothetical situations.

BRAIN-STORMING.   In brainstorming, students form groups and rapidly exchange ideas and possible solutions to problems. Brainstorming allows individual students to share knowledge with each other, thereby expanding the information base of the entire group. Ideas and creativity are sparked by the interplay of energy and facts offered by group members.

GAMING/SIMULATION.   In gaming and simulation, students create models of actual situations or problems and learn from the experience of model situations. As an example of simulation in a social studies class, students could set up a simulated lobby group and attempt to apply pressure on hypothetical legislators (also class members). Through simulation, students often uncover the fallacies in theories and can then determine better solutions through logic and thought.

RESOURCE CENTERS.   The resource center can be either one area of a classroom or a separate room in the school in which a student can find reference materials, equipment, and other learning aids to assist in understanding of various subjects. Resource centers can be staffed by a resource specialist, or they can be completely independent spaces used solely by students.

GUIDED DISCOVERY.   Guided discovery is a technique in which a teacher presents a particular subject for exploration. Students then are guided by the teacher and by classroom materials to investigate the subject. Books, dialogue, and lectures can be included in the discovery, as can outside research. Students may work on separate subjects (projects) or can work together in obtaining information and understanding.

PROGRAMMED LEARNING.   Programmed learning is a technique in which a student follows a planned, well-structured resource guide or workbook to obtain knowledge about a particular subject. The programmed learning book usually

Profile

William H. Kilpatrick, 1871–1965

W. H. Kilpatrick was a progressivist and one of John Dewey's most avid and successful disciples. His contributions to curriculum development included the "Project Method" to implement Dewey's child-centered philosophy.

A native of Georgia, Kilpatrick attended graduate school at Columbia University. Although he had intended to return to Georgia, he began teaching at Columbia as a graduate student and remained there most of his life.

He felt that strong curriculum, in addition to helping the child develop skills necessary to be responsive to a changing environment, must meet the needs of the total child. He emphasized the social aspects so strongly because he realized society itself was changing rapidly; the structure of the family was changing, as was the American way of life. Traditional concentration on the simple transfer of factual information was no longer adequate. He believed the democratic ethic was in danger of losing potency through the maintenance of antiquated educational tradition, and he feared the possibility of vested interests controlling the majority "good." A problem-solving methodology that stressed learning *how* to think rather than *what* to think would guard against this.

Kilpatrick believed this could be implemented through the activity approach of an integrated curriculum which emphasized the importance of the individual learner. He parted ways with Dewey in emphasizing that the purposes and plans of education are those of the learners, not the teachers.

Kilpatrick's greatest impact came from his mastery of the art of teaching. During his years at Columbia, he taught some 35,000 students. Today his influence is seen in the inquiry method of teaching, which emphasizes social interaction, role-playing, and concrete, experiential learning. His advice that schools should integrate character development with the teaching of concepts and skills is certainly applicable to today's education.

includes much repetition of materials as well as self-testing devices. The student decides when to move on to advanced material; if the student does not "pass" the self-tests, he or she returns to the beginning of a section or turns to a special section of the workbook for review. Students move at their own speed and with the amount of drill and explanation that they need.

TECHNOLOGY: A TOOL OF CURRICULUM

In this section, we briefly discuss some of the more common technologies in use in classrooms today.

Types of Educational Technologies

ITV. Instructional television (ITV) is closed-circuit television which brings lectures, demonstrations, and programs into the classroom. Individual school systems can create their own programs or purchase programs from various foundations and video companies. Television instruction offers the possibility of providing students with knowledge from a specialist or expert in the field, or with providing all students from a particular school system with the same type of information. Interactive television is growing rapidly. In this arrangement, those receiving transmission have the opportunity, visually and orally, to interact with those sending it. It is also increasingly common for high schools to work with cable systems in making their own television productions.

ETV. Educational television consists simply of those programs of an educational nature shown on the commercial networks or on the Public Broadcasting System. Frequently, educational television programs are funded by the federal government or by foundations. The subject matter varies in quality and value—as do all learning materials. ETV also allows students to keep up with important current events. It is definitely instant communication.

VIDEO TAPE RECORDERS. Video recorders have greatly aided the feasibility of classroom use of ETV. Teachers may tape a program at one time and play it back to the students at another. Further, teachers may create their own video programs in class using small video recorders. Another use for this equipment is that of taping students themselves. For example, students in a dance or gym class may be recorded and the tape may then be shown to them to assist them in perfecting their skills; or students may be taped giving oral presentations or while reading so that they may analyze and correct their own problems by observing their strengths and weaknesses.

Microcomputers

The microcomputer has rapidly become a familiar tool to people in all walks of life and certainly to college students like yourselves. It is also becoming an increasingly common instructional tool in elementary and secondary classrooms. Many youngsters come to the classroom with considerable experience and skill in using this technology, largely because of their involvement in their home with the computer.

Because of its interactive nature, the microcomputer is an excellent learning and teaching resource. Computers are becoming more and more affordable. Also, the increasing amount of software programs in different subject areas is adding to the likelihood that, as a teacher, you will be applying this technology in a variety of ways and to different age and grade levels.

Fundamental principles in teaching include: acquiring active student involvement, achieving individual attention, and providing continuing and accurate feedback about performance. The microcomputer is able to maximize these principles. It is also able to accommodate diverse instructional goals

Points of View

Is There a Message in the Media?

What Message?

All television is educational television. The question is: *What is it teaching?*

Nicholas Johnson, former director, Federal Communication Commission (FCC).

Teachers versus TV

The classroom teacher is in stiff competition with one of the most common items of furniture in the American home—the television set. . . . From that first day of school, there is never a day when a pupil will not spend more time in front of a television set than in a classroom.

George Comstock in "The Second Teacher: Recent Reseach on Television," *Phi Delta Kappan*, (March 1979).

TV and the Teacher

Using video involves children in ways few other materials can: students respond naturally to a medium they have grown up with all their lives, shared with their friends, and are natural "authorities" on. . . . Teachers who are concerned about being replaced by television need more than ever to operate it, produce programs, direct student projects, and teach the new communications.

Don Kaplan in "Television: The Mediums Inside The Medium," *Phi Delta Kappan* (March 1979).

including: the acquisition of information, drill and practice, dialogue in a tutorial or mentorial situation, and the simulation of a variety of experiences not otherwise possible in the classroom.

The computer can store vast amounts of information and retrieve such information in a rapid fashion. Thus, as more and better software is developed, students can access all sorts of desired information in a very efficient fashion. The quality of this information is dependent upon the ability of those in the educational enterprise—especially teachers—to assist in adapting this subject matter or software into a structure and a form which embraces learning by students at different ages and levels of ability.

When employed in an information-accessing manner, the computer can be of additional assistance to teachers as well. For example, several curriculum programs rely heavily on a continuing diagnostic-prescriptive approach and demand an efficient means of storing and retrieving information on students' progress. Computers can also store information on student backgrounds, interests, aptitudes and specific needs to assist teachers in accommodating the range of individual differences found in classrooms.

Drill and practice, while in many respects a lower-order form of learning, nonetheless, is critical. The acquisition of basic concepts and skills are often requisite to more complex ones. Many learnings represent a hierarchical or development ordering of skills and concepts. The advantages of the computer are that it can relieve you, as the teacher, of monitoring and correcting more routine assignments of this nature and allow you to interact with other students in more diverse and demanding ways. The computer allows the student to proceed as rapidly or slowly as able, provides immediate feedback, and keeps an ongoing accurate record of each student's progress.

More complex forms of dialogue can, of course, occur with the computer. Major inroads are being made into the science of artificial intelligence, which, in turn, allows the computer to interact in more complex and logically consistent ways with the user. The computer takes on more of a monitoring function, probing and challenging the student and allowing for more divergent and inductive modes of learning.

Finally, the computer can simulate a number of complex situations. These simulations often involve a game-type format. For example, in the Sumerian game, the student assumes the role of the ruler of an ancient city and is faced with a number of options in terms of how to protect, support, and govern this municipality. In the Sierra Leone game, students are placed in the role of key persons in the U.S. Agency for International Development, and they must make difficult choices about how best to allocate funds for resolving the problems of a developing nation. There are many other simulations which allow students to gain practice in decision making, problem solving, and testing hypotheses in complex and abstract situations. There is also an interpersonal dimension to many simulations which call for group problem solving or some form of collaboration.

Instructional technology is the combination of nonhuman resources employed in a systematic way in the design, implementation, and evaluation of instruction. Microcomputer technology is still relatively new (in the classroom), and there is much to be learned about how it can be used most effectively in teaching and learning situations. As we have tried to illustrate here, microcomputers can be used in a variety of ways to achieve different goals. Computers can be the medium of delivery or the topic of discussion.

In summary, the teacher can use the computer to assist instruction through drill and practice, tutorials, simulations, instructional games, problem solving, and word processing. The computer can also manage class records, keep students' progress records, route students through appropriate curriculum, store communications, test, diagnose, keep inventories, and so on. You will be in a position to contribute further to the already growing body of knowledge of how to effectively use the microcomputer in the classroom.

Training Teachers in Technology*

Computers and other advanced technologies can spur major improvements in education, but "educational technologies are not self-implementing, and they do not replace the teacher," says the Congressional Office of Technology Assessment (OTA).

A major part of the drive to improve education in the United States focuses on raising professional teaching standards. Technology "could be an important lever for change," according to OTA. Unlike their pupils, most of today's teachers did not grow up in a computerized society, so the success of educational technologies may depend to a great extent on teachers' ability to adapt to advanced classroom technologies, including videocassette recorders, cable and satellite transmission, electronic telecommunications, and—especially—computers.

Yet, only about a third of U.S. teachers have had even 10 hours of computer training, most of which is devoted to learning *about* computers rather than how to teach with them, says OTA in a new report, *Power On! New Tools for Teaching and Learning.* "Despite a nationwide call to improve teaching, there is almost no federal money for the training of new teachers," the report points out.

Some states have already taken steps to develop the technological capabilities of teachers. The state of New Hampshire provided $2.5 million for the purchase of computers for teachers' personal use, whether at school or at home or both. Nearly 2,000 teachers have received a computer and completed initial training. Of these, 130 teachers received two weeks of advanced computer training during the summer of 1988 and will train other teachers in their home districts, forming an active resource network.

New York has established Teacher Resource and Computer Training Centers, which are organized and operated by and for teachers across the state. Much of the focus is on technology and on how computers, videodiscs, and other technologies can be used effectively in the classroom. Through the use of satellite broadcasts, information services and databases, and electronic networks and bulletin boards, teachers share ideas and support each other in developing materials, collaborating on research, and helping less-experienced teachers gain technological confidence.

Congress could support these efforts and others, OTA suggests. For instance, funding for "Star Schools" programs—the use of satellite and other technologies for long-distance education—could be broadened to include teacher training.

Other steps that Congress might take to enhance technology training for teachers include:

- Provide grants and low-interest (or forgivable) loans for students entering teacher-training programs.

- Expand support for training activities to include in-service teacher training in technology.
- Provide funds to schools of education to purchase more-current equipment on which to train teachers.
- Provide grants for workshops and courses to upgrade the technology skills of education-school faculty.

*From Office of Technology Assessment, *Power On! New Tools for Teaching and Learning* (Washington, D.C.: U.S. Government Printing Office).

SUMMARY

The purposes of education are closely related to the development of a curriculum. There is more involved in teaching than just presenting information to youngsters. Many theorists have ideas about how to achieve successful learning environments, how to enhance motivation, and how to deal with individual students' needs. Among the important theorists in these areas are Jerome Bruner, David Ausubel, Jerome Kagan, Jean Piaget, and Abraham Maslow. Traditional curriculum patterns usually involve single-teacher/single-subject/single-classroom organization; but many variations of organization exist. For example, curriculum may be fused, integrated, or single-subject. Classrooms may or may not be organized by age, may be graded or ungraded, and may be tracked or grouped at random. Team teaching is common in some school systems. Many patterns of instruction exist. They are all expansions of the three basic teaching models: didactic (fact-oriented); problem-solving (inquiry/discovery); and interpersonal. There are many technologies available to teachers now. These technologies, including television and computers, can enhance any of the basic teaching models.

ACTIVITIES

1. How would you create an environment suitable for inquiry teaching? Describe the learning setting and how you would encourage students to pursue discovery.
2. Many people say that when it comes right down to it, the curriculum does not affect the student as much as the teacher who teaches it. Discuss whether you agree or disagree.
3. How might you employ the use of a microcomputer in your classroom?

4. Make a list of what you consider to be the necessary characteristics of a successful learning environment.

5. Discuss the three models of instruction (problem solving or inquiry, didactic, and interpersonal). Which approach do you prefer and why?

6. Form a discussion group and explore the following types of organization patterns: (a) multiage classrooms; (b) tracking; (c) nongraded schooling; (d) modular/flexible scheduling.

7. Among your classmates, see how many different types of instruction you can identify, such as lecture, brainstorming, or role-playing.

SUGGESTED READINGS

BRUNER, JEROME, *The Process of Education.* Cambridge, Mass.: Harvard University Press, 1960.

CHENEY, LYNNE V., *American Memory: A Report on the Humanities in the Nation's Public Schools.* Washington, D.C.: National Endowment for the Humanities, 1987.

COOPER, JAMES M., *Developing Skills for Instructional Supervision.* New York: Longman, 1984.

ELLIS, A. K., J. A. MACKEY, AND A. D. GLENN, *The School Curriculum.* Boston: Allyn & Bacon, 1988.

GREENE, MAXINE, *Teacher As Stranger.* Belmont, Calif.: Wadsworth, 1973.

JOHNSON, D. W., AND R. T. JOHNSON, *Cooperation and Competition: Theory and Research.* Edina, Minn.: Interaction Book, 1989.

JOYCE, BRUCE, AND MARSHA WEIL, *Models of Teaching.* Englewood Cliffs, N. J.: Prentice-Hall, 1986.

LEMLECH, J. L., *Curriculum and Instructional Methods for the Elementary School.* New York: Macmillan, 1984.

MASLOW, ABRAHAM, *Motivation and Personality* (2nd ed.). New York: Harper & Row, 1970.

RUCHLIS, HYMAN, AND BELLE SHAREFKIN, *Reality-Centered Learning.* New York: Citation Press, 1973.

RYAN, FRANK L., AND ARTHUR K. ELLIS, *Instructional Implications of Inquiry.* Englewood Cliffs, N.J.: Prentice-Hall, 1974.

UNRUH, G. G., AND A. UNRUH, *Curriculum Development: Problems, Processes, and Programs.* Berkeley, Calif.: McCutcheon, 1984.

WILES, JONN, AND JOSEPH BONDI, *Curriculum Development: A Guide to Practice.* Columbus, Ohio: Merrill, 1989.

Chapter 16

FUTURE DIRECTIONS

We live in an age in which change is the one thing we can take for granted. It is all around us. The tape player you bought last year has been replaced on the market shelves with a newer, more compact model. The pasture you used to drive by has been subdivided, and workers are busy building apartment houses where cows were grazing a few short months ago. The research in the area of brain function renders much of the psychology taught a few years ago obsolete. And so on.

What will schools be like in the twenty-first century? What methods of teaching will be used? How will children learn? Will technology change the very meaning of school? What will we expect of teachers in the future? How much formal training will they need? How will teacher training differ qualitatively from the teacher training of today? There is no end to the questions we could ask about the role of education and educators in the future.

The great scientist, Niels Bohr, once wrote that "prediction is very difficult, especially about the future." Bohr's tongue-in-cheek observation is quite aptly applied to the field of education. As we reach the final years of this century the pace of change in our society is dizzying. It has been observed that if the amount of printed knowledge were placed in a frame of reference we could all understand, it might look something like this: from the dawn of history to the year 1850 (Abraham Lincoln's time), we could say the amount of printed knowledge was about one inch deep; from 1850 to 1950, the amount of printed knowledge doubled, giving us two inches; using our same yardstick, from 1950 to 1990, the amount of printed knowledge increased in depth to about 36 inches! Given the exponential nature of the expansion of new knowledge, imagine what the future holds!

Of course the picture is more complicated than the sheer quantitative explosion of knowledge. The nature of knowledge itself is changing. Old "facts" are swept aside. Old truths are called into question. What seemed so certain yesterday seems less so today, and who knows about tomorrow?

A reasonably useful guide to the future has always been the past, but because of the acceleration of the rate of change, the past is not quite so accurate a barometer as it used to be. Nevertheless, it gives us a place to start. With regard to the schools and classrooms of the future, we can be assured that technology, particularly in the area of microcomputers, will increase its already rapidly expanding influence. The use of databases in history, science, and humanities classes is already rather widespread and will continue to expand. The use of calculators and computers will continue to change our definition of what is basic in mathematics. School libraries will increasingly use on-line networking to expand the amount of information available to students and faculty members.

We can expect a future where schools will have access to up-links and down-links in satellite telemetry, making it possible for a class of students in, say, Missouri, to work directly with a class of students in Australia. Textbooks will, in many cases, be accompanied by discs filled with possibilities for extending learning beyond the bounds of bookcovers. The Encyclopedia Britannica and others are already on disc, and this trend will continue.

On the other hand, researcher John Goodlad has pointed out that, in many ways, very little has changed in classrooms since the turn of the twentieth century. We still have, predictably, one teacher up in front of thirty students trying to motivate, discipline, and teach them. So, while change will continue its upward spiral, much will no doubt remain the same. Human emotions and basic needs seem to change very little. Perhaps in the schools of the future, teachers will be freed from much of the routine and will be able to spend more time truly interacting with students.

THE STATE OF THE PROFESSION

What does the future hold in store? Some people directly challenge the belief in a future that will yield a better world in general and a more ideal approach to schooling in particular. Others chide us for heeding pervasive prophecies of doom and suggest unlimited potential for improvement and major advances in education. Certainly, we have no special crystal ball nor privileged power to see accurately into the future. We wish to paint neither an unrealistically rosy picture nor an unnecessarily harsh one of what is ahead. Teaching, as is the situation in many vocations, has its fair share of both problems and rewards. Major adjustments in the teaching role are generally unlikely in the near future. Thus, we believe that we can offer you some assistance in considering various aspects of your future career.

We should all be concerned about the future because we will have to spend the rest of our lives there.

Charles Kettering

In this chapter, we will first look backward briefly to ascertain what recent changes have occurred in schools that affect teachers; then, we will project what may be on the horizon.

Since changing social conditions will also determine the future of schools, we will briefly explore alternative future global scenarios. We ask you to think about what is likely to occur in the future, and what the implications will be for the classroom teacher. We have chosen this approach to underscore that we need both to anticipate and to *influence* the future to the greatest extent possible.

Future Possibilities in Teaching

In summary, then, we interpret the data to suggest that there will be continued, but gradual, improvements in working conditions for teachers. There is likely to be further intervention through funded programs, especially at the federal level, to ensure a more pluralistic professional work force. The number of women and members of minorities will be better represented on administrative and teaching levels. Finally, there will be only limited efforts at more radical experimentation with the process of schooling (at least until more fundamental populist priorities such as increased literacy and improved career opportunity are better achieved for more students).

What changes lie ahead for the children you teach whose careers will span the first half of the twenty-first century? One answer to that question is, of course, that no one knows. But there are perhaps more people than you realize who are trying to formulate answers. A fascinating source of ideas about changes in the coming decades is in the

Omni Future Almanac. It is available from:
Robert Weil, Editor
Omni Future Almanac
World Almanac Publications,
200 Park Avenue
New York, New York 10166

Here are some events the writers of the *Omni Future Almanac* believe may occur in the decades to come:

1990s

- A NASA-manned spacecraft will travel to the planet Mars. Curiously, this will occur right around the 100th anniversary of the invention of the airplane.
- For the first time in human history, more than half the world's population will live in cities.

2000–2010

- More than 1,000 people will live and work on the moon, a slight majority of them female. Meanwhile, 600 million people on earth will live in the worst poverty imaginable. The earth's population will be six billion.
- The following animals will probably be extinct: California condor, giant panda, gray whale, Central African mountain gorilla, Indus dolphin.
- A 6,000-mile-per-hour subway could connect New York to Los Angeles. (This means about a 30 minute ride between the cities for those of you in a hurry.)

2010–2020

- Life expectancy for Americans will surpass eighty years. Americans born in this decade may live 120 years, the span that the *Bible* mentions as the ideal length for human life.

- Terraforming, the changing of an alien environment to support human life, may begin in this decade with a temporary colony on the planet Mars or Venus.

2020–2030

- Tests continue on long-range propulsion systems that attain velocities just below light-speed. (That's right; 186,000 miles per second.)
- By 2025, a satellite power system could provide most of North America's electricity.

2030–2040

- New tools such as deep-ground mapping machines unlock the mysteries of the past and help settle arguments about Atlantis and other sunken civilizations.
- Time begins to run out on the water supply of the western United States, possibly reducing the output of American farmers.

2040–2050

- Skyhooks—elevators run on cables connecting satellites with various space bodies—may be constructed for Earth's moon, Jupiter's Ganymede, and Saturn's moon Titan.
- A method for sustaining human brains outside the body is perfected.
- The human population of outer space exceeds 7,500 people.

Teachers on the Future of Teaching

Another way to project what the future might hold in store is to ascertain what changes experienced teachers have observed and to examine what these imply for the future. The data just examined focused primarily on the teacher's working conditions, including the number of students a teacher is assigned. Certainly the type of student one works with is a factor equally as important as the number of students. For example, would a teacher plan differently for a class composed of twenty boys and ten girls than for the reverse? Certainly, critical periods of a child's development warrant special consideration, as in the case of a group of pre-adolescent twelve-year-olds, a group of nine- and ten-year-olds moving out of a pattern of thinking which has been limited primarily to concrete rather than abstract concepts. Adjustments would have to be made for a teaching position with multiage or bi- or multiethnic populations as opposed to single-age or single-culture groups.

Education for the Class of 2000*

America's school system today is clearly overburdened, even by the traditional demands placed on it. How can the school system be strengthened to bring high-quality education to all members of the class of 2000? And what can be done about the growing demand for adult education in the years to come? Over half a dozen measures come to mind, most of them embarrassingly simple:

- Lengthen the school day and year. In any field, you can get more work done in eight hours than in six, in 10 days than in seven. Japan's school year consists of 240 eight-hour days. America's averages 180 days of about 6.5 hours. So let's split the difference: Give us 210 seven-hour school days a year.
- Cut the median class size down from 17.8 to 10 students. Naturally, this means hiring more teachers. This will give teachers more time to focus on the *average* student.

  Not too long ago, schools were just beginning to recognize the needs of special students with learning disabilities or exceptional talents. Now there are programs for the learning disabled and the gifted and talented, as there should be. But, in focusing attention and resources on the needs of the minority at the extremes, the nation's schools have neglected the needs of the majority in the middle. American students' dismal performance on standardized tests attests to this.

  Inadequate attention at school is exacerbated by inadequate attention at home for the average student. The big advantage that schools like Mantua enjoy over less-successful institutions is not their specialized programs, but the fact that their students are drawn largely from traditional families where parents are available and are actively interested in the child's education. Where one-parent homes are the rule, teachers must provide the individual attention that parents cannot. In crowded classrooms, they simply can't do it. The answer is to cut class size.
- Computerize. Computer-aided learning programs are already replacing drill books; as software improves, they will begin to replace some kinds of textbooks as well. More teachers should be actively involved in writing the software. The best computerized learning programs already include primitive forms of artificial intelligence that can diagnose the student's learning problems and tailor instruction to compensate for them. "We can put 30 computers in a room, and they will go as fast or as slow as each child needs; the child controls it," observes Representative James Scheuer (Democrat, New York). "He has an equal and comfortable relationship, building his morale and self-esteem, which can only enhance the learning process." The result may not be as good as having

highly skilled, caring teachers give hours of personal attention to each student, but computerization is a lot easier to achieve, and it's a big improvement over today's situation. This should be an easy notion to sell to taxpayers; in a survey of parents of Mantua kindergartners, fully two-thirds cited computers as one of the most important topics their children should learn in school.

But making this transition won't be cheap. By 1990, the United States will already have spent $1 billion on computerized learning, but two-thirds of that will have been spent by affluent parents for their own children. If public school systems fail to develop their own programs, the less-affluent students could suffer an irreparable educational disadvantage.

- Tailor courses to the needs of individual students. Individualized education programs (IEPs) are already used in many schools; they suggest which skills the student should practice and recommend ways of testing to make sure they have been learned. But far more is possible.

In the future, IEPs will look at the students' learning style: whether they learn best in small groups or large classes; whether they learn best from reading, lectures, or computer programs; how much supervision they need; and so on. Teachers will be evaluated in the same way and assigned to large or small classes, good readers or good listeners, as best suits them. These programs may not be adopted in time to help the class of 2000, but the sooner the better.

- Promote students based on performance, not on time served in class. Students starting school in 2000 will move up not by conventional grade levels, but by development levels, ensuring that each child can work on each topic until it's mastered.

- Recruit teachers from business and industry, not just university educational programs. Get chemists to teach chemistry, accountants to teach arithmetic, and so on. These specialists could become teachers in areas where teachers are scarce. Give them the required courses in education necessary to meet teaching standards. But start by making sure that would-be teachers actually know something worth teaching.

- Set new priorities for school systems that today are overregulated and underaccountable. In many communities, the curriculum is so standardized that teachers in any given course on any given day will be covering the same material. It's time to cut through that kind of red tape and give teachers the right to do the job they supposedly were trained for. Then make teachers and their supervisors responsible for the performance of their students. Teachers who turn out well-educated students should be paid and promoted accordingly. If students don't advance, neither should their would-be educators.

- Bring business and industry into the public school system. Corporations must train and retrain workers constantly, and that requirement will grow ever more pressing. The obvious answer is for them to contract with schools to do the teaching. The money earned from such services can go toward teachers' salaries and investments in computers, software, and such things as air conditioning needed to keep schools open all year.

For students not headed toward college, businesses may also provide internships that give high-school students practical experience in the working world they are about to enter. When public schools turn out graduates who haven't mastered reading, writing, or math, business suffers.

- Finally, if Americans really want quality education, they must be willing to pay for it. Since the National Commission on Excellence in Education published its landmark report, *A Nation at Risk,* in 1983, the Reagan administration has never asked for a significant increase in federal aid to education. In fact, since 1984, the White House has attempted to cut the national education budget by more than $10 billion. Though Congress has always restored most of those proposed cuts, the federal government is actually spending, after inflation, about 14 percent less for education than it did five years ago.

Teachers are still dramatically underpaid compared with other professions that require a college education. In 1987, the average starting salary for an accountant was $21,200, new computer specialists received $26,170, and engineers began at $28,500. The average starting salary for teachers was only $17,500.

Today's education system cannot begin to prepare students for the world they will enter on graduation from high school. By 2030, when the class of 2000 will still be working, they will have had to assimilate more inventions and more new information than have appeared in the last 150 years. By 2010, there will be hardly a job in the country that does not require skill in using powerful computers and telecommunications systems.

America needs to enact all the reforms outlined above, and many others as well. It is up to concerned citizens, parents, and teachers to equip our children with the knowledge and skills necessary to survive and thrive in the twenty-first century. In this election year, education should be a major political issue, for time is running out: The class of 2000 is already with us.

*Excerpted from Marvin Cetron, "Class of 2000," *Futurist.* Nov. 88, pp. 9–15. Used with permission.

It is also apparent that children and adolescents in general may change somewhat in terms of interests, needs, and behavior as the times change. For example, what were elementary-aged children like ten years ago? What were adolescents like in the 1960s? We are concerned less with the extent to which they differ from or resemble those of today, as with the need to understand how the teacher's behavior may have to be altered to accommodate differences in children over time, to realize that future events can and probably will influence future students in several ways. Let us compare these reflections on whether students have changed with the views of teachers we talked with recently.

Peter L. teaches at a suburban junior high school in the Southeast:

> I have finished my ninth year of teaching, and I have seen a remarkable change in their attention span, activity levels, family backgrounds, and respect for others. Children seem to be very much a part of the mobile society. They have moved several times. They have had many more experiences outside their home life than previously. They have traveled a lot. They are more concerned about material things. Yet their greatest need seems to be attention from peers, teachers, and parents.
>
> They have changed greatly from kids five to ten years ago; today these kids *want* to be heard. They seem to need more animated-action, such as filmstrips and film for learning concepts—more so than kids of the early '70s.
>
> Kids from the '50s when I was a child, respected authority a lot more than now. Kids from the '50s seemed to have fun with other friends in their own homes. Today, they need to "get away" to have fun. Kids from the '50s seemed to listen to their parents and teachers better, and parents backed up the teachers. Today, parents seem to protect their children more from any heartaches or disputes. I think they are overprotected.

Adele K. is a high school science teacher at a large urban school:

> Kids are definitely different—they are so much more aware of the adult world and there are also greater differences among children (socially and academically), mostly because of home influences.
>
> Many know a great deal more. Some don't have the respect for authority that students did when I grew up. Yet, it's hard to believe some of them can survive at all in the family situations they come from.
>
> I think students are smarter than when I began teaching seven years ago. They are becoming more knowledgeable every year. They ask better questions every year and this is making teaching more challenging and, I might add more enjoyable.
>
> I feel kids today are more open, and that change doesn't seem to bother them as much. They appear to be less fearful and more sophisticated. However, I feel that they really need structure, discipline, and to be given *responsibility* with *high expectations* and standards. One of the major differences between kids today and of the '50s when I was a kid is that today's kids need to be *entertained* whereas I feel we were much better at entertaining ourselves.
>
> Also, kids today are materialistic, aware, in a hurry to mature, and the degree of sophistication, age for age, has increased. I think the greatest need is in the area of parenting. The parents are not fulfilling their responsibilities to their children. They are not holding their youngsters accountable for learning.

Herb R. teaches elementary school in a suburban school in a medium-sized city:

> I don't feel kids have changed that noticeably over the last five to ten years, but they have changed since the kids of the '50s. I feel this is due to society which has changed greatly over the years, especially in the family structure and unit.
>
> Children tend to be more active than reflective. I'm not saying that they can't be reflective or that they can't be led to be more reflective. I would say that they

experience a great confusion: at times consciously and at other times subconsciously. Perhaps they are not spending time reflecting. There is some confusion in regard to values, particularly moral issues, and that is because of the confusion in society as a whole and in the family, in the church.

What are their strengths? Intelligence, their leadership potential, which is a direct outflow of their intelligence.

Their need is to see the responsibility they have for their own learning and others. The great need is to develop self-direction.

Doris S. teaches junior high school and serves as an advisor to students in a school in the Midwest:

> I feel that the children haven't changed as much as the schools. We now have busing instead of walking, and less-than-aesthetic lunches at school instead of lunch at home. The curriculum has accelerated with more subjects to be taught in less time. This puts more pressure on both the teachers and children. The increased hyperactivity of the children is related to the noisy, crowded day.
>
> Many children today have a great deal of inconsistency in their lives—I think they need more consistency. I think the children today also have less self-respect.

Teachers are also concerned with certain pressures society has placed on educators. Demands of the public place heavy burdens on teachers. Carlos R. teaches history at a high school in Arizona:

> There is too much emphasis on basic curriculum materials. More integration needs to be made with the aesthetic, performing arts, and current social problems.
>
> There are problems in class size. Over twenty-five or thirty students makes it close to impossible to deal with individualization well. The minutes divided by kids just don't work out. However, the teacher can frequently meet individual needs just as effectively in small groups, with the added benefit of the children learning to adjust and to function in group situations.

Maynard W. teaches elementary school in Missouri:

> I feel no long-term pressures but there are occasional, short-term administrative pressures. I also sometimes feel *competitive* pressures from my colleagues. I think that accountability in connection with standardized achievement tests is becoming much more of a pressure.
>
> There is not enough time to do everything the way you want to do it. Also, there are financial pressures; the pay is not enough for a teacher. Many teachers I know work at two jobs, or their spouse works. I'm only teaching because I like it, certainly not for the money.

Dorothy A. teaches junior high school in Oregon.

> There is simply too much paperwork! I have less and less time to spend on students because of more and more time needed for paperwork. There are too many students to adequately individualize learning. Not enough money is being spent on educating students. Too much money is spent on assessment and evaluation and not enough on rewarding effective teachers.

Certainly not all teachers feel all these pressures and certainly not at all times. Many teachers believe that while working conditions are not ideal, there are probably few if any jobs where they are. It should also be emphasized that as the NEA data illustrates, teaching conditions have generally improved over the years. And teaching, like many very challenging jobs, can also be very rewarding.

Our intent here was to provide classroom teachers' perceptions of present conditions. When we consider this information along with the demographic data examined earlier, we are able to conjecture somewhat further about the future. It is obvious there are considerable demands to teaching. To do an effective job as a teacher does take time; it is not—or at least should not be—an eight-to-four job. On the other hand, there are signs that more collaborative and less competitive teaching arrangements will evolve and, through these more cooperative staffing arrangements, more time for planning and better division of labor can be achieved as well.

Teachers are also concerned about the overcrowded curriculum; this is symptomatic of a complex problem in our society and, with the rapid growth of information, not likely to be resolved easily. Different curricular problems present themselves in different situations. Illustrative of this are the responses which we got when we asked teachers about the adequacy of present curriculum. Some responded that the curriculum is more than adequate. Others made statements similar to this: "We live in an integrated society. Too much of the curriculum is fractionalized. The curriculum should try to be more futuristic. Students need to be involved more than they are now." Still other teachers considered literacy to be a fundamental problem. Others were concerned that curriculum trends are becoming too factual and not conceptual enough.

One person's problem is another person's pleasure. These varied perceptions about the adequacy of the curriculum point out how crucial the teacher's role is in many curriculum decisions, as well as how diverse conditions may be from one place to the next. In order to make needed curricular adjustments from time to time, the individual teacher must fill many roles. As a scholar, the teacher must look into the suggestions of research and the experience of others concerning what should be done. As a clinician, the teacher must investigate how changing conditions dictate what learners need. As a politician, the teacher must examine ways of working with others whose vested interests may disagree with sound educational principles. Whatever the future holds in store, the teacher will have to make continuing adjustments in the curriculum to meet constantly changing demands.

Teachers on Parents and Families

In Chapter 14 we noted that parental expectations exert one of the most pervasive influences on the teacher. We asked teachers these specific questions about changing parental expectations: What do you believe parents and the community expect from you? How is this changing? How do these expectations affect your role? The responses of several teachers follow.

Ralph V. teaches English at a high school in California:

I feel that parents are expecting more from the schools but are giving the school less support. I think we are expected to take over many of the family's jobs—especially that of the daily talking with individual children. Why do I think this is happening? I think parents are more insecure. They tend to think that everything will happen and you don't really need to work at it. My role is affected because I feel we as teachers try to provide too much as a result of parental pressure. The problem with that is you don't do a good job at any of it.

Parents expect me to effectively deal with their child in the classroom, socially, emotionally, and educationally. I see parents' expectations of me increasing. I believe there is a generally increasing reliance on institutions to assume responsibilities formerly considered parental or familial. I see this as tending to increase the scope of my role within an institution that is either unwilling or unable to provide the necessary resources to do this adequately.

Karen B. is an elementary school teacher in Iowa:

Today, parents and community expect accountability—in all areas of education. Test scores have more meaning now. Parents ask how they can help their child at home and reinforce skills. Parents expect teachers to move their children vertically up the academic ladder, rather than giving them a broad range of experiences. They seem more concerned about a narrow difinition of "success" rather than the attitudes and skills needed for a well-rounded individual.

Carla M. teaches third grade at a parochial school in Pennsylvania:

Today I think parents and community expect teachers to "produce" well-rounded kids that are able to meet standard requirements. They are especially concerned that their kids succeed in standardized tests. They want teachers to stress the basics. The idea of accountability now is an important factor. With this comes more recordkeeping and planning on my part.

Besides the basics, parents also expect me to provide opportunities to explore and discover. Parents also expect the teacher to be unbiased—nonsexist, nonracist. Parents want to know exactly how their child is progressing and as I teach I keep these expectations in mind.

Rita T. teaches eighth grade at a school in a large Eastern city:

I believe that many parents have given us much of their responsibility. I don't feel that most parents know that much about schools, and therefore, their expectations are unrealistic. They only get involved if problems occur or if their child is failing a class. I think they expect the school to educate their child and not to have any problems in the process. That's simply not realistic.

Adam B. teaches in a midwest suburban middle school:

I have taught for longer than I want to admit, and I think I appreciate parents more than ever today. They're more intelligent and informed, and I think quite sensitive to the difficulties of teaching and raising youngsters with care and intelligence. We've certainly come a long way since the era of "if he gets out of line, belt him one," which existed when I first started. Parents expect a lot, but they are really supportive of the teacher who puts some effort into teaching.

While these are only the selected opinions of a few teachers, surveys indicate that a great many teachers feel the same pressures described in these excerpts. We concur with these teachers' perceptions that the schools and teachers are being asked to do more than ever. The concern for the child to achieve the basics, and to achieve them well and quickly, in many cases—is explicit and pervasive. While many challenge the appropriateness of the role of the school in some of the more personal, emotional, social, and moral aspects of a child's education, conditions in many homes suggest that parents are unable (for whatever reasons) to adequately provide for what is, in many respects, their primary responsibility. Thus, we have a dilemma. In some ways this dilemma is long standing, but in many ways it is attenuated today. What is an *appropriate* and *feasible* role for schools?

What of the future? Will the concept of the nuclear family as we historically know it continue to break down, or do conditions suggest this concept will be reaffirmed? Will new and emerging concepts of familial structure become more prevalent? Will various communal arrangements be established that might share not only their material resources but the responsibility for the education and socialization of children as well? Whatever the family concept of the future, the relationship between home and school will be a critical one. While it appears that concept of the family itself as well as of that of the appropriate home-school relationship is not altogether clear, the teacher can be reassured that his or her role in the future will be directly affected by these. Therefore, the continuing study of the family as a logical partner in education, and of alternative modes of communication and cooperation with the home and community, are essential to the teacher's work and training.

THE STATE OF THE WORLD: EFFECTS ON TEACHING

We have examined some recent changes in schools and school-home relations in terms of what these suggest for the future. But what of the changes in global or societal conditions, which are more difficult to predict?

This time, like all times, is a very good one, if we but know what to do with it.

Ralph Waldo Emerson

As the human race expands at a rate of 200,000 people per day, or 73 million people per year, several vital questions emerge:

- Where will we get our food, and how can it be fairly distributed?
- How can we get enough energy for everyone, and how can it be equitably shared?
- How can we reduce the poisons in the atmosphere?

- Can we have a proper balance between the number of people and the resources they need for life?
- How can we live together, with civility and in peace?

In spite of the critical importance of these questions, most citizens and most teachers do not examine them from a global perspective. For example, surveys taken at the beginning of the major oil shortage crises of the late 1970s showed that only 52 percent of the public knew that the United States must import oil to satisfy its energy demands. In another area—foreign languages—studies showed that fewer than 2 percent of all high school graduates had studied any foreign language. Further, fewer than 5 percent of the teachers trained today have studied international or comparative education, or have taken any other intercultural courses in their work for certification. Nevertheless, despite the fact that many Americans ignore the global situation, the fact remains that issues in the global society affect each of us. And what happens in the world enters the realm of the classroom as well.

What does the future hold for us—for society in general and for the school? Here are some general alternative beliefs about the future:

1. Global conditions will rapidly and drastically worsen.
2. Global conditions will slowly degenerate.
3. Global conditions will remain the same.
4. Global conditions will improve gradually.
5. Global conditions will rapidly and dramatically improve.

Let us explore examples of future possibilities. We have arbitrarily selected the issue of available resources to help you think briefly about the future. Applying each of the above possibilities to the natural resources situation, we end up with five different future scenarios:

1. Obvious shortages of resources will lead to global conflict by the end of the century.
2. The present rate of consumption of natural resources will yield major shortages within fifty to a hundred years.
3. The development of new resources will ensure that present levels of consumption can continue.
4. The development of new and alternative sources of food and energy will gradually bring everyone out of poverty conditions.
5. Dramatic advances in terms of food and energy sources will make these things available to all.

What do you think? Are you generally pessimistic, optimistic, or (like the authors, in many respects) uncertain. Only time itself will provide us with the answers. We all know which scenario we hope will come to pass, but even experts differ on what the likelihood of achieving these goals will be. Our intent here is simply to underscore the dramatic effects our changing global condition will have on us in the future. Basic questions, such as availability of resources, must be addressed in a global context. Although the conditions noted above have been with us for some time, many behave as if they do not really exist. "Out of sight, out of mind" too often becomes the mode of behavior. The fact that millions of people are starving is not a reality to many. It is shunted aside as a distant problem that will resolve itself. We know this is not so. The resolution of many of these problems—to the extent that they can be resolved—will only come about through the countless efforts of many individuals. The teacher has a personal and professional responsibility to ensure that the school curriculum in some way sensitizes young people to the globally interdependent nature of many issues and problems especially as we help them look to the future.

Global events and conditions will impinge upon the teacher, on teaching, and on the curriculum in various ways at different times. The day of the classroom teacher who is expected to remain divorced from political activity and larger social concerns is long past. It is difficult to understand how anyone can see very clearly into the future unless he or she has struggled somewhat to shape the present.

The teacher's awareness of major unresolved issues and potential problems is important if, as a professional educator, he or she is going to rationally plan for the future. There are some aspects of the future that appear to be quite obvious and predictable—for example, there will be a need for basic literary skills. Other aspects of the future, however, are not so readily apparent. What impact home computers will have on how these basic skills are acquired and on the function of schools and roles of teachers relative to the microcomputer, is not as clear.

Future Opportunities for Those with Education Degrees

It seems appropriate to us to conclude with a look into the future as it affects the teacher-in-training most directly and personally. We hope that you will find teaching or at least a teaching-related or human services career attractive. As we read earlier, it is no secret that a decreasing number of young people have been entering the teaching profession in recent years. This reduction in the number of new teachers is related to the sharp decline in school enrollment that existed into the middle 1980s in most parts of the country. This situation is changing. The Bureau of the Census, for example, has predicted an increase (a trend forecast) in birthrate from 14.7 per 1000 population in 1976 to 17.1 by 1985. Beginning in the early 1980s school enrollments, especially in elementary schools, began to rise once again. (See Table 16.1.)

It should also be noted that the demand for teachers will vary considerably from one geographic location to another. Rarely is there any surplus of qualified teachers in the inner cities or the more remote rural areas. Part of the recent lack of demand for general elementary and certain secondary teachers was created by the many potential teachers who either would not or could not move to

Table 16–1 Estimates of live births, birthrates, and increases in school enrollments from birth, six years earlier, 1976–85

BIRTH YEAR	YEAR ENTERING SCHOOL	LIVE BIRTHS	BIRTHRATE
1976	1982	3,165,000	14.7
1977	1983	3.386,550	15.3
1978	1984	3,412,000	15.6
1979	1985	3,575,000	16.2
1980	1986	3,733,000	16.7
1981	1987	3,839,000	17.0
1982	1988	3,904,000	17.2
1983	1989	3,951,000	17.2
1984	1990	3,985,000	17.2
1985	1991	4,007,000	17.1

Bureau of the Census, *Projections of the Population of the United States: 1977 to 2050* (Series II Projections), p. 23.

another location to pursue a teaching career. One reason that teachers are needed in certain locations more than others is that students are hardly distributed equally in all parts of the country. There are major patterns of immigration within the country. The Sunbelt should continue to grow rapidly in the immediate future, and the large increases in the Hispanic population in the Southwest and Far West should continue. The majority of white children are located in the suburbs, smaller cities, or rural areas, but minority populations such as blacks and Hispanics are more likely to live in the central portions of the cities.

In summary, then, in spite of falloffs in student population, the best available data for the 1980s indicates that many teaching opportunities exist now and will be even more numerous in the near future. Many are even predicting teacher shortages.

There are numerous teaching and teaching-related opportunities outside the *public school* domain available for those who wish to pursue such careers. The following sections illustrate this.

OPPORTUNITIES IN PRIVATE SCHOOLS. The dramatic increase in the number of private schools also brings with it increased opportunities for teaching. This increase is partly because of the growth of religious sects in this country. More and more religious-based schools are opening. Further, parents concerned about the quality of education in public schools, as well as parents who are opposed to busing, often send their children to private neighborhood schools. For a variety of reasons, opportunities in private schools are growing.

OPPORTUNITIES FOR TEACHING THE HANDICAPPED. Although great strides have been made, there are still millions of youngsters today in this country who are classified as handicapped in some way and who are not receiving the education they could. Thus, there will continue to be multiple opportunities to work with the handicapped in a variety of educational settings both in and out of the public school structure.

OPPORTUNITIES IN PARENT AND FAMILY EDUCATION. The large and apparently growing number of abused and neglected children is but one of many indications of the need for enhanced parent and family education. Study in parenting is required before anyone under the age of nineteen be granted a marriage license in some locations.

The estimates of child abuse in this country range from tens of thousands of children to even millions. Clearly, the increased public awareness of neglect, and of physical and sexual abuse, has led to increased reporting of abuse and neglect of children. Tragically, child abuse appears to be a common and widespread problem, and now there is an opportunity to offer parent and family education courses to help remedy this epidemic.

OPPORTUNITIES IN HEALTH EDUCATION. While we tend to think of the United States as a world leader in health care, there is nonetheless wide variability in this country in terms of health services provided. Part of this variability is attributable to economics and part to lack of *education,* for often services available without cost are not taken advantage of. In the 1980s, fifteen other countries had lower infant mortality rates than the United States, and thirty had lower infant mortality rates than that for non-white Americans.

Among the many opportunities in health is the need for nutrition educators. For example, iron is commonly lacking in the American diet and it is estimated that 30 to 40 percent of all children between the ages of one and five years have iron deficiencies. By age two, one out of two children already has tooth decay, and approximately 50 percent of all school-age children suffer from even more serious gum disease. The prevalence of general nutritional deficiencies is especially common in economically deprived minority populations.

Through education, any of these health problems can be eradicated. Opportunities for educators exist in social assistance organizations, clinics, community centers, hospitals, and government agencies.

OPPORTUNITIES IN GENERAL SOCIAL AND WELFARE SERVICES. While real income has increased for many, the number of children in poverty situations is still considerable. Educators are needed to help alleviate poverty conditions. Conservative estimates suggest that more than one in seven children suffer from economic deprivation. The problem is acute in terms of the need for extrafamilial child care resources for children in single-parent families headed by women. A great many of the children in this type of family situation are likely to be deprived of needed services.

The number of children being affected by divorce has increased by 100 percent during the twentieth century. The number of children living in families

- Legislative aid
- Sales and promotion
- Claims adjustment
- Care and planning for elderly
- Federal, state, and regional government education and human service
- Parent and family education

SUMMARY

In this final chapter, we briefly examined recent changes in schools or school conditions in terms of what they might suggest for you in the future as you pursue your own teaching career. We talked with experienced teachers about changes they had witnessed as a way of thinking about what further changes might occur in the future. Some of the more salient and obvious issues and problems in society today were noted, and you were asked to think about the implications of these for the future as well.

Whatever the immediate future holds in store, there appears to be little lack of opportunity or challenge in terms of both teaching and teaching-related opportunities for those who would seek them out. Not only are there increasing needs for teachers in public schools, but there are also a variety of teaching-related opportunities as well. Whatever you decide eventually, we hope that the time spent in reading and discussing the material here has helped you see more clearly both the challenge and rewards that lie ahead.

ACTIVITIES

1. Map out a scenario of what the world will be like in twenty years; in fifty years. How will your future scenarios affect the teaching role? (Recall the changes in society which have occurred over the last twenty years and the fact that there is a good chance that you will be teaching twenty years from now.)

2. What do you think about the expectations parents have for teachers? Do you agree with these expectations? Do you feel that the schools should abandon some of their responsibilities?

3. Investigate the trend in single-parent families. Are many men also raising children alone? What arrangements do working parents make for care of their children? What effect might this condition have on children entering school?

4. Check into current teachers' salaries. Compare teachers' salaries with salaries of occupations such as: journalists; secretaries; computer operators; nurses; city sanitation employees; insurance claims adjustors. What benefits of teaching can you think of?

5. Reflect on trends that you have seen in educational priorities and educational philosophy. Use your own schooling experiences as a reference. Do educational trends appear to be changing? What do you think educational priorities will be in ten years?

SUGGESTED READINGS

BECKUM, L. C., "The Urban Landscape: Educating for the 21st Century," *Journal of Negro Education* (Summer 1989), pp. 430–441.

CETRON, MARVIN, "Class of 2000," *Futurist* (November 1988), pp. 9–15.

CETRON, MARVIN, *Schools of the Future.* New York: McGraw-Hill, 1985.

COGAN, JOHN, ED., "Citizens for the 21st Century: The Role of the Social Studies," *Social Education* (October 1988, November 1988, January 1989, March 1989).

DIDHAM, C. K., AND B. J. SCHOOLEY, "Recruiting Quality Teachers for Tomorrow," *American Secondary Education*, No. 1 (1988), pp. 12–16.

FREDERICKS, A. D., "Almost Tomorrow," *Teaching PreK–8* (August 1989), pp. 26–28.

HARRIS, L., "2001: The World Our Students Will Enter," *College Board Review* (Summer 1988), pp. 5–27.

HIPPLE, T., ED., "Education in the Year 2000," *Clearing House* (Winter 1989), pp. 20–24.

NOTHEM, A. H., "On the Future of Teaching," *NASSP Bulletin* (April 1989), pp. 113–117.

INDEX